P9-DVE-503

DATE DUE

DEMCO 38-296

Coleridge in Italy

Colorists in Italy

Coleridge in Italy

Edoardo Zuccato

ST. MARTIN'S PRESS
NEW YORK

Riverside Community College
Library
4800 Magnolia Avenue
Riverside, California 92506

To my parents, Ferdinando and Fernanda,
to Rosi, and Angela

Riverside Community College
Library
4800 Magnolia Avenue
Riverside, California 92506

Coleridge in Italy

Copyright © 1996 by Edoardo Zuccato

PR 4487 .I8 Z83 1996

Zuccato, Edoardo.

Coleridge in Italy

used or reproduced in any manner
1 the case of brief quotations
rmation, address:

ion,

First published in the United States of America in 1996

Printed in Great Britain

ISBN: 0-312-16572-2

Library of Congress Cataloging-in-Publication Data

Zuccato. Edoardo.
    Coleridge in Italy / Edoardo Zuccato.
        p.   cm.
    Includes bibliographical references (p.   ) and index.
    ISBN 0-312-16572-2 (cloth)
    1. Coleridge, Samuel Taylor, 1772–1834 – Knowledge – Italy.
2. Coleridge, Samuel Taylor, 1772–1834 – Knowledge – Literature.
3. Italian literature – History and criticism – Theory, etc.
4. Coleridge, Samuel Taylor, 1772–1834 – Philosophy. 5. English
poetry – Italian influences. 6. Philosophy in literature. 7. Italy – In literature.
I. Title
PR4487.I8Z83   1996
821'.7–dc20   96-38240
                                                              CIP

Contents

Acknowledgements

Two main debts have made this work possible: the former is to James Mays, who advised me to undertake the research and supervised it as a true 'maestro di filologia'; the latter is to my father and my mother, my aunt Rosi and my grandmother Angela†, who generously provided financial support. The book is dedicated to them.

I am also grateful to Amanda Lillie, Marianne Mays, and Franco Buffoni for their advice; to John Beer and Graham Parry for their valuable comments; to Patrizia Nerozzi Bellman for her help; to Victoria College Library, Toronto, and Mr Brian Lake, who allowed me to read manuscript material; to the University of York for the grant I received in 1990; and to the library staff of University College Dublin, where the research was begun, to the J. B. Morrell Library, York, and to the British Library, London, all of whom never let me down.

Parts of the book have appeared in a different form as articles: 'S. T. Coleridge, Italy, and the Fine Arts', *Textus*, III (1990); 'La tradizione cavalleresca da Boccaccio a Tasso nel pensiero critico di S. T. Coleridge', *Lingua e letteratura*, X, No 19 (1992); 'S. T. Coleridge as a Critic of Dante', *Il confronto letterario*, IX, No 18 (1992); 'Italian Petrarchism in S. T. Coleridge's Theory of Poetry', *Textus*, VII (1994).

The publication of this book has been funded partially by the Consiglio Nazionale delle Ricerche (CNR).

Illustrations

Abbreviations

AR (CC)	COLERIDGE, S. T. *Aids to Reflection*, ed. John Beer, Routledge: London; Princeton UP: Princeton (N. J.), 1993.
Barry	BARRY, Kevin. *Language, Music and the Sign. A Study in Aesthetics, Poetics and Poetic Practice from Collins to Coleridge*, CUP 1987.
BL (1907)	COLERIDGE, S. T. *Biographia Literaria*, ed. with his *Aesthetical Essays* by J. Shawcross, 2 vols., OUP: Oxford (rpt. 1969).
BL (CC)	*Biographia Literaria or Biographical Sketches of My Literary Life and Opinions*, eds. James Engell and Walter Jackson Bate, 2 vols., Routledge & K. Paul: London; Princeton UP: Princeton (N. J.), 1983.
BL&J	*Byron's Letters and Journals*, ed. Leslie A. Marchand, 12 vols., Murray: London 1973–82.
BPW	Byron. *The Complete Poetical Works*, ed. Jerome McGann, 6 vols. of 7 (vol. 6 with Barry Weller), Clarendon Press: Oxford 1980–.
Branca (1964)	BRANCA, Vittore. *Boccaccio medievale*, Sansoni: Firenze.
Brand (1957)	BRAND, C. P. *Italy and the English Romantics. The Italianate Fashion in Early Nineteenth-Century England*, CUP.
Brand (1965)	*Torquato Tasso. A Study of the Poet and of His Contribution to English Literature*, CUP.

Butler	BUTLER, Marilyn. *Romantics, Rebels and Reactionaries. English Literature and Its Background 1760–1830*, OUP: Oxford.
C on Bruno	SNYDER, Alice Dorothea. 'Coleridge on Giordano Bruno', *Modern Language Notes*, XLII (1927), 427–36.
C 17th C	*Coleridge on the Seventeenth Century*, ed. Roberta Florence Brinkley, Duke UP: Durham (N. C.) 1955.
C Talker	*Coleridge the Talker. A Series of Contemporary Descriptions and Comments*, ed. Richard W. Armour and Raymond F. Howes, Cornell UP: Ithaca (New York); OUP: London, 1940.
Cary M	CARY, Henry Francis. *Memoir, with his Literary Journals and Letters*, by Henry Cary, 2 vols., Edward Moxon: London 1847.
C&S (CC)	COLERIDGE, S. T. *On the Constitution of the Church and State*, ed. John Colmer, Routledge & K. Paul: London; Princeton UP: Princeton (N. J.), 1976.
CC	*The Collected Works of Samuel Taylor Coleridge*, ed. Kathleen Coburn, Routledge & K. Paul: London; Princeton UP: Princeton (N. J.), 1969–.
CH	*Coleridge. The Critical Heritage*, ed. J. R. de J. Jackson, Routledge & K. Paul: London 1970.
Churchill	CHURCHILL, Kenneth. *Italy and English Literature, 1764–1930*, Macmillan: London 1980.
CIS	COLERIDGE, S. T. *Confessions of an Inquiring Spirit* (rpt. from the 3rd edn 1853 with the intr. by J. H. Green and the note by Sara Coleridge), ed. H. StJ. Hart, A. & C. Black: London 1956.
CL	*Collected Letters of Samuel Taylor Coleridge*, ed. Earl Leslie Griggs, 6 vols., Clarendon Press: Oxford 1956–71.
CM (CC)	COLERIDGE, S. T. *Marginalia*, ed. George Whalley (vol. 3 with H. J. Jackson), 3 vols. of 5, Routledge & K. Paul: London; Princeton UP: Princeton (N. J.), 1980–.
CN	*The Notebooks of Samuel Taylor Coleridge*, ed. Kathleen Coburn, 4 vols. of 5, Bollingen Foundation, New York, Princeton (N. J.) and London, 1957–.
Coffman	COFFMAN, Ralph J. *Coleridge's Library. A Bibliography of Books Owned or Read by Samuel Taylor Coleridge*, Hall: Boston (Mass.) 1987. [Unreliable].
Cormorant	WHALLEY, George. 'Samuel Taylor Coleridge: Library Cormorant. A Study of Purpose and Pattern in His

Reading', unpubl. Ph.D. thesis, 2 vols., Univ. of London (King's College), 1950.

Corrigan   CORRIGAN, Beatrice (ed.). *Italian Poets and English Critics, 1755–1859. A Collection of Critical Essays*, Univ. of Chicago Press: Chicago and London, 1969.

CRB   *Henry Crabb Robinson on Books and Their Writers*, ed. Edith J. Morley, 3 vols., J. M. Dent: London 1938.

CRD   *Diary, Reminiscences, and Correspondence of Henry Crabb Robinson*, selected and ed. Thomas Sadler, 2 vols., Macmillan: London and New York 1872 (3rd edn).

Dialoghi   BRUNO, Giordano. *Dialoghi italiani*, ed. Giovanni Gentile, rev. Giovanni Aquilecchia, 2 vols., Sansoni: Firenze 1958 (rpt. 1985).

DNB   *Dictionary of National Biography*, 1885–.

Ellis   ELLIS, Steve. *Dante and English Poetry. Shelley to T. S. Eliot*, CUP 1983.

Elwert (1967)   ELWERT, Theodor W. *La poesia lirica italiana del Seicento. Studio sullo stile barocco*, Olschki: Firenze.

Elwert (1973)   *Versificazione italiana dalle origini ai giorni nostri*, Le Monnier: Firenze (rpt. 1989).

EOT (CC)   COLERIDGE, S. T. *Essays on His Times, in The Morning Post and The Courier*, ed. David V. Erdman, 3 vols., Routledge & K. Paul: London; Princeton UP: Princeton (N. J.), 1978.

Ferguson   FERGUSON, Wallace K. *The Renaissance in Historical Thought. Four Centuries of Interpretation*, Riverside Press: Cambridge (Mass.) 1948.

Field   FIELD, Arthur. *The Origins of the Platonic Academy of Florence*, Princeton UP: Princeton (N. J.) 1988.

Friend (CC)   COLERIDGE, S. T. *The Friend*, ed. Barbara E. Rooke, 2 vols., Routledge & K. Paul: London; Princeton UP: Princeton (N. J.), 1969.

Garin (1989)   GARIN, Eugenio. *Umanisti artisti scienziati. Studi sul Rinascimento italiano*, Editori Riuniti: Roma.

Geschichte   SCHLEGEL, Friedrich. *Geschichte der alten und neuen Literatur* (*Kritische Ausgabe*, vol. VI; orig. edn Wien 1815).

Hale (1954)   HALE, J. R. *England and the Italian Renaissance. The Growth of Interest in Its History and Art*, Faber and Faber: London.

Hallam   HALLAM, Henry. *View of the State of Europe during the Middle Ages*, 2 vols., Murray: London 1846 (orig. edn 1818).

Havens   HAVENS, Raymond Dexter. *The Influence of Milton on*
                        English Poetry, Harvard UP 1922 (rpt. Russell & Russell:
                        New York 1961).

Heffernan   HEFFERNAN, James A. W. *The Re-creation of Landscape.*
   (1985)   *A Study of Wordsworth, Coleridge, Constable and Turner*,
                        UP of New England: Hanover and London.

Histoire   SISMONDI, Sismonde de. *Histoire des républiques*
                        italiennes du Moyen Age, 16 vols., Treuttel & Würtz: Paris
                        1826 (first publ. Paris 1809–18).

Hunt (1956)   *Leigh Hunt's Literary Criticism*, eds. Lawrence Huston
                        Houtchens and Carolyn Washburn Houtchens, with an
                        essay by Clarence DeWitt Thorpe, Columbia UP: New
                        York; OUP: London.

IS   *Inquiring Spirit. A New Presentation of Coleridge from His*
                        Published and Unpublished Prose Writings, ed. Kathleen
                        Coburn, Routledge & K. Paul: London 1951 (rev. edn
                        Univ. of Toronto Press: Toronto, Buffalo and London,
                        1979).

King (1925)   KING, R. W. *The Translator of Dante. The Life, Work and*
                        Friendships of Henry Francis Cary (1772–1844), Martin
                        Secker: London.

Klibansky   KLIBANSKY, Raymond. *The Continuity of the Platonic*
                        Tradition during the Middle Ages, with a new preface and
                        four supplementary chapters, together with *Plato's*
                        Parmenides in the Middle Ages and the Renaissance, with a
                        new introductory preface, The Warburg Institute: London
                        1939 and 1943 (rpt. Kraus-Thomson: München 1981).

Kristeller   KRISTELLER, Paul Oskar. *Renaissance Thought II. Papers*
   (1965)   *on Humanism and the Arts*, Harper: New York, Evanston
                        and London.

Kritische   *Kritische Friedrich-Schlegel-Ausgabe*, eds. Ernst Behler,
   Ausgabe   Hans Eichner and Jean-Jacques Anstett, 35 vols.,
                        Schöning: München, Padeborn and Wien; Thomas:
                        Zürich, 1951–87.

Logic (CC)   COLERIDGE, S. T. *Logic*, ed. J. R. de J. Jackson,
                        Routledge & K. Paul: London; Princeton UP: Princeton
                        (N. J.), 1981.

Lowes   LOWES, John Livingston. *The Road to Xanadu. A Study in*
                        the Ways of the Imagination, Constable: London 1927,
                        rev. edn 1930 (rpt. 1934).

LS (CC)   COLERIDGE, S. T. *A Lay Sermon* in *Lay Sermons*, ed.

R. J. White, Routledge & K. Paul: London; Princeton UP: Princeton (N. J.), 1972.

Lects 1795 (CC)   COLERIDGE, S. T. *Lectures 1795 on Politics and Religion*, eds. Lewis Patton and Peter Mann, Routledge & K. Paul: London; Princeton UP: Princeton (N. J.), 1971.

L Lects (CC)   COLERIDGE, S. T. *Lectures 1808–1819. On Literature*, ed. R. A. Foakes, 2 vols., Routledge & K. Paul: London; Princeton UP: Princeton (N. J.), 1987.

Marshall   MARSHALL, Roderick. *Italy in English Literature 1755–1815. Origins of the Romantic Interest in Italy*, Columbia UP: New York 1934.

MC   *Coleridge's Miscellaneous Criticism*, ed. T. M. Raysor, Constable: London 1936.

McFarland   McFARLAND, Thomas. *Coleridge and the Pantheist*
(1969)   *Tradition*, Clarendon Press: Oxford.

Minnow   *Minnow among Tritons. Mrs S. T. Coleridge's Letters to Thomas Poole 1799–1834*, ed. Stephen Potter, Nonesuch Press: London 1934.

N   Notebook of S. T. Coleridge (numbered or lettered) in ms. References are given by folio.

Olc   BRUNO, Giordano. *Opera latine conscripta*, 3 vols., Morano: Napoli; Le Monnier: Firenze, 1879–91.

Omniana   *Omniana, or Horae Otiosiores*, by Robert Southey and S. T. Coleridge, ed. Robert Gittings, Centaur Press: Fontwell (Sussex) 1969.

Opere l   BRUNO, Giordano. *Opere latine*, ed. and tr. Carlo Monti, UTET: Torino 1980.

P Lects   *The Philosophical Lectures of Samuel Taylor Coleridge*, ed. Kathleen Coburn, Pilot Press: London 1949.

Prose   PETRARCA, Francesco. *Prose*, eds. G. Martellotti, P. G. Ricci, E. Carrara and E. Bianchi, Ricciardi: Milano–Napoli 1955.

PW (CC)   COLERIDGE, S. T. *Poetical Works*, ed. J. C. C. Mays, 3 vols., Routledge & K. Paul: London; Princeton UP: Princeton (N. J.), forthcoming (quoted from the typescript).

PW (EHC)   *The Complete Poetical Works of Samuel Taylor Coleridge*, ed. E. H. Coleridge, 2 vols., Clarendon Press: Oxford 1912 (vol. 1 rpt. 1988; vol. 2 rpt. 1968).

Sapegno (1963)   SAPEGNO, Natalino. *Storia letteraria del Trecento*, Ricciardi: Milano–Napoli.

Shaffer (1975)   SHAFFER, Elinor S. *'Kubla Khan' and 'The Fall of Jerusalem'. The Mythological School in Biblical Criticism and Secular Literature 1770–1880*, CUP.

Scienza nuova   VICO, Giambattista. *Principi di scienza nuova* (1744), in *Opere*, ed. A. Battistini, 2 vols., Mondadori: Milano 1990.

SCW   *The Complete Works of Percy Bysshe Shelley*, eds. Roger Ingpen and Walter E. Peck, 10 vols., Benn Press: London; Gordian Press: New York, 1965 (orig. edn 1926–30).

SL   *The Letters of Percy Bysshe Shelley*, ed. Frederick L. Jones, 2 vols., Clarendon Press: Oxford 1964 (all references to vol. II only).

SM (CC)   COLERIDGE, S. T. *The Statesman's Manual* in *Lay Sermons*, ed. R. J. White, Routledge & K. Paul: London; Princeton UP: Princeton (N. J.), 1972.

South   SISMONDI, Sismonde de. *Historical View of the Literature of the South of Europe*, tr. Thomas Roscoe, 2 vols., Bohn: London 1846 (orig. edn Paris 1813).

Sturrock   STURROCK, June. 'Wordsworth's Italian Teacher',
   (1984–5)   *Bulletin of the John Rylands University Library of Manchester*, LXVII, 797–812.

Sultana (1969)   SULTANA, Donald. *Samuel Taylor Coleridge in Malta and Italy*, Blackwell: Oxford.

Thorndike   THORNDIKE, Lynn. *A History of Magic and Experimental Science*, Columbia UP: New York, vol. IV: 1934 (rpt. 1960), vol. V: 1941 (rpt. 1959).

TL   COLERIDGE, S. T. *Hints Towards the Formation of a More Comprehensive Theory of Life*, ed. Seth B. Watson, J. Churchill: London 1848 (rpt. Gregg International Pub.: Farnborough, Hants, 1970).

Toynbee (1909)   TOYNBEE, Paget. *Dante in English Literature from Chaucer to Cary* (c. *1830–1844*), 2 vols., Methuen: London.

TT (CC)   COLERIDGE, S. T. *Table Talk, Recorded by Henry Nelson Coleridge (and John Taylor Coleridge)*, ed. Carl Woodring, 2 vols., Routledge & K. Paul: London; Princeton UP: Princeton (N. J.), 1990. [Ref. to Woodring's edn given by date; ref. to HNC's edn as rpt. in vol. II given by vol. and p.].

Warton   WARTON, Thomas. *The History of English Poetry from the*

Eleventh to the Seventeenth Century, Ward, Lock & Co.: London, n.d. (rpt. of the London 1778 and 1781 edn).

Watchman (CC) COLERIDGE, S. T. *The Watchman*, ed. Lewis Patton, Routledge & K. Paul: London; Princeton UP: Princeton (N. J.), 1970.

Wright WRIGHT, H. G. *Boccaccio in England from Chaucer to Tennyson*, Univ. of London, Athlone Press: London 1957.

W Prose *The Prose Works of William Wordsworth*, eds. W. J. B. Owen and Jane Worthington Smyser, 3 vols., Clarendon Press: Oxford 1974.

WPW *The Poetical Works of William Wordsworth*, ed. E. de Selincourt, 5 vols. (vols. 3–5 rev. Helen Darbishire), Clarendon Press: Oxford 1940–9.

Yates (1964) YATES, Frances. *Giordano Bruno and the Hermetic Tradition*, Univ. of Chicago Press: Chicago and London 1991 (1st edn, London 1964).

Yates (1966) *The Art of Memory*, Routledge & K. Paul: London.

Introduction

The world is a book: he who stays
at home reads only one page.
Augustine

WHEN THE EDUCATED English-speaking readers think of Italy
and British Romanticism, Byron and Shelley immediately cross
their minds. Though English interest in Italy developed without
interruption from the mid-eighteenth century, the particular image of
Italy held by the younger Romantics is usually illustrated by comparison
with eighteenth-century views alone, whereas the role and attitude of the
elder Romantics are left unspecified. Critical attempts at defining the
Romantic image of Italy are based on principles introduced by the
Romantics themselves. The central idea appeared in Mme de Staël's *De la
Littérature* (1800) and *De l'Allemagne* (1810), in which she popularized an
oppositional view of the north and the south of Europe that belonged to
the cultural climate of the time. Northerners were introverted, gloomy
and reflective; their spirit was Romantic, their aesthetics – the Gothic –
sublime. Southerners were extroverted, jolly and spontaneous; their spirit
and aesthetics were classical because they were balanced and lived in
harmony with nature. The dichotomy of south and north Europe came to
represent the contrast between past and present, but also, in the wake of
eighteenth-century primitivism, between nature and culture.

I assume only travel agents and tourists would give much credit to
Mme de Staël's dichotomy today. While the German and English
Romantics speculated on southern spontaneity and incapability of
thought, there lived a Giacomo Leopardi. Other examples which
contradicted the dichotomy in its aesthetical or cultural sense were

1

available – for instance, the Greek tragedians, Lucretius and Dante – but they do not seem to have troubled nineteenth-century English poets and critics, despite their familiarity with Italian and Classical culture.

However, this dichotomy is still the ultimate source for the contemporary critical evaluation of Romantic interest in Italy. In hindsight, the opposition has been applied to the two generations of English Romantics: the elder understood as northerners (introverted, sublime, 'Gothic'), the younger as southerners (extroverted and more Classical). One of the most persuasive recent studies is a chapter in Marilyn Butler's *Romantics, Rebels and Reactionaries* (1981) entitled 'The Cult of the South', in which she interprets the dichotomy in political terms. She argues that the ultimate meaning of the contrast between north and south was political: the elder Romantics were reactionaries and stood for 'German' culture, which was nationalist and conservative; the younger Romantics created a fictional view of the south as non-repressive, cosmopolitan and progressive to counteract it. My objections to such a view do not concern the cultural dichotomy of north–south in itself, however unfounded it may be; Marilyn Butler's retrospective application of the dichotomy would be historically correct, if such an opposition between northern and southern culture appeared in both generations of Romantics. But does it?

The present study of Coleridge and Italy has a bearing on two histories. In the first place, it challenges the dominant critical view of the relations between Italy and the English Romantics, of which Marilyn Butler's is the most powerful example. This is, as it were, the external history, since it is an attempt to define Coleridge's place in the history of Anglo–Italian literary relationships. I shall not take it as my starting point, because such a discussion requires the analysis of Coleridge's knowledge of Italian culture, a subject which has received little critical attention. This is the 'internal' aspect of my study, the aspect concerning the influence Italian culture exerted on Coleridge's intellectual life. In other words, this book has not only a bearing on the cultural history of the Romantic age, but is also a study in the history of criticism. Coleridge's opinions on Italian poets, artists, and philosophers intrigue me in themselves, and not only as material for an ideological critique of English interest in Italy.

Henry Crabb Robinson thought that Coleridge's mind was 'much more German than English' (*CRD* I 181). Such an opinion has become so apparently indisputable that scholars consider English and German as the essential components of Coleridge's culture (Greek is given a significant place in his philosophical background only). I do not intend to propound an improbable Coleridge more Italian than German; however, over three decades he read Dante, Petrarch, Boccaccio, Pulci, Ariosto, Giambattista Strozzi, Tasso, Guarini, Marino, Chiabrera, Metastasio, Goldoni, Carlo Gozzi, Ficino, Pico della Mirandola, Machiavelli, Bruno, Vico. Although the list does not include the Italian authors he read only in part, it shows that his interest was not occasional. Since he was not a passive reader, it is reasonable to assume that he must have learnt something from such an army of Italian authors.

The conviction that German alone was important to Coleridge goes along with the view of the 1800s as an unproductive period of his life. The *Norton Anthology of English Literature*, which for the most part reflects established critical opinion, describes the decade as follows:

> *Dejection: An Ode*, published in 1802, was Coleridge's despairing farewell to health, happiness, and poetic creativity. A two-year [sic] sojourn on the Mediterranean island of Malta, intended to restore his health, instead completed his decline. When he returned to England in the late summer of 1806 he was a broken man, an inveterate drug addict, estranged from his wife, suffering from agonies of remorse, and subject to terrifying nightmares of guilt and despair. . . . A bitter quarrel with Wordsworth in 1810 marked the nadir of his life and expectations.[1]

A hole seems to exist between the formative journey to Germany in 1798–1799 and his renewed life as a critic in the 1810s. No doubt the 1800s were marked by terrible existential troubles; but his mind did not go into hibernation. Far from being a dead period, the years between 1803 and 1810 were crucial to the development of his critical thought, whose genesis is otherwise difficult to explain.

The 1800s were Coleridge's Italian phase, with its peaks between 1804 and 1806, and in the first *Friend* period. The journey to Malta was neither an escape nor the 'voyage in vain' of which Alethea Hayter wrote: he set off for Malta with literary projects which led him to explore Italian poetry. The one year of travel through Italy and the contact with a new literature disclosed to him new areas of knowledge – in particular the fine arts and Renaissance lyric poetry – which helped him develop the critical thought we consider today as peculiarly his.

Coleridge wrote in 1805 that 'Dante, Ariosto, Giordano Bruno' would be his Italy (*CN* II 2598). The statement is a useful starting-point for the study of his experience of Italian culture, provided that it is interpreted as follows: Ariosto as a symbol for Renaissance poetry; Bruno for philosophy; and Dante for himself. The summary is incomplete without the fine arts, which are not mentioned because he 'discovered' them in

Italy in 1806. The variety of subjects suggests that the peculiarity of his approach to Italy lies in the interrelation of different interests – a distinctive feature of his mind.

His interest in Petrarch and the Petrarchan tradition is a case in point. His reading was stimulated by two projects: the 'Soother of Absence', a collection of love poetry, and an essay on prosody. However, his return to Petrarch's poetry in 1804 after the conventional interest of the 1790s cannot be separated from his interest in Petrarch's Latin writings, which is linked to his philosophical studies. His reading of Metastasio, which led to his first distinction between copy and imitation, was a consequence of his plans for the 'Soother of Absence' and the essay on metrics, but was also linked to his interest in opera, which in turn is inseparable from his interest in music and drama; and so on. The analysis of the material obliges me to separate the topics, but it is important to remember that they coexisted in Coleridge's mind: some of his most illuminating ideas are in fact combinations of elements belonging to distant cultural contexts.

The most remarkable example in this respect is his experience of Renaissance lyric poetry and the fine arts. Petrarch and Petrarchism influenced the love poetry he wrote after 1804; above all, they gave him a new sense of the value of poetic technique, or, more exactly, of artistic technique, since the fine arts were involved in the process. Although his critical views of painting were belated and often commonplace, his experience of the fine arts played a significant role in the development of his idea of style. The formal polish of Renaissance poetry and art led him to reconsider Classicism, upon which he had not meditated enough, given his antipathy for English and French Neoclassicism. Admiration for the perfection of Renaissance art was common in his time, but he gave it a twist of his own, since his experience was part of a wider speculation on poetics which involved English, classical and German sources. The fine arts also played a significant role in the general theory of aesthetics he attempted to develop in his lectures.

The critical results of his experience of Italy appear in the lectures and works he published in the 1810s. However, only the lecture on Dante is worthy of his fame, whereas the one on romances from Boccaccio to Tasso, which shows a scanty interest in narrative poetry, is condensed and even misleading. Dante was for Coleridge, as for his contemporaries, the symbol of the Middle Ages and, at the same time, the initiator of the Renaissance. Coleridge's emphasis on the encyclopedic character of Dante's mind and on the importance of Scholasticism in his poetry was uncommon in England, whereas it is parallel to the view of Schelling and the Schlegels. The English Romantic image of Dante came to be dominated by Shelley's and, above all, Byron's interpretations of his work, which although in part unhistorical contributed to making him a popular figure. Coleridge's comments on Dante show that his understanding of the Middle Ages was in advance of his time, though it was inferior to his knowledge of the Renaissance.

Since Coleridge's lectures make evident that the principles of his criticism were philosophical rather than historical, his observations on Italian philosophy are an essential part of his view of Italy. He always emphasized the philosophical implications of poetry and art, and his enthusiasm for Renaissance painting and lyrical poetry was interlocked with his knowledge of Florentine Platonism. The interconnection led him to believe that Platonism was the distinctive and unifying character of the Renaissance, which he considered as an age of great scholarship and art rather than philosophy in a strict sense – a view to which his acquaintance with writing in Latin made a significant contribution.

Although Italian philosophy was not for Coleridge a unique experience – like that of the fine arts, Dante and Petrarch – its impact on some aspects of his thought was considerable. His Trinitarian conversion in Malta rendered his response to Italian Platonism less enthusiastic than it had earlier been to other Platonisms, but his view of Plato was ultimately based on Ficino, whom he admired and commended.

Giordano Bruno was one of Coleridge's heroes, and seems to have represented to Coleridge a trend of Renaissance thought, that is, natural philosophy. At the same time, Bruno was a precursor of Romantic *Naturphilosophie*, both in his 'polar logic' and his conception of nature. Coleridge's attitude to Bruno cannot be understood from a solely philosophical viewpoint: Coleridge came to reject all the doctrines central to Bruno's thought, but continued to admire his personality.

The other Italian philosopher who stood high in Coleridge's favour was Vico. His philosophy of history influenced the late Coleridge, who, it should not be forgotten, rejected Hegel. Coleridge's attitude is not contradictory: his response to Vico shows that he was never inclined to accept a strong form of historicism; he also became suspicious of the doctrines of Vico which were incompatible with Christianity.

Since ethics was so decisive in Coleridge's thought, the significance of his moral affinity with Petrarch must be emphasized. Besides the philosophy of love, Coleridge was attracted by Petrarch's reflections on intellectuals and society, which have a bearing both on his own political opinions and his view of the Renaissance. Figures like Petrarch and Ficino contributed to forming his image of the Renaissance as a golden age of scholarship and art; and it is significant that as a symbol of the epoch he portrayed Boccaccio the Humanist in his garden, rather than Dante or Tasso.

It is evident that the Renaissance was the centre of Coleridge's interest in Italy. Harold Bloom pointed out that 'English Romanticism, as opposed to Continental, was a renaissance of the Renaissance'; but Bloom was probably referring to the English Renaissance, and the importance Spenser, Shakespeare and Milton had for the Romantics.[2] If the relation between the younger Romantics and Italian Renaissance poetry is well known, Coleridge's view of the Italian Renaissance, the role it played in his understanding of Elizabethan England, and the place it has in his history of European literature have so far been neglected. Though Italian culture was not for Coleridge the renewal it was for Byron and Shelley, it represents a significant part of his intellectual life.

The evaluation of Coleridge's place in the history of Anglo–Italian relationships would be incomplete if it considered only his view of poetry and art. The English image of Italy includes other, inevitable, elements like contemporary society, politics and the Grand Tour. Coleridge's response to them provides the background to the analysis of his literary opinions, and it helps us understand the peculiarity of his attitude to Italy.

English interest in Italian culture cannot be separated from the tradition of the Grand Tour. The subject is so well known that I need only recall some basic facts. I select as ideal limits 1705, the year of the publication of Addison's *Remarks on Several Parts of Italy*, and 1864, the year in which Thomas Cook's first organized tour of Italy took place. Coleridge stands between the eighteenth-century aristocratic traveller and the mass tourism of which the travel agent Cook was the initiator.

Coleridge's tour of Italy was unusual in several respects. It took place at a time when the Continent was closed to English people as a consequence of war with France. It was only after 1814–1815, as Mary Shelley wrote, that British travellers were free to visit Italy again in their thousands.[3] The geography of Coleridge's tour was no less unusual than its chronology. As far as I know, nobody else travelled through Italy as he did: following a sojourn in Malta and a long tour of Sicily, he went to Naples via Calabria, then to Rome, where he stayed for about two months, Loreto, Florence, Pisa and Leghorn, whence he sailed back to England.[4] His tour reversed the standard route of the Grand Tourist, which included Turin, Bologna, Florence, Rome, Naples (where winter was spent), Rome again for Carnival and Holy Week, Loreto via Umbria, Venice, then the return to England before winter (the three last places were often omitted in the first half of the century). Coleridge's tour, which did not include the north of Italy, must be kept in mind whenever we discuss his attitude to the country: Italy was for him more Mediterranean than it was for most British travellers.

His departure from the standard route, though unintentional, seems to anticipate the Romantic tour and its eagerness to discover new aspects of Italy. Though he was not the only traveller who visited the south, a journey through the region was considered as a daring enterprise at the time and still much later in the century. Everybody – including Neapolitans – thought civilized Europe ended in Naples. François Lenormant related that as late as 1880 Neapolitans would make their wills before undertaking a journey to the south.[5] Local inhabitants were described as savages (for example by Patrick Brydone, whom Coleridge knew), roads for wheeled traffic hardly existed and the miserable inns were top on the list of complaints of all travellers.[6] Nonetheless, they visited the region for diverse reasons, such as a taste for the classical world and for the primitive, both in its human and natural aspect.

Coleridge was a Romantic traveller, though he preserved some eighteenth-century attitudes. For example, as a member of the British administration in Malta, he travelled part of the way with letters of intro-duction. This method was characteristic of eighteenth-century aristocrats, whose contacts with Italian natives were limited to local nobility. Despite the introductions, Coleridge did become acquainted with Italians of different social rank, even though his best friends belonged to circles of artists and poets – both foreign and Italian – who gathered in Rome. These made up the new kind of tourists who had emerged in the 1770s: they were intellectual members of the middle classes who visited Italy for specific cultural reasons. They did not replace aristocratic tourists, whom they criticized for their idleness, but coexisted with them for some decades. A cosmopolitan intelligentsia joined a cosmopolitan aristocracy, which still had a leading role in the patronage of the arts.[7]

If such was the milieu in which Coleridge moved in Italy, his main interests were religion, politics, landscape and the arts. The subjects in themselves would not characterize him as a Romantic traveller, if we did not notice that he responded to landscape in as lively a manner as to art, and that he neglected Classical for Renaissance art.

It is not necessary in this context to discuss Coleridge's impressions of Italian landscape; it is enough to remember that his detailed descriptions of nature are characteristic of Romantic travelling. He paid special attention to mountains and volcanoes, which were favourite objects of the Romantic interest in nature.[8] It is emblematic of his taste that he ascended

Mt Etna twice, but he visited few Greek and Roman remains (or, at least, he did not make any note on them).

Grand Tourists used to visit places associated with the Classics, which they frequently quoted in their travel journals. Addison's *Remarks*, full as they are of Classical reminiscences rather than direct observations, are a monument to this attitude. Conversely, Coleridge noted that he would not feel anything for Shakespeare's mulberry tree 'if it were a Tree of no notice in itself': 'a Shakespeare, a Milton, a Bruno exist in the mind as pure *Action*, defecated of all that is material & passive' (*CN* II 2026 Apr 1804; cf. *TT* (*CC*) 4 Aug 1833). It is not surprising that a fabulous image of Sicily cannot be found in Coleridge. Atanasio Mozzillo points out that such a realistic attitude was typical of the last representatives of the Enlightenment, and that it was short-lived.[9] The younger Romantics would resume and renew the former fictional attitude.

Coleridge's interest in contemporary society and customs focused on two aspects: religion and politics. They were hardly separable at the time, since clerical influence on politics and daily life was enormous.[10] His response to both was very much in the tradition of British Protestantism, whose importance for all English travellers in Italy cannot be overestimated.

His objections to Roman Catholicism were of two kinds: doctrinal and social. The former reflect Protestant commonplaces: the main mistakes of the Roman Church were its doctrine of works and faith, which led it to consider the consequences of an action as more important than its nature, and to a sort of moral utilitarianism; its conception of miracles and the worship of saints; the higher value attributed to faith than charity; and its doctrine of Purgatory.[11]

It is more interesting to observe the way in which Coleridge's view of the Church as an institution changed through the years. In his early, Unitarian period he expressed radical objections to the Church. The mark 'of the antichrist' was on both the English and the Roman Church, between which there was no 'real difference' (*Lects 1795* (*CC*) 210–11). In 1802 he still considered religious deism as more Christian than the idolatry of institutional Churches (*CL* II 893). However, Napoleon's Concordat in 1801, the Union with Ireland in 1802 and the Italian sojourn led him to reconsider the political role of the Church.

Unlike the aesthetes who would multiply in the nineteenth century, Coleridge disliked Catholic worship and its ministers. Clergy threatened people with the fear of death and exploited them financially. Ignorance was the true foundation of Catholic power: the Bible was not read and illiteracy was widespread. His antipathy to monastic orders was due to their hostility to culture. Complacent friars led the processions he saw in Sicily, which struck him as noisy and fetishistic. His irritation was due to his conviction that wisdom could not be obtained by pilgrimages and worship; faith and reason were for him inseparable. He preferred ancient paganism to such ceremonies.[12] Although Sicilian fanaticism amazed him, he found it 'much more pleasing and good natured' than Spanish religiosity (though he did not travel in Spain):

> The popular superstition of Italy is the offspring of the climate, the old associations, the manners – the very names of the places. It is pure paganism, undisturbed by any anxiety about orthodoxy, or animosity against heretics.[13]

The suppression of Roman Catholic doctrines was not a theological question, but depended on the destruction of the practical aspects of Roman religion, in particular clerical celibacy (*C&S* (*CC*) 138; TT (*CC*) 4 May 1833). Though Coleridge's attitude to sexuality was ambiguous, he did not regard compulsory chastity as a religious value. He thought St Teresa's ecstasies did not differ from orgasms; he believed nymphomania was common in nunneries (*CM* (*CC*) I 505, 518, 1825), though he disapproved of the love stories about nuns and escapes from convents which are almost a convention of the Gothic novel. He said such gossips had ruined more than one family in the south of Europe (*CM* (*CC*) II 92–3). The official repression went alongside the sensuousness of Catholicism: a sensuousness sometimes censured by Coleridge, despite his awareness that it benefited the arts (*CM* (*CC*) II 1043, 1824 or 1826; N 37.74 f62, 1828).

The experience of Italy confirmed what Napoleon's Concordat and the Union with Ireland had suggested: that doctrines and political power were inseparable. Although Coleridge thought, as may be expected, that the policy of the Church was based on Machiavellian principles, he noticed that in practice improvization thrived in Roman territories – for instance, the notorious papal censorship was inefficient, and books on the *Index* were easily available. Nonetheless, the inseparability of Roman Catholicism and papal power led him to oppose the Act of Catholic Emancipation in 1829.[14]

Coleridge's attitude to the Church had changed profoundly from his early, radical opposition. He abandoned Unitarianism early on, and came now, in Malta in 1805, to regard it as Catholic epicureanism in rational disguise (*CN II* 2717). The consequence was a revaluation of the Church of England: in an allegory brought out in 1795 he had identified it with superstition; but when he republished an expanded version of his text in 1811, he substituted the Roman Church for the English as a main character. However, he still thought the gap between them was not unbridgeable.[15]

Italian history was not for Coleridge the inexhaustible source of inspiration it was for his contemporaries and the younger Romantics. Even though he considered the history of Venice as the most perfect subject for historical research and he was struck by the stories of the Foscaris and Marino Faliero, his interest focused on contemporary politics.[16] This is shown by the articles on Italy he wrote before the journey to the Mediterranean, which were based on second-hand knowledge.[17] It was only after his sojourn in Malta and Italy that his observations became more personal, and they focused on the south rather than the north of Italy, of which he had no direct experience.[18] When we discuss his political comments on Italy, we must remember that France and England were fighting for the control of the Mediterranean while Coleridge resided there. His observations are those of a loyal British citizen, and they are characterized by a realism and matter-of-factness at odds with his reputation as a visionary.

He thought 'every thing in Sicily had been exaggerated by travellers, except two things – the wretchedness of the people, and the folly of the Government'.[19] Sicilian aristocracy was incompetent; heavy taxation was absurd in a country without a free circulation of capital, labour and commodities; justice was fraudulent; and the government enacted the opposite of what ought to be done.[20] Sicilians were slaves of the Roman Church and a despotic government, but a parliament was improbable in a country characterized by incompetence and civil disobedience.[21] Such conditions seemed to justify the presence of the British in the region: 'Italians desire to be English, confirmed to me by the most intelligent'.[22] The alternative at the time was to be French, which is what happened to Naples, where English people were not welcomed (*Friend* (*CC*) I 559–60, 217).

In the articles on Italy he published in 1798 and 1800, Coleridge repeated current English opinions, that is, he emphasized the contrast between past glory and present decay (*EOT* (*CC*) I 23–6, III 60–3). He thought disunity was the main characteristic of Italian history and society even before his journey to Italy, and he did not change his mind afterwards (*CN* II 1923, Feb–Mar 1804). He noted that Austrian and Spanish domination did not do any good: their hostility to industry and trade hindered the improvement of civil rights (*C&S* (*CC*) 25–6). The patronising attitude of Italian aristocracy, on the other hand, prevented citizens from becoming responsible and independent (N 45.3 flv, May 1830). Although Italy demonstrated that 'a bad and wicked constitution' renders freedom impossible, he never openly supported political independence as a remedy (*IS* 317). He thought the spirit of a race depended on a few great minds, and could degenerate if the political situation became too fragmentary. Greek independence was possible because, unlike Italy, Greece was not divided into small states. Germany was in the same condition as Italy, but its national spirit had survived, whereas the Neapolitans, for example, had been under foreign rule for too long and had lost the sense of their origins. Despite such scepticism, he condemned the Holy Alliance.[23]

The French Revolution, Napoleon and the Congress of Vienna turned Italy into a very different country from that which Boswell and Goethe had known. If Coleridge, who was in Italy when the changes were taking place, still travelled as a member of a foreign community consisting of aristocrats and intellectuals alike, Romantic travellers found themselves in a new world after 1815. The changes in Italy were profound – the end of the Venetian Republic is the most obvious example – but they were in a way not so dramatic as the changes abroad. The structure of Italian society was still that of the *ancien régime*, whereas in England the role of aristocracy had been eroded by the middle class in substantial areas of public life. Tourism, like any other aspect of society, underwent significant modifications: new forms of travelling and sojourn emerged.

The most striking change concerned foreign aristocracy, which had played the most important part among visitors to Italy for over a century. Byron, who travelled in a carriage with servants and friends – in the way nobles used to travel – was now considered a curiosity. Travel became standardized well before the end of the period, and one is left with the impression that by 1825, when Hazlitt made his Tour, a journey through Italy could hardly be an adventure, except perhaps in the far south.

Hazlitt exemplifies a form of sojourn which became very common – a tour of a few months – which points to mass tourism, however sophisticated.[24] Other forms of Romantic sojourn ranged from Hunt's long residence; to Shelley's and Landor's 'exile', an attitude which attracted later poets like the Brownings and Pound; to that of Byron, who almost became Italian.[25] Though the reasons which motivated English residents in Italy were various, one reason was common: the low living expenses in comparison to England.

The new attitudes developed tendencies which for the most part existed in the eighteenth century. If a traveller like Hazlitt can be described as a middle-class version of the average eighteenth-century tourist, Byron seems to have collected women and impressions of social life with the same accumulative passion with which eighteenth-century nobles collected paintings and statues. The 'exiles' themselves acted under the influence of eighteenth-century primitivism, which had induced the earlier Romantics to move to the country.

The combination of novelty and convention which characterizes the practical side of English interest in Italy also emerges in the theoretical attitude toward the myth of Italy; but, surprisingly, the transformation of the intellectual view was slower. Those who are acquainted with Romantic interpretations of Italy have probably come across political and social opinions like Coleridge's elsewhere. This is the reason why I mentioned them before. The English view of Italy was based on a set of ideas which, in my opinion, the younger Romantics did not alter fundamentally. No doubt their affinity with Italy was unique; but their vision was in part traditional. The view of the south as pagan and of Roman Catholicism as a form of paganism was commonplace since the Reformation, and had not been discarded in the eighteenth century. Byron and Shelley did not lay the foundations of a new interpretation: they reversed the values of the current British view of Italy, but their reversal remained within the schemes of the old system.

The originality of the approach of the younger Romantics is limited by other elements. If Byron's understanding of the Italian way of life became exceptionally deep and relativistic, Shelley lived in isolation and confined himself to despising Italians as savages.[26] But, as Philip Martin noted, Byron was an impoverished aristocrat for whom Italy, a cheap country where the abhorred middle class hardly existed, signified the opportunity to continue playing a social role which had become problematic in England.[27] Most English residents in Italy did not mix with natives: like Shelley, they were bourgeois who had little in common either with Italian aristocracy, which seemed to them vicious and decayed, or the lower classes, which seemed to belong to another world.[28] Byron's example was not imitated because it was socially inimitable, and the traditional attitude of suspicion toward Italians remained the norm.[29]

The distance between the two generations is even smaller in terms of literature. Marilyn Butler's opposition of the elder Romantics as northern and the younger as southern is problematic for several reasons. In the first place, the elder Romantics had a lifelong interest in and admiration for southern culture, be it Southey's Spain and Portugal, Wordsworth's France and Italy, or Coleridge's Greece and Italy.[30] In turn, Byron and

Shelley did not hold German culture in low regard despite their limited knowledge of it. Byron made use of German settings and themes even in his Italian years, as in *Werner*; Shelley was influenced by Goethe and preferred German to French philosophy.[31]

It may be assumed – it often is – that the attitude of the younger Romantics to Italian culture was less prejudiced than the attitude of their elder colleagues. However, this is only a half-truth, since they preserved some traditional prejudices and even reintroduced others which the previous generation had abandoned. Shelley abhorred the Church as much as Coleridge did, though for different reasons; Byron admired it as an aesthete could, that is, for the theatricality of its rituals – which is what Protestants had always thought of them. In other words, the Protestant influence on Byron and Shelley was stronger than is often supposed, and is also evident in their aesthetic preferences, as, for example, in their dislike of religious painting. C. P. Brand neatly summarized the opinion of most British travellers: 'If Italy had been a great country, it was in spite of Catholicism; if she was now decadent it was because of it' (Brand, 1957, 223). Nobody was free enough to acknowledge that Italian history, like the history of the other Catholic countries, is inseparable from the history of the Roman Church, regardless of one's antipathy to it. Such an attitude, rather than a Protestant, a materialist or an aestheticizing stand-point, would have helped any foreigner understand Italian culture better.

Hostility to the Church was a component of the anti-medievalism which the younger Romantics embraced in spite of their enthusiasm for Dante, Petrarch and Boccaccio,[32] whereas Coleridge's dislike for the Church did not limit his view of the Italian Middle Ages, a view which was historically more plausible than that of Byron and Shelley. Shelley's hasty view of the age, which is condensed in his *On the Revival of Literature*, influenced his attitude to Dante, whom he admired as alien to the Middle Ages.[33] The unhistoricity of Byron's interpretation is even more evident. Of course, both attitudes were wonderfully productive in terms of poetry; but they should not be presented as monuments of unprejudiced originality. Coleridge's uneasiness with the eroticism of Italian Renaissance romances, which is often quoted as evidence of his limited affinity with Italian culture, therefore demonstrates very little. The aspects of Italy Coleridge was unable to accept are not more essential than those Byron and Shelley disliked. If there is an Italy which corresponds to Shelley's and Byron's, there is one corresponding to Coleridge's – Christian, Platonic, sublime.

Since the younger Romantics changed the value of a pre-existing inter-pretation of Italy rather than the interpretation itself, their innovations are not to be found in their ideas, but in the form in which they were presented. A radically new interpretation should have reconsidered the role of the Roman Church in Italian history, or the opposition between England and Italy (culture vs. nature, rationality vs. irrationality, etc.). It might be argued that such observations are beside the point because the younger Romantics were interested in criticizing contemporary England rather than understanding Italy; or that I am asking of them an historicized approach which did not exist at the time.

Although England was always their main concern and the public for which they wrote was English, I think their interest in Italy was genuine. The limits of their understanding cannot be ascribed to their aims only – criticism of contemporary society, etc. – but it must also be traced to their background. As far as the latter objection is concerned, the present study will show that Coleridge's attitude to Italian philosophy and art pointed to a more correct historicization. If his achievement may seem normal today, it is because it represents a substantial contribution to the foundation of the scholarly building in which we are still working.

I do not think the present remarks flatten our image of Romanticism. The light they shed on Coleridge make him at the same time more and less original than he seemed: less original, since they show he was not interested in German culture alone, but that he took part in the literary fashion of his time, that is, Italian; more original, since he gave the interest a twist of his own. The English reader who is acquainted with Italian literature through other Romantics will find many unusual names in the present study – a sign of the originality of Coleridge's approach.

Unusual writers and unusual works of popular writers, like Petrarch's Latin writings or Boccaccio's romances, were not a vain display of culture to impress an audience. They testify to Coleridge's effort to push public thinking out of stereotypes: Dante had been petrified into a few picturesque passages of the *Inferno*, Petrarch into a dozen sonnets, and Italian literature into a small group of excellent poets. Coleridge endeavoured to provide a wider historical image of Italian literature, and to communicate the complexity of a tradition beyond the widespread simplistic view. Though not all his remarks are original or equally important, he helped to raise public interest in diverse aspects of Italian culture, like Petrarchism or philosophy, to which his contemporaries paid little attention.

If such are Coleridge's peculiarities, the attitudes he had in common with the other Romantics must not be excluded from a complete discussion of Romantic interest in Italy. A view which ignores all the similarities creates artificial dichotomies which conceal important aspects of the matter at issue. In terms of literature, the model of Romantic interest in Italy was the English Renaissance, of which Romantic poetry intended to be a revival; in terms of culture, Protestant background and Classical education conditioned the English idea of Italy as pagan. Besides, a comparison between Coleridge's ideal image of Italy, as illustrated in *The Garden of Boccaccio*, and the myth of Italy created by the younger Romantics, reveals interesting similarities in terms of political implications, despite the differences between the images themselves. I believe that only an approach which takes into account both similarities and differences between the two generations of Romantics can lead us to a plausible cultural history of the age.

I

Coleridge and Italian Lyric Poetry

Coleridge and the Sonnet

A STUDY OF COLERIDGE and Italian poetry ought to begin with Petrarch rather than Dante, as might be expected. The experience of Petrarch and the Petrarchan tradition influenced both Coleridge's love poetry after 1804 and his critical understanding of the Renaissance. The originality of his later ideas was achieved slowly, and can be appreciated if it is measured against his early attitude to Petrarch, which was largely conventional and based on second-hand knowledge.

In the introduction to *A Sheet of Sonnets*, a miscellany Coleridge compiled and edited in 1796, he expressed a view of the sonnet which supported William Lisle Bowles in opposition to Petrarch – or what Coleridge thought Petrarch represented. Boileau and William Preston codified sonnet-writing in rules based on the practice of Petrarch;[1] but Coleridge had 'never yet been able to discover either sense, nature, or poetic fancy in Petrarch's poems; they appear to me all one cold glitter of heavy conceits and metaphysical abstractions.' The models he brought forward as alternatives were Charlotte Smith and Bowles, 'who first made the Sonnet popular among the present English'.[2]

Coleridge thought the sonnet a poetic form 'in which some lonely feeling is developed'; and such feelings are developed best in the context of 'the scenery of Nature.' The poet is free to decide about metre and rhymes – 'many or few, or no rhymes at all' (*PW* (EHC) II 1139). English sonnets in the Italian form are often tortuous in syntax and unnatural in vocabulary, since the rhyme scheme of the Italian sonnet is not suited to the English language. Therefore, they can hardly be the proper form for bursts of passion, as Preston claimed.[3]

Coleridge's introduction echoes several critical commonplaces of the time, and shows that his education at twenty-four was up to date in terms of poetry and conventional in terms of critical theory.

Petrarch was not a Romantic rediscovery: he had been popular since the 1770s thanks to the reviving interest in the sonnet, a form with which he is commonly associated. It is well known that after the Renaissance enthusiasm, during the seventeenth and eighteenth centuries he was blamed for monotony and artificiality. With the important exception of Milton, in England the sonnet declined together with Petrarch's reputation.[4] Milton and Petrarch, in fact, were the strongest forces underlying the revival of the sonnet: Gray, Thomas Edwards and Thomas Warton, the main forerunners of the new attitude, admired and studied both Milton and early Italian literature, even though they paid little attention to Dante and the *stilnovo* poets.[5]

The book which marked and introduced a decisive change of attitude to Petrarch was Susannah Dobson's *Life of Petrarch* (1775), which is a selected translation of the Abba Jacques-François de Sade's monumental *Mémoires pour la vie de François Pétrarque* (1754–67), a work still valuable today for its wealth of information.[6] De Sade and Susannah Dobson helped to raise that public interest in Petrarch's biography which became characteristic of the Romantic approach.[7]

Translations from Petrarch's sonnets began to appear from about 1770 and increased in number in the following years. The second part of *Canzoniere*, which contains the poems *in morte*, drew more attention than the first, *in vita*, which the Elizabethans preferred. The number of translators is too large to be enumerated and commented on here; suffice it to say that virtually all sonneteers – Raymond D. Havens counted over 130 – tried their hand at translating or imitating Petrarch.[8]

The poets who influenced Coleridge were William Preston, Charlotte Smith and William Lisle Bowles. Preston was probably the most devoted admirer of Petrarch among them. His *Poetical Works* include a section entitled 'Sonnets, Love Elegies, and Amatory Poems', which is preceded by the preface to which Coleridge referred. Preston's sonnets are an intermixture of translations and imitations of Petrarch in which it is difficult to discover any originality. If he was a mediocre theoretician, he was no better as a poet or a translator.[9] Charlotte Smith belonged to the opposite party: her *Elegiac Sonnets and Other Essays* (1784) deal with natural themes in melancholy moods. Even her collection of poetry, however, included the translation of three sonnets of Petrarch and several imitations.[10] Bowles' sonnets, first published in 1789, enjoyed a remarkable popularity, and were admired by young Coleridge. Most of them are irregular or vaguely Shakespearean in form, since Bowles claimed he 'thought nothing about the strict Italian model'.[11] As far as syntax and vocabulary are concerned, the difference between Bowles' spontaneity and Anna Seward's artificiality today appears much smaller than Coleridge claimed.[12] Coleridge's view of the sonnet may have been affected by other poets, like the Della Cruscans,[13] Charles Lamb, Charles Lloyd and Robert Southey, but their influence seems negligible.[14]

Most of Coleridge's sonnets were written before 1797, and although his early critical opinions were conventional, his interest was genuine: 'The Sonnet has ever been a favourite species of composition with me' (PW (EHC) II 1146). His sonnets can be thematically divided into two groups: sonnets dealing with nature and with politics; a vigorous morality pervades both. Bowles' influence is evident in the former group,[15] whereas the latter testifies to Coleridge's political commitment at the time.[16] Though Petrarch was not his model, he mentioned Laura a few times in his early poems – a sign that he was not far from the conventions he was critical of.[17]

Coleridge's poetic interest in the sonnet is at odds with the reservations about its structure he expressed in some of his writings. In the preface to his *Poems on Various Subjects* (1796), he maintained he might have called most of his poems sonnets, 'but they do not possess that *oneness* of thought which I deem indispensible [sic] in a Sonnet' (PW (EHC) II 1137). His conviction that the fourteen-line structure is an accidental feature of the form was reiterated even as late as 1832, when he published an article on the English sonnet in *Blackwood's Magazine*.[18]

If Coleridge's insistence on the unity of feeling and thought as the condition essential to the accomplishment of genuine poetry is the most original aspect of his introduction, his opinions on the codification of the sonnet, the artificiality of Petrarch's feelings, and the unsuitability of the Italian sonnets for the English language are significant not as critical judgements, but as evidence of the resistance to a tradition which had dominated European lyric for centuries.[19] The most surprising aspect of Coleridge's introduction is not his scanty knowledge of Italian poetry, but his disregard of English Renaissance poetry, however common such a lack of interest may have been.

Coleridge's reaction against his earlier attitudes was twofold, that is, poetic and critical. In 1797 he parodied the 'affectation of unaffectedness, of jumping and misplaced accents in common-place epithets, flat lines forced into poetry by italics . . . puny pathos, etc., etc.' in three sonnets

Attempted in the Manner of Contemporary Writers, which he signed 'Nehemiah Higginbottom' (*PW* (EHC) I 210 n.). He got rid of the old mannerisms while he was writing his best poems – although I find his early sonnets, within the limits of their conventions, not so bad as he himself seemed to believe. Besides, he reacted against the opinions on Petrarch he had expressed in the introduction to *A Sheet of Sonnets*. He wrote in a copy of the 1797 edition of *Poems* that his former judgement was

> a piece of petulant presumption, of which I should be more ashamed if I did not flatter myself that it stands alone in my writings. The best of the joke is that at the time I wrote it, I did not understand a word of Italian, and could therefore judge of this divine Poet only by bald translations of some half-dozen of his Sonnets. (*PW* (EHC) II 1147)

The marginal note, which according to James Mays dates from between 1808 and 1810 (*PW* (CC), Introduction, Annex C), expresses the attitude to Petrarch and Italian lyric poetry which Coleridge developed during his sojourn in Italy.

Coleridge's Grand Tour of Italian Lyric Poetry

Coleridge's period in the Mediterranean is currently viewed as a kind of escape from a situation which in several respects had become intolerable: the intellectual expectations of his German tour had partly failed, his financial problems were not solved, the relationship with his wife had deteriorated as a result of his friendship with Sara Hutchinson, his health was degenerating and, last but not least, his 'shaping spirit of Imagination' was failing. Such was his condition in the early 1800s, which might confirm the view of his journey to Malta and Italy as escapist, especially if compared to his German tour. However, the contrast is not as clear as it seems, and can be modified on both sides by showing that his sojourn in Germany had been planned less carefully than is often assumed, and that his journey to Italy was not purposeless.

Coleridge wrote that he desired to leave for Germany to study theology and philosophy (*CL* I 209, 6 May 1796). It was Thomas Beddoes who stimulated his interest in German science and philosophy in particular, so that Coleridge decided to go to Blumenbach's Göttingen instead of Schiller's Jena.[20] In other words, Coleridge had come across some authors who stimulated his curiosity, and decided to improve his knowledge of them and the culture they belonged to. Once in Germany, however, he spent most of his time studying Old German poetry and collecting material for a planned 'Life of Lessing'. If George Whalley managed to see in the 'Life of Lessing' a prefiguration of *Biographia Literaria*,[21] the interest in Old German is more baffling, though I think it was motivated by the desire to provide a philological background to his knowledge of the English language. His knowledge of Latin and Greek, which he had studied at school, was sufficient in this respect, whereas he knew little of the Germanic roots of English.[22] Whatever may have happened, the important point is the discrepancy between his plan and the following events, which shows that the aim of his journey was not clear.

There is an analogy between Coleridge's approach to German culture and Italian culture. In 1802 and 1803, when one would expect him to continue his exploration of German, he surprisingly turned to Italian. Either German had disappointed him for some reason, or he felt his intellectual development still lacked something he had not found in Germany. Several motives underlie his decision to learn Italian. As in the case of German, he discovered some writers who attracted his attention, and wanted to read them in the original. These authors are Giordano Bruno and Pico della Mirandola, whom he first heard of in Germany, and Dante, Petrarch and Boccaccio.[23] The Wordsworths helped him develop his new interest: he began the study of Italian with them in 1802, and urged William to send him 'Dante & a Dictionary' before leaving for Malta.[24] Nevertheless, their influence cannot be considered decisive, since they were reading Italian during the Alfoxden period, and this had not stimulated Coleridge's curiosity.

Coleridge made his first note on the Italian language after a visit to the Wedgwoods in the autumn of 1802.[25] In July 1801 Wordsworth had written to Thomas Poole on Coleridge's behalf about the possibility of a journey to the Azores. Poole replied directly to Coleridge that 'he had proposed to the Wedgwoods that Coleridge accompany Tom to Sicily, but that he had received no answer'.[26] Coleridge was uncertain of the destination of his journey: he mentioned Madeira, the Azores, Spain, Portugal, France, Malta and Italy.[27] Although the reason for his hesitation was mainly practical – he could not afford to decide where to go –, I think that his growing attention to Italian culture between 1802 and 1804 might have stimulated his interest in a journey to Italy. However important the financial element of the tour may have been, other events must be considered.

In 1803 Coleridge became acquainted with Sir George Beaumont, who helped him develop a new interest in the fine arts – Italian Renaissance painting in particular. Coleridge visited some English galleries on the recommendation of Beaumont in 1803 and 1804, so that it can be assumed that painting was in his mind when he left for Italy.

As far as poetry is concerned, Coleridge had two main projects at the time: an essay on prosody and the 'Soother of Absence'. The essay on prosody is linked to his lifelong interest in metrics and testifies to a new, comparative, approach to the subject; the 'Soother of Absence' was a planned collection of love poetry related to his passion for Sara Hutchinson. Italian lyric was an appropriate source for both plans, as he soon discovered.

Altogether, Coleridge had even too many reasons for a journey to Italy: his bad health, the presence of Napoleon elsewhere on the Continent, a moment of emotional bewilderment (his relationship with Sara Hutchinson), an interest in Italian philosophy and poetry, a fresh enthusiasm for the fine arts, and two literary plans (the essay on prosody and 'Soother of Absence') for which new knowledge was required. Poetry, philosophy and art, to which the tradition of the Grand Tour and fashion can be added, as Italian culture attained the height of its popularity in the first two decades of the nineteenth century. His Italian journey, therefore, does not appear less motivated than his German tour.

The 'Soother of Absence', Petrarch, and Love

> *Tra la spiga e la man qual muro è messo?*
> Giorgio Caproni

Coleridge's exploration of Italian literature in Malta and Italy focused on two subjects: love poetry, with an eye to his 'Soother of Absence', and metrics, for the planned essay on prosody. Renaissance lyric poetry was the natural ground for his research, though it was not his sole reading.

The 'Soother of Absence' was conceived in 1802 as a long topographical poem, and it soon evolved into a collection of short love poems (*CN* I 1225). The project was linked to Coleridge's passion for Sara Hutchinson, and although it was never completed, it underlies much of his reading and writing between 1804 and 1808. The Malta notebooks show that his frustrated passion preoccupied him, and his peculiar psychological condition must be kept in mind as we approach the topic. His attitude is perceivable in a note he made on his journey to Malta:

> In my Soother of Absence to note my utter want of Sympathy with all
> the ordinary Love-poems, complaining of the Cruelty of the Mistress, of

her attachment to another &c – in short, all that supposes that I could love with no knowledge of being loved in return – or even with the knowledge of the contrary. – In short, I shall have abundant matter for contemplation on the Subject in my Perusal of the Italian Love-poems. (*CN* II 2062, May 1804)

Ironically, the bold tone of the note is at odds with his sentimental condition, since his intense feelings for Sara were not reciprocated. His dissatisfaction with the love poetry he was familiar with and his desire to read Italian lyric poetry are important to the present argument. He fulfilled his desire in Malta, where he began to read Italian poetry as soon as he could, that is, after improving his knowledge of the language. The poet most natural to discuss first, though not chronologically first in his reading list, is Petrarch, both for the influence he had on Italian poetry and the importance he had for Coleridge.

After the conventional, critical attitude of the *Sheet of Sonnets*, Coleridge turned to Petrarch in 1803, when he borrowed William Sotheby's complete edition of Petrarch.[28] Though it is not clear what he read before leaving for the Mediterranean, the discovery of Petrarch's Latin writings was a turning-point. He must have found Petrarch's introspection congenial, and it is noteworthy that he returned to the Latin works after his sojourn in Italy, where he experienced Petrarch's poetry and the Petrarchan tradition more deeply. It must not be forgotten that Coleridge's knowledge of Italian in 1803 was not sufficient for him to read Petrarch's Italian poetry in the original, whereas Latin was not a problem. Nothing demonstrates that he read or scanned Petrarch's poems in the fourth volume of the Basel edition at the time.[29]

Coleridge probably bought and read his edition of Petrarch's poems (*Le Rime di Francesco Petrarca*, 1778) in Malta or in Italy. I say probably because there is no chronological certainty: only internal evidence and contemporary reading suggest such a date.[30] The marginal notes in the volume are short, like most of his early marginalia, but they reveal a new attitude to Petrarch. He divided the poems which struck him as 'good', 'pleasing', and 'dignified', and commented briefly on some. It is worth analysing his preferences.

The group classified as 'good' includes sonnets and one *canzone*. Some of Petrarch's masterpieces are part of the list, as the first sonnet of *Canzoniere*, 'Voi ch'ascoltate', and 'Solo et pensoso' (XXXV),[31] a favourite with the Romantics, since it deals with wandering in nature in the company of one's thoughts. Most of the preferences are love poems: Coleridge was struck by 'Quando fra l'altre donne' (XIII), which expresses a view of the poet's woman as a mediator between man and God – a concept repeated by the *canzone* 'Gentil mia donna' (LXXII), which treats the theme of the mistress's eyes. 'Vergognando talor' (XX) is a rhetorical statement on Petrarch's poetic skill: his mistress is so beautiful that he is not able to write about her as he wished.

Coleridge did not neglect Petrarch's moral meditations. 'La gola e 'l somno' (VII) is a proud statement of Petrarch's sense of his own cultural mission in a world which only pursues physical pleasure ('La gola e 'l somno', that is, 'Greed and sleep'). 'S'io credesse' (XXXVI) anticipates Hamlet's proverbial monologue and argues that the poet would commit suicide to stop his torments, if death meant peace; since he does not know, he lives on. The theme is repeated in a passage of *canzone* 'Perché la vita è breve' (LXXI, lines 37–45), which Coleridge admired for its 'vigour and chastity' (*MC* 25) – it is in effect unusually vigorous for Petrarch.[32]

Coleridge seems to have preferred the first part of *Canzoniere*; the only two poems of the second part he commented upon are 'Che debb'io far?' (CCLXVIII) and 'Amor, se vuo' ch'i' torni' (CCLXX). Both deal with writing as consolation.[33] He regarded the *canzone* 'Amor, se vuo' ch'i' torni' as superior to 'Che debb'io far?', even though he did not like some of its images. The poem is a plea to Love, that he may bring Laura back to life, since Petrarch feels free but melancholic, and it anticipates sixteenth-century taste in the paradoxical nature of its argument and its imagery, which Coleridge disliked. He would have deleted 'half-a-dozen conceits and Petrarchisms of *hooks*, *baits*, *flames*, and *torches*'.[34] Such disparaging observations on Petrarchism make it probable that the note was made before the summer of 1805, when his judgement changed.[35]

Coleridge's notes focus on poems of love and moral reflections – subjects prominent both in *Canzoniere* and Coleridge. The marginalia relate to the first hundred pages of part I of *Canzoniere* and to the beginning of part II. *Canzoni* attracted his attention more than sonnets; he found the ballad 'Lassare il velo' (XI) pleasing, but was not struck by any *sestina*. Coleridge's disregard for pre-Dantesque poetry has perhaps something to do with his indifference toward highly complex poetic structures, although the *stilnovo* poets were not popular in his time. George M. Ridenour has argued however that the first line of Coleridge's *First Advent of Love* (*PW* (EHC) I 443, ?1824), 'O FAIR is Love's first hope to the gentle mind!', is 'an unmistakable reminiscence of the opening line' of Guido Guinizelli's 'Al cor gentil repara sempre Amore' ('Love always returns to gentle hearts'). I find the reminiscence unconvincing, both for internal reasons – the resemblance is generic – and for external reasons:

the late date of the poem, and the lack of other references to the *stilnovo* poets.[36]

Petrarch's influence on Coleridge's idea of love is instead worth pursuing. In the 1817 edition of *Sibylline Leaves*, the love poems were arranged in a section to which the following motto was prefixed:

Quas humilis tenero stylus olim effudit in aevo,
Perlegis his lacrymas, et quod pharetratus acuta
Ille puer puero fecit mihi cuspide vulnus.
Omnia paulatim consumit longior aetas,
Vivendoque simul morimur, rapimurque manendo.
Ipse mihi collatus enim non ille videbor:
Frons alia est, moresque alii, nova mentis imago,
Voxque aliud sonat –
Pectore nunc gelido calidos miseremur amantes,
Jamque arsisse pudet. Veteres tranquilla tumultus
Mens horret, relegensque alium putat ista locutum.[37]

It is an excerpt from Petrarch's metric epistle to Barbato da Sulmona (lines 42–9, and 63–5), which Coleridge read and transcribed in 1813. Here I am not concerned with his reading in Petrarch's Latin writings, but with the fact that he regarded Petrarch's view of love as a reference point. An analysis of Coleridge's philosophy of love will make clear the significance Petrarch had for him.

Coleridge's love poetry can be divided into three phases or modes: first, a period of apprenticeship, in which the main influences were eighteenth-century and Classical poetry.[38] The second mode, the ballad, is narrative and sets sentimental situations in the context of romance. The form includes some of Coleridge's masterpieces, like *Christabel* and *Love*. It is evident that Coleridge was ignorant of the Petrarchan tradition, to which most love poetry written between the fourteenth and the seventeenth century belongs, when he went to Italy. He had created a new kind of love poetry which had to do with the daemonic and supernatural in the wake of late eighteenth-century enthusiasm for medieval poetry, but his knowledge of the Renaissance tradition was still superficial. Renaissance love poetry is introspective rather than narrative, made up of subtle reasoning – from which the notorious conceits derive – rather than exotic stories, and depends on a philosophy of love which proved to be congenial to Coleridge. Petrarch's impact on Coleridge will be clearer if we compare their conceptions of love.

Petrarch had no cosmological interests and was mainly concerned with himself, as the story of his ascent to Mount Ventoux epitomizes.[39] The result was a systematic exploration of his own soul, in which he discovered contradictions rather than the certainties of revealed truth. Petrarch found the cause of his interior fluctuation in the weakness of his will, which was in its turn due to his *acedia*, 'a lack of spiritual energy which hampers any resolute choice . . . and which radically destroys any possibility of action, because it shows the substantial vanity of every action'.[40] Consequently, hesitation characterizes Petrarch's sentimental life. His love for Laura possessed 'something obscure and morbid as a desire always unfulfilled and that lasted beyond her death';[41] it was nonetheless – or because of it – 'a means by which Petrarch could give lyric reality to the complexity of his sentiments, and the imaginative centre at which the wavering lines of contradictory feelings converge'.[42] Petrarch ignored the *stilnovo* code of love and its implications – a conventional psychology and the aristocratic court of lovers,[43] and his main theme was, 'instead of the metaphysical power of the "benevolent angelic salvation", the irremediable contradiction of his feelings considered as a value in themselves, outside any logical and moral rationalisation'.[44] A different conception of beauty stemmed from the new attitude. Unlike the *stilnovo* poets, Petrarch tended to oppose soul and body, not only because of his Platonism, 'but above all because his experience included the "time" factor'.[45] His description of Laura is realistic despite its vagueness because she is a mortal woman in time rather than an incarnated metaphysical entity.[46] In other words, Petrarch's temper was not metaphysical but psychological, and his strength was a stubborn need for self-analysis, whose discoveries were disciplined by his literary culture. The result was a kind of technical language consisting of a vocabulary of selected words by which he could represent his interior experience without becoming visceral.[47]

If we turn to Coleridge, it is not difficult to discover where his vision of love overlaps with Petrarch's. Coleridge's central problem was the relation between body and spirit. He wanted love to involve the whole human being in its action, but it was not easy for him to define the role of physical sensation alongside the metaphysical meaning authentic love was supposed to imply. In so far as this has a bearing on sexuality, I agree with Lawrence S. Lockridge when he writes that though Coleridge 'does imply in his poetry and elsewhere that sexual feeling plays a crucial role mediating between nature and spirit, one can speculate that sex loathing prevents him from formulating that role fully'.[48] But despite the fact that the subject embarrassed him, he never dismissed its importance explicitly. On the contrary, he went so far as to write: 'Is it true what is constantly affirmed, that there is no Sex in Souls? – I doubt it – I doubt it exceedingly' (*CN* III 3531, Jul–Sept 1809). Although it has often been repeated that Coleridge conceived of love in its ideal form as a sort of extension of friendship, he emphasised the radical difference between them. He noted in Thomas Browne's *Religio Medici* that

> friendship satisfies the *highest* part of our nature; but a wife, who is capable of friendship, satisfies all. The great business of unostentatious Virtue is – not to eradicate any . . . genuine instinct or appetite of human nature; but – to establish a concord and unity betwixt all parts of our nature, to give . . . a Feeling & a Passion to our purer Intellect, and to intellectualize our feelings and passions. (*CM* (*CC*) I 751, probably after 1806 or 1810)

The attitude strengthened late in life, as *Love and Friendship Opposite* shows (*PW* (EHC) I 484 (?1830), lines 3–6): 'Friendship/. . . Gives no accord to Love, however refined./Love, that meets not with Love . . ./ Grows ashamed of itself, and demurs.'

The next problem was the relation of friendship and love with passion and desire. Coleridge solved the riddle in symbolic terms:

> WHERE true Love burns Desire is Love's pure flame;
> It is the reflex of our earthly frame,
> That takes its meaning from the nobler part,
> And but translates the language of the heart.[49]

Coleridge could not accept the idea that pain and pleasure, 'Great Springs of human conduct . . . main Springs perhaps', were the basic powers of human behaviour. 'The Will = the Ego is the prime mover – & what is Reason? – And Love too – No! That too is no Creature of Pain & Pleasure – say rather the Parent *nursed* & sustained by its Children' (*CN* II 2058, 30 Apr 1804).

If love could not be reduced to its corporeal components, beauty could not be reduced to its bodily appearance. Coleridge's view can be inscribed into the Christian and Platonic traditions, in which physical beauty is a sign of spiritual beauty, and this in turn symbolizes the eternal and the divine.[50] The authentic amorous relationship is Platonic and consists in a spiritual exchange by which each lover obliterates in the other and regains the original unity of being that was lost:

> The Lover worships in his Beloved that final consummation <of itself which is> produced in his own soul by the action of the Soul of the

Beloved upon it, and that final perfection of the Soul of the Beloved, <which is in part> the consequence of the reaction of his (so ameliorated & regenerated) Soul upon the Soul of his Beloved/till it contemplates the Soul of the other as involving his own, both in its givings and its receivings . . . and thus still keeping alive its *outness*, its *self-oblivion* united with *Self-warmth*, & still approximates to God! (*CN* II 2540 (Apr 1805))

Or, to sum up,

Real + symbolical . . . Love – and the grandeur of loving the Supreme in her – the real and symbolical united . . . In loving her thus I love two Souls as one, as compleat . . . as the *ever improving* Symbol of Deity to us. (*CN* II 2530, Apr 1805)

Knowledge, or more exactly self-knowledge, is a momentous result of the process, since love is

a sense of Substance/Being seeking to be self-conscious, I. of itself in a Symbol. 2. of the Symbol as not being itself. 3. of the Symbol as being nothing but in relation to itself – & necessitating a return to the first state, Scientia absoluta. (*CN* II 3026, Feb-May 1807)

Petrarch's philosophy of love, which is a Christianized Platonism mixed with courtly elements, is based on similar ideas. However, Coleridge might have found them in other poets, so that his admiration for Petrarch requires a deeper explanation. I believe Coleridge found in Petrarch not only congenial ideas on love, but above all a congenial blend of them. In other words, the ratio between the body and the spirit, between Christianity and Platonism, in Petrarch's vision of love was the closest to Coleridge's own ideal. His reaction to other poets who might have been his models in this respect confirms it.[51]

The philosophy of love has crucial resonances in Coleridge's ethics. A 'most important' subject for *The Friend* was to argue

That Love, however sudden, as affirmed of it – *fall in love* – which is perhaps *always* the case of Love in its highest sense, as defined by me elsewhere, is yet an act of the will – and that too one of the *primary* & therefore unbewusst, & ineffable Acts. (*CN* III 3562, Jul–Sept 1809)

If love did not imply an unconscious act of the will, it would be impossible to distinguish it from mere sensuousness, however conceived.[52] Coleridge objected to Boccaccio's and Ariosto's amorous situations, and charged them with 'degrading and deforming passion into appetite' (*BL (CC)* II 22). His disagreement with Kant is even more important.

Kant was echoing an eighteenth-century commonplace when he argued in the *Metaphysik der Sitten* that '*Liebe* ist eine Sache der Empfindung, nicht des Wollens'. Coleridge wrote an extensive marginal note to the passage:

> If, I say, I doubt this independence of Love on the Will, and doubt even Love's being in its essence merely eine Sache der Empfindung, a mere matter of *feeling*, i.e. a somewhat *found* in us which is not of and from us/Emp. – (= in sich) – Findung, I mean only that my Thoughts are not distinct much less adequate on the subject – and I am not able to convey any grounds of my Belief of the contrary. But the contrary I *do* believe. What Kant affirms of Man in the state of Adam, an ineffable act of the will choosing evil & which is underneath or within *consciousness* tho' incarnate in the *conscience*, inasmuch as it must be conceived as taking place in the Homo *Noumenon*, not the Homo *phainomenon* – something like this I conceive of *Love* – in that highest sense of the Word, which Petrarch understood.[53]

This is the core of Coleridge's uneasiness with Kant and Stoicism: he could not accept Kant's idea that feeling did not play any role in ethics, after collapsing love into feeling. Coleridge objected to Stoicism as early as the *Lectures 1795*, where he pointed out that the Stoic idea of happiness as ataraxy consisted in the attempt to be 'totally unaffected by external objects, to feel neither Love or Pity' (*Lects 1795 (CC)* 157). Ten years later, however, he was ruminating on Kant's argument probably in order to try to moralize his passion for Sara:

> Ours is a life of Probation/we are to contemplate and obey *Duty* for its own sake, and in order to this we . . . must see it not merely abstracted from, but in direct opposition to the *Wish*, the *Inclination/*. . . To perform Duties absolutely from the sense of Duty is the *Ideal*. (*CN* II 2556, Apr 1805)

This attitude was short-lived and he soon resumed his former idea that morality should aim at harmonizing duty and inclination (*CN* II 3026, Feb-May 1807). Coleridge did not change his mind again:

> I reject Kant's *stoic* principle, as false, unnatural, and even immoral, where in his Critik der Practischen Vernun[f]t he treats the affections as

indifferent (*adiaphora*) in ethics, and would persuade us that a man who disliking, and without any feeling of Love for, Virtue yet *acted* virtuously, because and only because it was his *Duty*, is more worthy of our esteem, than the man whose *affections* were aidant to, and congruous with, his Conscience. (*CL* IV 791-2, 13 Dec 1817)

To sum up, Coleridge reacted against two apparently opposite views of love. On the one hand, writers like Pope, Sterne, Ariosto and Boccaccio acknowledged the importance of love for human behaviour, but regarded it as a mere corporeal phenomenon. Love was for them an embellished form of feeling and sensation – what Coleridge called lust. On the other hand, Spinoza, Kant, Godwin and Wordsworth – i.e., Stoic ethics – also regarded love as an offspring of feeling, but found it undesirable or morally meaningless.[54] Coleridge adjudged such ideas immoral and illusory. Feeling was everything to the former and nothing to the latter: both refused to see any sacred or transcendental value in love. If his reaction against the former was predictable, his ethical disappointment with German philosophy and Wordsworth was not the least reason why he turned to other subjects and another culture around 1802. The paradoxical aspect of his admiration for Petrarch's philosophy of love was that he overlooked that the Petrarchan tradition is an uninterrupted hymn to adultery. Despite the failure of his own conjugal life, Coleridge continued to believe in the religious and institutional value of marriage.

Coleridge's attempt at reviving a metaphysics of love may seem anachronistic or a consequence of his prudery. It was certainly an isolated episode in his time, but it must not be forgotten that Shelley tried to do something similar, even if his approach to the same tradition was different. Both were intrigued by the philosophical implications of love; but whereas the tone of Shelley's best love poetry is high and lofty, Coleridge's is intense and intimate.[55] Another important difference between them is frustration. Sara Hutchinson, Coleridge's only true passion, did not return his love, although their friendship compromised his marriage. Coleridge had mocked love poetry 'complaining of the Cruelty of [the] Mistress', yet he painfully discovered that there could be a grain of truth even in trite conventions.[56]

Coleridge was affected both by Petrarch's vision of love and his poetic technique. His responses may seem independent of one another, since they concern different areas of knowledge, but they stem from the same experience. His interest in Petrarch's Latin works and his formal interest in the Petrarchan tradition show the importance the experience had to him.

Coleridge planned what became the 'Soother of Absence' as

> a *series* of Love Poems – truly Sapphic, save that they shall have a large Interfusion of moral Sentiment & calm Imagery on Love in all moods of mind – Philosophic, fantastic, in moods of high enthusiasm, of simple Feeling, of mysticism, of Religion – /comprize in it all the practice, & all the philosophy of Love. (*CN* I 1064, Dec 1801)

He did not seem to realize at the time that a love poetry which combined Classical polish – I take Sapphic to mean this in the context – and detailed psychological analysis had been introduced into modern Europe by Petrarch and adapted by his numerous followers. The note shows that Coleridge was looking for a new style in love poetry beyond the ballad form. Such a style characterizes the last phase of his love poetry, and is easily distinguished from the ballad: it is analytic and descriptive rather than narrative, and it borders on abstract thought rather than story-telling. As such, it fitted Coleridge's taste after 1800, which had become more philosophic. Some of his best poems were written in forms which derived from a reinterpretation of the recovered medieval tradition; Renaissance poetry was not equally fruitful for his poetic writing, although it underlies much of the love poetry he composed in his maturity.

The new, intimate and meditative mood first appears in the sonnet *To Asra* and in the epigrammatic *Love's Sanctuary*, both composed in 1801.[57] In the former, I and Thou replace knights and damsels, who became rare in his love poetry; *Love's Sanctuary* reveals a bent for emblematic poetry which emerged fully in his late period. The character of his interest in the Petrarchan tradition became clearer in the following years, when he mentioned flushing cheeks, smooth necks, shining eyes, in sum the stock-in-trade of Petrarchism, in some poems.[58] The presence of such imagery, however, does not testify to a profound understanding of the Petrarchan tradition, but to an approach as superficial as the *querelle* on the Italian sonnet form in the late eighteenth century. Petrarchist conventions played a marginal role in Coleridge, who repeatedly made fun of them.[59]

Coleridge's serious love poems may seem to have little in common with Petrarch, since they do not imitate his imagery and structures. However, an accurate reading shows the profound affinity of their vision, due to their common Christian and Platonic background. I have already mentioned some images and concepts which recur in Coleridge's love poetry. His idea that the lover regained himself through the other underlies the poems dealing with spiritual exchange, of which the exchange of hearts is a favourite image, as in *The Exchange* or in the fragment 'I STAND alone, nor tho' my heart should break'.[60] Many poems are concerned with the symbolic value of the body, which reveals its soul in love; but the idea did not lead him to extensive descriptions of the body, as in the Renaissance. He focused on few general images, repeating time and again that love spiritualizes the body and makes the spirit shine through and around it.[61] Beauty is such a revelation of the essence of things:

> O Beauty, in a beauteous Body dight!
> Body! that veiling Brightness becom'st bright/
> Fair Cloud which less we see, than by thee see the Light!
>   in avvenenti spoglie
> Bellissim' Alma![62]

A short poem written in 1830, *Song ex improviso on Hearing a Song in Praise of a Lady's Beauty*, summarizes his attitude:

> 'Tis not the lily-brow I prize,
> Nor roseate cheeks, nor sunny eyes,
>   Enough of lilies and of roses!
> A thousand-fold more dear to me
> The gentle look that Love discloses, –
>   The look that Love alone can see!
>   (*PW* (EHC) I 483)

But I hardly need mention that gentle looks, exchanged hearts and shining souls belong to the Provençal and Petrarchan tradition as much as roseate cheeks and lily-brows. Coleridge seems to have dismissed the descriptions of the Petrarchan tradition and to have focused on concepts. His approach accounts for the limits of his love poetry after 1800, which, far from including 'a large Interfusion of moral Sentiment & calm Imagery on Love in all moods of mind' and comprising 'all the practice, & all the philosophy of Love' as he had planned in 1801, does not manage to turn love into the catalyst of a complete view of the world. Coleridge's love poems became epigrammatic late in life, and often consist of one or two rhymed quatrains.[63] However, it is significant that in the late 1820s he successfully returned to longer poetic forms in *Alice du Clos* (if it was composed at the time) and *The Garden of Boccaccio*.

In terms of content, Coleridge's love poems expressed increasing disillusion with frustrated love. Absence and separation characterize them from the beginning, and in the long run took over his hopes, as an impressive number of poems shows.[64]

The meaning of Petrarch's Latin lines prefixed to the love poems in *Sibylline Leaves* should be clearer now. The motto expresses in a more prosaic form concepts often repeated in *Canzoniere*, as for example in the opening sonnet, 'Voi ch'ascoltate': the force of love and its vanity, its irresistible fascination and its cruelty. It is not the least valuable aspect of Petrarch that he managed to turn such commonplaces into fascinating poetry.

The ethical affinities between Petrarch and Coleridge must not over-shadow Coleridge's interest in the formal values of the Petrarchan tradition. Besides his marginalia on *Canzoniere*, his translation of the sonnet 'I dolci colli' (*Canz.* CCIX) testifies to his interest in Petrarch's poetry. He translated from the Italian with an eye either to the 'Soother of Absence' or to the education of his children, as his notes on Giambattista Marino show (*CN* II 2625, ?Jul–Oct 1805). The translation, which will first appear in the *Collected Coleridge* edition, goes as follows:

> Those pleasant hills high tow'ring into air
> Where lingers with delight my captive soul
> Are ever in mine eyes: and still I bear
> Love's burden e'en to earth's extremest pole.
> Oft do I strive to free myself in vain
> From the sad yoke imposed by despot Love;
> Nor time, nor distance can relieve his pain,
> Who's doom'd such bitter pangs as mine to prove.
> Swift bounding o'er the plain the wretched hart
> Whom cruel huntsman from afar espies
> Receives into his side the envenom'd dart
> Which galls him all the more, the more he flies.
> Thus rankling in my heart love's shaft doth lie:
> Tis death to tarry, but what pain to fly!

The original:

> I dolci colli ov'io lasciai me stesso,
> partendo onde partir già mai non posso,
> mi vanno innanzi, et èmmi ognor adosso
> quel caro peso ch'Amor m'à commesso.

Meco di me mi meraviglio spesso,
ch'i' pur vo sempre, et non son anchor mosso
dal bel giogo piú volte indarno scosso,
ma com piú me n'allungo, et piú m'appresso.

Et qual cervo ferito di saetta,
col ferro avelenato dentr'al fianco,
fugge, et piú duolsi quanto piú s'affretta,

tal io, con quello stral dal lato manco,
che mi consuma, et parte mi diletta,
di duol mi struggo, et di fuggir mi stanco.[65]

Coleridge's version diverges from the original in several points, first of all in its Shakespearean form; but the most interesting aspect is that it preserves few of the original antitheses. Line 2, a typical Petrarchan antithesis, is turned by Coleridge into 'Where lingers with delight my captive soul'. The second quatrain consists of an antithesis repeated in a varied form (lines 6 and 8); Coleridge preserved the idea that it is impossible to get rid of Love's yoke, but suppressed Petrarch's conceit that the farther from the hills he travels, the closer he is to them. The antithesis at line 11 is preserved, but the one at line 13 is not. Coleridge made his final line more like an antithesis than the original probably on account of the rhyme.

Some elements of the translation do not appear in the original. Images of nature are expanded: Petrarch's hills are just 'sweet', whereas Coleridge's are 'high tow'ring into air'; Coleridge bears Love's burden 'e'en to earth's extremest pole' (a very Coleridgean word, line 4), whereas the burden – i.e., the yoke – was simply 'imposed' on Petrarch. The hart of Coleridge's sestet is traced by a 'cruel huntsman', whom the original does not mention. Such additions are probably due to the suppression of the antitheses, which compelled Coleridge to expand other elements of the original.

The changes in the second quatrain illustrate the different temper of the two poets. Petrarch is more objective and less self-complacent in his pain: he simply relates his surprise at discovering that he fails to get rid of his haunting recollections. Coleridge turns Love's 'bel giogo' ('beautiful yoke', line 7) into a 'sad yoke', and above all puts lines 7–8 in the third person: 'Nor time, nor distance can relieve his pain,/Who's doom'd such bitter pangs as mine to prove.' Line 8, which is completely Coleridge's, is more querulous and moralizing than the original. Coleridge's view of his amorous condition was more pessimistic than Petrarch's: the original antitheses emphasize that love is painful and delightful at the same time, as at line 13, where love's dart 'mi consuma, et parte mi diletta', while delight disappears in the English text: 'Thus rankling in my heart love's shaft doth lie'.

Coleridge's version is perhaps better defined as an adaptation than a translation. The natural imagery of the original appealed to Romantic taste, and the filter of Coleridge's interpretation is landscape poetry – Wordsworth and perhaps still Bowles' style which he had mocked, as the expansion of natural images and the effort to make the conceited style of the original simple and 'natural' show. Nonetheless, its link with the 'Soother of Absence' is evident: it is a love poem which deals with the pain of absence, and the version implicitly transforms the hills of Vaucluse into the hills of Yorkshire, where he first met Sara. Besides, the translation demonstrates that Coleridge's reading of Petrarch is wider than it seemed, since his marginal notes only concern the beginnings of part I and II of *Canzoniere*. Finally, it is worth noting that Coleridge focused on the poetry and the philosophy of Petrarch's *Canzoniere* and ignored the biographical details of its love story, which was the centre of contemporary attention.[66] But the full meaning of Coleridge's translation from Petrarch cannot be understood without a discussion of his metrical and formal interests in Italian Renaissance poetry.

The 'Essay on Prosody' and Italian Metrics

Wordsworth is reported to have said that Coleridge was 'quite an epicure in sound', and that 'he attributed in part, his writing so little, to the extreme care and labour which he applied in elaborating his metres' (*PW* (EHC) II 1014 n. 1). Coleridge's metrical studies concerned several languages, but mainly English, Greek, Latin and German. His abundant notes on the subject were made with an eye to an essay on poetry or metre which he planned in 1801 and never completed.[67] Observations on Italian prosody appear in the Malta notebooks, where he transcribed and analysed poems by Giovan Battista Strozzi il Vecchio, Marino, Metastasio, and other minor librettists. More exactly, he analysed only Metastasio and the librettists in terms of metrics, whereas he read Marino, Strozzi, Dante and Petrarch from a formal viewpoint – that is, with an eye to their style. I think his interests were interdependent, so that it is illuminating to discuss them together. Their link to the 'Soother of Absence' must not be overlooked, since most of the poems he analysed are love poems or deal with sentimental situations.

A long notebook entry contains several of Coleridge's notes on Italian metrics (*CN* II 2224). It seems to date from October 1804, even though it is too long to have been made on a single occasion. His earliest note on Italian metre dates from between May and July of 1804, and, if his notation is reliable, the untraced poem might be an operatic aria, since its metre seems seven-syllable verse, the particular metre of arias.[68]

Coleridge began to copy out arias from operas and to analyse them metrically in the following months. Kathleen Coburn remarked that his immediate curiosity for Italian prosody recalls his response to metre in Germany in 1798 (*CN* II 2224 n.). But despite his enthusiasm, it was too early for so difficult a task. The notes show that Coleridge was not familiar enough with the rules of Italian metre and language. He applied Classical rules to Italian metrics uncritically, or, to be more precise, the pseudo-classical system which was imposed on English verse. But a system based on long and short syllables (–, ⌣) is suited to the English language if they are understood as metaphors for stressed and unstressed syllables, whereas it is unfit for Italian.

The basic elements of Italian metre are the number of syllables and accents. The main accent is placed on the penultimate syllable of the line, whereas other accents vary in number and place. Coleridge ignored the number of syllables and tried to discover long and short – i.e., stressed and unstressed – syllables. His shaky knowledge of the Italian language helped him to misplace many accents, and the predictable result was confusion.

He believed Italian poets made free and unlimited use of trochees instead of iambics, and ascribed it to

> their more spondaic mode of speaking which is the custom to *caricature*, as it were, when they read poetry. If you listen to an Italian who speaks with propriety, you cannot but observe this more equable *diffusion* of *accent* – words either spondees or pyrrhics (– –, or ⌣ ⌣), not as with us all Iambics or Trochees or Anapæsts. (*CN* II 2224 *f20*)

He was learning empirically that the Italian accent is weaker than the English, although each word, unlike French, 'has its own strong accent which is preserved in sentences and consequently also in verses'. Despite such confusion, Coleridge was able to note different kinds of verse, and continued to collect arias for metrical purposes.[69] His sources include Metastasio, Valentino Fioravanti (1764–1837), Pietro Alessandro Guglielmi (1728–1804) and Sebastiano Nasolini (*c.* 1768–*c.* 1806), whose operas he may have heard in Syracuse in 1804.[70]

Although he commented later that these notes were 'all one blunder, but a blunder inevitable on the common rules of Italian verse' (*CN* II 2224 *f20*), he tried to improve his knowledge of Italian metrics, since he acquired Girolamo Ruscelli's *Del modo di comporre in versi nella lingua italiana*.[71] The treatise is not considered a masterpiece; the only valuable part is its rhyming dictionary, which ran through several reprints. Coleridge made some short marginalia in the volume, but there is no definite evidence that he read much of it. Below his notes on the above-mentioned arias, he classified some Morlack lines as 'endecasyllables' or 'decasyll[ables]', terms he had not used before (*CN* II 2224 *f23v*), which he may have learnt from Ruscelli or during a literary talk.

Operatic arias were not the sole subject of his metrical interests: the marginalia in his copy of Ariosto's *Orlando furioso* probably date from the same time (*CM* (*CC*) I 116–17). Coleridge preferred Spenser's stanza to Ariosto's, and jotted down the rhymes for an Italian Spenserian stanza, in which hendecasyllables should have replaced pentameters and a thirteen-syllable line the final Alexandrine. The correspondence between hendecasyllable and iambic pentameter is acceptable; the other is incorrect, since thirteen-syllable lines do not exist in traditional Italian metrics.[72]

Coleridge never developed a proper understanding of Italian metrics. An undated note shows that he continued conceiving of Italian lines in terms of accents: 'The heroic verse of the Italians has been regarded by all Grammarians and Lexicographers hitherto as Paniambic according to its Rule' (*IS* 153). It is not easy to imagine who these grammarians and lexicographers are. He went so far as to define Italian 'heroic verse', an oblique name for the hendecasyllable, as 'Pan-imabic pentameter hyperacetalectic' [*sic*] (*IS* 154). Dante's and Ariosto's verse was 'composed of five Iambics, the fifth having a superabundant unaccented Syllable'. His conclusion was that, 'If this statement is indeed the true one, the loftiest and most learned Italians are licentious beyond all modern precedent' and even beyond the ancients 'except in the loose Iambics of Latin Comedy' (*IS* 154). The reason he gave for this opinion is no less curious.

The arbitrariness of Italian prosody, 'invented by the Grammar-writers in order to reduce the Italian Verses to the Possibility of Iambic movement', was due to synalephe and synaeresis, two of its characteristic features he could never make sense of. Synalephe and synaeresis are similar principles: in both cases two consecutive vowels, whether belonging to the same word or not, can form one metrical syllable, although they are otherwise two syllables. Coleridge regarded the fact that '"Suo" and "pria", except at the end of the line, form but one syllable', though they are in fact two syllables, as an arbitrament of grammarians (*IS* 154). Even though he objected to 'the whole doctrine of Elisions' – i.e., synalephe – which had been borrowed improperly from Classical metrics, he understood elision as such, that is, the actual omission of the final vowel in a word.[73]

Even if the system may seem arbitrary, it is not, and Coleridge himself intuited the reason for it. He noted that the Italian language as spoken by middle- and lower-class women contained 'no *words*, but a fusion of sounds' (*CN* II 2812, Mar–Apr 1806). In other words, he realised that the glottal stop does not exist in Italian, so that pronunciation does not separate consecutive vowels but runs uninterrupted through them. In Italian verse, therefore, 'two consecutive vowels can form one syllable as a rule, that is, according to the actual pronunciation'.[74] This accounts for synalephe and synaeresis.

In spite of his theoretical hostility, Coleridge appreciated the effects of synalephe and synaeresis. He argued that Classical metres were superior to modern metres, and the main reason was

> That the common manner of talking was far less caught from *spelling* & *reading*/consequently more streamy & tho' less intellectual in the colder <might I not say meaner> and contradistinctive sense of the word, and less facilitative of Intellect (as contra-distinguished from Passion, or Feeling) yet was necessarily more passionate and musical. (*CN* II 2835, Apr–May 1806)

He found a modern instance of it in Italian metrics, especially in comparison to German and English. Italians

> not only run lines into each other more easily & happily than we – at least, in all our lyric poetry – but with perfect ease fused words together, not only in the same Line, but even from one into the another. This latter had already become impracticable among the Romans, a less impassioned people. (*CN* II 2835, Apr–May 1806)

Although it is not clear what he means by running lines into each other, the note expresses admiration for the flowing sound of Italian poetry and, consequently, for the metrical figures he criticized.[75] I do not need to emphasize how important this was to his view of poetry. He often repeated that 'the ancients *sang* their poetry', whereas the English 'have substituted *reading*, impassioned and tuneful *reading*, I grant, but still *reading*, for *recitative*'.[76] He read his own poetry almost as if it was recitative, that is, in a musical rather than a rhetorical way.[77]

Metastasio and Melodrama

The fact that Metastasio and other librettists rather than the great early poets were the first subjects of Coleridge's metrical studies is not surprising to the readers who are aware of Metastasio's fame in the early nineteenth century. Coleridge's notes cannot be separated from his interest in Italian opera.

The popularity of melodrama in eighteenth- and early nineteenth-century England is well known, and it played a significant role in the developing interest in Italian literature.[78] Students of Italian were often motivated by the desire to understand and sometimes to sing the librettoes in the original. Metastasio was very popular in the last decades of the eighteenth century: he was considered as the master of the poets who wrote for the opera, and his style was refined and easy. Opera-goers who began the study of the Italian language could not pretend more. Besides, Metastasio's fame was equally great among literary critics.

Giuseppe Baretti, who popularized Italian literature around the mid-eighteenth century, regarded Metastasio as the greatest Italian poet. In 1784 Agostino Isola edited an anthology of Italian poetry translated by his students at Cambridge which included twenty-six of Metastasio's poems and none of Dante. A copy of the volume was owned by William Wordsworth, who was an admirer of Metastasio.[79] In other words, Metastasio was part of the cultural climate of the time, and his fame declined very slowly, since his selected works enjoyed at least four English editions between 1815 and 1835.[80]

Coleridge, whose interest in music and the opera developed in the 1790s, shared such enthusiasm. At Cambridge he took violin lessons, attended concerts, and was in touch with the Madrigal Society, some of whose members set to music a few of his early poems. He even planned to write a serious opera which one of the Clagget brothers would set to music and stage in London.[81] The concerts he attended in London between 1802 and 1804 revived his enthusiasm for melodrama.[82]

Coleridge's interest did not decrease in Italy, where he frequently attended opera-houses, beginning from the season at Syracuse in the early autumn of 1804. Here he became acquainted with Cecilia Bertozzi, the prima donna of the Palermo company performing at Syracuse, who tried to seduce him.[83] He even attempted to improve his technical knowledge of music, since he mentioned Vincenzo Manfredini's treatise of harmonics (Venice 1775). Manfredini reminded him of Tartini's harmonic system, with which he was acquainted.[84] However, Coleridge's familiarity with musical theory must not be overrated: he always regretted he had not acquired a deeper knowledge of it.[85] Nor was he too talented for music: 'An Ear for Music is a very different thing from a Taste for Music. I have no Ear whatever. I could not for my life sing an air. But I have the intensest delight in Music' (*TT* (*CC*) 5 Oct 1830).

Metastasio and Cimarosa were the Italian artists involved in the melodrama he preferred. His attitude to Cimarosa shows he was more interested in the *opera seria* than comic opera. Cimarosa is first of all the author of *Il matrimonio segreto* (1792), a popular work which is considered the highest achievement of *opera buffa*. Coleridge never mentioned *Il matrimonio segreto*, but only *Gli Orazi e i Curiazi* (1796), Cimarosa's most popular *opera seria*.[86] Coleridge considered Cimarosa mainly as a harmonious composer, since Cimarosa appears as an example in his definitions of harmony and of the effects of music on the mind. He mentioned him as one of the greatest composers together with Purcell, Handel, Haydn, Mozart and Beethoven, although he substituted Palestrina for him late in life.[87]

Coleridge's attitude to Rossini reveals the limits of his musical taste, which were 'in the tradition of the enlightened concert-goers of his day' (Barry 139). Rossini was first staged in England in 1818 and soon became the most popular Italian composer; his fame was also enormous on the Continent. Like the faithful followers of Cimarosa and Paisiello, Coleridge was hostile to Rossini, and thought his music sounded like 'nonsense verse' (*CH* 628; *TT* (*CC*) 5 Oct 1830; N 52.6 f6, 1833). I suspect there might be some elitist affectation in Coleridge's judgement, since he once praised Rossini's *Tancredi* after taking it for a work of Mozart's (*CN* IV 4927, 1822). His attitude was not isolated: Hegel regarded his taste as corrupted because he preferred Rossini to Mozart; Giacomo Leopardi thought Rossini's melodies were popular because they were predictable.[88]

Coleridge left us more comments on operatic librettoes than music, since his involvement was always literary rather than musical. The recent discovery of a copy of Metastasio's works inscribed and annotated by him shows that his knowledge of the Italian dramatist was deeper than it seemed.[89] The volumes were probably purchased soon after his arrival in Malta, where he read Metastasio's letters (*CN* II 2222), but his interest continued after the Italian period. In 1807 he copied out the titles of two arias of Metastasio, one of which, 'Amo te solo', he may have heard in Syracuse (*CN* II 3190). Interestingly, it is a love aria in Metastasio's typical style. Both titles appear again with reference to his sentimental situation in an 1811 entry in which they precede a poetic fragment.[90]

The links with the 'Soother of Absence' are in this case subordinated to the theoretical interest in theatre. Despite the limits of Coleridge's musical knowledge, he developed a view of the opera which became part of his general theory of drama. His initial reaction to Metastasio was the same as Addison's and Johnson's: he criticized melodrama for the improbability of its characters and situations.[91] This point is made repeatedly in the notes to *Semiramide* (1729), which he thought the worst play of the collection.

He disliked it for its treatment of love and its unlikely representation of Oriental culture, and was surprised it could be performed at Court.[92] However, he became aware of the limits of his opinion, even though his admiration for the opera was never devoid of reservations. He noted that

> To defend the *Opera* = all the objections against *equally* applicable to Tragedy & Comedy without music, & all proceed on the false principle, that Theatrical representations are *Copies* of nature whereas they are imitations. (*CN* II 2211, Oct 1804)

This is his first distinction between copy and imitation, which, being cardinal in his aesthetics, has led scholars to tangle with the familiar question of German sources. The distinction was in effect prompted by Metastasio, who discussed imitation in the first part of his *Estratto dell'arte poetica d'Aristotile e considerazioni su la medesima*, a work which Coleridge annotated. Chapter IV promises to analyse the '*differences between imitation* (imitazione) *and copy* (copia), *which lead to very noxious sophisms if ignored*'. Copyists aim at *vero*: they try to reproduce the original exactly in order to create illusion; imitators aim at *verosimile* (verisimilar), something like the original but which does not conceal its difference.[93] Coleridge's idea of copy and imitation is dissimilar from Metastasio's, which was thought-provoking for this reason.

Coleridge found the opera a stimulating subject for his reflections on the problem of imitation, since he returned to it. When he discussed realism in drama, he referred to the opera as the most artificial extreme, to domestic tragedy as the most realistic, and to Shakespeare as a sort of middle ground between them. Despite its artificiality, melodrama can give us great delight with its music and dance (*L Lects* (*CC*) I 226–7, 1811). Operatic characters, who are conventional types rather than tridimensional figures, confirm that melodrama is non-realistic.[94] In other words, the opera gave him the opportunity to experience a form of theatre radically different from non-musical modern drama. Greek tragedy was in his mind more like Italian opera than Shakespearian drama, although music was subordinated to poetry in Greece, whereas it was the contrary with melodrama. That is why 'little pleasure is lost by ignorance of the Italian Language' and little is 'gained by the knowledge of it' (*L Lects* (*CC*) I 441, 1812; II 120, 1818). Choral church music was perhaps a better analogy.[95]

Despite the comparisons Coleridge drew between melodrama and Greek theatre, he praised the suppression of the chorus, 'a barbarous and wearisome superfluity', in Paisiello's *Elfrida*, whose performance he reviewed in 1811 (*EOT* (*CC*) II 195–7). He saw a parallel between the dance included in some operas, like Cimarosa's *Gli Orazi e i Curiazi*, and the dance of Greek drama ('On Poesy or Art', *BL*, 1907, II 256). He had seen Cimarosa's work in Leghorn, and referred to it as a perfect example of imitation, that is, of balance between likeness and difference (N Q f33, after 1829). He thought French and Italian tragedy were less like Greek drama than Shakespeare was, since the former were mere copies of the classics, whereas Shakespeare used different means to achieve results analogous to the classics (*L Lects* (*CC*) II 511).

Racine and Metastasio were unfavourably compared to 'our myriad-minded Shakespeare' (*SM* (*CC*) 79), but the mere fact of putting Metastasio on a level with Racine would seem surprising today. Coleridge also complained that Metastasio's 'melodious dialogues' were preferred to Milton's poetry (*Friend* (*CC*) I 12–13); but despite such reservations, he never questioned Metastasio's taste. He praised him for placing the aria always at the end of the scene and for raising the style of the preceding recitative, so that there was no abrupt change of feeling, as there is in comic opera (*BL* (*CC*) II 122). However, Coleridge contrasted the structure of the aria in Metastasio with the song in Shakespeare: the former is placed at the end of the scene as the character's exit speech, thereby combining lyrical and dramatic values, whereas Shakespeare's songs are given as songs and not as speeches. They are part of the dramatic and not only combined with it.[96] Coleridge was involved in the problem as a critic and a playwright: parts of his *Remorse* were set to music by Michael Kelly.

Metastasio became in Coleridge's mind the emblem of Italian drama, of which he knew little else. In a long marginal note at the end of *L'eroe cinese* (1752; *Opere*, vol. VII), he argued that the play was imperfect, but its plot was interesting and could have been used better. The play embodied the ideal of Italian drama, which Metastasio expressed better than his successors – that is, the later Italian librettists.[97] It was a poor ideal, since it was too remote from life, and it was necessary to aim at something higher.

Coleridge's observations are not profound, but the other leading Romantics had nothing more substantial to say on melodrama, which was perhaps the most popular Italian form of art in contemporary England. But they were all poets and literary critics, and the native influence of Elizabethan drama was overwhelming in comparison to the opera, despite the pleasure they took in it.

Giambattista Marino and Baroque Poetry

Coleridge's exploration of Italian lyric poetry for the 'Soother of Absence' and the essay on prosody was not confined to Petrarch and Metastasio;

but instead of using an anthology, he preferred to make his own selection from original sources. The poets he chose show that his reading was intended to provide a general view of Italian lyric poetry, from which only the fifteenth century remained excluded: Dante and Petrarch were specimens of the *Trecento*, Ariosto of the early sixteenth century, Strozzi and Guarini of the late sixteenth century, Chiabrera and Marino of the seventeenth century, and Metastasio of the eighteenth century.

The transcription of four sonnets of Giambattista Marino (1564–1625) – most likely during the summer of 1805 – was Coleridge's next step into Italian poetry. The comments on Marino, Guarini and Chiabrera, provide a view of his attitude to Italian Baroque poetry. Style rather than metre seems to have been Coleridge's concern at the time: he transcribed Marino's *Sonetto alla Principessa di Stigliano che va in barca per la Riviera di Posillipo* 'for the sake of the Diction', and *Il rossignuol cantante* 'for the sweetness and simple Flow of the Style and of the Narration'. Although he admired their style, he blamed the view of nature they embodied: 'I cannot but think, that this mode of belying the lovely countenance of Things & *red-ochring* the rose, must be injurious to the moral tact both of the authors & their admirers'.[98]

Marino's hedonistic sensualism did not engage Coleridge, who was more intrigued by two sonnets on metaphysical and moral subjects. *Tratta delle miserie umane*, a sonnet commonly anthologised, deals with the hardness and shortness of human life.[99] Coleridge found it 'superior to all the imitations & copies' he had seen, which probably means all the poems on the same subject he had read. He only objected to one word, 'serena' ('serene') at line 7. Although it is a small objection, it confirms his attitude to Marino's optimism. The line defines adult age as 'more sure and more serene' than childhood, a view Coleridge could not accept, as his attempts to rephrase the line show.[100]

The last sonnet he transcribed was 'Sotto caliginose ombre profonde', which he analysed in detail.[101] Coleridge thought it was 'a noble poem', even if it contained 'too many defects and botches'; in this case, he preferred the subject of the poem to its style.[102] Coleridge's interest in the subject of the poem was genuine, whereas Marino considered it as a chance for virtuoso variations on a difficult theme. In spite of the objections, Coleridge noted that he read the sonnet 'at first *well contented*, saving the "Argo"': in other words, melody at first prevailed over any other element.

It is noteworthy that Coleridge's reading of Marino focused on the sonnets. The edition he used is not known; if it was an *opera omnia*, he remarkably ignored *L'Adone*, Marino's long poem and most characteristic achievement, as well as other poems like madrigals, eclogues and *canzoni*. However, even *La Lira*, the collection of Marino's shorter poems, does not include only sonnets.[103]

The poems Coleridge transcribed deal with three subjects: nature, metaphysics and love. His reaction against the Baroque view of nature was predictable: Baroque nature is mythologized and physiocentric, and as such unpalatable to Romantic sensibility. Marino's main interest was external reality, which he extensively described in his works.[104] It is not surprising that Coleridge found Marino's moral and metaphysical poems more to his taste. The sonnets he transcribed, *Tratta delle miserie umane* and 'Sotto caliginose ombre profonde', are based on Celio Magno's *canzone Deus* (1597). Marino's use of his source shows that his interest in grave subjects, unlike Celio Magno's, was stylistic rather than philosophical.[105] Coleridge would probably have found Magno's meditative tone more congenial than Marino's descriptiveness. His response to Marino's love poetry confirms that his taste inclined to sixteenth- rather than seventeenth-century Italian lyric.

When Coleridge transcribed Marino's sonnet to the Princess of Stigliano, he commented: 'the Style being its whole, my attention will be concentrated and confined to this one Object while I am attempting to translate it . . . in order to catch its graces in English' (*CN* II 2625). Although no hypothetical version of the Maltese period is extant, he translated a sonnet of Marino in September 1808.[106] The translation and the notes may have been made with an eye to Hartley's and Derwent's education or to teaching young Sara and her mother Italian.[107] It is remarkable that Coleridge decided to teach his daughter and wife Italian, but it is more important at this point to highlight the links between his translation from Marino and the 'Soother of Absence'. Whatever the reason for his translation, the two purposes are not incompatible.

Marino's sonnet *Alla sua amica* goes as follows:

> Donna, siam rei di morte. Errasti, errai;
> Di perdon non son degni i nostri errori,
> Tu che avventasti in me sí fieri ardori;
> Io che le fiamme a sí bel sol furai.
>   Io che una fiera rigida adorai,
> Tu che fosti sord'aspe a' miei dolori;
> Tu nell'ire ostinata, io negli amori:
> Tu pur troppo sdegnasti, io troppo amai.
>   Or la pena laggiú nel cieco averno:
> Pari al fallo n'aspetta. Arderà poi,
> Chi visse in foco, in vivo foco eterno

Quivi: se Amor fia giusto amboduo noi
All'incendio dannati, avrem l'inferno,
Tu nel mio core, ed io negli occhi tuoi.

Coleridge's version:

LADY, to Death we're doom'd, our crime the same!
Thou, that in me thou kindled'st such fierce heat;
I, that my heart did of a Sun so sweet
The rays concentre to so hot a flame.
I, fascinated by an Adder's eye –
Deaf as an Adder thou to all my pain;
Thou obstinate in Scorn, in Passion I –
I lov'd too much, too much didst thou disdain.
Hear then our doom in Hell as just as stern,
Our sentence equal as our crimes conspire –
Who living bask'd at Beauty's earthly fire,
In living flames eternal there must burn –
Hell for us both fit places too supplies –
In *my* heart thou wilt burn, I *roast* before thine eyes.[108]

The translation shows that Coleridge continued to read Marino after his
return to England, and its context seems to be the 'Soother of Absence', as
the entry is surrounded by notes on Sara Hutchinson and fragments of
love poems. Since he planned to write a love poem 'in simple & elegant
verse, as an imitation of Marini – and of too large a part of the Madrigals of
Guarini' (*CN* III 3379, Sept 1808), it is worth analysing his view of them.

His version from Marino shows how far his attitude to traditional love
poetry had changed after the experience of Italian lyric. He had noted in
1804 his 'utter want of Sympathy with all the ordinary Love-poems,
complaining of the Cruelty of my Mistress' (*CN* II 2062); four years later,
he admired and intended to imitate Marino, who insisted on the theme of
his mistress's indifference.

Coleridge's attitude to conceits had also changed. We earlier saw him
mock Petrarch in this respect; later he did not object to Marino's conceits,
which are more frequent and extreme than Petrarch's.[109] His version of
Marino's *Alla sua amica* shows that his understanding of the
Petrarchesque tradition had widened. The translation is closer to its
original than his version from Petrarch was, and, above all, it is
distinguished by its stylistic faithfulness. The flamboyant rhetoric of
Marino's text was neither suppressed nor made more 'simple and natural'
in English; on the contrary, some devices were carried to extremes.

Marino's sonnet is constructed on repeated binary parallelisms: each sentence involving the 'I' is counterbalanced by a sentence involving the 'Thou'. Coleridge preserved the binary structure as far as he could, and even stressed it by adding two chiasmi that are not in the original at lines 7 and 8. Besides, 'I, fascinated by an Adder's eye' has more 'point' than Marino's line 6 ('I, who adored an implacable monster'). He was perhaps developing a taste for artifice, since the sonnet is structurally like 'Sotto caliginose ombre profonde': it is based on a single image – love as fire – expanded over fourteen lines. Its irreverent tone is also noteworthy: it turns the idea of eternal damnation to burlesque by stating that lovers will suffer in hell as on earth, that is, in each other's hearts and eyes. The hyperbolic overtones of the sonnet are due to such mock-metaphysics, and to the innuendo in 'morte', which may mean *petite mort* in the context.

Coleridge's intention to write a poem in Marino's style is surprising, since Marino's view of women is very far from his own. The two sonnets portraying women he transcribed are not in Marino's characteristic manner. The sonnet for the Princess of Stigliano is an encomiastic piece, which accounts for the large presence of mythology in it.[110] The picture is elegant and learned but cool. Feeling is more lively in *Alla sua amica*, but neither are particularly descriptive, unlike most of Marino's love poems, which represent love by external signs and not by interior events. The poet usually describes the physical look of women – lips, eyes, forehead, hair, hands etc. – so that women are generically portrayed by 'traditional elements which might be traced back to the abstract profile of Classical lyric'.[111] Marino's eroticism, the only thing he took seriously and that could move him, was the offspring of such objectivism.[112] Personal feelings for a lover are rare in Marino, but despite his anti-Petrarchism, Petrarch and Petrarchism remained his major poetic sources. Marino expanded Petrarch's themes in number but did not renew them radically. From a stylistic viewpoint, he used in a new way the technique he inherited from Petrarchism.[113]

The implications of Coleridge's transcriptions from Marino should now be clearer. Marino and his followers expanded those aspects of Petrarch Coleridge was less interested in: his descriptions. The transcriptions show that Coleridge tended to link Marino either with seventeenth-century sacred poetry or with Renaissance lyric. 'Sotto caliginose ombre profonde' and *Tratta delle miserie umane* belong to a moral, philosophic mode which is not as prominent as sensuousness in Marino.

I pointed out that the source of both sonnets is Celio Magno, a late sixteenth-century Petrarchist. But Petrarchism is also the immediate source of *Alla sua amica*.[114] This sonnet, though different from its models, has wider intellectual implications than the love poems of Marino which are merely descriptive.[115] Besides, it is worth noting that Coleridge was struck by Marino's flowing melody rather than his uninterrupted metaphorizing. His admiration is justified: musical compositions based on Marino's texts are innumerable.[116]

Coleridge's interest in Marino is especially noteworthy if we consider that he was an unpopular writer in the early nineteenth century. He was included in anthologies of Italian poetry and had his admirers, but none of the great Romantics took interest in him.[117] Anti-Marinists from Chiabrera to Guidi and Filicaia drew more public attention. Coleridge's final judgement on Marino shows how far his taste changed in two decades:

> The seductive faults, the *dulcia vita* of Cowley, Marini, or Darwin might reasonably be thought capable of corrupting the public judgement for half a century, and require a twenty years war . . . in order to dethrone the usurper and re-establish the legitimate taste. But that a downright simpleness, under the affectation of simplicity, prosaic words in feeble metre, silly thoughts in childish phrases . . . should succeed in forming a school of imitators . . . and that this bare and bald *counterfeit* of poetry, which is characterized as *below* criticism, should for nearly twenty years have well-nigh *engrossed* criticism, as the main, if not the only, butt of review, magazine, poem, and paragraph; – this is indeed matter of wonder! (*BL (CC)* I 74–5)

Although his view of Marino was not positive, he now considered him as less dangerous than the late eighteenth-century manner of which he got rid only after the experience of Italian lyric poetry, as his translations from Petrarch and Marino demonstrate. Cowley, Marino and Darwin have in common not only their 'seductive faults', but also their descriptiveness.[118]

Gabriello Chiabrera (1552–1638) has long been considered as the anti-Marino, the champion of healthy, classicist taste in a corrupted age. He was the main poetic model in eighteenth-century Italy, when Marino's reputation was very low. Modern research has demonstrated that such a critical view is untenable: far from being a stranger to his own age, Chiabrera was as Baroque as Marino, though in a different way. Theodor Elwert has compared the relation between Marino and Chiabrera to the relation between Bernini and Borromini or Caravaggio and the Carraccis: a revolutionary aesthetics was countered by a more conservative aesthetics which was nonetheless innovating.[119] The most significant difference between Marino and Chiabrera is their metrics. Marino's metres are relatively traditional, whereas one of Chiabrera's greatest merits was the invention of metrical and stanzaic forms which were imitated and varied in the following centuries. The *canzonetta melica* ('melic canzonetta') and the ode are prominent among his innovations.[120]

It is remarkable that Coleridge and Wordsworth paid attention to Chiabrera's loftiest mode – the ode – and ignored the lighter *canzonette*. Coleridge's interest is confined to the 1809 *Friend* period, though he probably discovered Chiabrera in Malta.[121] The passages he transcribed from Chiabrera's odes in the May of 1808 confirm attitudes to the Baroque which emerged in his reading of Marino. The substitution of 'Il Sole' ('the Sun') for 'Febo' ('Phoebus') is due to his dislike of mythology; it also shows that his knowledge of Italian metrics had not improved, since the correction adds a syllable to the original line.[122] The passages he transcribed were quoted and translated in *The Friend*, in which a few of Chiabrera's epitaphs appeared.[123] They were translated by Wordsworth, who admired them particularly. Wordsworth's essays on epitaphs were a kind of conclusion to the enterprise.[124]

The reason for Coleridge's and Wordsworth's interest is evident. Coleridge said that Chiabrera's ode on Columbus 'in the strength of the thought and the lofty majesty of the poetry, has but "few peers in ancient or in modern song"' (*Friend (CC)* I 480, 1818). Wordsworth stated that monuments and epitaphs derive 'from two sources of feeling: but these do in fact resolve themselves into one' (*Friend (CC)* II 336). In other words, they appreciated in Chiabrera a monumental, dignified style which they probably linked with Milton's and Gray's.[125] Their enthusiasm had some antecedents: Thomas J. Mathias, for example, found in Chiabrera's Pindaric odes the same lofty and exalted tone as in the odes of ancient Greece.[126]

Coleridge's view of Chiabrera explains a poem like A *Tombless Epitaph*, composed in the same period. It is an idealized self-portrait adapted from Chiabrera's epitaph for Ambrosio Salinero, and it owes something to Wordsworth's version of the original.[127] Although Chiabrera's lofty style is not as turgid as Marino's, it is mannered and easily becomes bombastic. I think it sounds bathetic when used for an epitaph on oneself, as in Coleridge's poem. It is difficult to understand how Wordsworth could demand that an epitaph should 'speak, in a tone which shall sink into the heart', and simultaneously admire Chiabrera's mannered rhetoric.[128] However unconvincing Coleridge's and Wordsworth's reasons may be, the interesting point for my argument is their preference for Chiabrera's classicizing odes above the *canzonette*, elegant proto-rococo arabesques of sound.

Coleridge's attitude to Battista Guarini is analogous to his attitude to Marino. He disliked Guarini's *Pastor fido*, the pastoral tragicomedy to which his fame is due, and was intrigued by his lyrical poetry.[129] Coleridge's interest, which lasted over ten years, was not superficial: I think the 'Soother of Absence', more than religious impulses, motivated his reading.[130]

Coleridge found in Guarini, as a transitional figure, different poetic modes: his madrigals can be regarded as Petrarchistic, the allegoric dialogue he translated as Baroque. The translation of Guarini's *Fede, Speranza, Carità* has probably something to do with his teaching Sara Coleridge Italian (*PW* (*CC*) No 497, editorial note). However, the reason why he translated *that* poem rather than any other may be found at lines 21–3, where Charity asks: 'What is Man's soul of Love deprived?', and Hope and Faith answer: 'It like a Harp untunéd is/That sounds, indeed, but sounds amiss' (*PW* (EHC) I 428). The image of the soul as a harp is Coleridgean, and probably struck him. The conclusion of the poem argues that 'From holy Love all good gifts are derived' (line 24).[131]

If the link of Coleridge's translation of the allegoric dialogue with Sara Hutchinson is indirect, his earlier transcriptions from Guarini are evidently part of his 'Soother of Absence' project. The two madrigals deal with the pain of love, and with desire as sin. Coleridge admired them, since in September 1808 he planned a love poem 'in simple & elegant verse, as an imitation of Marini – and of too large a part of the Madrigals of Guarini himself'.[132]

It is not surprising that Coleridge preferred Guarini's madrigals, which are formally close to Petrarchism, to the *Pastor fido*.[133] However, his remark on 'too large a part of the Madrigals of Guarini' expresses implicit reservations about them, and the reason is to be found in the character of Guarini's short poems, about which I agree with Ettora Bonora:

> The *Rime* do not contain the warmth of poetry, but great literary skill. The rhythms and learned balance of the Bembesque poetic language are observed, but without participating in the vital reasons of Petrarchism . . . The *Rime*, like other contemporary *canzonieri*, contain encomiastic, occasional and love poems; besides, a more refined grace appears in the numerous madrigals, whose witticisms often embody the languid music which belongs to many passages of the *Pastor fido*.[134]

Coleridge wrote two versions of a poetic fragment after his translation from Marino and his plan for a poem in Marino's and Guarini's manner:

> Two wedded hearts, if ere were such,
> Imprison'd in adjoining cells,
> Across whose thin partition-wall
> The builder left one narrow rent,
> And where, most content in discontent,
> A joy with itself at strife –
> Die into an intenser life. (PW (EHC) II 1003)

> The Builder left one narrow rent,
> Two wedded hearts, if ere were such,
> Contented most in discontent
> [Still] There cling, and try in vain to touch!
> O Joy with thy own Joy at Strife,
> That yearning for the Realm above
> Would'st die into intenser Life
> And union absolute of Love.
> (CN III 3379, Sept 1808)[135]

Marino's and Guarini's influence is perceivable in the antithesis at line 7 and the anaclasis at line 5 of the second fragment. The short structure and the tone of the poem derive from Coleridge's idea of the madrigal.[136] The poem he planned to write in Marino's and Guarini's 'simple & elegant verse' is even more interesting:

> If love be the genial Sun of human nature, unkindly has he divided his rays in acting on me and {Sara} – on her poured all his Light and Splendor, & permeated my Being with his invisible Rays of Heat alone/ She shines and is *cold*, as the tropic Firefly – I dark and uncomely would better resemble the Cricket in hot ashes – my Soul at least might be considered as a Cricket eradiating the heat which gradually cinerizing the Heart produced the embery ashes, from among which it chirps, out of his hiding-place. (CN III 3379, Sept 1808)

This remarkable note shows how far Coleridge's enthusiasm for the Petrarchan tradition had gone. The central image of the plan is the oxymoron 'icy fire', the most peculiar of Petrarchistic conventions. Moreover, the image of the soul as a cricket is extravagant and very much like a conceit.[137] The reason for such enthusiasm can be found in his reading of Italian Renaissance lyrics. According to Elwert, the continuity between Renaissance and Baroque lyric poetry is nowhere so evident as in

Italy.[138] There are differences, of course, but the development of Coleridge's view of poetry was stimulated by the intuition of the continuity rather than the differences between them.[139]

Giovan Battista Strozzi il Vecchio

Coleridge's comments on Giovan Battista Strozzi il Vecchio are crucial to my argument. Coleridge read the first edition of Strozzi's poems (Sermartelli, Firenze 1593) probably in the summer of 1805, and transcribed twenty-seven madrigals whose formal polish struck him. The transcription is preceded by a long comparison between the Renaissance poetic style and early nineteenth-century poetry which, in an expanded but similar form, became chapter XVI of *Biographia Literaria*. It is not exaggerating to argue that this note introduced a new perspective in Coleridge's view of poetry. The annotation is worth citing in full:

> In the present age the Poet proposes to himself as his main Object & most characteristic of his art, new and striking Images, incidents that interest the Affections or excite the curiosity of the Reader; and both his characters and his descriptions he individualizes and specifies as much as possible, even to a degree of Portraiture/Meanwhile in his diction and metre he is either careless (W. Scott) or adopts some mechanical measure, of which one couplet or stanza is an adequate specimen, with a language which claims to be poetical for no better reason, than that it would be intolerable in conversation or prose . . . Now in the polished elder poets, especially of Italy, all is reversed – . . . The imagery is almost always *general*, Sun, Moon, Flowers, Breezes, Murmuring Streams, warbling Songsters, delicious Shades, &c – their thoughts seldom novel or very striking, while in a faulty extreme they placed the essence of Poetry in the *art* of Poetry, that is, in the exquisite polish of the Diction with perfect simplicity, equally avoiding every word which a man of rank would not use in common conversation, and every phrase, which none but a bookish man would use – in the studied position of these words, so as not only to be melodious, but that the melody of each should refer to, assist, & be assisted by, all the foregoing & following words of the same period, or Stanza, and in like labor, the greater because unbetrayed, in the variety of harmony in the metres – not as now by invention of new Metres, which have a specific overpowering tune of their own (such as Monk Lewis's Alonzo & Imogen, from the German, or Campbell's Hohenlinden, &c) but by countless subtleties in the common metre of the class of Poetry in which they are composing.[140]

The 'endless Rage of Novelty' (*CN* II 2598, May–Jun 1805) of modern poets led them to concentrate on their subjects in order to invent something unusual; metre and diction – i.e., style – were neglected. Here is the first important result of Coleridge's interest in Italian metrics, despite his imperfect understanding of them. Modern ballad metres were either flat and mechanic, like Scott's, or insupportably galloping, like Lewis' and Campbell's, if they were new. Pope's version of Homer, Darwin's *Temple of Nature*, and metres derived from German ballads would be quoted in the *Biographia* as similar examples ((*CC*) II 30, 33–4).

It may seem arrogant to claim that Coleridge, the author of *Kubla Khan, The Rhyme of the Ancient Mariner* and *Christabel*, could discover the value of polished versification as late as 1805. The point is that he discovered a form of metre he had previously neglected. In his transcendental ballads he invented an accentual type of verse distinct from the accentual–syllabic system which was predominant in the eighteenth century. The metres of his major poems are linked to the recovery of the medieval poetic tradition begun by Percy and Thomas Warton, and the poetic movement in the wake of it. If Coleridge had not paid much attention to Renaissance poetry in terms of metrics before 1804, he could not ignore it as a critic, since its influence on European poetry was enormous. This is why it can be argued that he discovered Renaissance metrics around 1805; and why Petrarch and Petrarchism played a more important role than Dante in his understanding of modern European lyric poetry, whose core is Petrarchan rather than Dantesque.

Coleridge's remarks on the language of poetry reflect the same attitude. Modern literature often used an exotic language, as if strange implicitly meant poetic. He wrote in 1809:

> that a poet ever uses a word as *poetical*, i.e. formally – which he – in the same mood & thought – would not use, in prose or conversation, Milton's Prose Works assist me in disproving . . . The sole difference, *in style*, is that poetry demands a *severer keeping* – it admits nothing that Prose may not often admit; but it *oftener* rejects. (*CN* III 3611)

He found evidence for this in modern German writers like Klopstock, Wieland, Schiller and Goethe, but he first became aware of it through Italian Renaissance poetry. It is surprising that Coleridge, who worked to create a modern ballad style, criticized it now so severely. His taste was undergoing a radical change, or was at least widening.

The praise of Renaissance polish, which was not uncommon in his time, should not conceal the important point of the note. Coleridge understood that Petrarchism provided the writer with a poetic grammar, as it were: syntax, vocabulary, rhetorical figures, imagery, metres and, to a certain extent, even thought – the notorious conceits – derived from Petrarch. The essence of poetry was identified as the art of arranging given material and not the invention of new images and metres, as in modern literature. Imagery was general and poets did not tend to individualize situations and characters: they aimed at *universalia*, not at *particularia*. Their language was courtly and excluded all technical codes except Petrarchan language and the jargon of the Neoplatonic theory of love. It is an anti-expressionist poetic in which single words do not stand out, but contribute to a whole. The result is a simple and melodious style, a harmony which Coleridge ascribed to the subordination of the individual components to the whole. This satisfied his holism as well as his ear. As he said later, 'to please me, a Poem must be either music or sense – if it is neither, I confess I cannot interest myself in it' (*TT* (*CC*) 5 Apr 1833).

But such insistence on simplicity implies a momentous discovery: that simplicity is the result of artifice. He wrote of Strozzi's poems that, 'trifles as they are, they were probably elaborated with great care; yet in the perusal we refer them to a spontaneous energy rather than to voluntary effort' (*BL* (*CC*) II 34). Coleridge's new awareness marked the definitive end of his participation in the naïve, primitivist poetics of Bowles, which was still perceivable in his translation from Petrarch. Simplicity now depended on 'exquisite polish', the 'perfection of Art', 'the greater because unbetrayed': it is Castiglione's courtly concept of *sprezzatura*. The consequence was a different view of the conceits and rhetorical devices he had dismissed previously.

Coleridge's new attitude emerged in his comments on Baroque poetry and his fragments for the 'Soother of Absence'. Moreover, he planned an

Essay in defence of Punning – (Apology for Paronomasy, alias Punning)
to defend those turn of words,

che l'onda chiara
    1   2

E l'ombra non men cara,
    1   2

in certain styles of writing, by proving that Language itself is formed upon associations of this kind . . . that words are not mere symbols of things & thoughts, but themselves things – and that any harmony in the things symbolized will perforce be presented to us more easily as well as with additional beauty by a correspondent harmony of the Symbols with each other. . . . This is the beauty of homogeneous Languages – So veni, vidi, vici. (*CN* III 3762, Apr–Jun 1810)

Surely Roman Jakobson would have been delighted by such ideas. The example cited in the note is taken from a madrigal of Strozzi he had transcribed, 'Aure dell'angoscioso viver mio'.[141] Paronomasy is frequent in Strozzi, and appears in other madrigals Coleridge copied out.[142] The important point is that the note shows new understanding of a poetic tradition in which such devices were common.

Although Coleridge argued that he turned to Italian Renaissance poetry as a source of Shakespeare's poems, the effects of his experience of Petrarchism influenced not only his conception of poetry, but also his view of Shakespeare's plays. His analysis of *Romeo and Juliet* focused on the same themes that emerged in his reading of Italian Renaissance lyric: conceits, the character of images and the philosophy of love. The opinions he expressed in his lectures on *Romeo and Juliet* – one of his favourite plays – are identical with the thoughts Petrarch and his followers prompted in him. They played a primary role in enlarging his understanding of an important aspect of Shakespeare's writing.[143]

Coleridge's ideas may seem timid today, after a century of the avant-garde, but their originality will be evident if they are compared to nineteenth-century attitudes to Italian Renaissance lyric. The eighteenth-century views of Petrarch and Petrarchism were interdependent: despite the contemporaneous neoclassical aesthetics and the popularity of sixteenth-century poets like Ariosto and Tasso, Petrarchism was considered as affected and artificial, and more often mocked than admired.[144] Something changed after the mid-eighteenth century, but hostility was still prevalent. Thomas Warton, for instance, mentioned Petrarch frequently, but praised Surrey for avoiding Petrarch's conceits, and disliked Wyatt's 'prolix and intricate comparisons, and unnatural allusions'.[145] Even the attitude of a champion of the Italian Renaissance like William Roscoe was similar. Though he wrote in his *Life of Lorenzo de' Medici* that 'in the works of Ariosto, the two Tassos, Costanzo, Tansillo, and Guarini, the poetry of Italy attained its highest degree of perfection',[146] the judgement on Petrarchism in his *Life of Leo X* was critical. He argued that Bembo's poetry was correct but cold, so that any reader felt he could write poems of equal value.[147]

Roscoe's *Life of Leo X* was published in 1805, the same year in which Coleridge's note on Strozzi was made, and it enjoyed a remarkable popularity. The numerous translations from lyric poets of the Italian Renaissance published at the time by Roscoe, Mathias and many others seem to have confirmed rather than renewed the old attitude: the poets had nothing to say but said it exquisitely.[148] Coleridge's view, though anticipated in many respects by the older Italophiles, had a different value due to his awareness of historical and aesthetic implications of Petrarchism previously overlooked. It is surprising that even a leading authority on the Renaissance as Roscoe could state:

> By the example of Bembo, the Italians would have written with correctness and with elegance, but they would have been read only by their countrymen. The delicate and attenuated sentiment which gives its faint animation to these writings, is lost when an attempt is made to transfuse it into another language; but the bold ideas of Ariosto bear without injury all change of climate; and his works have contributed more than those of any other author to diffuse a true poetical spirit throughout Europe.[149]

Ariosto was undoubtedly influential in Europe, but Roscoe's view of Petrarchism is historically incorrect. Modern French, Spanish and Portuguese lyric poetry grew out of the early Petrarchan tradition, which also played a significant role in the development of Renaissance literature in England. Petrarchism appears in the literatures of most European countries and Latin America.

Coleridge realized that his opinion of Petrarchism was unusual when the *Biographia Literaria* was published: 'I am aware, that the sentiments which I have avowed concerning the points of difference between the poetry of the present age, and that of the period between 1500 and 1650, are the reverse of the opinion commonly entertained' (*BL (CC)* II 35). C. P. Brand argues that after 1815 Renaissance lyrics were usually regarded as 'too classical in sentiment and language and too artificial in their imitation of Petrarch', and that interest in them diminished.[150]

It is significant that Coleridge discovered the value of Renaissance lyric poetry through Italian literature. He rarely mentioned sixteenth-century English sonneteers, and seems to have held them in low regard early in life.[151] He disliked Spenser's *Shepheardes Calender*, and if he knew other lyric poems of Sydney and Spenser, he must have found them unexciting, since he hardly ever referred to them. The praise of the linguistic purity of Renaissance poets at large in *Biographia* is a consequence of his experience of sixteenth-century Italian poetry specifically.[152] The intensity of his enthusiasm is demonstrated not only by the fact that most of the books he purchased in Italy were editions of Renaissance lyrics, but also by the comments and projects related to Italian lyric poetry analysed in the present chapter.[153]

A second, remarkable, point is that Coleridge's discovery focused on the madrigal, which Renaissance theoreticians regarded as a minor poetic form. It was canonic, since it appeared in Petrarch's *Canzoniere*, but the sonnet and the *canzone* were considered more perfect structures. The sixteenth-century madrigal is in fact flexible and open, as it consists of a free combination of hendecasyllables and seven-syllable verses, which are usually less than fourteen in number.[154] Since Strozzi is considered with Tasso as the best madrigalist of the age, some observations on him have a bearing on the discussion.

The traditional evaluation of Giovan Battista Strozzi il Vecchio as a melodious, idyllic poet has changed in recent years, in the light of previously unpublished poems. The Sermartelli imprint, which Coleridge owned, was a partial selection edited by his sons Lorenzo and Filippo. Their choice was based on conservative aesthetic principles, that is, a mannered Petrarchism to which Strozzi's poems belonged only in part. The most innovative texts were excluded, so that the Sermartelli Strozzi seems more conventional than he was.[155]

Some of his madrigals transgress the limits of the Petrarchist conventions as Bembo had codified them. Erotic conceits play a secondary role in Strozzi's poems, whereas landscape is lively in comparison to the usual Petrarchist backcloths.[156] His syntax is often irregular and sinuous, qualities commonly associated with Mannerism. The shortness of the madrigal is partly responsible for its compactness – the wholeness Coleridge admired so much. Conceptual coagulation is evident in the

> *senhal* full of surrealist-metaphysical possibilities (*emeralds, stones, moons, thorns, lights, breezes, marygolds*), on which the madrigal is constructed as a progressive double exposure of symbolic nuances which . . . produce around themselves a *Stimmung* of spicy reconversion of the world of dreams into courtliness and vice-versa.[157]

There are groups of madrigals built on the same *senhal* – often spelt in full capitals – which shows the potentially endless repetitiousness of mannerist writing. For example, Coleridge copied out seven madrigals on 'AURE' (Breezes) and four on 'FIORE' (Flower). Strozzi's 'hermeticism', therefore, is perceivable also in the conventional areas of his poetry. The consequence is a 'taste for a *préciosité* which is the almost necessary sediment of any valuable Petrarchesque experience'.[158] Strozzi's 'private' madrigals are characterized by an existential anguish which recalls Michelangelo's, whose poems are often compared with Strozzi's. Such bleakness appears in parts of the Sermartelli imprint, especially in the poems of *Death*, some of which were transcribed by Coleridge. Strozzi's poetry, then, hinges on two divergent elements: 'on the one hand a sensuous naturalism of idyllic, Petrarchesque origin; on the other a precious, hermetic mannerism', which are not separated, but perceivable in each text in variable degrees.[159]

Dante's Lyric Poetry

Coleridge's reading of Dante's lyric poetry is continuous with the interests analysed so far, and his comments are an excellent test of the validity of my argument concerning Petrarch and Petrarchism. Dante was included in the group of authors who stimulated Coleridge's desire to learn Italian.[160] Coleridge's curiosity, unlike the curiosity of his contemporaries, was not limited to the *Divine Comedy*, though his enthusiasm for it led him to plan a poem on metamorphosis 'in the manner of Dante'.[161] Soon after returning to England from Italy, he read Dante's minor works, which suited his interests at the time – metrics and love poetry – better than the *Comedy*. It cannot be a coincidence that the work on which Coleridge's attention focused was the *Rime*, which collects most of Dante's short poems.

Though Coleridge's reading was careful, his comments show that he was not familiar with pre-Petrarchan poetry. He transcribed in full 'Tre donne intorno al cor mi son venute' because it 'is a poem of wild and interesting Images, intended as an Enigma, and to me an Enigma it remains, spite all my efforts. . . . AD 1806' (*CN* II 3014). He added later:

> 2 Sept. 1819. Ramsgate. I *begin* to understand the above poem: after an interval from 1805, during which no year passed in which I did not reperuse, I might say construe, *parse*, and spell it, 12 times at least, such a fascination had it, spite of its obscurity! A good instance, by the bye, of that soul of *universal* {meaning} <significance> in a true poet's compositions in addition to the specific meaning. (*CN* IV 4590)

It would not be surprising if he had first read the poem in Malta in 1805; in any event, his response is significant. The *canzone*, one of Dante's most perfect, deals with his exile.[162] Since Coleridge's admiration was mainly stylistic, it is worth noting that Dante's particular directness characterizes the poem's style and syntax.[163]

As far as the 'wild and interesting Images' which impressed Coleridge are concerned, Patrick Boyde points out that 'metaphor is still not an important element' in Dante's lyric poetry, excluding the *rime petrose*; 'the sequence of ideas, and the course of the argument are still determined by logic'.[164] However, 'Tre donne' is in part beyond such limits, and not only thanks to images like 'il nudo braccio, di dolor colonna' (line 22), whose analogic speed Contini defines as 'symbolist'.[165] In the poem 'the interpenetration of proper and tropological language is unique',

> because it is grounded in unique circumstances; and I think it does much to explain the poem's lasting fascination. The allegorical passages have the urgency and immediacy of lived experience; the 'proper' passages take on a splendour and nobility from a context in which Dante's exile is itself the type or figure of the exile of justice.[166]

Such features explain Coleridge's view of the poem as 'a good instance . . . of that soul of *universal* . . . <significance> in a true poet's compositions in addition to the specific meaning' (*CN* IV 4590). In other words, he realised that the experience of poetry does not imply the full understanding of its meaning and subtlest resonances, but precedes them – an idea repeated by T. S. Eliot with reference to Dante's allegories.

The other transcriptions from Dante's lyrics confirm that Coleridge was not familiar with their conventions. He copied out the sonnets 'Di donne io vidi una gentile schiera' and 'Un dí si venne a me Malinconia' 'for their singularity' (*CN* II 3019): but the former is, in Contini's words, an 'anthology of the most common *stilnovo* themes'.[167] The fact that he preferred some spurious poems to many of Dante's originals is in itself significant.

Coleridge seems to have understood Dante's early view of love only in part. He intended to introduce in the 'Soother of Absence' 'love singing the ordinary song of desire from beauty as for instance th[a]t of Dante': – and here he transcribed a passage from a spurious *canzone*, 'Io miro i crespi e gli biondi capegli' – '& then to describe myself unaffected uninfluenced t[i]ll the soul within through the face & form declares a primary sympathy' (*CN* II 3017 and n.). The *canzone* is excluded from the spurious poems of modern editions of the *Rime*, and in fact both the passage and the sentiments he ascribed to Dante are not Dantesque at all. The poem's images, puns and conceits sound Petrarchan rather than Dantesque. Coleridge preferred to the *canzone* the sonnet 'Questa donna che andar mi fa pensoso', ascribed to Dante or Cino da Pistoia, which treats the *stilnovo* convention of Love shining through the mistress' eyes (*CN* II 3012). Dante's philosophy of love is clearer in *Vita nuova* than in the *Rime*, but Coleridge must have found *stilnovo* conventions unusual. Some sonnets he transcribed might have been included in *Vita nuova*, but, interestingly, he chose among them a sonnet like 'Ne le man vostre, gentil donna mia' whose concluding tercet seems to anticipate Petrarch.[168]

Coleridge's response to Dante's lyric poetry shows that he did not find Dante's love poems congenial. He was attracted by the philosophic and moral meditations of *canzoni* like 'Tre donne' or 'Doglia mi reca', which should have been included in *Convivio*.[169] However, the background of both these poems and *Convivio* is Aristotelian Scholasticism, a tradition Coleridge was less at home with than the Platonism of Petrarch and his followers. As far as love poetry is concerned, he preferred spurious or conventional poems to texts considered as peculiarly Dantesque like the *rime petrose*. His response confirms his indifference to Provençal technicality, which emerged in relation to Petrarch's sestine. Nonetheless, Coleridge's interest in Dante's minor works, and the *Rime* in particular, is noteworthy. These works were neglected even by the Italian Romantics in the early nineteenth century, since contemporary attention focused on the *Divine Comedy*.[170]

Biographia Literaria, Chapter XVI: Renaissance Lyric in Coleridge's Theory of Poetry

If we reconsider chapter XVI of *Biographia*, we notice that Coleridge's note on Strozzi is set in a wider context. Coleridge now provides a specific reason for his interest in Renaissance poetry:

> The study of Shakespeare's *poems* (I do not include his dramatic works . . .) led me to a more careful examination of the contemporary poets both in this and in other countries. But my attention was especially fixed on those of Italy, from the birth to the death of Shakespeare; that being the country in which the fine arts had been most sedulously, and hitherto most successfully cultivated. (*BL* (*CC*) II 29)

Coleridge discovered Shakespeare's non-dramatic works considerably late: the *Sonnets*, for example, had been ignored in the introduction to *A Sheet of Sonnets*. In November 1803, however, he reacted against a derogatory note of Wordsworth's on Shakespeare's sonnets. Wordsworth had written that

> these sonnets <beginning at 127,> to his Mistress, are worse than . . . a puzzle-peg. They <are> abominably harsh obscure & worthless. The others are for the most part much better. . . . Their chief faults, and heavy ones they are, are sameness, tediousness, {laboriousness}, quaintness, & elaborate obscurity.[171]

Coleridge's opinion diverged from Wordsworth's: 'I see no <elaborate> obscurity . . . and very little quaintness – nor do I know any Sonnets that will bear such frequent reperusal: so rich in metre, so full of Thought &

exquisitest Diction'.[172] His note contains themes on which his reading of Italian Renaissance poetry would focus. It is significant, therefore, that some sonnets of Shakespeare – all dealing with absence – appear in a notebook entry dating from February 1805.[173]

But the whole chapter XVI must be considered in the context of the theory of poetic language introduced in this section of *Biographia*. Chapter XVI is preceded by chapter XIV, which attempts to define poetry in general, and chapter XV, in which such definition is *'elucidated in a critical analysis of Shakespeare's Venus and Adonis, and Lucrece'*, as the subheading goes. Chapters XVII-XX propound a theory of poetic language which diverges from Wordsworth's, whose poetry is analysed in chapter XXII. The two themes which have a bearing on the present essay are the link Coleridge saw between Shakespeare's poems and Italian Renaissance poetry, and its value within his theory of diction.

Coleridge's admiration for Shakespeare's poems, and for *Venus and Adonis* in particular, developed during and after his Italian sojourn. *Venus and Adonis* was first mentioned in an 1805 note on paronomasy, in which he defended the work against the charge of being a mere display of rhetorical skill by pointing out that its style was exquisitely harmonious (*CN* II 2396, Jan 1805). The observations which appear in chapter XV of *Biographia* are based on notes dating from 1808 (*CN* III 3246, 3247, 3290) and 1811 (*CN* III 4113, 4115), that is, immediately after his period of full immersion in Italian lyric poetry.

I am not concerned with Shakespeare's sources here, but I want to emphasize that Coleridge could hardly overlook the kinship between Shakespeare's poems and Italian Renaissance lyrics, even though none of the Italian lyric poets he read is an immediate source of Shakespeare. The conventions which dominated Italian poetry in the Renaissance abound in Shakespeare's poems. It might be argued that Shakespeare's sonnets are more akin to Petrarchism and his poems to Italian Baroque poetry, though Petrarchist conceits are more evident in early plays like *Romeo and Juliet*, and Petrarchist conventions are not rare in the poems.[174] Mario Praz points out that

> The taste for *ekphráseis* according to the old recipe of *ut pictura poesis* and for women in pathetic circumstances is indulged in by Shakespeare in his early poems to an extent equaled only by Marino in Italy.[175]

However, we noted that Coleridge paid little attention to descriptions, so he must have found other elements more attractive. In fact, he argued that Shakespeare's sonnets and poems are characterized by boundless fertility, and laboured condensation of thought, with perfection of sweetness in rhythm and metre. These are the essential in the budding of a great Poet. (*TT (CC)* 13 May 1833)

These ideas are the core of chapter XV of *Biographia*. Chapter XVI, therefore, is a bridge between a general view of the natural talents a poet must possess and a discussion on the technique he must acquire.

Italian lyric influenced another aspect of Coleridge's theory of poetry. Coleridge mentioned Dante's *De vulgari eloquentia* in corroboration of his idea that the first duty of a poet is to safeguard the purity of their native tongue.[176] Since Dante's treatise does not contain such a remark, the editor rightly believes that Coleridge was referring to its spirit rather than to any specific passage.[177] To be more precise, I think that Coleridge's observation must not be considered as a comment on a particular passage of Dante's treatise, but as an anticipation of the argument of the following chapters of *Biographia*: poetic diction.

Coleridge mentioned Dante again when he criticized Wordsworth's view of poetic language as "'*a selection of the REAL language of men*'" (*BL (CC)* II 55). He pointed out that ordinary language, or *lingua communis*, should be substituted for Wordsworth's 'real language' of rustic men – although Wordsworth was not supporting vernacular or uneducated language, but simply a kind of *sermo humilis*. If poets aim at creating and preserving a flexible language for everybody, they cannot derive it all from one social milieu. Poetic language must be abstracted from reality: 'Anterior to cultivation the lingua communis of every country, as Dante has well observed, exists every where in parts, and no where as a whole'.[178] Such linguistic purity was to be found in Renaissance rather than modern poetry; pre-Restoration poets were quoted to exemplify his ideas in the *Biographia*.

However, Coleridge did not desire a mere revival of Renaissance poetics. He wrote at the end of his note on Strozzi:

> Of this exquisite Polish, of this perfection of Art, the following Madrigals are given as specimens, and as mementos to myself, if ever I should once more be happy enough to resume poetic composition, to attempt a union of these – taking the whole of the latter [i.e. madrigals], and as much of the former [i.e. ballads] as is compatible with a poem's being perused with greater pleasure the second or the 20th time, than the first. (*CN* II 2599)

Or, as he rephrased it in *Biographia*, 'a lasting and enviable reputation awaits that man of genius' who will be able to combine the delicacy, polish and wholeness of Anacreon, Catullus and the Florentine poets with the deep pathos, vivid imagery and profound thoughts of the best modern poets, like Shakespeare and Milton (*BL (CC)* II 34–6). The consistency of Coleridge's taste is undeniable if we recall his early attachment to Anacreon and Catullus, and that Ovid and the Greek Anthology were major sources for both English Renaissance and Italian Baroque poetry.[179]

A note on the improvement of taste since Johnson's time that Coleridge made after 1820 resumes his programme:

> The revived attention to our elder Poets, which Percy and Garrick had perhaps equal share in awakening, the revulsion against the French Taste which was so far successful as to confine the Usurper within the natural limits of the French Language; the re-establishment of the Romantic and Italian School in Germany and G. Britain by the genius of Wieland, Goethe, Tieck, Southey, Scott, and Byron among the poets, and the Lectures of Coleridge, Schlegel, Campbell and others among the Critics; these, at once aided and corrected by the increased ardor with which the study of ancient literature and especially the Greek Poets and Dramatists, is pursued, esteemed and encouraged by the Gentry of the Country, and men of the highest rank and office, have given a spread and a fashion to predilections of higher hope and . . . to principles of Preference at once more general and more just. (*IS* 158–9)

The combination of the Romantic and Italian school as opposed to the French school is meaningful. The model underlying the idea was the Renaissance, since he talked of 're-establishment'. The great example he had in mind was Shakespeare, or, in other words, the way in which Italian culture was used in Elizabethan England. German taste was not recommended for its own sake, but as a means of rereading Italian matter. The list of writers mentioned as belonging to the new school is surprising, because it includes poets like Wieland, Southey and Scott, about whom he had reservations, and excludes Wordsworth. Coleridge elsewhere dismissed the idea that a School of the Lakes, to which he himself, Wordsworth and Southey were supposed to belong, had ever existed:

> how utterly unfounded was the supposition, that we considered ourselves, as belonging to any common school, but that of good sense confirmed by the long-established models of the best times of Greece, Rome, Italy, and England. (*BL (CC)* I 51 n.)

His statement should remind us that he did not consider German as his only background besides English.

Coleridge was not alone in supporting such an 'improvement of taste': similar ideas belonged to the cultural climate of his time, and had in part been propounded by Italophiles like Thomas J. Mathias. But the role they play in Coleridge's aesthetics and the meaning they have in his theory of poetry is distinct from his predecessors. There is, in fact, another aspect of Coleridge's argument which has not been mentioned so far. Both in the 1805 note on Strozzi and in chapter XVI of *Biographia*, the comparison between Renaissance and modern poetry is extended to the fine arts. Therefore, it is necessary to turn to the 1818 and 1819 lectures, in which his view of Italian taste and the fine arts is applied to modern literature.

II

The Fine Arts

*Those writers who lay on the watch for novelty could have little hope
of greatness; for great things cannot have escaped former observation.*
Samuel Johnson

S INCE COLERIDGE IS a literary critic and the fine arts is a marginal
interest, most studies of his view of painting focus on particular
aspects like his sense of colour and landscape, or the relation between his
poetry and his idea of images, while his opinion of the fine arts is often
left in the background. Carl Woodring and Kevin Barry have discussed in
different contexts Coleridge's attitude to painting.[1] Barry compares
Coleridge's ideas of painting and music and concludes that music was
much more important than painting in Coleridge's system of the arts. I
disagree with him, and I shall return to the point at the end of the
chapter. Woodring's discussion is correct, but it measures Coleridge's
opinions against the wrong background. Taking for granted that
Coleridge is a German mind, Woodring endeavours to point out the links
between Coleridge's idea of painting and Germany, so far as to give
considerable space to a supposed interest in early German art, to which
Coleridge paid no attention. All these comparisons – Coleridge's sense of
colour and English Romantic painting, his idea of music and painting, his
German background and painting – are desirable and sometimes
illuminating, since Coleridge's glamour is in the variety of his interests
and their interrelation. However, such comparisons ought to be drawn
after an historical assessment of his experience of the fine arts, which
owes little to Germany because it is part of his Italian background.

The fine arts were Coleridge's second important discovery in Italy. His
previous artistic education was very limited, and consisted of occasional

63

visits to collections like Oakover, 'a seat famous for a few first-rates of Raphael & Titian', and Beireis's (*CL* I 231, 22 Aug 1796; I 522, 6 Jul 1799). His interest in the fine arts increased in 1803, when he became acquainted with Sir George Beaumont, the amateur painter whose collection of old masters today belongs to the National Gallery:[2]

> I have learnt as much f[rom] Sir George Beaumont respecting Pictures & Paintings and Painte[rs as] I ever learnt on any subject from any man in the same Space or Time. A man may employ time far worse than in learning how to look at a picture judiciously. (*CL* II 1063, 15 Feb 1804)

Although Coleridge visited other important collections on the recommendation of Beaumont before leaving for Malta, his most profound experience of the fine arts took place in Rome.[3] He wrote to Daniel Stuart:

> by my regula[r atten]tion to the best of the good things in Rom[e,] and associating almost wholly with the Artists of acknowledged highest reputation I acquired more insight into the fine arts in the three months, than I could have done in England in 20 years. (*CL* II 1178, 22 Aug 1806)

Who were these artists 'of acknowledged highest reputation'? In the first place, the American painter Washington Allston, in the company of whom he visited the city and its surroundings, and who introduced him to the circle of his friends. Most of them were German artists who met at the Caffè Greco and Villa Malta, the residence of the Prussian Consul and patron of the arts Wilhelm von Humboldt. The most notable figures were Thorwaldsen, Asmus Jakob Carstens, Gottlieb Schick, Joseph Anton Koch, and writers like Ludwig Tieck and August Wilhelm Schlegel.[4]

Though we have no reason to question that Coleridge learnt much from them, it is noteworthy that they did not modify the substance of his taste. In a way, it may be argued that it was Coleridge who influenced or anticipated the development of their taste. Classical art was the chief model for the circle at the time, whereas Coleridge advised Allston to study Christian rather than Greek or Roman art. In other words, the canon of their taste was still neoclassical, whereas Coleridge's was Romantic. The Nazarenes arrived in Rome soon afterwards, and Allston's painting showed an increasing interest in religious subjects in the following decades.[5]

Helped by such friends, Coleridge discovered the works of art which became his favourites: the church of S. Paolo fuori le Mura,

Michelangelo's *Moses* and the frescoes in the Sistine Chapel, Raphael's Vatican *Stanze* and *Logge*, and the frescoes in the Camposanto at Pisa.

The effect of his experience was a new enthusiasm for painting, which is demonstrated by his intention, after returning to England, to lecture 'on the Principles common to all Fine Arts' (*CL* II 1181, 16 Sept 1806). However, the lectures he gave at the Royal Institution in 1808 were on the principles of poetry only, so that in 1814 he was still planning essays 'on the Principles of *genial* criticism concerning the Fine Arts, especially those of Statuary and Painting', whose immediate aim was to 'serve poor Allston, who is now exhibiting his Pictures at Bristol' (*CL* III 534, 12 Sept 1814). Four essays had already been published in *Felix Farley's Bristol Journal*; besides, in the same letter Coleridge promised a series of essays 'containing animated descriptions of all the *best* pictures of the great Masters in England, with characteristics of the great Masters from Giotto to Correggio' (*CL* III 535). The plan, like many others, was never realized, but his fragmentary comments on the Italian masters provide a sufficient view of his critical opinions.

Modern painting began in Coleridge's mind with the Italian artists of the thirteenth and fourteenth centuries. The works he habitually quoted to illustrate this idea were the frescoes in the Camposanto at Pisa, which he visited in June 1806 (*CN* II 2857 and 2858). Though the frescoes were not for him the revelation of a vocation, as they came to be for Ruskin, they were an unforgettable experience. The special meaning they acquired in his philosophy of art emerged in the 1818 and 1819 lectures.

In Lecture I of the 1818 series on European literature, Coleridge tried to distinguish Classical and Gothic art. He believed painting and architecture were 'of native growth' among the Gothic races. Their distinctive features were 'complexity, variety, and symbolical character', as for instance in the works of 'Giotto and his associates in the cemetery at Pisa' (*L Lects* (*CC*) II 59–60). However, he pointed out the differences between early and late medieval art. In the early Viennese school, for example, superficies and outlines were sometimes 'wonderfully vivid', but devoid of life, and 'every figure was imprisoned within its own outline'. A radical change took place with Cimabue, Giotto and their followers

> who, with all the awkwardness of composition and stiffness of outline of their predecessors, gave such a bewitching grace that one remains in looking at the pictures in perfect astonishment how such a feeling of grace could be conveyed through such a media. (*P Lects*, 1949, 167)

The example he gave was his experience of the *Triumph of Death* in the Pisan Camposanto.

> The impression was greater, I may say, than that which any poem had ever made upon me. There, from all the laws of drawing, all the absence of color ... it was one mighty idea that spoke to you everywhere the same. In the other pictures the presence of an idea acting on that which was not formed was evident, because the forms there outraged all notions of that which was to be impressed, had there not been something more; but it was the adoption of a symbol which, though not in as polished a language as could be wished for, which though in a hoarser voice and less tempered modulation, uttered the same words to that mind which is the source of all that we really enjoy or that is worth enjoying. (*P Lects*, 1949, 168)

In other words, Coleridge was struck by the half-faded fresco which only consisted of a set of proportional relations. He seems to have regarded it almost as a visual representation of essence in the Aristotelian sense, a kind of empty structure on and out of which outward reality is constructed. The rhythmic relations of the outlines reminded him of harmony in music, which he defined as 'the best symbol <*of the Idea*>' (*P Lects* (1949) 168); and as symbols they succeed in transforming the material means into an image of internal beauty. The Pisan fresco illustrated the Plotinian conception of beauty as a victory of the spirit over the body, whose effect is a sense of depth which attracts the beholder:

> Why, having seen their outlines, why, having determined what they appear to the eye, do we still continue to muse on them, but that there is a divine something corresponding to <*something*> within, which no image can exhaust but which we are reminded of when in the South of Europe we look at the deep blue sky? The same unwearied form presents itself, yet still we look on, sinking deeper and deeper, and therein offering homage to the infinity of our souls which no mere form can satisfy. (*P Lects*, 1949, 193–4)

Such a view of early Italian painting clarifies the comparison Coleridge drew between Dante and Giotto as precursors of the Platonic revival, and the relation he saw between the Pisan muralists and Michelangelo and Raphael.

Despite the fact that nearly all the English collections he visited included items of early painting, he paid little attention to them, with the exception of the frescoes in the Camposanto at Pisa.[6] His interest was not altogether unusual: the frescoes struck numerous English travellers in the eighteenth century, and admirers multiplied in Coleridge's time. It is not easy to understand why *these* frescoes caught the fancy of so many amateurs from Smollett to Keats: probably because they included scenes of secular life, unlike most medieval pictures, whose golden, religious iconography was alien to early nineteenth-century taste.[7] The view of Giotto as the precursor and initiator of the Renaissance in painting is Vasarian, but it is significant that the Pisan frescoes, rather than any work definitely ascribed to Giotto, became Coleridge's favourite example of the concept.[8]

The *Triumph of Death* at Pisa is the first part of a trilogy including the *Last Judgement* and the *Thebaid*. The cycle, and the *Triumph of Death* in particular, is characterized by a unique variety: it includes angels, devils, hermits, beggars, knights, courtiers playing in a garden, corpses, and it mixes allegoric and realistic, popular and aristocratic elements (plates I–III). Though the debate on the author of the fresco has continued for decades and is still open, there is general agreement on one point: the work is one of the most Gothic in early fourteenth-century Tuscany, equally opposed both to Sienese aristocratic art and Giotto's rationality. The image is tendentially bidimensional, and the realism of the details is at variance with the non-realism of the composition – a technique which recalls

Plate I: *Triumph of Death*, left half.

Plate II: *Triumph of Death*, detail.

Plate III: *Triumph of Death*, detail.

illumination. A strong northern component belonged to the style of its author, whoever he was.[9]

It is symptomatic of Coleridge's taste that he was struck by such a work rather than by other early paintings or sculptures he saw or might have seen in Tuscany – for example, Nicola Pisano's sculptures in the Pisa cathedral or Giotto's frescoes in Florence.

Coleridge's enthusiasm for Michelangelo and Raphael is more conventional, though convention does not mean mere fashion when it involves artists of such value. Coleridge considered Michelangelo chiefly as a painter, since he never mentioned his architectural and poetical works, and neglected his sculpture with the exception of the *Moses*.[10] Raphael also interested Coleridge as a painter only: his *Logge* and *Rooms* in the Vatican, his *Galatea* in the Farnesina, his Cartoons and some of his Madonnas were Coleridge's favourite works.[11] A peculiar aspect of his approach was that he did not get involved in the dispute on Michelangelo's supremacy over Raphael or vice versa. As an external observer, he admired both, and his thinking was more stimulated by the elements they had in common than their differences.

Michelangelo and Raphael were in Coleridge's mind the pinnacle of the artistic movement which Giotto had begun under the influence of Platonism.[12] Such a periodization of art history, which had prevailed since the sixteenth century and was still commonplace in his time, can be traced back to Vasari.

Coleridge emphasized the idealism of Michelangelo and Raphael, whom he mentioned in his attempts to define art in general.[13] The character of Michelangelo's painting was already stressed in a note made in 1806 in which he tried to define the Ideal:

> Ideal = the subtle hieroglyphical *felt*-by-all though not without abstruse and difficult analysis detected & understood, consonance of the *physiognomic* total & substance (Stoff) with the obvious *Path*ognomic. (*CN* II 2828, 3 Apr 1806).

He found a perfect instance of it in a figure of Michelangelo's *Last Judgement,* whose character he distinguished from the 'unmeaning abstractions' of coldest neoclassicism – probably Giovanni Battista Cipriani (1727–85) is meant here – from Marie Vigée-Lebrun's empty sentimentalism, and from 'Opie-ism, i.e. passions planted in a common face <or portrait> that might equally well have been the accidental

Substrate of any other Passion'.[14] Ideal art is on the contrary '"*Forma formans per formam formatam translucens*"' (*BL (CC)* II 215).

Moreover, Coleridge distinguished the generalizing idealism of the Italians from the individualizing mimesis of the Dutch and Flemish painters – which does not mean that he was unable to appreciate the latter:

> the infant that a Madonna [of an Italian master] holds in her arms cannot be guessed of any particular age – it is humanity in infancy. The babe in the manger in a Dutch painting is a facsimile of some real new born bantling (*TT (CC)* 24 Jul 1831).

In Lecture I of the 1818–1819 course on Shakespeare, on the character of illusion, he maintained that Raphael would have smiled at the remark that his landscapes were not realistic (*L Lects (CC)* II 267).

> It is a poor compliment to pay to a painter to tell him that his figure stands out of the canvas . . . take one of Mrs Salmon's wax queens or generals, and you will feel the difference between a Copy, as they are, and an Imitation, of the Human Form, as a good portrait ought to be. (*TT (CC)* 1 Jul 1833)

Coleridge emphasized that the artist should take the image of things from her or his own mind and not from the senses.

Though the observations may seem commonplace, they are important, as they involve the problem of imitation, which is crucial for any theory of artistic creation. Painting helped Coleridge to reflect on it. He wrote in the *Biographia* that

> the formation of a copy is not solved by the pre-existence of an original; the copyist of Raphael's Transfiguration must repeat more or less perfectly the process of Raphael. (*CC* I 137)

The artist should not copy the external form or *natura naturata*, but master the essence or *natura naturans* – '& this presupposes a bond between *Nature* in this higher sense and the soul of Man'.[15] Michelangelo and Raphael did not copy the ancients, as Dante did not copy Virgil, and Ariosto Homer: not only, as Coleridge said, following August Wilhelm Schlegel, because genius is rooted in human nature, but because art is an 'imitation of nature' in this particular sense (*L Lects (CC)* I 492; and I 83–4).

The correspondence between the essence and the material, between soul and body, clarifies Coleridge's critical attitude to Opie, Mme Lebrun and Cipriani.[16] He thought a spontaneous love of beauty was more important for a young painter than the realism or sensationalism of his subjects (*CL* III 352, 7 Dec 1811). The subjects of Michelangelo's and Raphael's works are known beforehand, so that the reason for their greatness must be another: their style (*BL* (*CC*) II 187).

Coleridge was obviously able to notice some peculiarities of Michelangelo as distinguished from Raphael. His observations are based on the traditional view of Michelangelo as 'sublime' and Raphael as 'beautiful'. He compared Dante's and Michelangelo's sublimity, even if he maintained that the scenes of Lear's madness were more powerful than any a Michelangelo inspired by Dante could have conceived.[17] However, despite his natural instinct for the sublime, Coleridge admired Raphael's art without reservations. Whereas Wordsworth seems to have regarded the Virgin and Child as a subject unworthy of a high mind, Coleridge praised the divinity of Raphael's Madonnas, and thought they displayed a 'Galvanic arc of infantine & maternal Love'.[18] Raphael had inspired even Milton, who did not otherwise take notice of any Italian painter (*TT* (*CC*) 6 Aug 1832). Raphael's and Domenichino's figures, like 'the Apollos & Jupiters of the Ancients' and unlike 'the physiognomy produced in all countries & all ages by Pietism', were the incarnation of an ideal humanity whose soul and body were perfectly balanced – almost *schöne Seelen* (*CN* III 3901, Jun 1810). Such an organic unity belonged both to the single figures and the composition of Raphael's paintings: the structure of his *Galatea* was geometrical but not stiff, that is, more like the skeleton of the human body than a scaffold ('On the Principles of Genial Criticism', *BL*, 1907, II 234–5).

> Painting went on in Power till in Raphael it attained its apex, and in him too I think it began to turn down the other side. The Painter began to think of overcoming difficulties.
>
> After this the descent was rapid, till sculptors began to work inveterate likenesses of perriwigs in marble – as see Algarotti's tomb in the cemetery at Pisa – and painters did nothing but *copy* . . . the external face of Nature. (*TT* (*CC*) 25 Jun 1830)

The substance of Coleridge's scanty comments on other Italian painters is resumed in this passage. Sixteenth-century art interested him, though superficially, more than the *Quattrocento*, which he ignored completely. He was acquainted with Mannerism and some artists linked to it, like Frà Bartolomeo, Andrea del Sarto, Bronzino, Parmigianino and Cellini, but he had little to say on them.[19] His admiration for the Venetian School was spontaneous but conventional: he liked Titian's colours and chiaroscuro effects, and mentioned him to illustrate his idea of the picturesqueness of modern art.[20] It is noteworthy that the latent empiricism of the Venetians attracted him less than the idealism of the Florentines, though this may be due to the fact that he visited Florence and Rome but not Venice.

There is an analogy between Coleridge's response to Baroque art and Baroque poetry. He preferred Caravaggio's and Spagnoletto's stern morality and strong chiaroscuro contrasts to the flamboyant technique of the Carraccis and Bernini, 'in whom a great genius was bewildered and lost by excess of fancy over imagination'.[21] He took an unexpected interest in 'devotional' painters like Bernardo Strozzi (1581–1644), Carlo Dolci (1616–86), Carlo Cignani (1628–1719) – who belongs to the Carraccesque academic tradition – and Ciro Ferri (1634–89), though he noted their affected sentimentalism.[22] But the obligatory Italian Baroque painter in eighteenth- and nineteenth-century England was Salvator Rosa.

Salvator's sublime landscapes were regarded as models together with those of Claude Lorrain and the Dutch masters; his fame was so great that he was frequently compared to Shakespeare, and even John Ruskin defined Turner's style in *Modern Painters* by comparing it to Claude's and Salvator's.[23] Coleridge admired Salvator's painting and associated it with craggy landscapes and broken trees, but did not overlook its extravagance.[24]

Salvator's landscapes of ruined civilization anticipate the *capriccios* of engravers like Piranesi, the only eighteenth-century Italian artist Coleridge mentioned beside the abhorred Giovanni Battista Cipriani. Piranesi's engravings were fashionable in early nineteenth-century England,[25] and Coleridge regarded them as representations of the unconscious, if the episode related by De Quincey in his *Confessions* is true.[26]

Coleridge's historical view of modern art was Vasarian, though the insistence on the Platonic character of the Renaissance sounds like his own. However, it seems likely he did not read Vasari's *Lives*, even if he mentioned them.[27] It is remarkable that both Coleridge's discovery of the fine arts and his historical view of them depended on the Italian Renaissance, despite his excellent Classical culture.

He included the Pantheon, the Venus de Medici and the Apollo Belvedere among 'the noblest productions of human genius' and purchased a list of papyri found at Ercolano, but his Italian notebooks contain very few entries on classical works of art.[28] He did not consider Italy primarily as a Classical land, as many of his contemporaries still did

– as for instance, in obvious ways, Goethe or Shelley. The most popular travel books in his day, Eustace's *Classical Tour* and Forsyth's *Remarks on Antiquities, Arts, etc.*, approached Italy 'from the viewpoint of the classical scholar',[29] although a sentimental attitude had generally replaced the former archaeological interest.

Coleridge thought that the Classics 'in History and the Fine Arts; and Architecture . . . still remain our masters – in Poetry . . . our equals – in Painting and in instrumental music probably our inferiors' (*L Lects (CC)* II 55). The comparisons he drew between Classical and modern art were based on German sources such as August Wilhelm Schlegel. Classical art was statuesque, and the components of a work were few and homogeneous; modern art is picturesque and admits of a greater variety of structure and subject. Raphael's and Titian's crowded group pictures, however, show that modern painting is no less harmonious than Classical sculpture.[30] Coleridge opposed the clarity of Classical art, in which everything is immediately given in phenomena, with the complexity and depth of Gothic art, in which phenomena have become symbols (*L Lects (CC)* II 60–1). Greek art was beautiful, Gothic art sublime (*L Lects (CC)* II 79). The beholder feels annihilated in a Gothic cathedral, whose constructive principle is 'Infinity, made imaginable. It is no doubt a sublimer effort of Genius than the Greek style, but then it more depends on execution for its effect' (*TT (CC)* 29 Jun 1833; *L Lects (CC)* II 74 and 79). According to H. H. Carwardine, Coleridge affirmed that Classical architecture excited him less than Gothic architecture (*L Lects (CC)* II 62).

Such comments must not conceal the fact that Coleridge's interest in architecture and sculpture was slight and subordinated to his interest in painting. Despite his conviction concerning the architectural 'genius of Italy', very few remarks on the topic are extant.[31] The *Piazza dei Miracoli* at Pisa was impressive 'especially by moonlight', but 'what interested [him] with a deeper interest' were the local hospitals (*CN* II 2856, Jun 1806). The only building in Rome which caught his fancy was the church of S. Paolo fuori le Mura, which he preferred to St Peter's (*CL* IV 569, 25 May 1815). The reason for such a preference is again pictorial rather than architectural. S. Paolo fuori le Mura, built in 384, was a vast basilican church with five aisles containing mosaics and frescoes. It was redecorated in the thirteenth century, and the main cycle of frescoes, traditionally attributed to Pietro Cavallini, was the largest of the Romanesque period in Rome. It included the life of St Paul, an Old Testament cycle and portraits of prophets, apostles, saints and popes. The church as it stands today is a reconstruction following the destruction of the original by fire in 1823. It is easy to infer on the basis of eighteenth-century engravings that Coleridge must have been impressed by the cycle of frescoes rather than the exterior of the church (Plate IV). Not all his contemporaries shared his admiration: Sismondi described the church as an 'ouvrage informe et barbare'.[32]

Since Coleridge thought that architecture 'exhibits the greatest extent of the difference from nature which may exist in works of art' ('On Poesy or Art', *BL*, 1907, II 261), it is noteworthy that he preferred the realism of painting to the abstraction of architecture. His attitude must be not overlooked when we discuss his response to Gothic art, which is essentially architectural.

Sculpture did not excite Coleridge any more than architecture. The excellence of Classical sculpture had not been equalled in modern times; he advised artists not to copy it, since it was inimitable.[33] The only great specimen of modern sculpture was Michelangelo's *Moses*, whereas Bernini's sculptures were an 'unhappy attempt at picture petrifications'.[34] (It must also be added that when he was asked to name three great sculptors, he specified 'Praxiteles, Thorwaldsen, and Flaxman' (*C Talker* 174)). On the whole, it is not enough to say that Coleridge preferred painting to the other arts: he was more interested in the general aesthetic principles of the fine arts than in painting itself.

Plate IV: *The Visit of the Cardinal of York.*

The essays 'On the Principles of Genial Criticism concerning the Fine Arts' (1814) analyse the philosophical principles common to all arts, though they mainly concern painting. Coleridge blamed recent art criticism for being too technical and therefore of interest to artists only. He stressed the universality of the pictorial language, even though he thought the possibilities of the medium were limited by its frailty.[35] Poetry was superior to painting because it did not suffer alterations in time.

The essays are constructed as a small 'dictionary' of aesthetic terms – 'agreeable', 'beautiful', 'multeity in unity', 'sense' and 'sensation', etc. – in eighteenth-century fashion. The most relevant point for the present argument is the definition of 'poesy' – or elsewhere 'poetry' – as the essence of all the arts. Such an attempt had already been made in the lectures 'On the Principles of Poetry'. Poesy consisted in 'the excitement of emotion for the immediate purpose of pleasure through the medium of beauty', and as such was distinguished from science, whose purposes were truth and utility.[36] It is difficult to understand how the conception of poetry he had been developing in terms of excitability can be harmonized with his contemporaneous definitions of fancy and imagination. Nonetheless, he regarded these essays as some of the best he had written (*BL* (1907) II 304–5 n.).

A unified discussion of the arts was again attempted in the 1818 lectures on European literature. The prospectus shows that Lecture XIII, 'ON Colour, Sound, and Form, in Nature, as connected with POESY' – otherwise known as 'On Poesy or Art' – was conceived as a discussion of the philosophical principles underlying the first twelve literary lectures of the course (*L Lects (CC)* II 42). Thereafter, Coleridge's desire to lecture again on the fine arts 'as far as the *philosophy* of the same alone is concerned' remained unfulfilled (*CL* IV 925, 28 Feb 1819).

Coleridge maintained that the theory of the fine arts could furnish a guide to the philosophical critic and even to the poet: 'to admire on principle, is the only way to imitate without loss of originality'.[37] His theoretical approach to painting was holistic; however, he did not show interest in all aspects of painting, but mainly in the idea embodied in form, which in its turn was interesting so far as the idea shined through it.[38] His comments on painting often seem to disembody the image, to atomize it into its components: he considers colour, or form, or drawing, but seldom the relations among them. Moreover, he tended to discuss these aspects in non-pictorial terms. He would have liked to investigate 'the symbolical characters or Significancy of Colors', and most of his notes on the subject appear in entries on the theory of colours in which painters are mentioned just as examples.[39]

Nonetheless, his emphasis on the idea explains why he disapproved of judging works of art by faults only, like critics who concentrate on some details of Raphael's backgrounds and ignore the other aspects of his pictures (*BL* (*CC*) I 61). He was equally suspicious of classifying artists by schools, some of which were in his opinion groundless (*CN* III 3952, Jul 1810), and of drawing parallelisms between scientists and artists (*CL* III 172, 1809). He thought each work of art ought to be considered in the first place from the viewpoint of its plan and aim (*CN* III 3952).

Coleridge always thought of painting in terms of words, even if in such contexts he considered the term 'word' in a general sense as an objective-subjective organism of sound and form. A picture of Michelangelo's or a musical composition were thus 'words'. Raphael's and Michelangelo's works were *one* poem, one objectivized subject of them.[40] Poetry was steadily above painting in his hierarchy of the arts, since the range of its power was wider than that of painting. Poetry could represent the abstract better than painting: Milton's description of Death produced in the reader an undefined feeling, whereas painters represented death by a definite image, like a skeleton, which 'reduced the mind to a mere state of inactivity & passivity' (*L Lects* (*CC*) I 311–12). As we saw before, Coleridge was struck by the image of Death in the Pisan Camposanto because the fresco was faded and left room for the imagination.

Coleridge's idea of the relation between poetry and painting is not surprising, since painters themselves shared it in his time. Reynolds believed that

> POETRY having a more extensive power than our art, exerts its influence over almost all the passions; ... The Painter's art is more confined, and has nothing that corresponds with, or perhaps is equivalent to, this power and advantage of leading the mind on, till attention is totally engaged. What is done by Painting, must be done at one blow.[41]

Reynolds is only one example, since the superiority of poetry over painting was a classicist tenet which few in the past questioned – the first, obvious exception is Leonardo da Vinci. Classicism does not mean that the critics labelled today as Romantic opposed it: Hazlitt believed that 'the evocative power of words far transcended that of pictures'; Shelley thought poetry superior to painting because it was purely mental, whereas the resistance of the material limited the power of painting. James Heffernan points out that the 'insistence on the difference between the sister arts was in large part motivated by the urge to rank poetry above painting'.[42]

The analogies between Reynolds and Coleridge are not confined to this point. Heffernan shows that Constable's, Turner's, Wordsworth's and Coleridge's idea of landscape and colour were all fundamentally Romantic and similar. His argument is convincing, but at the end of his book, after two hundred pages of parallels between them, he is unable to explain why neither Wordsworth nor Coleridge took any interest in Constable and Turner. He points out that only two persons were acquainted with all four figures: Beaumont and Hazlitt.[43] But Beaumont was 'the chief legislator of the Reynolds tradition during the first quarter of the century', and reduced 'Reynolds' principles to the simpler one, that the artist should imitate seventeenth-century painters'.[44] As such, he became the fiercest adversary of Turner and had little enthusiasm for Constable. Hazlitt had more sympathy for Turner's art, but his critical interests developed when his friendship with Coleridge and Wordsworth had deteriorated.[45]

However, Coleridge's and Wordsworth's indifference cannot be reduced to a question of acquaintances. Heffernan's puzzlement at their attitude is due to his assumption that Coleridge's sense of images and colour in nature and in painting was identical. I think it was not, though a relation between Coleridge's ideas can be discovered. Heffernan's assumption derives from the idealistic doctrine that vision depends on the beholder alone. No doubt the perception of a painting is physiologically the same as the perception of a natural prospect; but the experience of a painting is not the same as the experience of a natural prospect. We do not respond to a work of art as to a work of nature, however modified by humans. Our expectations are different; the knowledge we activate to receive the new experience is different.

Coleridge's response to landscape was less conditioned than his view of the arts because he was more familiar with the conventions of the former than those of the latter. Familiarity gave him the freedom to respond personally, whereas his limited knowledge of painting constrained him within traditional attitudes which Turner and Constable had abandoned. However, the differences between Coleridge and the Romantic painters were not only a matter of knowledge, but also of taste. I do not agree with Heffernan when he affirms that Coleridge, like the Romantic painters, 'drastically revalues colour itself' against the line.[46] He may have done so in his notes on landscape colour, but he certainly did not in his comments on painting. The frescoes in the Camposanto at Pisa struck him because their colours were faded: there he discovered the force of form, which, as Keats put it, left so much room to the imagination. Another proof is his preference for the Roman and Florentine schools over the Venetian.

Coleridge held contemporary landscape painting in low regard, and the reasons he gave for it are consistent with his general view of art. In recent landscape painting

> the foregrounds and intermediate distances are comparatively unattractive: while the main interest of the landscape is thrown into the back ground, where mountains and torrents and castles forbid the eye to proceed, and nothing tempts it to trace its way back again. But in the works of the great Italian and Flemish masters, the front and middle objects of the landscape are the obvious and determinate, the interest gradually dies away in the back ground, and the charm and peculiar worth of the picture consists, not so much in the specific objects which it conveys to the understanding in a visual language formed by the substitution of figures for words, as in the beauty and harmony of the colours, lines and expression, with which the objects are represented. Superior excellence in the manner of treating the same subjects was the trial and test of the artist's merit. (*BL* (*CC*) II 32)

The example he gave to illustrate the passage was a comparison between 'a masterly etching by Salvator Rosa' and 'a pinky-coloured plate of the day', about which he asked a servant to express her preference. Since she liked the '*ware* from Fleet-street print artist' better than Salvator's etching, he quoted Reynolds and James Harris in support of the idea that taste needs cultivating.[47] Although here Coleridge is referring to the industrial artistic production, his opinion of contemporary painting was also critical.

> The more I see of pictures the more I am convinced that the ancient art of painting is gone and something substituted for it very pleasing, but different and that in kind not in degree only. Portraits by the old masters . . . fill not merely occupy a space – they represent individuals: – modern portraits . . . give you not the man – not the inward humanity, but merely the external mask. (*TT* (*CC*) 24 Jul 1831)

The intuition that the sense of space was undergoing a change in contemporary art is not banal. However, he objected to the individualizing tendency of modern art and preferred the old generalizing representation of reality, as any classicist would have done. He felt there was 'a sort of reviviscence, not, I fear, of the Power – but of a Taste for the Power' of early painting in his day (*TT* (*CC*) 25 Jun 1830), but he was probably thinking of painters like Allston rather than Blake or Constable.[48]

Coleridge's enthusiastic response to Michelangelo's and Raphael's frescoes makes it clear that the revival of power he was thinking of was a revival of history painting – the so-called 'grand style'. This genre had been considered as supreme by Renaissance and neoclassical theorists, and was also the centre of Reynolds' system. 'A History-painter paints man in general; a Portrait-Painter, a particular man, and consequently a defective model': perfect form can be produced 'by leaving out particularities, and retaining only general ideas'. The principle comprises all aspects of grand style, as invention, composition, expression and colour.[49] Who are the chief models of grand style? Obviously Raphael and Michelangelo, who in the Sistine Chapel

> from a dry, Gothick, and even insipid manner, which attends to the minute accidental discriminations of particular and individual objects, assumed the grand style of painting, which improves partial representation by the general and invariable ideas of nature.

The history painter 'must sometimes deviate from vulgar and strict historical truth' if he wants to represent humans as they ought to be and not as they are. In Aristotelian language, history-painting ought 'to be called Poetical, as in reality it is'.[50]

The hostile attitude to illusionism which emerges from Coleridge's response to Italian painting was closer to Reynolds' ideas than to Blake's, Hazlitt's or Turner's. Both Blake and Hazlitt 'detested the generalising bias of Reynolds *Discourses*, which urged the painters to "get above" all particularities.' Turner detested details, but in Coleridge's mind he probably fell into the opposite error.[51] It is noteworthy that the same anti-illusionist attitude recurs in Coleridge's reading of poetry: one of the defects of Wordsworth's poetry was his 'minute accuracy in the painting of local imagery' (*BL (CC)* II 127). Conversely, Coleridge thought that images in poetry should not be discursive: he demanded illumination, not ekphrasis. The power of Shakespeare's, Dante's and Milton's genius

> was not shewn in elaborating a picture of which many specimens were given in Poems of modern date, where the work was so dutchified by minute touches that the reader naturally asked why words & not . . . painting were used . . . The power of Poetry is by a single word to produce that energy in the mind as compels the imagination to produce the picture. (*L Lects (CC)* I 362)

Coleridge considered painting as 'the intermediate somewhat between a Thought and a Thing' (*TT (CC)* 29–30 Aug 1827; also *CN* III 4397, Mar 1818). He consequently distrusted the naïve realism which obliterated the symbol into the thing, but also Turner who, in Gombrich's words, forgot what he knew to paint what he saw, and Blake who, to paraphrase Gombrich, forgot what he saw to paint what he knew. The thing and the symbol: Coleridge wanted to preserve both, and he developed a view of painting which places him in the mainstream of Western taste from Giotto's to his own time. The analogies with Reynolds exist because both share some basic tenets of this tradition. Coleridge was in fact suspicious of Joshua Reynolds' 'semi-Platonism' and expressed reservations about his painting, even though he admired his taste (*CL* IV 759, 28 Jul 1817; *TT* (*CC*), 24 Jul 1831). Coleridge's preference for painters like Allston coincides with the preferences of his friend Beaumont, who was a devoted follower of Reynolds. Beaumont criticized Turner's foregrounds for their lack of precision as early as 1803[52] – an opinion which may have influenced Coleridge's analogous view of contemporary foregrounds – but 'responded warmly to other aspects of Romanticism, Wilkie's intimate genre and even the bombastic heroics of B. R. Haydon, as well as the emotionally suggestive neo-classicism of Washington Allston's religious paintings'.[53] Coleridge was more realistic: he liked Allston, but thought that these contemporaries brought about 'a sort of reviviscence, not, I fear, of the Power – but of a Taste for the Power' of the great masters (*TT* (*CC*) 25 Jun 1830; and N Q.69 f.67, 1833 or 1834).

After his Italian journey, Coleridge 'impressed even Hazlitt with his knowledge of the old masters'; a decade later Bryan Waller Procter thought that 'he knew little or nothing of the art of painting'.[54] I think Coleridge's knowledge of painting was neither impressive nor null. Despite his own late assertion that his mind at work was in a state probably closer to Mozart's or Beethoven's than Wren's or Titian's (*IS* 214, Sept 1833), he knew far more about painting than music. Kevin Barry believes that Coleridge's 'enthusiasm for music was greater than his enthusiasm for painting';[55] but I would be more cautious. Whatever the implicit place of music in Coleridge's aesthetics may be – he never developed such a theory – it must not be forgotten that his experience of painting was deeper than his experience of music, as the greater number of remarks on art shows. It is difficult to explain why he did not expand his knowledge of music, which was very slight, if he considered it as indispensable to his understanding of the arts. His interest in painting, which is at least documentable, was a secondary but genuine interest which may have played a more significant role than it seems in the development of his aesthetics.[56]

Biographia Literaria Chapter XVI Again

If we return to chapter XVI of *Biographia*, the meaning of the double comparison between art and poetry in the Renaissance and in modern times should now be clearer. Modern poetry and modern landscape painting are analogous, since both focus on details rather than on the whole. As early as 1805 Coleridge had noted:

> Modern Poetry characterized by the Poets [*sic*] ANXIETY to be always *striking* – The same march in the Greek and Latin Poets/Claudian, who had powers to have been anything – observe in him the anxious craving Vanity! every Line, nay, every word *stops*, looks full in your face, & asks & *begs* for Praise. A Chinese Painting no distances no perspective/all in the fore-ground/and this is all *Vanity*.[57]

The opposite was true of the Italian poets and painters of the fifteenth and sixteenth centuries: they used general imagery and traditional themes. Even the subject was frequently known beforehand, as for example in Michelangelo's and Raphael's frescoes in the Vatican. Analogously, there is nothing in Ariosto's stories that cannot be traced back to some older romance or poem, as in Classical Greece several tragedies were written on the same subject. The story was regarded as the painter regards the canvas: that on which, not by which, he had to show his art. 'To a cultivated taste there is delight in *perfection* for its own sake, independent of the material in which it is manifested' (*BL* (*CC*) II 34–5). The essence of poetry was placed in art, that is, style, which should be a combination of 'exquisite polish of diction' and simplicity. Learned words and words a gentleman would not use were excluded. Everything had to contribute to the harmony of the whole and could not be considered in itself separately. Coleridge contrasted the heavy, mechanical rhythms of the German ballad style to the graceful polish of Anacreon and Catullus; a grace that was revived in Tuscany and also belonged to the elder poets of England. These thoughts were suggested to Coleridge 'during the perusal of the Madrigals of GIOVAMBATTISTA STROZZI', nine of whose poems were included as instances. The chapter is concluded by an analogy with painting – Salvator Rosa compared to a contemporary landscape painter.

If this argument was a late example introduced in *Biographia* merely to fill up some pages, as scholars believe, it would not be noteworthy. But Coleridge had developed these ideas as early as 1805, when he read Strozzi. Some of them, like the admiration for Renaissance polish, were widespread in Coleridge's time; but again, the chapter is not a mere

statement of formalist taste. It must be considered in its context in the
Biographia, that is, between the theory of imagination and the theory of
the language of poetry. My opinion is that the experience of Italian
Renaissance poetry and art helped develop Coleridge's thinking in several
respects. More precisely, they helped him verify in practice theories as he
developed them from English and German sources. (The description of
the process as 'development' or 'verification' depends ultimately on the
inductivist or deductivist approach of the scholar, since it is impossible to
decide on the basis of facts.)

The chapter is near the beginning of the second volume of *Biographia*,
in an area of transition from the theoretical principles of volume I to the
practical criticism of volume II. But *Biographia* is a literary autobiography:
the chapter, therefore, is not a digression but testifies to an important
phase of Coleridge's intellectual life, although it fails to provide a
theoretical link between the two parts of the book.

When Coleridge came across sixteenth-century Petrarchism, he must
have realized that the material of Shakespeare's non-dramatic works he
liked so much had been used countless times before; yet it had been
possible to achieve extraordinary masterpieces with it. This confirmed his
view that poetry depends on the way of arranging a given material rather
than on the material itself. But since the arrangement of the material is a
mental process, poetry must depend on the mental faculty 'imagination',
whose early definitions date from the period in which he was immersed in
Italian lyric poetry. In other words, he worked out the main consequences
of what is known today as the poetic of imagination between 1804 and
1808, but he wanted a detailed account of the underlying mental processes
– which he never accomplished – and a name for it. A favourite example of
imaginative poetry was Shakespeare's 'Full gently now she takes him by the
hand, /A lily prison'd in a gaol of snow, (*Venus and Adonis*, lines 361–2),
which combines the Petrarchistic commonplaces of the mistress's hand and
whiteness. However, other observations must be added in order to clarify
why Petrarchism stimulated Coleridge's thought so much.

Karl Popper argues that any new theory which wants to supersede
another must explain and include it in the new context.[58] Does
Coleridge's theory of artistic creation, based on imagination, include and
explain in a new way the theory of artistic creation as imitation? And if so,
how did he become familiar with it?

As a poet, Coleridge could afford to scorn or ignore neoclassicism – i.e.,
the latest form of imitative aesthetics – and act according to a different,
implicit poetic; but as a critic he could not. In order to develop a new
theory which would supersede Neoclassicism, he had to assimilate and

understand the poetics of imitation, which had prevailed in various forms in Western art for centuries. German literature could offer him little in this respect; English Neoclassicism seemed a short episode in a longer and different story; and his antipathy for anything French prevented him from reading and evaluating French Neoclassicism correctly. Coleridge's disagreement with mechanicism was not the least reason for his uneasiness with English and French Neoclassicism.

It is not surprising, then, that he discovered certain aspects of classicism in Italian culture, where classicism was neither a short-lived episode nor coincided with a philosophy he disapproved of. A cultural climate which had produced Ficino and Pico, Michelangelo and Raphael, Ariosto and Machiavelli convinced him more than eighteenth-century France and England. It is emblematic that Coleridge's only extant notes on Aristotle are the marginalia to Metastasio's reflections on the *Poetics*.[59] The experience of Italian culture even helped him modify his attitude to English Neoclassicism.[60]

Coleridge's experience of the Italian Renaissance was not exclusively an experience of classicism. The Renaissance was less classicist than it seemed in the seventeenth and eighteenth centuries, and Coleridge was not indifferent to the elements of Renaissance culture which anticipate Romantic aesthetics, like some Gothic aspects of Renaissance art or the idea of beauty as illumination. Nevertheless, the Italian Renaissance poets, however anti- or un-classical they are, always retain a formal polish which is usually associated with classicism. For example, the plot of Ariosto's *Orlando furioso* has no unity in the Aristotelian sense and its subject matter is the same as that of medieval romances, but the style is so infallible and polished that was it praised even by the staunchest classicists.

It is not important that Coleridge associated poets and artists who are considered today as belonging to different aesthetic contexts: in the first place, because some concepts – like Mannerism – did not exist in his age; secondly, because the categorization of history available at the time made such associations possible – for example it was neoclassical art theory that indicated some Renaissance artists as models. If we want to label Coleridge's experience of Italy, it is possible to define it as a stylistic experience of classicism, provided the word is understood in a general, atemporal sense as signifying art as technique and material work. Coleridge noticed the polish of Italian poets from Petrarch to Marino, but it was the Mannerist Strozzi who impressed him with the force of form, and it is not difficult to understand why: Petrarchism is so rigidly codified that it exhibits a 'zero degree' of content. It is in a way one of the most imitative poetics, being an imitation of Petrarch as a man and a poet.

Conversely, Baroque poetry is varied in subject and neoclassical poetry is socially committed, so their formal polish is less prominent.

The choice of Mannerism is significant from another point of view. The two volumes of *Biographia* can be described as Platonic (vol. I) and Aristotelian (vol. II). Volume II does not represent a turn toward conservative principles: whenever we deal with poetic technique we become Aristotelian, since Aristotle's *Poetics* is the first systematic treatise of art as technique and describes some processes inevitable in any such discussion. What is more interesting is that the historical model for poetic technique propounded in volume II of *Biographia* is Mannerism (Shakespeare's Manneristic poems and Italian Renaissance poetry). Mannerism is a metaphysics of technique, a Platonizing form of an Aristotelian attitude (art as an artifact). The choice confirms Coleridge's Platonic temper, which tended to Platonism even in an Aristotelian context such as volume II of *Biographia*.

However, Coleridge was not a formalist, and the comparison of Shakespeare's poems with other Petrarchist works confirmed his view of poetry as ideal, as based on an imaginative arrangement of the material rather than mere technical skill. But if such is the poetic process, it must work analogously in all the arts. That is why the experience of Italian Renaissance painting was more important than it seems: because painting was the only art besides poetry to which he attempted to apply his theory, as the definition of poesy in the 'Essays on the Principles of Genial Criticism' demonstrates. The great Italian masters reinforced his hypothesis concerning artistic creation by showing that art was essentially ideal. It is not a coincidence that Coleridge's interpretation of painting, though not very original, insists on this aspect.

Finally, he probably became aware of the danger implicit in his theory of imagination. His emphasis on mental process might induce writers to disregard poetic technique, as many of his careless contemporaries did. But

> whatever *specific* import we attach to the word, poetry, there will be found involved in it, as a necessary consequence, that a poem of any length neither can be, or ought to be, all poetry. Yet if an harmonious whole is to be produced, the remaining parts must be preserved *in keeping* with the poetry; and this can be no otherwise effected than by such a studied selection and artificial arrangement, as will partake of one, though not a *peculiar*, property of poetry. (*BL* (*CC*) II 15)

The formal perfection of the Renaissance lyrical poets was the best example he could provide to counteract the potentially Crocean element of his theory.

III

Italy and Modern European Literature

COLERIDGE'S LECTURES ON Italian poetry are only in part equal to his fame as a talker. His plans were numerous, but he devoted only two lectures to Italian poetry: one on the romances of chivalry from Boccaccio to Tasso, the other on Dante. The former is so general as to be misleading: Coleridge discussed too many authors, and the opinions he expressed do not correspond to his complete view of them – Boccaccio's case is emblematic in this respect. Conversely, the lecture on Dante is Coleridge's longest discussion on the Florentine poet, and, though it is not so analytic as the lectures on Shakespeare, it represents his criticism at its best.

However uneven the value of the lectures, the view of Dante and Italian romances they contain differs from the prevalent Romantic view. The modernity of Coleridge's Dante is striking: Dante was not for him a Byronic hero, the author of a few picturesque passages of *Inferno* and much unreadable theology in verse, as his contemporaries believed, but a philosophic poet who wrote an encyclopedic poem. Coleridge's originality is not limited to such an unusual understanding of Dante's mind and the structure of the *Comedy*, but also emerges from his attitude to Dante's style, which was often criticized at the time according to eighteenth-century standards. Coleridge's interpretation deserves to be considered, together with Friedrich Schlegel's and Foscolo's, as one of the greatest Romantic contributions to Dante studies.

The same judgement cannot be expressed of Coleridge's lecture on the

Italian romance. Despite occasional intuitions, it is clear that he found the romance uncongenial both in terms of subject matter and style. Coleridge was not impressed by *ottava rima*, since he was not a narrative poet; and he could hardly sympathize with the spirit of the major poets of chivalry, be it Pulci's burlesque irony, Ariosto's serene scepticism or Tasso's sensuous dramaticism.

Coleridge's lectures contain, beside his opinions on the aspects of Italian poetry most popular in Romantic England, his view of the role of Italy in the history of European literature. Though his desire for comparative criticism can be traced back to his early maturity, he fulfilled it only in the *Lectures on European Literature* he gave in 1818.[1] The syllabus of the course shows the structure of his history of modern European literature (*L Lects* (*CC*) II 39–42). Lecture I dealt with Christianity in the Middle Ages, which Coleridge regarded as the common origin of two branches or tendencies of literature: the romantic, and the religious-metaphysical. The romantic branch appeared first in the tales and metrical romances of Germany and France (Lecture II), then in the Italian romance, Petrarch, Chaucer and Spenser (III). He discussed these aspects with an eye to Shakespeare (IV, V, VI; VII on other Elizabethan playwrights). During the Renaissance, the romantic branch parted again into two, and the latter sub-section was characterized by wit and humour (VIII: Cervantes; IX: Rabelais, Swift and Sterne). In other words, the romantic branch consisted of two sub-sections: the former was dramatic, the latter linked to narrative poetry and fiction.

The alternative branch from the common medieval stem was metaphysical and religious. Coleridge introduced it with Dante, Donne and Milton in Lecture X, followed by a discussion of the romantic use of the supernatural in literature (XI), and of magic and witchcraft (XII). Lecture XIII was a sort of general summary and a discussion of the aesthetic principles of the course: it dealt with the arts in general and their relation to philosophy and religion. Lecture XIV was a conclusion leading to the present: it analysed the corruption of style in eighteenth-century England, which the 're-establishment of the Romantic and Italian School in Germany and Great Britain' had recently contributed to correcting (*IS* 158).

The Italian contribution to Coleridge's scheme is evident. He was interested in Renaissance romances in verse and lyrical poetry as steps towards modern lyric and Shakespeare. Dante, as the first great religious poet of Europe, had opened a path which led to Milton. The fine arts and music (more with reference to the opera as a form of drama than to instrumental music) were the means by which Coleridge tried to develop a general theory of aesthetics. The Italian Renaissance was therefore the centre of his interest, which focused on the art of verse from Petrarch – as the heir of the troubadours – to Renaissance lyric, and on the romantic element of narrative poetry, both considered as leading to Shakespeare. The fine arts, and Renaissance painting in particular, helped him develop the aesthetic foundation of his literary criticism.

The time available for a lecture is so short that Coleridge was compelled to discuss Italian poets briefly in the 1818 course; therefore, an accurate assessment of his critical thought must include the opinions he expressed on the same authors elsewhere.

Dante

The patterns of Coleridge's reading of Dante and Petrarch are similar: both began as a conventional interest and developed into an original view. The conventions were in both cases those of late eighteenth-century England: the vogue for Petrarch depended on the revived interest in love poetry and the sonnet; the discovery of Dante's *Comedy* was due to the revived interest in the Middle Ages and exoticism.

Dante was a common interest in the circle of Coleridge's friends in the 1790s. Southey and Coleridge borrowed Boyd's translation of the *Divine Comedy* in 1794 and 1796, and the result was a plan for a 'Poem in ~~three~~ one Books [sic] in the manner of Dantè on the excursion of Thor'.[2] The epic poem on Thor remained a project, but Coleridge wrote *The Ancient Mariner* and *Kubla Khan*, in which Dantesque echoes have been discovered. Although no precise borrowings from *The Divine Comedy* have been traced, there is an undeniable correspondence between the visionary and nightmarish atmosphere of Dante's *Hell* and Coleridge's *Mariner*, whose journey may owe something to the Ulysses episode in the *Comedy*.[3] Other conjectural references to Dante in Coleridge's early poems are too vague to be significant.[4]

Coleridge's real acquaintance with Dante dates from his Italian decade. His interest revived before his journey to the Mediterranean, where he bought a complete edition of Dante's works. Between 1804 and 1808 he read the *Comedy* and the minor works in the original.[5] The other decisive episode behind his criticism of Dante was his encounter with Henry Francis Cary. Coleridge had referred to Dante with admiration but only occasionally before 1818, despite his intention to 'give a course of

Lectures on Dante, Ariosto, Don Quixote, Calderon, Shakspere, Milton, and Klopstock – assigning, on the average, two lectures to each'.[6]

In October 1817 Coleridge met Cary by chance on the beach at Littlehampton. Cary was not unknown to Coleridge, who had read his *Sonnets and Odes* (1787) before 1796 (*PW* (EHC) II 1140). They soon became friends, and Cary gave Coleridge a copy of his translation of the *Comedy* which revived Coleridge's interest.[7] The translation, published in 1814, had not attracted public attention, in part because it was printed in an uninvitingly small type. Critical response had also been cold.[8] Coleridge's reaction to Cary's version, which he had never heard of before meeting its author, was enthusiastic: he was able to repeat and comment on long passages of it the morning following their first meeting at Littlehampton. He also expressed his intention to bring it to public notice.[9]

The value of Cary's *Divine Comedy* is undeniable, measured against the other English translations available at the time. The only complete version of Dante was Boyd's (1802), the mediocre translation in rhymed six-line stanzas whose *Inferno*, published separately in 1785, Coleridge knew.[10] Whereas his version did not recreate the spirit of Dante's poem in English, Cary's translation 'may now & then not be Dante's *Words*, but always, always, *Dante*' – a fact that 'those only who see the difficulty of the Original' could understand and appreciate (*CM* (*CC*) II 136). Cary was faithful to the meaning of the original, but his version is a living poem because its style recreates the original in English terms. *Paradise Lost* is the great religious epic in English, so that it was natural for Cary to adopt a Miltonic language. Coleridge wrote:

> I still affirm, that . . . both your Metre and your Rhythm have in a far greater degree, than I know of any other instance of, the variety of Milton without any mere *Miltonisms* – that . . . the Verse has this variety without any loss of *continuity* – and that this is the *excellence* of the Work, considered as a translation of Dante – that it gives the reader a similar feeling of wandering onward and onward. Of the diction, I can only say that [it] is Dantesque, even in that the Florentine must be preferred to our English Giant – namely, that it is not only pure *Language* but pure *English* – the language differs from that of a Mother or a well-bred Lady who has read little but her Bible and a few good books – only as far as the Thoughts and Things to be expressed require learned words from a learned Poet. – Perhaps, I may be thought to appreciate this merit too highly; but you have seen, what I have said in defence of this in the Literary Life.[11]

Coleridge's sincerity is demonstrated not only by his marginal notes in his copy of Cary's *Comedy*; he found new publishers – Taylor and Hessey –

who reprinted Cary's work, and he quoted and commended the translation in the lecture on Dante and Milton he gave on 27 February 1818.[12] The effect was immediate: the remaining copies of the old edition sold out quickly, and a new edition was published with Wordsworth's and Rogers' support in 1819. The other decisive element which contributed to Cary's popularity was Ugo Foscolo's review of the translation in the *Edinburgh Review* in February 1818.[13]

The importance of Coleridge and Foscolo can be evaluated if we remember that it was through Cary that most nineteenth-century English readers approached Dante. Not all of them were as enthusiastic as Ruskin, who wrote in *The Stones of Venice* that he would rather have Cary's *Comedy* than Milton himself. Some, like Taaffe and Shelley, found Cary monotonous. However, such readers were comparing him to the original, of which they had a first-hand knowledge.[14] Since Cary recreated Dante in Miltonic terms, it is true that his language lacks the conciseness of the original, and that it is softer and more paraphrastic, especially in some parts of the *Inferno*. Cary's *Divine Comedy* cannot be considered a great, classic translation in the same way as, for instance, Chapman's and Pope's Homer, since Cary's language does not possess a distinctive originality – it looks backward rather than forward. Byron's and Shelley's versions from Dante are instead examples of creative translation, as they pointed to a kind of metre and poetic language new to the English tradition. However, they could sustain the effort for a few lines only. As a complete version, Cary's enterprise remained without a serious rival for a long time, despite more than forty translations which appeared in English between 1818 and 1900.[15]

The effect of Coleridge's rereading of Dante through Cary can be observed both in his criticism and his poetry. Dante's limbo, located in the superior part of hell, inspired Coleridge's *Limbo* (1817). The Dantesque element is particularly clear in a variant portraying a figure which can be identified with Charon. The names of the places also derive from *Inferno*:

> For skimming in the wake it mock'd the care
> Of the old Boat-God for his farthing fare;
> Tho' Irus' Ghost itself ne'er frown'd blacker on
> The skin and skin-pent Druggist cross'd the Acheron,
> Styx, and with Periphlegeton Cocytus, –
> (The very names, methinks, might frighten us)
> Unchang'd it cross'd –
> (*PW* (EHC) I 429–30)

Above all, Cary's *Divine Comedy* helped Coleridge expand his under-standing of Dante's poem. Coleridge said to John Payne Collier in 1811 that he 'had the grandest opinion of Dante', but that he was not 'a sufficient master of the language to form a proper estimate' (*C Talker* 174).

Coleridge's role as a mediator of Dante is not confined to his discovery and advertisement of Cary's translation of the *Comedy*: the lecture he gave on Dante is valuable as criticism, regardless of the help it gave Cary. Although several of Coleridge's comments on Dante are commonplaces of contemporary criticism, some are not: in England he alone understood the significance of philosophy in Dante's poem, and very few appreciated Dante's style as deeply as he did. The result was a remarkable widening of the current image of Dante.

Coleridge gave two lectures on Dante. Notes for the latter, which is part of the course on European literature he held in 1819, are still extant, and show that he drew on Cary, Henry Hallam, Schiller and the Schlegels for the general background.[16] The lecture, as in 1818, began with an outline of the age of Dante.

Coleridge pointed out that the Gothic character spread only super-ficially in Italy, where the imitation of Latin literature had begun early. The political situation was characterized by the existence of small independent cities such as had existed in classical Greece or pre-imperial Rome. Scholasticism attained its height before Dante's time, but it was less influential in Italy than anywhere else in Europe. Coleridge argued that it is impossible to understand Dante without a good knowledge of Scholastic philosophy. In the philosophical lectures he gave during the same period, he complained of the neglect in which Scholasticism was held. It was a legitimate reproach at a time when Dante was a fashionable subject, but few cared for the theology and philosophy embodied in his works. Sismondi's *Histoire des républiques italiennes du moyen âge* (16 vols., Paris 1809–18) and Henry Hallam's *View of the State of Europe during the Middle Ages* (2 vols., 1818), which provided the historical background to Dante, enjoyed instead great popularity.[17]

However, Coleridge added that the medieval revival of philosophy, whose aim was the mere defence of superstition – i.e., Roman Catholicism – caused a reaction. Coleridge seems to have regarded Dante as a precursor of the Reformation, as his opinion of Gabriele Rossetti's commentary on the *Divine Comedy* shows. Rossetti, an Italian political exile he had met in 1824, interpreted the whole *Divine Comedy* as a political allegory aiming to undermine the Roman Church.[18] Coleridge found it 'in great part just; but he has pushed it beyond all bounds of common sense' (*TT (CC)* 17 Aug 1833).

The view of Dante as anti-clerical, which was traditional in England from the Reformation onwards, was based on Dante's invectives against the corruption of the Church in *Monarchia* and the *Comedy*. It appears, for example, in the writings of John Foxe, John Jewel and Milton, and later in Roscoe and Shelley.[19] Rossetti's stance must be understood in the context of the Italian Risorgimento and its anti-clericalism. Dante the patriot dominates Foscolo's criticism, which is a polemic against Jesuit scholarship of Dante like Venturi's.[20] Byron and Shelley helped to diffuse the image of Dante as a political rebel and an apostle of liberty which remained popular throughout the century, though it was historically false. It is not true, as Steve Ellis states, that Coleridge's view of Dante in this respect is 'exactly opposed to Shelley's' (Ellis 249–50): Coleridge, who wrote that 'in Pindar, Chaucer, Dante, Milton, &c. &c. we have instances of the close connection of poetic genius with the love of liberty and of genuine reformation' (BL (CC) I 209), included politics among the elements necessary to understand Dante's poetry. He emphasized the intensity and violence of political life in medieval Italy, epitomized by the struggle between the Guelph and Ghibelline factions and, on an individual scale, by Dante's own biography.[21] The important point, however, is that he did not make politics the core of his interpretation of Dante, as Byron and Shelley (in part) did.

By way of concluding his introductory section, Coleridge noted that the chivalric element played a minor role in medieval Italy. The Christian element appeared in a purer form in Italian poetry because a proper chivalry was introduced after the Crusades and through Venice at a later date. Both Friedrich Schlegel and Hallam wrote extensive chapters on chivalry and its literature, which Coleridge probably had in mind.[22] But in this context I think he was simply trying to explain how a work like *The Divine Comedy*, full of theology and philosophy, could appear so early in Italy, whereas metrical romances of chivalry flourished from Boccaccio to Tasso at a time when they were declining everywhere else in Europe.

After the historical preamble, Coleridge defined the new elements Christianity introduced to poetry. Friedrich Schlegel thought the characteristic elements of medieval poetry were 'das Rittergedichte, de[r] Minnesang und die Allegorie';[23] Coleridge disagreed and provided a different and longer list. The first element he mentioned was allegory, which he only hinted at here, because he postponed it to a successive lecture. He argued that Dante's poem was not an allegory, but 'a system of moral, political, and theological Truths with arbitrary personal exemplifications – <the punishments indeed allegorical *perhaps* –>' (*CN* III 4498). Such an opinion, which may seem surprising, is understandable in the light of Coleridge's conception of allegory as mechanical and inferior to symbol. He probably intended to emphasize the radical difference between most medieval allegories, specimens of which appear also in Dante (the 'arbitrary personal exemplifications'), and the symbolic power emerging in many parts of the *Comedy*. Schelling thought that Dante's poem contained 'ein ganz eigenthümliches Mittel' between allegory and 'symbolisch-objektiver Gestaltung.' Friedrich Schlegel solved the problem in a different way: he argued that Dante had put realistic representations of life within an allegoric frame – that is, the general structure of his poem – whereas the poems of chivalry concealed allegoric meanings under a realistic story.[24]

This interpretation of Coleridge's statement is confirmed by the second element which, according to him, Christianity had introduced in poetry: a new conception of the infinite. In Classical Greece the infinite was seen in the finite, whereas in Christianity the finite is seen in the infinite. The Greeks derived their gods from Egypt, depriving them of universality and making them mere embodiments of ideas; but 'to interest, the Ideas must be turned into Finites, and these into Finites anthropomorphic – Their Religion, their Poetry, their very pictures, statues &c &c'. Christianity, on the contrary, sees everything in 'connection with the Infinite – . . . in some shadowy, or enduring relation – Soul, Futurity &c' (*CN* III 4498). Schelling made a similar point in his *Philosophie der Kunst*, but drew different conclusions: in religion the finite becomes a reflection of the infinite in which it is intuited, whereas the infinite embodied in the finite becomes symbolic and therefore mythology. As such, Greek mythology was not a religion.[25] In Coleridge's mind, it was Christian and not Classical art which was eminently symbolic.

An immediate consequence was his idea that in Christianity poetry and doctrine are always combined. The combination is evident in Dante, who failed far more than Milton to blend poetry and philosophy – although he was Milton's model for it. The marginalia on Cary's Dante show that Coleridge's opinion was a consequence of his reading of *Paradiso*. The implications of *Par*. I 13–14 were that,

> Hitherto, the Poet & Moralist has sufficed; but henceforward the *Philosopher* must be added: my 'Paradiso' *must* be metaphysical. Yet how to make this compatible & co-present with the equally necessary Element of Poetry – hic labor est! Both the Powers of Intellect, the Discursive & Sensuous, and the Rational Super-sensuous, must unite at their summits. (*CM* (*CC*) II 135)

Despite Coleridge's reservations, which Friedrich Schlegel shared,[26] it is worth noting that he characterized Dante's poem as a system of moral, philosophical and poetical truths instead of focusing on some favourite aspect.[27] Coleridge was probably the only critic in England who grasped and emphasized that the outstanding character of Dante's work is encyclopedic; most readers selected some aspect and ignored or condemned the rest. Whether the selection was based on eighteenth-century principles, like Landor's or Hunt's, or on Romantic principles, like Byron's and Shelley's, the approach was similar.[28] Even Foscolo, whose criticism is a milestone in Dante studies, ignored the theology of the *Comedy* to turn Dante into an enemy of the Church and a patriot. This approach was still the basis of Croce's view of Dante, which delimited some lyric passages of poetry within a structure of non-poetry – philosophy, theology and allegory. If today we have learnt to admire and appreciate *The Divine Comedy* for its structure, very few did in Coleridge's time: the Schlegels and Schelling are the only names which occur to me. In addition, Coleridge intuited and pointed out more clearly than them the role abstract knowledge plays in shaping the mind of a poet, and the way in which it later emerges in poetry:

> Nothing can be more absurd than this belief of the necessary opposition of poetry to science. In all great poets the reverse is manifest. You see it in Homer, in Dante, and above all, in Milton. Perhaps I ought rather to say, that you *feel* its influence, in shaping the conception of the poet, and preserving those fine proportions whose combination makes the harmony of a structure. (*C 17th C* 55)

He even spoke of a 'higher Logic' authenticated by the 'reasonableness . . . of Passion', without which it is impossible to understand Dante, Shakespeare and Milton (*TT* (*CC*) 1 Jul 1833).

But Coleridge had more to say about the philosophical element in Dante. He stated that this aspect was so important that the *Comedy* could indeed be read as philosophy.[29] Dante was

> the Link of Christian poetry and Christianized Philosophy, and in this union, the Link again of the Platonic, christianized into the Mystic, and the *Aristot*otelean, by the numerous minute articles of Fact & Ceremony & converted into Hair-splitting. (*CN* III 4498)

It is an interesting remark, which Coleridge repeated in the *Philosophical Lectures* (1949, 292).

Dante's philosophy is a controversial issue. Although Thomism has often been considered as the dominant element in his thought, Nardi, Gilson and other twentieth-century scholars have argued that Dante could not be a Thomist. His philosophical view was a personal combination of mystical and rationalist, of Platonizing and Aristotelian Scholasticism.[30] Coleridge, who had a good knowledge of Scholasticism, intuited it, perhaps with the help of the notes in the editions of Dante he read. Generic assertions about Dante's learning have always been common, but no other English Romantic critic beside Coleridge was able to define successfully, though in general terms, the philosophical tone of Dante's thought.[31]

The Christian combination of poetry and philosophy does not mean that modern art was devoid of feeling. On the contrary, the association of poetry and sentiment was characteristic of Christianity, which turned 'the mind inward on its own *essence* instead of its circumstances & communities', so that 'the re-action of the Poet's general reflections on any Act or Image [were] more *fore-grounded* than the act itself' (*CN* III 4498). Coleridge was rephrasing Schiller's theory of naïve and sentimental poetry: the ancients were naïve poets because they felt; the moderns are sentimental because they feel their feelings. The example Coleridge gave to illustrate the concept – a comparison between Homer and Ariosto – derived in fact from Schiller.[32]

The new amalgam of thought and feeling emerges in Dante's images, which are 'not only taken from obvious Nature & all intelligible to all; but ever conjoined with the universal feeling received from them – opposed to the idiosyncracies of some meritorious modern Poet'. Coleridge quoted some lines from Inferno (II 127 ff.) to illustrate his assertion – a passage he also cited in the section on Time in *Logic* to exemplify the interaction between external and internal knowledge (*CC* 166). 'Dante's Charm, and that which makes him indeed a *Poet*' is what Coleridge calls Topographic Reality: 'Nature worse than Chaos, a thousand delusive forms have reality *only* for the Passions, they excite: the Poet compels them into the service of the Permanent.'[33] Even though some of Dante's images were imperfect – for example, his Satan was inferior to Milton's[34] – Dante's graphic power reminded Coleridge of Giotto, that is, the frescoes in the Camposanto at Pisa which impressed him.[35]

Coleridge was not content with highlighting Dante's picturesqueness, but tried to define the nature of the phenomenon. He compared his nightmares to the wanderings of a Dante without his guide through Swedenborg's Devildom (*CL* V 489, 6 Sept 1825), and he associated *The*

Divine Comedy with dreams when he argued that the imagery of the poem had in part been suggested by the trances of a monk. In his 'Life of Dante', Cary pointed out some visions, and the 'Vision of Alberico' in particular, as sources of Dante. In addition, Coleridge was certain that 'the monkish *áskēsis* may produce the magnetic sleep', and in support of his idea he quoted chapter 9 of Tertullianus' *De anima*, which describes the visions of a Montanist woman during an ecstasis (CL VI 714, 28 Nov 1827). In 1814 he had associated Dante with the *broukolaka*, in Greek religion the corpse of an excommunicate who wanders reanimated by the devil. As Kathleen Coburn points out, he was probably thinking of Canto XXXIII of *Inferno* (lines 115–33), in which Friar Alberigo describes himself in similar terms (*CN* III 4211, Jun 1814). But, to return to Dante's imagery, Coleridge's point is clear: images in themselves, however original, do not make a poet. It was his usual anti-ekphrastic stance, which is evident in his response to painting.

Though in *Biographia* Coleridge described Shakespeare as more picturesque than Dante, he habitually quoted Dante and Pindar as examples of picturesque poetry, whose peculiarity is to 'present every thing in the completeness of actual objectivity'. The other great category, in which Coleridge included Milton and himself, was that of musical poets, who had 'few or no proper pictures, but a magnificent mirage of words instead'.[36]

Dante's picturesqueness is a commonplace of nineteenth-century criticism, but Coleridge tried to provide a psychological and historical explanation for it. The background to his attempt is August Wilhelm Schlegel's idea that Classical art is statuesque and modern art picturesque – a distinction underlying Coleridge's comparison between Classical and modern art and their different sense of beauty.[37] In the Pantheon the parts are subordinated to the whole, whereas in Christian art – he was probably thinking of Gothic architecture – they are 'sharply distinct, and this distinction counterbalanced only by their multitude & variety – while the Whole . . . is altogether a Feeling, in which all the thousand several impressions lose themselves as in a universal Solvent'. The accumulative, empirical character of modern art, distinguished from Greek and Roman centripetal idealism, appears in the encyclopedic structure of Dante's poem. The comparison between the *Comedy* and Gothic architecture was not unusual, and was, for example, drawn by William Roscoe and August Wilhelm Schlegel.[38]

In the second part of Lecture X, Coleridge discussed Dante's excellencies, which he illustrated by quoting passages from the *Divine Comedy*. It is worth pointing out that whereas his marginalia to Dante concern *Purgatorio* and *Paradiso*, in the lecture he referred chiefly to the *Inferno*, probably in order to put the audience at ease. The peculiarity of Coleridge's approach emerges even in such a descriptive section, in which he expressed his view of Dante's poetic technique.

Style was the first evidence of Dante's greatness. Coleridge considered it superior to Milton's because of 'the passion and miracle of Words after a slumber in Barbarism, which of itself gives a romantic somewhat not felt by the original Classics themselves'. The passages he quoted as examples were Dante's encounter with Virgil (*Inf.* I 64–99) and the description of the Wood of the Suicides in which the Harpies live (XIII 1–30).

The language of the *Comedy* has always been a debated issue in Dante criticism. Hostility to it was normal during the eighteenth century, and appeared even in critics and poets who admired *The Divine Comedy*: Alfieri, Cesarotti and Baretti, who extolled Dante in many respects, found his style inelegant. It was an aspect of contemporary taste, and 'the last sign of the Bembesque and the Crusca Academy's heritage, the flattening voice of a Petrarchesque tradition which had spread inexorably in time, and which was more constraining than any norm'.[39] Though neoclassical taste had different origins in England, the attitude to Dante was similar.

The recovery of medieval literature helped to modify this attitude, but the process was slow. Thomas Warton, whose *History of English Poetry* includes a long summary of *The Divine Comedy*, quoted a paraphrase of Dante by Voltaire to demonstrate that Dante would have more readers if his style was like Voltaire's.[40] The attitude did not disappear in Coleridge's time. Walter Savage Landor, who thought Dante inferior to Shakespeare alone, could not accept rhetorical figures like ploce, onomatopoeia, and paronomasy.[41] Leigh Hunt lamented Dante's mixture of styles, as well as of characters and facts, belonging to different cultural contexts. Though 'when Dante is great, nobody surpasses him', his style 'is nervous, concise, full as it can hold, picturesque, mighty, primeval; but it is often obscure, often harsh, and forced in its constructions, defective in melody, and wilful and superfluous in the rhyme'.[42]

Coleridge's admiration for Milton does not need to be illustrated here; the mere preference for Dante's style above Milton's implies an unconditionally positive judgement. The idea that the excellence of Dante's style is in part due to the expressiveness inherent in archaic language derives from eighteenth-century primitivism. He would find the same argument fully developed in Vico. However, Coleridge was aware that the archaic flavour of language was not a sufficient explanation for Dante's greatness, which derived from his craftmanship and philosophical power. As early as 1808 or 1809, he had written about 'the absurdity of tracing the growth of poetic Genius by *ancestry*: as if Dante or Milton were *creatures* of *wandering Bards* – Ritson & other Dullards are full of this nonsense' (*CN* III 3437). The 'wonderful sublimity' of the beginning of Canto III of the *Inferno* could only be 'explained from the true nature of RELIGION. The Reason+Understanding' (*CN* III 4498). Dante was not a 'gratuitous logician', as Hunt claimed, quoting the same lines as absurd. Moreover, one of the passages Coleridge cited to exemplify the beauty of Dante's style contains the line 'Cred'io ch'ei credette ch'io credessi' ('I think he must have thought that I was thinking', *Inf.* XIII 25, tr. D. L. Sayers; Cary has 'He, as it seemed, believed/That I had thought'), which Landor found intolerable. The Canto to which the line belongs is characterized by a tortuous syntax and a difficult style which echo the prose of Pier delle Vigne, who speaks in the episode. As Leo Spitzer suggested, such a style is the linguistic representation of the torture the damned suffer. An attitude like Landor's prevented most readers from understanding the stylistic expressiveness of the *Comedy*.

The presence of Dante in Coleridge's writings after 1819 is occasional.[43] However, the lasting importance Dante had for Coleridge emerges from an episode related by Philarète Chasles, who visited him at Highgate in the late 1820s. After refuting Spinozism, Coleridge illustrated his religious principles, 'till, reached to the summit . . . he bowed himself in humility and reverence to the earth, and murmuring some sweet and mysterious verses from Dante's Paradise, he closed' (*TT (CC)* I 556).

Romances from Boccaccio to Tasso

Though Coleridge's attitude to Italian romances was as unusual as his attitude to Dante, it did not lead to critical results of equal value. The character of his approach emerges if compared with that of Byron, whom the English reader usually associates with the Italian romance. Whereas both the tone and metres of the mock-heroic Italian tradition were of crucial importance to Byron, they signified much less for Coleridge. When Coleridge read Ariosto in the original, he did not try to adapt his stanza to the English language: conversely, he sketched an Italian Spenserian stanza, which he preferred to Ariosto's. What happened afterwards is well known: *ottava rima* as Byron adapted it was fruitful as late as Yeats and beyond, whereas Coleridge's option was a blind alley, since no Italian poet I know of made use of Spenserian stanzas. The example is telling, but Coleridge's response to the Italian romance is more complex and involves elements other than metrics.

Coleridge's view was formed on Boccaccio, Ariosto and Tasso, since his knowledge of Pulci and Berni was superficial. The mixture of admiration and suspicion he expressed for them all was in large part due to ethical reasons: the thought embodied in their poems was as uncongenial as their metres and stories, to which he also paid little attention. Although none of them, perhaps with the exception of Tasso, was a philosophical poet, Coleridge did not overlook the philosophical implications of their works, as he had not overlooked Dante's and Petrarch's thought. The result was not a total rejection of the Italian romance tradition, but a formal interest in some of its aspects – the only possible interest given such premises.

Coleridge discussed Italian romances in Lecture III of the 1818 course, the first three lectures of which can be considered as an introduction to the literature of the Middle Ages. It is not necessary to analyse Coleridge's argument and sources (mainly the Schlegel brothers and Ritson). Suffice it to say that Lecture I, a brief sketch which includes references to history, anthropology, religion, literature and the fine arts, summarizes themes which were later discussed in detail. Lecture II is devoted to the migration of the Indoeuropean races, and to the relations between Goths, Latins and Greeks, and Celts.[44] Coleridge compared the Graeco–Roman with the Gothic world, but above all he emphasized the 'amalgamating Genius of the middle ages', when 'the philosophy and the loveliness' of Greece and 'the legislatorial and ordonnant Mind of civilizing Rome joined with the deep feelings, the high imagination, the chivalrous courtesies and the breathings after immortality of the Goths' under the egis of Christianity (*CN* III 4384).

Lecture III deals with the Italian romance. The introduction describes the birth of the romance tongues from a combination of Latin and German elements. He believed that their external form was Latin, but their spirit was Gothic.[45] If the romantic spirit first appeared in France, it blossomed later in Italy 'from Boccaccio to Tasso'. Coleridge promised he would discuss the Italian romances not for their own sake but as antecedents to the literature of Elizabethan England (*L Lects* (*CC*) II 89–90; *CN* III 4388). In Lecture IV, he argued that English and Italian poetry grew out of the same root, that is, 'the allegorical, chivalrous and . . . amalgamating Genius of the middle ages' (*L Lects* (*CC*) II 111). The pinnacle of the whole process was Shakespeare, who assimilated everything preceding him, even if he shows fewer specific traces of each individual influence than any other writer (*L Lects* (*CC*) II 114). Since

Coleridge's comments on the Italian poets were brief and sometimes partial in the lecture, supplementary references are necessary.

Coleridge's analysis rightly started from Boccaccio, a writer toward whom his attitude was always ambiguous. On the one hand, the reservations he had about Boccaccio's ethics made his judgement censorious at times; on the other, he expressed genuine admiration for some of Boccaccio's works, which stimulated his desire to learn Italian in the early 1800s. His appreciation did not disappear late in life, since he used Boccaccio as a symbol for the Italian Renaissance in *The Garden of Boccaccio*.[46]

Boccaccio was discussed in Lecture III of the 1818 course as the founder of Italian prose and narrative poetry. Coleridge praised his 'happy art of narration', the finesse of his psychological analysis, and the variety of his tales which furnished the subject to many literary works (*CN* III 4388, Feb 1818). After such a beginning, which acknowledged the value of Boccaccio's style and subjects, one would expect an admiring or at least a positive analysis of his works; however, it was not so.

Boccaccio had the doubtful merit of introducing the Latinate prose style made of

> long inwoven Periods, which arose from the very nature of their language in the Greek writers, but which already in the Latin Orators and Historians betrayed a something of effort . . . – but far, far too alien from that individualizing and tho' confederating yet not blending character of the North, to be permanent – tho' the magnificence & stateliness &c yet it diminished the controll over the feelings of men – made too great a chasm between Books and Life – hence abandoned by Luther. (*CN* III 4388)

Kathleen Coburn points out that the comment seems to combine two different passages from Friedrich Schlegel's *Geschichte der alten und neuen Literatur*. However, her observation can be misleading, since Friedrich Schlegel extolled Boccaccio's style: 'Boccaccio ist in Rücksicht der Prosa ein unerreichbarer Meister wie Petrarca in Rücksicht der Versifikation'.[47] Whatever its source, Coleridge's comment expresses a view of prose which is difficult to reconcile with his own prose and with other remarks he made on the subject.

In Lecture XIV of the same course, he argued that the English inheritors of the Latinate style introduced to Italy by Boccaccio were Hooker, Bacon, Milton and Taylor: 'In all these the language is dignified but plain, genuine English, although elevated and brightened by superiority of intellect in the writer'.[48] Even if Coleridge's English authors appear to be a mixed group to modern eyes, they were the models of his own style in prose, which he hoped would supersede the eighteenth-century frenchified manner. Boccaccio's style had been criticized for its tortuousness in the eighteenth century,[49] and if such an indictment is comprehensible in Landor, whose admiration for Boccaccio was otherwise boundless, it is surprising in Coleridge, who loved some of Boccaccio's stories and above all his prose romances.[50]

Coleridge liked Boccaccio's 'almost neglected Romances' better than the *Decameron*. He thought they excelled it in psychological analysis and 'in the wild and imaginative character of the situations'. As far as I know, he was the only reader in his time who preferred the minor works to *Decameron*. Instead of comparing Boccaccio with Chaucer,[51] Coleridge compared Boccaccio's romances to Cervantes' minor works and proposed their translation to John Murray. Since Murray did not answer, Coleridge tried to interest Byron, Rogers and Daniel Stuart, but the project was finally abandoned.[52] In any event, the interest he showed in these works, or even in a part of them, is noteworthy, since they were not as popular as *Decameron*. Between the Renaissance and the Romantic age, only *Teseida* and *Filostrato* had attracted English attention in the wake of Chaucer's use of them.[53]

It is difficult to know how many of Boccaccio's minor works Coleridge read. He referred to *Filocolo* and *Teseida*, and was aware that Boccaccio's romances in verse were the models of the other Italian narrative poets, since he discussed them in the context of the Italian metrical romance. It is surprising, therefore, that he argued that Boccaccio 'has little interest as a metrical poet in any respect, and none for our present purpose' (*L Lects (CC)* II 92). In other words, Coleridge believed that Boccaccio's poems had no intrinsic poetic value, but only a historic value as models of the later Italian romances, as the fact that he discussed them in a lecture on the Italian poems of chivalry shows.

An important consequence was that Coleridge overlooked the vital interaction between Boccaccio's verse and prose. His analysis of Boccaccio's prose focused on the logical structure of sentences in order to trace its classicism, as most critics after Bembo had done.[54] If the centrality of the medieval *cursus* and rhythmical patterns in Boccaccio's prose has waited till the twentieth century to be discussed at length, some readers were responsive to it even in Coleridge's time. Shelley wrote that Boccaccio 'is, in the high sense of the word a poet, and his language has the rhythm and harmony of verse'; Vittore Branca points out a similar intuition in Foscolo.[55]

Style also played a major role in stimulating Coleridge's interest in Ariosto, which developed during his Italian journey, when he read him in the original. The lateness of his curiosity is surprising, since Ariosto was fashionable in the circle of his friends in the 1790s. Ariosto was an early acquaintance of Wordsworth, who always preferred him to Dante;[56] a similar enthusiasm appears in Southey, whose 'first Epic Dream' was conceived in his childhood after reading Hoole's translation of Ariosto.[57]

If the vogue for the *Furioso* did not involve young Coleridge, Ariosto was one of the first poets he turned to when he began to read Italian poetry in the original. The short notes he made in his copy of *Orlando furioso* (Venice 1713) and in his journal show an ambivalent attitude. Although he affirmed in 1805 that 'Dante, Ariosto, Giordano Bruno' would be his Italy (*CN* II 2598), he was never at ease with Ariosto, whose serene wisdom and acceptance of life in all its aspects were not congenial to a moralist like himself. His objections to Ariosto and Boccaccio were similar, since he blamed Ariosto for his sensuousness and for paganizing Christianity.[58]

Nevertheless, Coleridge admired other aspects of Ariosto, whom he included among the greatest geniuses (*L Lects* (*CC*) I 229). His approach was, from the beginning, formal: he focused on Ariosto's poetic technique, which he found exquisite. This is related to his interest in Renaissance lyric poetry, which led him to read Ariosto's Italian and Latin lyrics, from which he reworked a Latin charade into a poem.[59] His interest in Ariosto's Latin poetry revived in 1808, when he noted that metrical reading of Latin verse according to Classical rules was dissonant to English ears, and used a line of Ariosto's *De Julia* to illustrate his thesis (*CN* III 3305). Metrics was the subject of the only marginal note he made to *Orlando furioso*, which is a sketch of an Italian Spenserian stanza, and shows that he found Ariosto's metre uncongenial (*CM* (*CC*) I 116–17, Sept–Oct 1804).

It is symptomatic of Coleridge's mind that he turned to the minor works, but also that he selected his lyric poetry, Italian and Latin, instead of his better-known comedies. Ariosto's short poems are the results of his literary training: his early lyric poetry was his way of absorbing Petrarchism, which he later abandoned for the larger forms of romance; Dante was the stylistic model of his satires, which are realistic and close to moral autobiography.[60] However, despite his attention to Ariosto's metre, Coleridge could learn less from him than from other sixteenth-century Italian poets. The reason is that

> the true originality of Ariosto's discourse consists in the fusion of a narra-
> tive syntax of a Boccaccian kind with Petrarch's lyric 'proportion'. It is
> from this fusion, in fact, that the character articulated and fused, dynamic
> and eurhythmic, 'narrative' and 'lyric' of the stanza of Furioso derives.[61]

I think Coleridge's temper was lyric, so that he was never at home with long narrative forms, despite his love for certain epic poems: for example, whenever he miltonized in long forms he became bombastic, unlike Wordsworth. The Italian *ottava rima* was in any sense too far from his poetic spirit to be for him the fertile model it was for Byron.[62]

Despite his unusual interest in Ariosto's Latin poetry and the reservations about his stanza, it was the Italian poetry which intrigued him most. Ariosto made him reflect on the peculiarities of the European tongues. His style showed the capacity of Italian to express things naturally but with dignity. Collier's report emphasizes Ariosto's flexibility, since he is described as a poet who '*displays to the utmost advantage the use of his native tongue for all purposes, whether of passion, sentiment, humour, or description*' (*L Lects* (*CC*) I 291, 1811; II 482). Elsewhere, Ariosto was mentioned as an instance of the facility with which the Italian language can pass from grave to light subjects. The inferiority of English and German in this respect was an apparent defect of the language which arose 'from the moral defect & false taste of a Nation' (*CN* III 3557, Jul–Sept 1809; *Omniana* 343). An interesting aspect of these notes is that they imply a moral judgement of Ariosto much less cut-and-dried than in the later lectures. But, to return to Ariosto's style, Coleridge pointed out that it was sometimes complicated: he mentioned his *Satire* alongside Dante and Berni as examples of difficult works which ought to be read as soon as possible to improve one's command of Italian (*CN* III 3283, 1808).

The poetic language of Italy was not superior to German and English in every respect. Coleridge argued that the language of poetry is distinguished from common language where illiteracy prevails, as in Italy from Dante to Metastasio; otherwise, prose and poetry possess the same vocabulary, of which they make a different use. It is foolish to imitate the regional peculiarities of authors who have become the classics of a nation in which the spoken language is not unified, as in Italy, where Dante's, Ariosto's and Alfieri's Tuscanisms were copied too often (*CN* III 3611, 1809). Coleridge did not realize that Ariosto and Alfieri, who were not Tuscans, were among those imitators: in fact, they suppressed regional peculiarities to render their literary language more neutrally Italian, as Ariosto's revisions of his poem show. Coleridge's idea implies an anti-purist attitude to the so-called *questione della lingua*, the problem of what literary Italian should be, which is a central issue in the history of Italian letters.

Ariosto's language convinced Coleridge that Ariosto's art was not based on the invention of new stories but on the way in which he reshaped old materials (*Friend* (*CC*) II 219; *BL* (*CC*) II 188). Following August Wilhelm

Schlegel and Schiller, he mentioned Ariosto's relation to Homer as an example of creative imitation (*L Lects* (*CC*) I 492, 1812; 511, 516, 1813). Ariosto was a sentimental poet, Homer a naïve poet (*CN* III 4498, 1819).

In the light of these observations, we must regret the fact that Coleridge never discussed Ariosto in greater detail in his lectures. Lecture III of the 1818 course, on the Italian romances, is disappointing: one would expect Ariosto to be central to the discussion, but Coleridge confined himself to blaming his licence and paganism.[63]

Coleridge's admiration for Ariosto, however bizarre, is demonstrated by the traditional comparison with Tasso: 'Well! I am for Ariosto against Tasso; though I would rather praise Ariosto's poetry than his poem' (*TT* (*CC*) II 68, Jul 1827). Coleridge did not partake of the Romantic enthusiasm for Tasso's biographic legend, on which he did not make any comment – excluding those on Goethe's *Torquato Tasso*, which he disliked on moral grounds (*CRB* I 89, 1812). The reason is evident: despite the introspection, which might have attracted him, he found Tasso's Catholicism and morbid sensuousness unpleasant.

The story of Tasso's popularity in the Romantic age is complex, but a brief discussion of it will clarify Coleridge's attitude. Critical debate on Tasso's works was lively in the eighteenth century, when both the *Jerusalem* and *Amyntas* were translated and ran through several editions. New complete versions of the *Jerusalem* in heroic couplets were published by Philip Doyne (1761) and John Hoole (1763); the latter became the standard Tasso for about five decades.[64] The peculiarity of the Romantic approach was an unprecedented interest in Tasso's life, which turned him into 'a prototype of the Romantic poet, loving passionately but hopelessly and beyond his station, the victim of political oppression, . . . the hypersensitive creative artist at odds with society'.[65] Hints at the Romantic interpretation of his life appeared in the eighteenth-century – for example, in Baretti and in the 'Life of Tasso' prefixed to Doyne's and Hoole's translations – but it was not the centre of their attention. Some works helped to create the new image of Tasso, and none perhaps more than Goethe's *Torquato Tasso* (1789). Critical debate on the subject intensified: Tiraboschi, Serassi, and in England John Black, whose *Life of Torquato Tasso* appeared in 1810, provided a documented and less fictional account of Tasso's life, which however did not modify the prevailing public belief in Tasso's impossible love for Leonora d'Este. The most significant of the numerous English works on Tasso's life is Byron's *Lament of Tasso* (1817).[66]

Coleridge disliked Tasso from the beginning: he thought Tasso was a poet for women (*CL* I 258, 19 Nov 1796). He evidently found Tasso's sensibility too tender and his sensuousness disturbing – two grounds of interest for other Romantics – even though he later praised Tasso's sentimental sincerity (*L Lects (CC)* II 104). Coleridge's attitude explains his indifference to Tasso before he went to Italy, when presumably he read him in the original, since he referred to his style in 1808.

However slight Coleridge's knowledge, he was able to blame Addison for his unfounded criticism of Tasso. Addison attributed 'to Tasso himself, the superabundance of Conceits, which exist only in Fairfax's licentious tho' beautiful Translation, or rather rifacciamento of the Italian Poem'.[67] Coleridge found Tasso's style easy, like a part of Ariosto's and Metastasio's – a strange judgement as far as Tasso is concerned (*CN* III 3283, 1808). He confirmed his view when he did not include Tasso in the golden age of the Italian language, which ran from Dante to Tasso's 'artificial style' excluded (*TT (CC)* 8 Jul 1827). Although the turgidity of Tasso's style explains his reaction, his hostility is in part puzzling, since he possessed the right ear to perceive and enjoy the beauty of Tasso's music. A comparison between Tasso and Milton in this respect was natural for English critics: Hunt, for instance, confronted Tasso's with Milton's use of proper names, and found the latter more harmonious.[68]

The presence of Tasso in Coleridge's criticism is occasional, and his silence about Tasso's lyric poetry is significant. His attitude to *Aminta*, which he ignored, recalls his response to Guarini's *Pastor fido* and Sannazaro, and it confirms that pastoral poetry was not his favourite genre.[69] By way of contrast I can recall Leigh Hunt's lifelong interest in pastoral poetry; his translation of *Aminta*, dedicated to Keats, appeared in 1820. Hunt was not alone in his enthusiasm, since critics like Ginguené, Sismondi, Mme de Staël and the Schlegels admired *Aminta*.

The most surprising aspect of Coleridge's observations on the style of the Italian Renaissance prose and romances is his preference for the simplicity of Ariosto over the complexity of Boccaccio and Tasso. Many an eighteenth-century critic could have expressed such a view, which is all the more surprising for those who know Coleridge as a 'Goth', a lover of obscurity and complication. In fact, his attitude can easily be explained in the context of his experience of Italian culture, which was a very significant part of his aesthetic education because it was different from his temperament.

Coleridge's attention to the style of the romances does not mean that his viewpoint was that of a formalist; on the contrary, the overall impression is that an excessive moralism prevented him from judging those poems correctly. Such an impression is particularly strong when we read that he could find no excuse for 'the gross and disgusting licentiousness, the daring profaneness of both together, which rendered the Decamerone of Boccace, as the Parent of an hundred worse children, fit to be classed among the enemies of the human Race', a licence which poisoned also Ariosto and Chaucer, and tempted even 'our pure-minded Spenser' (*L Lects (CC)* II 95). Boccaccio's attitude to sentimental life was too frank – at least in the *Decameron* – to appeal to Coleridge and most Romantics, who preferred something more idealized or morbid. Coleridge also disagreed with Boccaccio's late misogyny (*BL (CC)* I 229).

Though Coleridge's judgement sounds unequivocally negative, his view was in effect many-faceted. In the same lecture where he attacked Boccaccio's licentiousness, he pointed out the finesse of Boccaccio's analysis of passion, as Hazlitt also did.[70] Carwardine's report of the lecture emphasized that Boccaccio, Pulci, Spenser and Tasso were said to be the first who wrote what they truly felt (*L Lects (CC)* II 104). Moreover, Hazlitt related he once heard Coleridge speak 'like one inspired' of the tale of the pot of basil – a favourite with the Romantics.[71] John Payne Collier confirms it, since he noted that Coleridge 'had the strongest liking for some of Boccaccio's tales, and spoke in praise of the old English translation of them.' He pointed out that Shakespeare 'had been indebted to several' (*C Talker* 175, 1811).

Another complication arises from the fact that Coleridge's reservations focused on the 'far-famed' *Decameron*, which, as we saw before, Boccaccio's 'almost neglected Romances' excelled in psychological analysis and sentimental intensity. His preference cannot be due to ethical reasons alone, since Boccaccio's view of love is similar in all his early works, and erotic situations in his romances are as frequent and explicit as in *Decameron*.[72] However irritating Coleridge's attitude seems today, it must be considered in the context of his philosophy of love, which led him to extol Petrarch and to refuse both Stoicism and open sensuousness.

Despite these significant nuances, which have often been neglected, it is true that Coleridge's interest in the plot of the romances was relative ('the prurient heroes and grotesque monsters of Italian Romances', *Friend (CC)* I 13), whereas it occupied the attention of his contemporaries.[73] Leigh Hunt's popular *Stories from the Italian Poets* (1846) contains prose abridgements from Pulci, Boiardo, Ariosto and Tasso, and embodies a view of them opposite to Coleridge's. The abridgements focus on the stories, and suppress the poetry of the original for those who could not read Italian or did not feel like reading the 40,000 lines of the *Furioso* in translation. Hunt's *Stories* could be compared to the twentieth-century productions of classics for television. On a higher level, Walter Scott was so influenced by the atmosphere and the narrative structures of the Italian romance as to deserve the epithet of 'Ariosto of the North'. References to Ariosto and other Italian narrative poets abound in his works, and he was almost alone in understanding Ariosto's intertwining of several stories – a technique he made use of in his own novels. *Orlando furioso* was usually criticized as formless because of its narrative structure, whose movement was compared by Foscolo to the long waves of the ocean.[74]

If Coleridge's objections to Boccaccio's and Ariosto's sentimental frankness is the most striking side of his uneasiness, his reservations about the Renaissance use of mythology are more complex. He believed that 'to Boccaccio's sanction we must trace a large portion of the mythological pedantry and incongruous paganisms which for so long a period deformed the poetry even of the truest Poets'.[75] Renaissance poets had 'transferred the functions & histories of <Hebrew> Prophets and Prophetesses and of Christian Saints and Apostles, nay the highest Mysteries & most aweful Objects of Christian Faith, to the names and drapery of Greek & Roman Mythology'. Coleridge's favourite example of this attitude was Boccaccio's definition of *Ars amandi* as 'il santo libro d'Ovidio', which he quoted in *The Garden of Boccaccio* to illustrate the effects of the revival of learning.[76]

Coleridge's discussion of Pulci in Lecture III of the 1818 course must be considered in the same context, that is, the modern use of mythology. Pulci was still an obscure figure at the time, even if his poem had inspired J. H. Merivale's *Orlando in Roncesvalles* (1814) and John Hookham Frere's *Whistlecraft* (1817; later included in *Monks and Giants*, 1818). Though these poems attracted some public attention, Pulci's fame in England is due to Byron, whose *Beppo*, inspired by Frere's use of *ottava rima*, appeared in February 1818.[77] As a close friend of Frere, Coleridge was aware of the growing interest in Pulci and the Italian mock-heroic tradition, which may have motivated his discussion.[78]

However, I think Pulci was mentioned in the lecture mainly to illustrate aspects of Coleridge's view of the Italian romance. Even though he expanded general remarks he had made on Boccaccio, his analysis of Pulci was superficial and did not add anything substantial to his criticism of romances.[79] Pulci's main merit was linguistic: he introduced the easy and colourful style based on the Florentine dialect which Berni brought to perfection.[80] But despite such praise – which was once again stylistic – Coleridge's did not partake of contemporary enthusiasm for *Il Morgante Maggiore*. Pulci enhanced the characteristic of the Italian romance which Coleridge found least attractive: the ironic, sceptical attitude to life which, in Pulci's case, was not redeemed by a formal polish like Ariosto's or Berni's. Pulci's main faults were for Coleridge superficiality and buffoonery, which appeared in the improper mixture of Classical mythology and Christian elements from the very first stanza of the poem.[81] Coleridge's attitude was not uncommon – it was even shared by Merivale – and C. P. Brand believes that Pulci's gross humour and light-hearted treatment of religion were responsible for the limited popularity he enjoyed in England (Brand, 1957, 79, 88).

If Coleridge disliked the modern poetic use of mythology, he might have preferred allegory as a Christian form of symbolic expression. Even though he mentioned the subject many times, his only extensive discussion of allegory was the final part of the lecture on the Italian romance. His desire for a history of allegory goes back to 1807–8, when he made a note on it after reading Cowley's *Davideis* and Dante's minor works. In Lecture III of the 1818 course, he tried to distinguish allegory from fable and metaphor, but failed to provide a satisfactory categorization. All that he could work out was that a metaphor was a fragment of an allegory, and a fable a short allegory. The distinction of allegory from symbol, which he repeated elsewhere, was implicit in the fact that in allegory 'the difference is everywhere presented to the eye or imagination while the Likeness is suggested to the mind' (*L Lects* (CC) II 99–101).

The brief history of allegory in the latter part of the notes is more interesting. Coleridge argued that the Classical world knew only 'picture allegory' but no narrative epic allegories, since 'the multiplicity of their Gods and Goddesses' precluded it (*L Lects* (CC) II 101). Allegory was a sort of substitute for the mythological imagery of polytheism (*CN* III 4498, 1819). In the Classical world idolatry consisted of a union of worship and corporeal personification of the idol; as the belief in the action of personified gods weakened, allegory developed – in allegory the signifier and the signified are disjointed (*CN* II 3203, 1807–8). If the allegoric figure is too individualized and attracts attention only to itself, it ceases to be allegoric; but if it does not, it need not be there. That is why Coleridge hesitated to call Dante's figures and his poem allegoric, whereas he referred to *La vita nuova, Il Convivio* and the contemporary works of other unspecified Italians as allegoric.

Coleridge did not share Friedrich Schlegel's enthusiasm for allegory, and was sometimes embarrassed about it: the allegoric parts of *The Faerie Queene* were the dullest; whether Milton's Sin and Death were allegoric remained a question; and Bunyan's allegory was admirable because 'the Bunyan of Parnassus had the better of Bunyan of the Conventicle'. But 'the most striking verdict against narrative Allegory is to be found in Tasso's own account of what he would have the reader understand by the persons and events of his Jerusalem' (*L Lects (CC)* II 103), which he probably found included in the edition he read. Coleridge believed the reader alone could have never developed the meanings suggested by Tasso, which were an arbitrary superimposition.[82]

Coleridge's scanty interest in the plot of romances and his objections to myth and allegory seem to indicate an indifference toward long poems, but, as Elinor S. Shaffer reminds us, he had a lifelong interest in the apocalyptic epic and planned a poem on the fall of Jerusalem.[83] The combination of fantastic and realistic elements provided an opportunity to deal with passionate situations, with contemporary politics under a thin symbolic mask, and to satirize society – an opportunity from which Southey, Landor and Byron, to mention the most significant names, profited in different ways. These aspects do not appear in Coleridge's criticism of Italian romances, though his hostility to their eroticism sets him closer to Southey than Byron. Coleridge associated the symbolic forms of epic and romance with a different context: allegory and religion. However, his notes on allegory make clear that he regarded it as inferior to symbol as a sign, and that he was not interested in its application as a frame for epic and romance. His attitude explains his cold response to the subject matter of romance and his interest in religious epic, although he did not always prefer the latter to the former, as his judgement on Ariosto and Tasso shows. Above all, his plans for an epic poem explain why Ariosto and Tasso interested him little.

Orlando furioso has been described as 'un libro perenne', a perpetual book: it lacks a true beginning – it starts as the continuation of another book, Boiardo's poem – and it lacks above all a proper end, since there is no final catharsis or resolutive catastrophe. Having no beginning and end, it is all middle, as it were: it is the 'golden chapter of a story which ignores any form of Providential plan', and which reproduces the endless and unpredictable flux of life.[84] Its structure is antithetic to Coleridge's desire for an epic modelled on the Bible and, in particular, on the *Revelation*, which hinges on the concept of the End. Ariosto's open, spiral structure was incompatible with Coleridge's teleological plans; but so was also Tasso's, though for different reasons: the structure of his *Jerusalem* was unified and teleological, but Coleridge disliked its allegoric frame saturated with Tasso's Catholicism which, however uneasy and rebellious, was at odds with his deepest beliefs. Moreover, the fact that Coleridge talked of 'romances from Boccaccio to Tasso' shows that he was not concerned with the distinction between romance and epic, a distinction on which the neoclassical theory of genre focused, and which still attracted Southey's and Wordsworth's attention.

Coleridge is often considered to possess a Gothic temper, that is, *inter alia*, as having a special feeling for the Middle Ages; but his response to romance, the only medieval literary genre common in his time, makes it clear that he was less interested in it than most of his contemporaries. We cannot speak of a Romantic rediscovery of Ariosto and Tasso as we speak of a rediscovery of Dante, since Italian romances were admired and discussed in the eighteenth century.[85] Thomas Hurd, William Hayley and Thomas Warton helped to create new interest in Ariosto and Tasso,[86] but it was John Hoole who played a central role in popularizing them.[87] Romantic interest in Ariosto and Tasso focused only on certain aspects of their works. Tasso's case is illuminating: despite general enthusiasm for his life, the leading Romantic poets had little to learn from his style, whose epic gravity was 'remote from the ideal of the times'.[88] Contemporary criticism confirmed this tendency: Tasso was a poet of passionate stories and pathetic situations, beside which other aspects even of his major poem passed unnoticed. Ariosto was treated in the same way: he was mainly admired for the *Furioso*, whereas his minor works were neglected even by the most devoted readers.[89] Coleridge's interest in the Renaissance romances, which he knew better than English medieval romances, is not not characterized by its limits, but by the reason for those limits.

Coleridge's tepid enthusiasm for Ariosto and Tasso, who were so popular in his time as to be identified, together with Dante, with Italian literature altogether, has contributed to the widespread belief that his interest in Italian poetry was marginal. But Italian literature is not only Ariosto and Tasso; and the fact that Coleridge's attention focused on other aspects should have rendered critics more curious about him.

Coleridge as a Critic of Comparative Literature

Coleridge's lectures on Italian poetry provide the opportunity to reconsider his idea of literary history and critical method. Italian poetry is part of the comparative interests which led to the 1818 lectures, the first English attempt at a comparative history of literature in the modern sense. Without denying the historical value and merit of what has been discussed in the preceding pages, it is necessary to point out further features and limits. I think the main defect of Coleridge's comparative criticism is its Anglocentrism or, to be more precise, a tendency to read everything in the light of Shakespeare – even though in Romantic criticism Shakespeare is sometimes a mere symbol for modern, 'romantic' poetry as distinguished from Classical and neoclassical poetry.

The brevity of the lectures, which did not allow him to discuss the foreign literatures for their own sake, is a partial justification. August Wilhelm Schlegel's *Ueber dramatische Kunst und Literatur* and Friedrich Schlegel's *Geschichte der alten und neuen Literatur* were also courses of lectures, but their point of view was less national than Coleridge's. It must be pointed out, however, that Coleridge never revised the notes for his lectures, though he attempted to do so in the 1820s. He did not lecture again after 1819, even though he tried to arrange a new course on English, Italian or German literature and the philosophical principles of the fine arts (*CL* IV 925, 28 Feb 1819; *L Lects (CC)* II 345–7).

The way in which he planned to collect and edit his lectures clarifies the principles on which his comparative criticism was based, and reveals his opinion of his own lectures. He reacted against the charge of fragmentariness by quoting those of his works he regarded as most valuable. He mentioned among them his lectures on 'Shakespear, Milton, Spenser, Dante, Ariosto and Don Quixote', and the course on the history of philosophy (*IS* 202). He considered his lectures on Dante and Ariosto as organic and homogeneous (*SM (CC)* 114 n.), and was satisfied with his performance when he gave them (*L Lects (CC)* II 33, 88). Such an opinion seems surprising in the light of what has survived in the case of Ariosto. Coleridge's 'Collected Criticism' should have been arranged as follows: vol. I, Shakespeare, and the history of English drama as distinguished from classical drama; vol. II, in two parts, 'philosophical analysis of Dante, Spenser, Milton, Cervantes, and Calderon – with similar but more compressed Criticisms of Chaucer, Ariosto, Donne, Rabelais, and others, during the predominance of the romantic Poesy' – these two books would form 'a complete Code of the Principles of Judgement & Feeling' applied to all the arts; vol. III, the history of philosophy (in two parts); vol. IV, on the Bible.[90]

What emerges from Coleridge's plans is the absence of a clear historical link between the individual great poets on whom his interest concentrated. The project which provides the closest approximation to the missing links is the 1818 course on European literature, which is, however, English-orientated. Such a pattern explains the limited attention paid to Spanish literature, the attention – at least in the lectures – to only a few aspects of Italian literature, and the absence of German literature, which had contributed too little to the English tradition in the past. Again his almost complete silence on French literature is embarrassing, as it is not possible to deny its influence on English.

The contemporary courses of lectures with which it is natural to compare Coleridge's are those of the Schlegel brothers. What characterizes

August Wilhelm Schlegel's *Ueber dramatische Kunst und Literatur* and Friedrich Schlegel's *Geschichte der alten und neuen Literatur*, in comparison to Coleridge's lectures, is a firmer sense of historical development. Of course, they did not invent everything: they drew on eighteenth-century antiquarians and learned scholars – for example, as far as Italian literature is concerned, Muratori, Denina and Tiraboschi – but they organized the older materials, which were often chaotic, according to clearer patterns. Conversely, the historical sections are the weakest in Coleridge's lectures, and it is not a coincidence that they contain the heaviest borrowings from his sources – the Schlegels, Hallam, and elsewhere Tennemann.[91] Coleridge is most original in textual analysis, whose principles modern scholarship has often compared to the principles of the Schlegels and other German thinkers. However, a fundamental difference remains, and it is not a mere difference between a systematic and an asystematic method (Friedrich Schlegel himself, a theorist of the fragment, was not so systematic): Coleridge's criticism was monographic, and his history consisted of spots, moments (Dante, Shakespeare, Cervantes, etc.) deeply analysed but unconnected. The sense of historical continuity is not evident in the lectures, and only emerges from the structure of the prospectus.

The absence of a defined national tradition may have helped the Schlegels to become better historians of European literature – even though their nationalism is evident, and underlay their admiration for the Gothic past as it did Herder's, and it even induced them to talk of Shakespeare as a German. The conclusion is not that Coleridge was a bad historian, but that he organized his criticism according to different principles, which in his mind provided a firmer and more important continuity. Such a continuity was philosophical rather than historical, and its definition involves his interest in Italian philosophy. In the present context, his criticism can be characterized as intermediate between the biographism of Johnson and the historicism of the Schlegels, and, as far as England is concerned, as forming the intermediate step from Johnson's poets to Carlyle's heroes.

IV

Philology and Philosophy:
The Italian Renaissance in Coleridge's Thought

THE RENAISSANCE WAS the centre of Coleridge's experience of Italy, which had two main consequences. On the one hand, Renaissance painting and lyric poetry, which modified his sense of technique in art, influenced his poetic style after 1804 and helped him develop his aesthetics; on the other, his experience of Italian culture enlarged his historical understanding of the Renaissance, and this changed his view of the English Renaissance and European literature in their turn.

Coleridge's originality does not lie in his preference for the Renaissance, which was common among his contemporaries, but in his image of the age. Whereas the essential components of the prevailing view were history, romance and the fine arts, his view included two further aspects which his contemporaries and other leading Romantics neglected, despite their historical relevance: poetry and prose in Latin and philosophy.

Although the impact of Italian philosophy on Coleridge was limited when compared to English, Greek and German, it was considerable on some aspects of his thought. The importance it had in forming his idea of Italy cannot be overestimated: his admiration for Dante's and Petrarch's poetry is inseparable from his admiration for their philosophy; his uneasiness with Italian romances was in large part due to their philosophical implications; philosophy played a major role in his understanding of the fine arts; and the principles on which he constructed his criticism were philosophical rather than historical.

In the *Philosophical Lectures* Coleridge described the Renaissance as a Platonic age: Platonism brooded 'over the birth of genius and revived with the restoration of literature and the fine arts' (1949, 393). Despite his usual enthusiasm for Platonism, he was aware that the Renaissance was not an age of great philosophers, like the thirteenth or the seventeenth centuries – the only exceptions were Bruno, Bacon and Boehme, who lived at the very end of the period. The Italian Renaissance was portrayed in the *Philosophical Lectures* as a cultural unity which included poets, artists, scholars and philosophers. Dante, Petrarch and the painters were given more space than the philosophers themselves, which means that in Coleridge's mind the significance of the Renaissance lay more in its impact as a movement than in the originality of its philosophers – a view that twentieth-century studies have corrected but in substance confirmed.[1]

His admiration for the Renaissance as a golden age of scholarship, which he portrayed in *The Garden of Boccaccio*, was not unconditional. His most often-repeated objections were interconnected and concerned ethics and philosophic style. The ideal balance between classicism and Christianity existed at an early time only, as in his favourite Petrarch; in the high Renaissance

> there was scarcely a man of learning in Italy . . . who was believed to be a serious Christian; some were open infidels . . . But the greater number were mystical infidels of the school of Proclus who felt the common notions of the school and Christianity too vulgar, and in the horror they felt for superstitions, passed into the opposite extreme of visionary enthusiasm. (*P Lects*, 1949, 297–8)

He specified that the Platonism, or rather the Plotinism, of the 'great Tuscan scholars, under the great [*Cosimo de Medici*] seems to have been unfavourable to the Reformation, strikingly so as compared with scholastic philosophy which was logical and analytic' (*P Lects*, 1949, 317). If Renaissance intellectuals rejected the Roman Church it was because it was not pagan enough: they 'were more in danger of becoming polytheists than PROTESTANTS'. There was a remarkable analogy in the fact that the German revival of Platonism in the late eighteenth century led either to mesmerism (that is, pantheism) or to Roman Catholicism.[2]

If the ethical consequences of the revival of learning preoccupied him, its philosophical consequences were also 'not an unmixed good'. The passion for classical Latin swept away the exactness of Scholastic terminology together with Scholastic style; Renaissance philosophy was written classically, 'i.e. without technical terms – therefore popularly.' The consequence was that sciences like mathematics, geometry and astronomy were permitted to have a technical vocabulary, whereas metaphysics 'sank & died and an empirical highly superficial Psychology took its place'.[3]

Coleridge's indictments are severe but must not be understood as definitive judgements: not only did he admire many aspects of Renaissance culture, like lyric poetry and painting, but he was also influenced by philosophers like Ficino and Bruno; and even when he extolled Scholasticism, he spoke of 'the MORE genial school of Platonism'.[4] His observations on the style of Platonism show that his interest in Renaissance Latin is part of his philosophical interests. His view would have been different, had he not read Petrarch's and other Humanist writings in Latin, which gave him a wider perspective on the theoretical problems of the times.

Renaissance Writing in Latin

Coleridge's reading of Renaissance Latin, though in itself not very extensive, was considerable, and it made him acquainted with essential aspects of Renaissance poetry and poetics. The debate on rhetoric, the imitation of the classics and the other themes characteristic of Renaissance poetics helped him develop his sense of Renaissance culture and, by extension, his view of poetry in general. The problem of imitation, in particular, is inevitable in neo-Latin writing.

A knowledge of non-Classical Latin poetry was common in eighteenth-century England – it was a consequence of the education of the time. Even though Coleridge's familiarity with it cannot be compared to his familiarity with English and Classical poetry, his interest was not occasional.[5] In 1805 he was using *Carmina illustrium poetarum italorum* (ed. by Giovanni Gaetano Bottari, 11 vols., Florence 1719–1726), which include about five hundred poets from the origins to the eighteenth century. Besides, he admired Benedetto Stay's *Fable of the Madning Rain* (1755), which was in his opinion one of the finest satires ever written.[6]

Among Italian poets in Latin, Coleridge most admired Petrarch, whom he read during and after the period in the Mediterranean. In Lecture III of the 1818 course he discussed *Africa*, which he held in low regard.[7] His response to Petrarch's metric epistles was different. Classical learning is not so prominent in them as in *Africa*; the rhetorical element is still evident, but is not an end in itself as in the epic poem, since it is counterbalanced by the subjects, which are characteristic Petrarchan musings on life and experience. Coleridge was enthusiastic about the first letter, to Barbato da Sulmona, which he transcribed and quoted.[8]

Despite his admiration for Petrarch, Coleridge did not undervalue the Latin poetry of the later Humanists. He opposed Johnson's opinion that Cowley's Latin poetry was superior to Milton's, and he was glad to discover that Ugo Foscolo agreed with him (*BL (CC)* II 235–6). Milton's Latin verse was comparable to the poems of fifteenth-century Italian Latinists for its combination of linguistic purity, depth of thought and unborrowed imagery, whereas Cowley's barbarisms reminded him of German Latin poetry (*IS* 157, after 1820). Petrarch's letter to Barbato da Sulmona would have been a classical gem, 'had Petrarch lived a century later, and retaining all his substantiality of Head, & Heart, <had> added to it the elegances & manly Politure of Fracastorius, Flaminius, Vida, & their Corrivals' (*CN* III 4178, 1813). Renaissance Latin poetry was impeccable in terms of style, but was inferior to Petrarch's in intellectual intensity; nonetheless, it deserved to be better known. In late 1809 Coleridge was still planning to 'make a Catalogue of the Greek and Latin Classics, and of those who like the author of the Argenis & Euphormio, Fracastorius, Flaminius, etc. deserve that name, tho' moderns' (*CN* III 3656).

Coleridge's attitude to neo-Latin poetry is clear enough. Leo Spitzer argues that whereas Petrarch 'shows himself to us as a spirit torn between two civilizations which he felt his duty to harmonize', Renaissance poets like Poliziano embody 'the independent existence . . . of two distinct poetic climates, ancient and modern'. The problem was to 'give the flavor of *new* personal emotion to the *traditional* Latin vocabulary'.[9] Coleridge was struck by Petrarch's metric epistles and in general by the letters, in which Classical learning is least evident, whereas he disliked the excesses of rhetoric, whether they led to *Africa* or that letter of Petrarch containing '177 phrases of human life, chiefly of 2 words each' (*CN* III 3634).

Living in a time in which neo-Latin writing has become exotic for everybody except scholars, we might be tempted to dismiss Coleridge's interest as a waste of time on a subject from which he seems to have learned hardly anything. This would be a mistake for various reasons. Coleridge himself practiced poetic imitation – an eminently neoclassical form of writing – throughout his life. He was perhaps referring to himself when he noted that

> To a Translator of Genius, & who possessed the English Language, as an unembarrassed Property, the defects of Style in the original (i.e., Petrarch's epistle to Barbato da Sulmona) would present no obstacles:

nay, rather an honorable motive in the well-grounded Hope of
rendering the Version a finer Poem than the original. (*CN* III 4178,
Feb–Jun 1813)

Coleridge always regarded Latin, including metrical composition in
Latin, as a necessary part of education. Since he was aware that Latin was
not any longer so common as in the fifteenth century, he recommended
students first to learn to develop their thoughts, then to embody them in
a mosaic of passages borrowed from the classics. The style of poetry
which consisted of translating 'prose thoughts into poetic language' – the
style of Pope and his followers – 'had been kept up by, if it did not wholly
arise from, the custom of writing Latin verses', which was regarded as
basic in the school (*BL* (*CC*) I 21). The implied negative tone of the
remark does not conceal his admiration for some Latin poems, even
though the point should not be overstated.[10] Coleridge observed that the
'prejudice in favor of classical learning' was so strong in Italy that Dante
and Ariosto intended to write their poems in Latin, while Petrarch
expected fame from his Latin works rather than his Italian poems.[11]

Coleridge's reading of Humanistic prose, to which Dante's *Convivio* and
De vulgari eloquentia can be added, made him acquainted with the
theoretical component of Italian Renaissance literature, which did not
exist for many of his contemporaries; it stimulated his thinking on the
problem of imitation; and it enlarged his historical sense of the age. A
complete evaluation of the subject would require a comparison with his
knowledge of the Classical literatures, a complete study of which is
unfortunately not available at the moment.

The first figure of some importance to Coleridge is, again, Petrarch,
whom he admired as a moral philosopher as much as a poet. Coleridge
gave Petrarch a significant place in his *Philosophical Lectures*. He called
him 'great in every respect because he was eminently good and desirable',
although he was aware that Petrarch was not a philosopher: 'He had, in
truth, too much of inward reality, too much of interest for his human
brethren, to find any gratification in forms of any sort (in mere *forms*)'
(*P Lects*, 1949, 292). However, Coleridge was right to include Petrarch in
his course of lectures. Dante, who was a philosophic mind, is
paradoxically less important than Petrarch in the history of philosophy.
Dante's philosophic writings are digests of medieval knowledge and only
have a bearing on his own intellectual life; Petrarch's Latin works, though
not philosophic in the technical sense, embody a new, epoch-making,

perspective on culture and therefore on philosophy, as his followers made evident. Nonetheless, Coleridge had reason to consider Dante as a fore-runner of the Renaissance: not so much because of his Platonism, as he believed, but on account of his *Vita nuova* and *Il Convivio*, which created Italian literary prose, as well as the *Comedy*, without which subsequent Italian poetry would be incomprehensible.

Coleridge's opinions were based on a first-hand knowledge of Petrarch's Latin writings, which changed his attitude to Petrarch in 1803: they induced him to read Petrarch's Italian poetry, which in turn stimulated him to take up again the Latin works after his sojourn in Italy. Between 1808 and 1813 he transcribed and marked long passages from *De vita solitaria, De origine et vita sua, De remediis utriusque fortune*, and the letters.[12]

Though Coleridge never discussed Petrarch's Latin works in detail, it is worth observing what aspects struck him most, since he quoted them in support of his own opinions in *The Friend, Biographia Literaria* and *Sibylline Leaves*. His excerpts, most of which were taken from *De vita solitaria* and the letters, mainly deal with the social role of intellectuals. *De vita solitaria* describes a way of life for the poet and the scholar which became a model in the following centuries. Petrarch opposed his life of knowledge both to monastic isolation and the emptiness of commercial life in town. His idea of solitude was closer to the classic *otium literarium* than medieval asceticism,[13] but he believed he had achieved a kind of balance between them, as the numerous references to Christian authors and figures in *De vita solitaria* show.[14] His ideal was aristocratic and elitist: he was aware that his model did not suit everybody, but only the chosen few (*Prose* 580–2). Petrarch proudly emphasized that he was self-taught, and the universities play a secondary role in his view of education and scholarship, whereas they were the centres of knowledge in the late Middle Ages (*Prose* 334).

Coleridge's interest in the story of Giovanni da Ravenna shows that he was interested by Petrarch's idea of education. Petrarch's letters on his disciple were Coleridge's favourite and led him to overvalue Giovanni's role as a mediator between Petrarch and the later humanists.[15] Coleridge considered these epistles as the most interesting documents of the relation between a teacher and a pupil: he admired, evidently, the model of education, a form of transmission of knowledge which became common in the Renaissance, and which suited his own view of intellectuals in society. Although Petrarch did not influence any aspect of Coleridge's thought in particular, the fact that his reflections on the life of the intellectual struck Coleridge has significant implications: it suggests that the affinities between them were profound and involved poetry and the philosophy of love as well as education, ethics and politics. It should not be forgotten that Coleridge's political interests, as he expressed them in *Lay Sermons* and *Church and State*, focused on the relation between intellectuals – the 'clerisy' – and society. The answer he gave to the problem has significant analogies with Petrarch's, though his reading of the Humanist tradition was influenced by the political theories of seventeenth-century England.

Coleridge's response to Petrarch has a bearing on the question of his acquaintance with literary criticism and scholarship in the Renaissance. The Renaissance reputation of Petrarch's Latin works, which preceded in this respect his Italian poetry,[16] rested on the fact that he propounded again the figure of the literary scholar by profession for the first time since the end of the Classical world.[17]

Coleridge did not pay much attention to the passages in Petrarch's Latin works which concern poetics. Giorgio Barberi Squarotti argues that Petrarch never wrote a treatise of poetry because 'moral problems prevailed and absorbed into their context any occasion of meditation on poetry'.[18] However, Petrarch may have influenced one aspect of Coleridge's thinking on poetry: the distinction between copy and imitation. Kathleen Coburn points out that Petrarch developed his ideas on imitation, a central theme for any classicist, in a letter to Boccaccio concerning Giovanni da Ravenna (*P Lects*, 1949, 442 n. 7). The imitator must produce something similar, not identical, to the original ('simile non idem'); the resemblance must be like that between father and son, something indefinite which painters call 'aerem' ('air, look').[19] Seneca and Horace argued that one should write as bees produce honey: not by picking up flowers, but by turning them into honey, so that various elements are melted into one, different and better ('non servatis floribus sed in favos versis, ut ex variis unum fiat, idque aliud et melius') (*Prose* 1018–20). If we remember that Petrarch's letters on Giovanni da Ravenna were Coleridge's favourite among the Latin writings; that he was reading them before leaving for Malta and Italy; and that his first distinction between copy and imitation was made in Malta in 1804 (*CN* II 2211), we can infer that Petrarch may well be one of his sources, even though Metastasio was the actual catalyst.

Boccaccio was the greatest scholar of his time together with Petrarch, and Coleridge was at least acquainted with two of his scholarly works: *Genealogia deorum gentilium* and *Trattatello in laude di Dante*. The

Genealogia is a vast and unfinished treatise of mythology on which
Boccaccio worked from his maturity onward.[20] Coleridge, who began to
read Giuseppe Betussi's Italian translation in 1803, was struck by the
figure of Demogorgon, whom Boccaccio considered as the father of pagan
gods and a terrifying figure.[21] In 1805 Coleridge noted that a proper
history of classical mythology was still wanting; Boccaccio's *Genealogia*,
Bacon's *De sapientia veterum*, and even recent works like Andrew Tooke's
The Pantheon did not satisfy him (*CN* II 2737). If he never found a
satisfactory history of mythology, he would later be intrigued by
Creuzer's, Schelling's and Vico's theories of mythology, a subject he
discussed in the 1818 and 1819 lectures and 'On the Prometheus of
Æschylus' in 1825.

The last two books of Boccaccio's *Genealogia*, which form a 'Defense of
Poetry', are today regarded as the most interesting part of the work. It is
not certain that Coleridge read them; his antipathy to the 'mythological
pedantry' of the Renaissance may have stopped him before. In any event,
the essential points of Boccaccio's theory of poetry also appear in the
Trattatello in laude di Dante, a much shorter work Coleridge read in full.
Since he never mentioned Boccaccio's theories, suffice it to say that they
are rooted in the medieval tradition, and develop themes Petrarch
discussed in his letters and in *Invectiva contra medicum quemdam*.
Boccaccio maintained that Classical literature was not dangerous or vain,
since it concealed profound truths under allegory in the same way as the
Bible: it was the standard medieval defence of the Classics. Poetry is
divine in its origin, because it derives from inspiration which is more than
human. However, Boccaccio thought the realistic element was necessary,
and opposed those who wanted to freeze poetry into a scholastic and
learned activity.[22] Whether Coleridge intended to include some of these
writings in the selected translation from Boccaccio's minor prose works
he proposed to John Murray is difficult to say, though it is possible.

Whereas Coleridge's reading of the three fathers of Italian literature was
extensive, his knowledge of the later generations of Humanists was patchy.
With the partial exception of Angelo Poliziano (1454–94), whom Coleridge
admired as a Latin poet and a Classical scholar, most Humanists were for
him undistinguished names in the revival of classical learning.[23] The other
major theorists he was acquainted with were not Humanists in the proper
sense, as they lived at a later date: Giulio Cesare Scaliger (1484–1558) and
Famiano Strada (1572–1649). Coleridge associated Scaliger with Samuel
Johnson probably on the grounds of their linguistic expertise, their
erudite classicism and their influence as critics. They were included
among the authors Coleridge intended to review in couples formed by

likeness or contrast.[24] Strada's *Prolusiones academicae* (1617) were for him an outstanding example of 'Art of Poetry', like Horace's or Quintilian's.[25]

Coleridge expressed his general view of neo-Latin writing in a note he made on Petrarch:

> The Latin of Petrarch is the Language of modernized Europe in Latin words – doubtless, the great Purifiers of Latin Eloquence, Laurentius Valla, & his learned tho' inveterate opponents, contributed greatly to prevent the Latin from becoming the Lingua Communis – by confining it to classical Purity they both impoverished it, & made the writing in it but a sort of Pedantry – . . . for in order to write Ciceronianly we must *think* in the age of Cicero. Erasmus fought nobly against this; but the fine gentlemen of Classical Literature, in Italy, were too hard for him. Perhaps, if some great Philosopher had arisen, laid down the foundations of philosophical Language, cleansed from Idioms; & made it the sole Law of Latin Style, that it should be equally intelligible to a Swede as to Sicilian, &c., something might have been done – we might have escaped the French. (*CN* III 3365, Sept 1808)

The view of language expressed in the passage recalls, in its essentials, the historic ideas of the German Romantics. Language and thought are inseparable: 'in order to write Ciceronianly we must *think* in the age of Cicero'. Besides, language is historical, and the exact reproduction of past styles is impossible: 'The Latin of Petrarch is the Language of modernized Europe in Latin words'. The later Humanists, however, thought otherwise, and their Latin was more distant than Petrarch's from everyday reality. The failure of Erasmus' attempt deprived the Europe of the learned of a common language – an issue which is still live today.

Coleridge's observations are correct, but give too much emphasis to the opposition between the various phases of Humanism. His knowledge of Valla and the later Humanists was not comparable to his knowledge of Petrarch,[26] so that he overlooked important facts – in particular Erasmus' debt to Valla.[27] The true object of Erasmus' polemic was not early Humanism, but sixteenth-century Ciceronianism.[28] Sixteenth-century strict Ciceronianism triumphed, in Luigi Baldacci's words, 'over the eclectic stance . . . which in the history of Humanism was linked to Poliziano's dispute with Cortese, and to the rich and conflicting ideas of Petrarch in his *Familiares*'.[29]

However debatable Coleridge's opinion is, what the note makes clear is that he regarded Latin writing not a as mere erudite exercise, but as a vital philosophical issue. His view, therefore, cannot be fully evaluated without discussing his knowledge of Renaissance philosophy.

Platonism and Aristotelianism

Since Coleridge considered the Renaissance as a Platonic age, it is important to define the way in which Italian philosophy, together with poetry and the fine arts, helped to form his conviction. The analogies between Petrarch's view of love and Coleridge's, which played a decisive role in stimulating his interest in Renaissance lyric poetry, can be reconsidered in the wider context of Petrarch's Platonism. Although Petrarch's direct knowledge of Plato was confined to the few dialogues available in Latin in the Middle Ages namely – *Timaeus, Phaedo* and *Meno* – he changed decisively the prevailing view of Plato.[30] The reason for his anti-Aristotelianism was moral: he reacted both against the scientific interests of natural philosophy and 'the tendencies to reduce any problem to a matter of terms, all fields of knowledge to a refined logic', as in Ockhamism.[31] True philosophy had to show 'the way to salvation; ethical, not logical, perfection is its object', for to will the good is wiser than to know the truth.[32]

Aristotle erred in the most important points, those which concern our salvation; he did not have any idea of true happiness (*Prose* 720). Plato was the Classical philosopher who came nearest to the Truth, as many Stoic, Neoplatonic and Christian philosophers acknowledged (*Prose* 742, 750). Charles Trinkaus points out that 'Petrarch's more pressing concern is to show Plato's compatibility with Christianity'.[33] There is no doubt, as Augustine believed, that Plato would have been a Christian had he lived in Christian times; the conversion of several Platonists contemporary with Augustine demonstrated it (*Prose* 760) – a point Coleridge also made in the *Philosophical Lectures* (1949, 295). Raymond Klibansky argues that

> the Augustinian origin of these ideas is obvious, and similar conceptions may be found in earlier mediaeval authors. But the significance they acquire for Petrarch is a different one. . . . the notion of Plato as the guide to Christianity which had been, for earlier thinkers, a bold construction of history, was for Petrarch an unquestionable truth confirmed by Augustine's life and dominating his own.[34]

Aristotle and Plato, therefore, were in Petrarch's mind the watchwords for two different attitudes to philosophy and knowledge; but although Petrarch's philosophical expertise was limited, the change he brought about was decisive.[35] His programme, as summarized in *De sui ipsius et multorum ignorantia*, consisted of Platonic wisdom, Christian dogma and Ciceronian eloquence, and it became a powerful model for Italian and

European Humanists. As Paul Oskar Kristeller argues, he showed that it was possible to reject Scholasticism

> while remaining convinced Christians, and to reconcile . . . classical learning . . . with religious faith. He is thus an early, Italian forerunner of that 'Christian Humanism' which recent historians have emphasized in the works of Colet, Erasmus, More, and other Northern scholars.[36]

Petrarch anticipated the Reformation in other aspects of his thought, mainly because of Augustine's influence. He developed the idea of salvation by grace alone; he endorsed the primacy of the will on the intellect; and his introspection precedes the Protestant solitary struggle with the conscience.[37] However, Petrarch's affinity with the Reformation must not be exaggerated; he always remained a convinced Roman Catholic – he took minor orders around 1330 – in spite of occasional invectives against the Church.

Coleridge's definition of Petrarch as a Platonist and a father of the Platonic revival of the Renaissance was historically grounded.[38] His admiration did not prevent him from pointing out that Petrarch's hostility to Scholastic philosophy was excessive, even though it was more comprehensible than the neglect in which Scholasticism was held in nineteenth-century England (*P Lects*, 1949, 292–3). If Scholastic philosophy was ignored, Petrarch's prose works were also not read. Sismondi, one of the few who commented on them, held them in low regard; Thomas Warton, who thought Petrarch would have benefited Italian literature if he had written his minor works in Italian, had nothing to say on their contents.[39] Coleridge was certain of the value of Petrarch's Latin works and tried to attract public attention by quoting them. The mottos for *The Friend* were selected with great care, because mottos 'are known to add considerably to the value of the Spectator'; and 'of two mottos equally appropriate', he always preferred 'that from the book which is least likely to have come into my Readers' hands' (*Friend* (*CC*) I 53). He specified that he quoted

> Petrarch often in the hope of drawing the attention of Scholars to his inestimable *Latin* Writings. Let me add, in the wish likewise of recommending a Translation of select passages from his Treatises and Letters to the London Publishers. If I except the German writings and original Letters of the heroic Luther, I do not remember a work from which so delightful and instructive a volume might be compiled.[40]

Whereas the philosophical relation between Petrarch and Coleridge was a matter of affinity, Marsilio Ficino influenced an essential aspect of

Coleridge's thought: the view of Plato and Platonism. Ficino translated and edited Plato, the Greek Neoplatonists and a large number of Hermetic works in the second half of the fifteenth century. The influence he exerted throughout Europe was indirect, that is, he spoke through the authors he translated. The core of his interpretation, as Eugenio Garin summarizes it, were the *Symposium* and the philosophy of love, and the *Parmenides* as interpreted by Proclus. Ficino insisted on the indispensability of Plotinus' reading of Plato, and on the Hermetic and Chaldean origins of Platonism.[41] In other words, 'Marsiglio and his friends endeavour to go back to the founder of the Academy; but the Plato they present is nearer to that of Christian Alexandria'.[42]

Raymond Klibansky emphasizes that 'the conception of Plato, and particularly that of the *Parmenides*, remained dominated by Marsilio's interpretation' until about the eighteenth century. In the wake of Proclus, Ficino interpreted the *Parmenides* as a dialogue on ontology rather than logic, so that the 'one' discussed by Plato was identified with 'the One'.

> The same tradition permeates the writings of the first English translator of the Parmenides, Thomas Taylor . . . Accordingly, his translation bears the sub-title 'A Dialogue on the Gods'. . . . Taylor's translations . . . may have given to [Coleridge's] Platonic studies their particular bent and may have stimulated his interest in Proclus and Marsilio.[43]

Despite Coleridge's awareness of the difference between Plato and the Neoplatonists, his reading of Plato was essentially Neoplatonic. I think Thomas McFarland overrates Coleridge's capacity for distinguishing between Plato and the Platonists (1969, 365). Coleridge spoke of 'the very little of proper Platonism contained in the *written* books of Plato, who himself, in an epistle . . . has declared all he had written to be substantially Socratic, and not a fair exponent of his tenets' (*CM* (*CC*) II 867). 'Proper Platonism' was to be found in Neoplatonism. The test for the Neoplatonic approach to Plato is the ontologic interpretation of the *Parmenides*, about which Coleridge wrote: 'in the Deity is an absolute Synthesis of opposites. Plato in *Parmenide* and Giordano Bruno *passim* have spoken many things well on this aweful Mystery' (*CM* (*CC*) I 568). The ontologic approach could hardly be clearer.

The study of Plato ought to begin with Sallustius, Proclus and Plotinus, and then 'proceed to Plato's works, using indeed the Bipont Edition with Tiedemann's Prolegomenon & the Dialogues; but still studying carefully Ficinus' Notes – & even collating his Translation with the sense attributed by the Bipontine Edition' (*CN* III 3934, Jun–Jul 1810). Accordingly, Coleridge made use of Ficino's editions of Plato and the Neoplatonists.[44]

In *Biographia Literaria*, Coleridge mentioned Ficino together with Plato, Plotinus, Proclus, Georgios Gemistos Plethon and other Platonists as the philosophers who prepared him to accept Descartes' *cogito*.[45] Above all, Plato and the Platonists were for Coleridge, in McFarland's words, guarantors 'of a unique and valuable tone for philosophical discourse. . . . It was this special tone of Platonism more than any arguments from logic – that 'kept alive the *heart* in the *head*'" (1969, 209).

In fact, Coleridge's admiration for Ficino's 'hyperplatonic Jargon' was stylistic. Ficino was not a great philosopher, but his writings were 'perfect models of philosophic *Vortrag* (style & manner). Even were it what the purblind Lockites affirm, groundless & visionary, yet even as poetry, even as a stationary *rainbow*, it deserves our gratitude & love'. He was certain that Ficino's name would 'once more be pronounced with honor and open reverence' (*CN* III 3861, Jun 1810). The judgement is specially remarkable in the light of the neglect in which Ficino was held in Coleridge's time; it also explains why Pico della Mirandola, in whose writings the Scholastic heritage is more prominent, did not strike Coleridge as much as Ficino, despite the admiration he expressed for him: Pico had 'little speculative power, but enormous & restless speculative curiosity – overlaid his genius or constructive power by his pantoïomathy' (i.e., 'miscellaneous learning').[46]

Although Coleridge understood the Renaissance to be essentially Platonic, he had some knowledge of Renaissance Aristotelianism, which he neglected in the *Philosophical Lectures*. His attention focused on Pietro Pomponazzi, whom he mainly knew through Tennemann. He regarded Tennemann's chapter on Pomponazzi as the most original part of his history of philosophy, even though Tennemann undermined Pomponazzi's debt to Scholastic nominalism and overvalued the Italian philosopher (*C on Bruno* 436; *P Lects*, 1949, 57).

Coleridge found several aspects of Pomponazzi's psychology intriguing. Following Aristotle, Pomponazzi affirmed in his *De immortalitate animi* that the human mind cannot know 'a universal unqualifiedly but always sees the universal in the singular'. Coleridge thought this was the philosophy of poetry, as Shakespeare, who excelled in the inter-penetration of the universal in the individual, demonstrates.[47]

Pomponazzi's work contains frequent references to the Aristotelian con-ception of imagination, to which Coleridge returned two decades later. He noted that Pomponazzi, following Averroes, explained miracles as effects of an '*active* Imagination capable of affecting the Imagination' in some individuals. Tennemann, who is the source of the note, discusses *De incantationibus*, in which Pomponazzi tried to give an explanation of magic and miracles founded on reason and nature.[48] Natural philosophy was approached in *De incantationibus* as ethics was in *De fato*, a work Coleridge recommended to those who were losing their Christian faith.[49]

Philosophy of Nature and Giordano Bruno

Coleridge's interest in the Renaissance philosophy of nature is part of his scientific studies. However fanciful they were, nature was for him and the *Naturphilosophen* a crucial problem. Coleridge's philosophical career began with the dismissal on ethical grounds of eighteenth-century science, that is, the dismissal of its moral and political consequences; thereafter, he turned to *Naturphilosophie* and other pantheist conceptions of nature, but soon discovered they were as unsatisfactory as materalism in terms of ethics. McFarland suggests that Coleridge's subsequent studies in science were attempts to develop a dynamic view of nature on the side of theism against hylozoism (1969, 324). He failed to achieve it and turned to other speculations in his late years.

Coleridge's exploration of Renaissance magic and later Italian science is part of the process. Beside Ficino's translations and editions, he knew the *Theologia platonica*, which he purchased in Messina in 1805 (*CM* (*CC*) II 647). Though the book is little concerned with the philosophy of nature, Coleridge made a marginal note on Platonic physics. He observed that modern science from Bacon to Condillac had a 'passion for merely sensuous phaenomena'; consequently, it rejected Platonic physics, which is not based on empirical observation, and it held Platonism in low regard. The moderns consider ancient philosophy with the scorn with which a peasant 'grins at an Astronomer's assertions of the motion & size of the Earth relatively to the Sun ... Common sense, cry the one! Mother-wit, cries the other' (*CM* (*CC*) II 648).

In the lectures Coleridge pointed out the similarities between Greek and Italian Neoplatonism, but he believed that the connection between magic and philosophy was stronger in the former than in the latter. Magic met with two kinds of opposition in Italy, deriving from the love of poetry and elegance, and the Church (*P Lects*, 1949, 297). Even though magic played a more important role in Renaissance philosophy than was often realized, Coleridge's opinion was substantially correct. Frances Yates argues that 'an atmosphere of unadulterated humanism is not one which is congenial to the Magus and his pretensions'.[50] The attitude of the

Church was equally hostile, despite attempts like Ficino's and Pico's to justify magic within theology. Some popes, like Paul III, Leo X and the notorious Alexander VI, were tolerant and even encouraged magic, but Pico had to escape to France when his theses were condemned as heretical. The most scandalous of them involved magic and religion.[51]

Although the various forms of Renaissance magic were interconnected, Coleridge's interest focused on alchemy as an anticipation of chemistry. Natural magic 'appears to be nothing more than a want of experimental philosophy' (*P Lects*, 1949, 296). Coleridge was critical of modern science, but he was aware of the oddity of magic. The constant 'intension of the Mind on an imaginary *End*, associated with an immense variety of Means', as it appeared in alchemy, was 'a specific form of Mania' (*CN* III 4414, May 1818). The alchemists wrote like 'the Pythagoreans on Music – viz – metaphysical, inaudible Music, as the basis of the Audible'. He noted the continuity between alchemy and *Naturphilosophie*, and believed the former only needed 'translating' into the latter: 'It is clear that by Sulphur they (the alchemists) meant the Solar Light or Rays, and by Mercury the principle of Ponderability'. The theory was similar to Heraclitic physics and *Naturphilosophie*, which derives everything 'from Light and Gravitation, each bipolar' (*CN* III 4414). Facts alone did not satisfy Coleridge: he gave the same value to the 'most absurd credulity' of Fracastoro's *De sympathia*, which related imaginary facts as real, and to modern empirical observation. Coleridge's attitude is unconvincing, even though he had a point in arguing that 'it is the your *relation* of the Facts, not the fact' which matters.[52]

Coleridge found an explanation for alchemy and magic in mesmerism.[53] Mesmerism 'may be traced . . . from the very earliest times to the present day'; it was 'one of the modes by which philosophy, through magic, gradually passed into experimental science and gave way finally itself to materialism' (*P Lects*, 1949, 305). Mesmerism accounted for 'a series of Phaenomena hitherto unexplained, or most unsatisfactorily explained away with Lies, Tricks, or the Devil, the Oracles of the ancients, Charms, Amulets, witchcraft, Prophecies, Divination'. Nevertheless, he was aware that mesmerism may suggest 'to the Infidel, plausible grounds for *explaining down* the Facts recorded by the Inspired Writers and Inspiration itself into a mere Natural Magic'. The attempt had already been made by the Greek Neoplatonists and 'was repeated by the Italian Paganists at the restoration of Literature'.[54]

If alchemy was the ancestor of modern chemistry, and as such became part of Coleridge's scientific interests, the other forms of magic were less attractive. The Cabbala was a species of pantheism whose Renaissance fortune shows the Italian tendency to paganism.[55] Astrology was hardly more interesting; there was no need for a new Pico della Mirandola to write a book against it, though indictments ought to be moderate, like Erasmus' and Newton's.[56]

Beside alchemy itself, the figure of the alchemist stimulated Coleridge's curiosity. In 1802 he borrowed Girolamo Cardano's autobiography, *De vita propria*. His conclusion was that Cardano, like Paracelsus, 'was a braggard and a quack', though they were blamed for their merits rather than their follies.[57]

Coleridge's interest in Galileo was equally perfunctory and biographic. Today no history of philosophy would give more space to Bruno, Boehme or Reuchlin than Galileo, as Coleridge did in the *Philosophical Lectures*. Galileo became for Coleridge a symbol of the persecution of true knowledge by prejudice and political interest.[58] He remembered Galileo's works for the elegant passages which show 'what awe and amazement' fill the mind which contemplates real space, although space and time in themselves are mere abstractions (*TL* 93). Such a poetic perspective fits Bruno better than Galileo, who 'was a great genius . . .; but it would take two or three Galileos and Newtons to make one Kepler' (*TT* (*CC*) 8 Oct 1830).

Coleridge's knowledge of Italian science was limited, despite his admiration for figures like the botanist Andrea Cesalpino and the anatomists Andrea Vesalio and Giambattista Morgagni.[59] The only scientist whose works he was familiar with was Giuseppe Ruggiero Boscovich (1711–87). Boscovich's atomic theory, to which he was led by his early Unitarian interests, became in his mind one of the clearest statements of the dynamic conception of matter.[60]

Coleridge's attitude to Renaissance science makes evident that he was more attracted by theology and mysticism than by the naturalism of the alchemists. The Renaissance philosophers he preferred were Bruno, Bacon and Boehme. Bruno and Bacon could represent a genuine interest in science: but Bacon was for Coleridge above all a Platonist, and Bruno did not interest him merely as a philosopher of nature. As McFarland argues, Coleridge's greatest debt was to Boehme as a trinitarian thinker (1969, 249). Physics was not the main problem: 'the gross errors of the Platonists' in this field 'do not affect the essential meaning' of their doctrine (*CM* (*CC*) II 648). Nature cannot be explained by physical principles, 'if there be not pre-adjoined the Spirit and the Word' (*CM* (*CC*) I 661).

Thomas McFarland provides two valuable suggestions to evaluate Coleridge's interest in Giordano Bruno. First, Bruno is part of the large group of pantheist philosophers (from the Greek Neoplatonists to Schelling) with whom Coleridge became familiar in the 1800s. Much scholarly work has been done on this aspect of Coleridge, and several of the following remarks are footnotes to it. The other suggestion, which I find more stimulating, is that the special attention Coleridge paid to Boehme and Bruno was due to their lives – Spinoza always remained the Pantheist *par excellence* thanks to the clarity of his thought.[61] Although Coleridge did not respond to the legends which had grown round Dante or Tasso, he was a man of his time and participated in his way in the 'cult of the hero'. His Italian hero was Bruno. The myth of Bruno's life attracted Coleridge's attention as much as the myth of Dante's and Tasso's lives created widespread public interest in their works.

Bruno was almost unknown in England in Coleridge's time. His Elizabethan reputation had faded, and an English translation of *Lo spaccio della bestia trionfante* waited till 1713, and John Toland did not publish his partial translation and abridgement of *De infinito* till 1726 (*Dialoghi* liv, xxxvii). Coleridge may first have heard of Bruno in Germany, where Bruno had become a popular figure among intellectuals. Jacobi included a summary of *De la causa, principio et uno* in the second edition of his *Ueber die Lehre des Spinoza*. His aim was to compare Bruno's thought with Spinoza's in order to provide a sort of summa of pantheism.[62] Even though Lessing, Hamann, Herder and Goethe had discovered Bruno by themselves, it was Jacobi who made him popular.[63] Schelling's *Bruno, oder, über das göttliche und natürliche Princip der Dinge* (1802) was the Romantic consecration.[64]

Ueber die Lehre des Spinoza was an important book for Coleridge, and he cannot have failed to take notice of Bruno. In any event, the first evidence of his acquaintance with Bruno dates from 1801, when he read two of his Frankfurt poems, *De monade, numero et figura* and *De immenso, innumerabilibus et infigurabilibus* (*CN* I 927, 928, 929). The Frankfurt poems contributed to attracting him to Italian culture: Giordano Bruno, with Dante and Ariosto, would be his Italy (*CN* II 2598, May 1805). In Malta and Italy he tried to acquire Bruno's works, but he only transcribed a list of them he probably found in Lecky's Library in Malta.[65] Given the rarity of Bruno's works, it is important to define which of them Coleridge perused. He himself said he had read six works of Bruno out of the eleven titles he knew (*Friend* (*CC*) II 82; I 118). Beside the two Latin works mentioned above and the extracts from *De la causa, principio et uno* in *Ueber die Lehre des Spinoza*, the works he read are *La cena de le ceneri*, *De umbris idearum* and *De progressu et lampade venatoria logicorum*. I have not found evidence he knew any of the other works included in the list, let alone those which are not.[66] Altogether, he perused two of Bruno's works on the art of memory (*De umbris* and *De progressu et lampade venatoria*); one of the Italian dialogues Bruno wrote in England (*La cena*), which is the best specimen of his art as a 'dramatist'; and two Latin poems written during the German period.

Coleridge's selection and his notes show that he focused on three aspects of Bruno: his logic, his philosophy of nature and his personality. A discussion of the first two aspects will render the third clearer.

Coleridge mentioned Bruno in *Biographia* among the philosophers who prepared him to accept Descartes' *cogito* (*CC*, I 143–6), and he specified Bruno's role when he defended himself from the charge of having plagiarised Schelling. He emphasized that he and Schelling had the same philosophical background, to which Bruno belonged as the father of the dynamic philosophy of nature later improved by Kant.[67] Coleridge's claims have often been sneered at as a pathetic defence against the charge of plagiarism, though they were not unfounded: most basic concepts of *Naturphilosophie* appear in Bruno, who was popular in Romantic Germany. A full account of Bruno's philosophy of nature is not necessary here; it is sufficient to discuss the aspects which struck Coleridge.

Coleridge's attitude to Bruno's philosophy of nature is part of his scientific ideas. Even though he mentioned Bruno with Boehme as a champion of pantheism, he admitted he had not read enough of Bruno to be certain whether he had made the same mistakes as Boehme, Spinoza and Schelling.[68] Above all, he had read Bruno when he was still unaware of the 'bitter root' of pantheism, that is, its ethical implications. Despite his uncertainty about Bruno's pantheism, it is significant that he refuted the basic doctrines of Bruno's cosmology: the infinity of worlds and universal animation.

Although Coleridge claimed he was familiar with Neoplatonic and pantheist writings from his youth, Bruno's view of universal animation surprised him in 1801, since he transcribed long passages on the subject from *De immenso*.[69] Bruno's central doctrine is that the universe is infinite and the same everywhere, and that all celestial bodies are similar. The moon, the sun and all planets are inhabited (*Olc* I ii 57, 37; *CN* I 10, 1795). There is no still centre, certainly not the earth, which is an ordinary body: the earth and the sun are both in motion (*Olc* I i 378–86; I ii 45, 97–8).

In the *Philosophical Lectures*, Coleridge said that Bruno's greatest merit was to have understood the implications of the Copernican revolution (1949, 326): but this is true so far as we speak of ethical implications rather than scientific implications. He noticed that Bruno's 'sublime panegyric on Nicolaus Copernicus' in *De immenso* only mentioned the faults of Copernicus' theory (*CN* I 928). Copernicus had not understood his own discovery because, as Bruno put it in *La cena de le ceneri*, 'he had studied mathematics more than nature' (*Dialoghi* 28). In other words, Bruno interpreted the Copernican theory as a reassertion of the cosmology of the *prisca theologia* of Hermes Trismegistus and the other pseudo-Egyptian sages who had been rediscovered in the Renaissance.[70] Thus he subverted both Aristotelian and Copernican cosmology.

The polemic against Aristotelian cosmology is a leitmotiv of Bruno's works and in particular of *De immenso*, which refutes it point by point. His anti-Aristotelianism does not mean that he was a champion of modern science, as the nineteenth century believed. Coleridge was in part aware of it, since he pointed out that Bruno considered 'himself a reviver of the Pythagorean system of the universe' (*P Lects*, 1949, 326). Aristotle, and much more the Aristotelians, epitomized for Bruno the pedants who refuse to admit hidden truths. Bruno's arch-enemy was the pedant-grammatician, that is, the Humanist.[71]

Bruno's idea of the infinity of worlds depends on the same attitude as his anti-Aristotelianism. The concept had for him the value of a hieroglyphic 'of the divine', an attempt 'to figure the infigurable' (Yates, 1964, 336–7). The infinity of worlds, and natural philosophy altogether, was for Bruno, in Cassirer's words, 'a question of *ethics*'. Bruno never asserted his doctrines on the basis of empirical observations or mathematical hypotheses, but as a result of intuition. Cassirer points out that the infinity of worlds was known to medieval philosophy, but had been refuted for moral reasons.[72] The idea of an infinite universe without a centre and infinitely inhabited was not shared by Copernicus, Brahe, Kepler and Galileo, and was debated in the seventeenth century: the doctrine raised theological problems, since it contradicted Moses and St John, who spoke of one world only.[73] Coleridge himself never felt 'any force in the arguments for a plurality of worlds' (*TT* (*CC*) 22 Feb 1834), which means that Bruno's cosmology did not have a great impact on him.

Some of Coleridge's observations on Bruno's cosmology were inaccurate. Such mistakes are not relevant in themselves, but as evidence that he did not accept the extreme consequences of Bruno's pantheism. Bruno never asserted 'the existence of an absolute vacuum which is necessary to motion but of which God is the sole plenitude' (*P Lects*, 1949, 326). The doctrine sounds Coleridgean rather than Brunonian. In *De immenso*, which Coleridge knew, Bruno repeatedly denied the existence of vacuum and admitted of 'a continuous, unique and immense space which encompassed all bodies located in a defined place, and which is therefore called plenum'.[74]

Another mistake of Coleridge was his belief that Bruno conceived of the souls of the planets as mere delegates 'of one Supreme Being and all-originating *Opifex*' (*C on Bruno* 433). Bruno attacked Plato's dualism in the last chapters of Book VIII of *De immenso*, where he stated that 'an artifex who governs from above and predisposes and shapes from without does not exist' (*Olc* I ii 312). Bruno reasserts his monism, in which 'God, Being, Unity, Truth, Fate, Reason, Order' coincide.[75]

Bruno's reflections on the macrocosm were based on the same principles as those on the microcosm, on which Coleridge focused in the *Philosophical Lectures*. He pointed out that Bruno's doctrines were similar to Michael Psellus' – he had earlier associated them with Proclus – but 'blended with a multitude of the wildest chemical fancies'. Bruno talked of excitability 'where a modern chemist would talk of attraction and affinity'. Excitability was the belief 'that every being . . . had a life if it could be called forth, and that all along that was called but the law of likeness'. The basic principle of their philosophy was 'the law of likeness' – what alchemists defined as *sympathia* – 'arising from what is called the polar principle'. They 'traced in their (*trichotomous*) philosophy all the facts in nature and oftentimes with most wonderful and happy effects'.[76]

Coleridge's chemical studies led him to believe that 'the Worlds *not* animantia as Giord. Bruno holds them' (*CN* IV 4639, Jan–Feb 1820), but his rejection of hylozoism dates from much before. The 1809 *Friend* included a favourite passage from *De immenso*, a significant point of which was translated as follows: Bruno (who is quoting a passage from Hermes Trismegistus): '*sicut Deus est omnia*'; Coleridge: 'even as in God all things are' (*CC*, I 116-17). As Coleridge had noted with respect to Plotinus in 1803, God is not everything, but everything is in God (*CM* (*CC*) I 602-3 and n.). The result of Coleridge's *ethical* rejection of pantheism was that he continued making use of its principles, as for example in the long letter he wrote to C. A. Tulk in September 1817 (*CL* IV 767–75), or in the lectures, when he referred to the concept of *natura naturans*. In other words, he did not develop an alternative view of nature; he abandoned the subject and turned to other speculation in his later years.

The other aspect of Bruno's philosophy which intrigued Coleridge was 'polar logic'. Since polar logic in Coleridge's sense, that is, a form of Romantic dialectic of which Hegel's is the most complex specimen, did not exist in Bruno, the question is to define what Brunonian concepts Coleridge associated with polarity. Owen Barfield, who has produced the longest study on the subject, observes that Bruno did not use the terms 'polarity' or 'pole' except in a geographical sense in *La cena de le ceneri*. The unanimous conclusion of Barfield, McFarland and Wheeler is that

Coleridge was referring to Bruno's principle of *coincidentia oppositorum*.[77] However, there are discrepancies in their interpretations: Barfield thinks that Coleridge's law of polarity has little to do with Bruno's *coincidentia oppositorum*, but Kathleen Wheeler suggests that Barfield overstates the difference between the two doctrines.[78]

The starting point must be that Bruno never wrote a treatise of formal logic; even *De progressu et lampade venatoria logicorum* belongs to the tradition of the art of memory more than logic. His polarities seem to have developed in another context, and are applied to various subjects: for example, mathematics (as in *De minimo*), physics and metaphysics (as in *De immenso* and *De monade*). The law of polarity is more evident in these works than in his mnemonic tracts, which are linked to his interest in magic and numerology rather than logic. Although mathematics – or rather mathesis – physics and metaphysics cannot be clearly separated in Bruno, the principle of *coincidentia oppositorum* probably belonged in origin to his physics.

As Coleridge put it, Bruno founded his cosmology on

> the centro-peripheric Process, or primary Law of Matter: which he elsewhere calls Law of Polarity, in this as in many other instances anticipating the Ideas & discoveries attributed to far later Philosophers, even those of the present age. (*C on Bruno* 432–3)

The theory implied that

> EVERY POWER IN NATURE AND IN SPIRIT *must evolve an opposite, as the sole means and condition of its manifestation*: AND ALL OPPOSITION IS A TENDENCY TO RE-UNION. This is the universal Law of Polarity or essential Dualism, first promulgated by Heraclitus, 2000 years afterwards re-published, and made the foundation both of Logic, of Physics, and of Metaphysics by Giordano Bruno. (*Friend* (*CC*) I 94)

Owen Barfield thought that Bruno's (and Lull's and Cusa's) principle of polarity was not so dynamic as Coleridge's: dynamism implies contrast, and Barfield finds it more in Boehme than Bruno. However, Barfield's distinction is unconvincing, since dynamism is prominent in Bruno's philosophy of nature.[79] I think what interested Coleridge was the interconnection of logic, physics and metaphysics, which made it possible for him to turn Bruno into a Platonist, however improbable it seems: 'in the Deity is an absolute Synthesis of opposites. Plato in *Parmenide* and Giordano Bruno passim have spoken many things well on this aweful Mystery/the latter more clearly'.[80]

If such were the consequences of the application of polar logic to metaphysics, Bruno himself provided the link between the physical and the logical application of the doctrine: 'It is profound magic to be able to extract the contrary after finding the point of union', and Aristotle did not achieve it. Aristotle considered deprivation 'as the origin, the relative and the mother of form', but did not descend 'into the species of contrariety', since he maintained that 'contraries cannot exist in the same subject' (*De la causa, Dialoghi* 340). It was neither a new nor an original observation, since, as Gentile remarks in a note to the passage, Cusa had made the same point. Before Cusa, the 'logic of contraries' appeared in Plato and developed in the Neoplatonic tradition.[81]

Coleridge ascribed to Richard Baxter the 'substitution of Trychotomy for the old & still general plan of Dychotomy' in logic (*CM* (*CC*) I 347). Baxter had anticipated Kant's logic, but he had in his turn been anticipated by Bruno:

> I have not indeed any distinct memory of Giordano Bruno's *Logica Venatrix Veritatis*; but doubtless the principle of Trichotomy is necessarily involved in the Polar Logic: this is again the same with the Pythagorean *Tetractys* – i.e. the eternal Fountain or Source of Nature. . . . Thus in
>
>
>
> Prothesis
>
> Thesis   Antithesis
>
> Synthesis
>
>
>
> we have the Tetrad indeed in the intellectual & intuitive Contemplation; but a Triad in discursive Arrangement, and a Tri-unity in Result. (*CM* (*CC*) I 347–8)

Owen Barfield is convincing when he argues that 'Polar Logic, Transcendental Logic and the Principle of Trychotomy appear, at most, slightly different aspects of the same idea' in Coleridge.[82] A sort of formalised assertion of Bruno's logic of contraries is not included in *De progressu et lampade venatoria logicorum*, as Coleridge vaguely recollected, but in *De monade*. In chapter IV, § vii, 'Application of triads', Bruno writes:

> The order of Beginning, MIDDLE AND END, that is, of the AGENT, MATTER AND FORMATION, is present in all things. . . .
> There is only one middle between two extremes, in whatever order.
> The middle which is linked with both extremes can be found in any third element which is united to some thing. (*Olc* I ii 373)

The Pythagorean conception of the Tetrad is discussed in chapter V of *De monade*, in which the logic of contraries is applied to cosmology (*Olc* I ii 382–401). However, Coleridge did not find *De monade* to his taste: 'It was far too numeral, lineal, & pythagorean for my Comprehension – it read very much like Thomas Taylor & Proclus &c'.[83] He thought Bruno's logic was to be found in his works on the art of memory.[84]

Words, Coleridge wrote in his *Logic*, are the most important philosophical subject, a subject 'worthy (of a Bruno)' (*Logic* (*CC*) 120). He sent to C. A. Tulk a reading list on logic which included Plato, Aristotle, Raymonde de Sabunde, Lull, Campanella, Cardano, 'Giordano Bruno – particularly, his De Umbris Idearum, Logici Venatrix Veritatis, in short, his *Mnemonic* Tracts generally', Leibniz and Kant. The conclusion was surprising: 'after all, Kant & Bacon supersede, I am convinced all the rest – except perhaps Giordano Bruno's Work'.[85]

Logic is not the main subject of Bruno's works on the art of memory, although they are part of the tradition which led to seventeenth-century attempts at universal calculus. Frances Yates argues that

> The memory tradition taught that everything is better remembered through an image, that these images should be striking and emotionally powerful, that they should be linked to one another associatively. Bruno tries to work memory systems based on these principles by linking them to the astrological system, using magically potent images, 'semi-mathematical' or magical places, and the associative orders of astrology. With this he mixes Lullist combinations and Cabalistic magic![86]

The art of memory is an essential part of Bruno's religion, which he conceived of as a revival of the ancient 'Egyptian' cult, whose aim was the re-establishment of the communication between man and the world interrupted by Christianity. Bruno's

> religion of Love and Magic is based on the Power of the Imagination, and on the Art of Memory through which the Magus attempts to grasp, and to hold within, the universe in all its ever changing forms, through images passing the one into the other in intricate associative orders, reflecting the ever changing movements of the heavens.[87]

Coleridge's reading of Bruno's mnemonic works is of outstanding originality, since he understood the value of a subject which has been neglected until recent years. The context in which he set them was correct, but he probably overrated their links with Romantic philosophy. Barfield points out that a few passages on the *coincidentia oppositorum* in Bruno's mnemonic tracts 'could well have made him (Coleridge) suspect that in the *De Progressu et Lampade Venatoria Logicorum* he had hit on what might prove an important attempt to develop a formal logic of trichotomy'.[88] This is plausible, but should not conceal the fact that Bruno's anticipations of dialectic are clearer in his works on cosmology than the art of memory.[89] If Bruno's mnemonic tracts deserve a place in the history of logic, they do not deserve it as precursors of Romantic dialectic but, together with Lull's, as part of the background to seventeenth-century projects for universal calculus.[90]

Coleridge's interest in Bruno's polarities was genuine, but, as Thomas McFarland emphasizes, his obligation to them 'is more symbolical than functional', since he 'did not use a polar logic, even though he loved to collect examples of how extremes meet'.[91] His drastic dismissal of Hegel confirms this. Coleridge admired Bruno not only as a philosopher of nature and a logician, but above all as a figure. Bruno was Sydney's and Greville's friend, the oracle whose conversation, if it was like his writing, made Coleridge think 'he would [have] talked with a trumpet'.[92] He was a great egotist too, like every original mind except Spinoza (*Omniana* 123; *CL* IV 938, 22 Apr 1819). All the projects of Coleridge on Bruno – they were numerous – included at least a section on Bruno's biography.[93]

That Coleridge's admiration was moral and biographical is evident from the use of Bruno he made in his works. The passage of Bruno he cited most often was a warning against thinking a writer mad without reading him with care.[94] Coleridge was fond of quoting Bruno's poetry, and particularly the ode at the beginning of *De monade*, '*Daedalias vacuis plumas nectere humeris*', which 'in grandeur of moral has been rarely surpassed'.[95] Bruno's poetry 'will place him high – for there are few [*such sublime enunciations of the dignity of the human soul as the De Immenso and the prose commentaries on it*]' (*P Lects*, 1949, 327). Coleridge was thinking in particular of the first commentary of *De immenso*, which contains such a 'sublime enunciation . . . according to the principles of Plato' (*CN* I 928). The excerpt, beginning 'Anima sapiens non timet mortem', is not Platonic but Neoplatonic, and contains the passage from the Hermetic *Asclepius* which defines man as a 'miraculum magnum'. The extract was quoted by Pico della Mirandola at the beginning of his oration 'On the Dignity of Man', which is regarded as the manifesto of the Renaissance view of humanity. Bruno was repeating a Renaissance commonplace, which Coleridge received through him.[96]

Bruno demonstrated, together with Plotinus, Boehme and Spinoza, that pantheism is 'not necessarily irreligious or heretical; tho' it may be taught atheistically' (*BL* (*CC*) I 247; *CN* III 4189). Bruno's death provided Coleridge with an opportunity to give vent to his anti-Catholic rhetoric. Bruno died at the stake in Rome for atheism, but his works are full of 'a lofty and enlightened piety, which was of course unintelligible to bigots, and dangerous to an apostate hierarchy'.[97] Addison misrepresented the sense of the *Spaccio della bestia trionfante*, whose aim was to show 'that all motives of hope and fear from invisible powers, which are not immediately derived from, and absolutely coincident with, the reverence due to the supreme reason of the universe, are all alike dangerous superstitions', like the Roman worship of saints or the African cult of fetishes. Bruno spoke as an enlightened Christian when he taught, like the apostles, that morality is not based on revelation, but on 'truths implanted in the hearts of men' (*Omniana* 136–7; *C on Bruno* 433). Despite Coleridge's eloquence, his Protestant interpretation of Bruno's religiosity is unfounded. Bruno's opposition to Christianity is nowhere so clear as in the *Spaccio*, even though the triumphant beast which should have been expelled was not the pope nor Christianity, but all vices as opposed to virtue (Yates, 1964, 218–19). Bruno's hermetic reformation, as Frances Yates called it, would restore the harmony between humanity, nature and God.[98]

Coleridge preferred Bruno's anthropology to evolutionism, which 'supposes the human Race to have been gradually perfecting itself from the darkest Savagery, or . . . contemplates Man as the last metamorphosis . . . of some lucky species of Ape or Baboon'; but in the end he preferred Christian creationism to both (*C on Bruno* 431).

Coleridge became aware that his ethics was irreconcilable with Bruno's as with any pantheist ethics. Bruno maintained that 'anima sapiens non timet mortem' because there was no death in his philosophy, but only the dissolution of material accidents, the transformation of the one and eternal substance, that is, metamorphosis.[99] However, Bruno did not accept Plato's theory of eternal return: his model of natural development was the spire, as in Goethe's *Steigerung* (*De immenso*, *Olc* I i 367–72, 350). Hazlitt accused Coleridge of deriving his conception of religion from Bruno's '"sublime piety"', but the charge was groundless (*CH* 250; *CL* IV 685–6, 25 Sept 1816).

Thomas McFarland argues that Coleridge's debt to Boehme was deeper than his debt to Bruno; his interest in Bruno was in part due to fashion and the glamour of Bruno's personality (McFarland, 1969, 249). I agree; and since Coleridge's interest was not purely philosophical, it cannot be measured against his philosophical background alone.

Bruno was one of the poetic philosophers Coleridge admired so much – a modern, minor version of Plato. But despite the admiration, the affinity between Coleridge and Bruno is limited, and goes little beyond the fact that they were both philosophers. The English Romantic whose personality recalls Bruno is Shelley – both indomitable rebels, fighters, restless exiles, exalted pantheists. It is obviously possible to admire someone who is different from oneself, but it is impossible to overlook the affinity between Coleridge and Petrarch. As Kathleen Coburn noted (*P Lects*, 1949, 443 n. 9), they were both poets, both torn between this and the other world, both frustrated lovers, both annotators of books, both given to self-analysis, both weak in their will, both Platonic Christians.

Bruno and Petrarch represent two different aspects of the Italian Renaissance. The former is the philosopher whose monism steamrolls the differences existing in reality. He aimed at reviving 'Egyptian' religion, regardless of its history; he belonged to the world of Ficino and Pico, even though he is less syncretic and Christian than they were. Petrarch was the founder of modern philology, which would slowly bring authorities back into history – first Aristotle, then the Bible. Therefore, a direct knowledge of Petrarch's and Humanist prose writings was for Coleridge of considerable *philosophical* importance, even though he was more excited by Ficino, Pico and Bruno.

Conversely, Bruno's influence on Coleridge's view of poetry was secondary. Some of Bruno's Latin poems were sublime, but one wonders what Coleridge would have thought of the bombastic anti-Petrarchism and misogyny of *De gli eroici furori*.[100] As far as poetics is concerned, Coleridge tried to define poetry in Brunonian terms as 'the Art of representing Objects in relation to the *excitability* of the human mind' (*CN* III 3827, May 1810). The concept of excitability derives from John Brown, whose works were well known to Beddoes and Blumenbach, and therefore to Coleridge. However, entry 3825 mentions Bruno; and Coleridge said that Bruno called excitability what modern chemists would call affinity or attraction (*P Lects*, 1949, 323). Since excitability depends on the law of likeness or sympathy, Bruno might lie in the background of Coleridge's definition of poetry as 'the communication of Thoughts and feelings so as to produce excitements by sympathy' (*CN* III 3827). Coleridge does not seem to have known of Bruno's attack on normative poetics in *De gli eroici furori*, which is often described as proto-Romantic.[101]

I think Coleridge's philosophical development would have hardly been different had he never read Bruno, since his Classical and German backgrounds would have filled the space. But if he had never read Petrarch, his understanding of poetry and criticism would have been different: he would have missed an essential chapter in the history of European culture – a chapter no Classical or German writer could have provided. This is neither meant to undermine the genuine admiration he had for Bruno, who was for him a rich source of reflection, nor to conceal the historical value of his understanding of Bruno's importance, but to form a correct balance of Italian influence on Coleridge. Bruno is a name which naturally crosses the mind of someone who thinks of Coleridge and Italy; it should not be forgotten that Coleridge's experience of Petrarch's poetry and thought was an event of at least equal importance, and that Ficino's influence on Coleridge's philosophy was more specific than Bruno's, even though he did not mention Ficino as frequently as Bruno.

The Philosophy of History and Giambattista Vico

Platonism, for Coleridge, supplied the unifying character of the Renaissance, as he argued repeatedly in the *Philosophical Lectures*: Platonism brooded 'over the birth of genius and revived with the restoration of literature and the fine arts' (*P Lects*, 1949, 393). A view of history which places ideas at its core is philosophic and, in Coleridge's case, idealistic. Coleridge would have agreed with Hegel that the spiritual essence of an epoch is contained in its philosophy, even though he never developed a complete historicist doctrine. Coleridge claimed he read 'all the famous histories', but never

> for the story itself as a story. The only thing interesting to me was the principles to be evolved from and illustrated by the Facts; after I had gotten my Principle, I pretty generally left the Facts to take care of themselves. (*TT (CC)* 7 Jul 1832)

His theoretical attitude explains his interest in Machiavelli, whom he frequently mentioned together with his favourite political philosophers – Hooker, Bacon, Harrington and Spinoza.[102] Even though no specific aspect of his political theories was influenced by Machiavelli, he admired him for bringing forward principles rather than mere facts.[103] Coleridge gave extraordinary prominence to principles in history: he believed, for instance, that all the recent failures of European politics were due to the neglect of some doctrine of Machiavelli, Bacon or Harrington.[104]

An important principle Coleridge deduced from his knowledge of history was a kind of idea of *Zeitgeist*. He noted that there was a

> common Consciousness, that in every age is the Mind of the State – This too, as in Individuals, is not undistinguishably continuous, in cycle or in stream; but evolutive, and revolutionary – It has its *Epochs* –

& the Epoch not the Circumstances constitutes the true ground & principle of political Insight, and herein consists the main value of History & the distinction of the Historical from the recordless Ages, of the Historical from the barbarous Nations. (*CN* IV 4941, May–Jul 1823)

Epochs, 'and all else as illustrative of these', are the sole materials of history; the Chinese have records but no history (*CN* IV 4941). Such an attitude to history seems inevitable whenever ideas are thought to precede facts, or, as McFarland would put it, the 'I am' precedes the 'it is'.[105]

Although philosophical speculation is unknown to most women and men, it is true for Coleridge that 'all the *epoch-forming* Revolutions of the Christian world' in all their aspects 'have coincided with the rise and fall of metaphysical systems'. In any age 'the Taste and the Character, the whole tone of Manners and Feeling, and above all the Religious (at least the Theological) and the Political tendencies of the public mind' have corresponded to the predominant system of philosophy (*SM* (*CC*) 14–15; *CL* IV 759, 28 Jul 1817). Society is governed by the ideas of few minds, whose effects are almost incalculable. Consequently, elitism is another feature of Coleridge's philosophy of history.[106]

The interconnection of metaphysics and events, as he noted, could be illustrated by a history of the fine arts from the tenth century onwards (*SM* (*CC*) 14–15). The rigid outlines of early medieval painting reflected the geometric structure of contemporary Aristotelianism; from Giotto, Dante and Petrarch to Raphael, Michelangelo and Titian, 'Platonism revived in the Noblest Minds', and was later replaced by Eclectic philosophy and the Carraccis' academicism (*LS* (*CC*) 103–4 and n.; *CL* IV 759). The experience of Renaissance painting, therefore, had a significant influence not only on Coleridge's idea of the fine arts and the development of his aesthetics, but also affected his philosophy of history.

The unifying principle which was seemingly wanting in his lectures on European literature should now be evident. Coleridge was interested in the continuity of a tradition: a Platonic and Christian tradition which developed in the Italian and English Renaissance, of which Romanticism should have been a revival. Dante, Petrarch, Raphael, Michelangelo, Spenser, Sidney, Shakespeare and Milton were Platonists; Dryden, Pope and Johnson were not. Coleridge was not supporting German taste against Italian taste; rather, he defined a poetic genealogy rooted in the Classical and medieval worlds whose trunk was the Italian and English Renaissance. Such a tradition was intended to replace the Anglo-French Neoclassicism which had dominated England since Dryden's time. Coleridge spent his critical life in defining and defending this tradition, which was not available as such before. The view on which it is based is conservative, since it aimed at preserving a form of thought which modern science had discarded; however, his conservatism was a renewal because it recovered a component of European culture which had become marginal. It is beyond the scope of the present work to discuss in detail whether his theory is justified – for example, I find his characterization of Dante and Shakespeare as Platonists untenable; my interest is to emphasize the philosophical consistency of his interpretation of history. His history of English and European poetry is not ours, but it was original and critical.

Coleridge developed his philosophical view of Renaissance history by the early 1820s. His ideas explain the enthusiasm he felt for Vico, who influenced his subsequent reflections on history. Like the German historicists, Coleridge 'hailed' Vico as a precursor: '*Pereant qui ante nos nostra dixere*' was his comment on first reading the *New Science* (*CL* V 454 (14 May 1825)). Unlike the Germans, however, he never developed a proper historicist doctrine, but eventually rejected the essentials of Vico's philosophy, since they were at variance with the Christian view of history.

Some of Vico's ideas were in themselves not new to Coleridge, since they were developed by eighteenth-century English philosophy from sources other than Vico. However, he found Vico's 'cultural anthropology' much more congenial than Hume's, Warburton's or Monboddo's, not to mention French scholars like Dupuis. The enthusiasm of his response is demonstrated on the one hand by his efforts to introduce Vico into English culture; on the other, by the presence of Vichian elements in his late works.

The story of Coleridge as a mediator of Vico in England has been traced in detail by Max H. Fisch and Thomas G. Bergin. We need only remember that in April 1825 Coleridge met Gioacchino de' Prati, an Italian exile who gave him a copy of the *New Science*.[107] Coleridge tried to attract public attention to the work in various ways: he used a maxim of Vico as a motto for the *Aids to Reflection*, which were being printed at the time (*CL* V 445, *c*. 10 May 1825); he planned – a characteristic conse-quence of his enthusiasms – a work on revolutionary minds which included an essay on Vico (*IS* 183); and he advised John Taylor Coleridge and de' Prati to write a 'spirited Sketch of Vico's Life and great Work', which he now preferred to the plan for Bruno's biography (*CL* V 470, 16 Jun 1825; VI 579, 9 May 1826). None of these works materialized, but Coleridge's influence, reinforced by Michelet's, was responsible for most English interest in Vico in the following decades.[108]

Coleridge had first heard of Vico some years before. A passage from Vico's *De antiquissima Italorum sapientia ex lingua Latina originibus eruenda* appeared in Jacobi's *Von den göttlichen Dingen* (1811), and Coleridge quoted it in the *Theory of Life*.[109] It is a short passage, but it contains one of Vico's most important principles: we can only know what we make. The passage opposes geometry, which can be demonstrated because it is a human product, to physics and metaphysics, which cannot be known completely since they are not man-made. Vico conceived his new science when he applied the Baconian doctrine to history.[110]

The principle became important for Coleridge, who must have been impressed by its applications in the *New Science*, even while he remained sceptical. In *Self-Knowledge*, one of his gloomiest poems, he used the doctrine in a way Vico would have never done:

> Say, canst thou make thyself? – Learn first that trade; –
> Haply thou mayst know what thyself had made.
> What hast thou, Man, that thou dar'st call thine own? –
> What is there in thee, Man, that can be known? –
> Dark fluxion, all unfixable by thought,
> A phantom dim of past and future wrought,
> Vain sister of the worm, – life, death, soul, clod –
> Ignore thyself, and strive to know thy God!
> (*PW* (EHC) I 487, ll. 3–10)

Vico's principle is accepted and rejected at the same time. Human beings might know what they themselves make, but the problem is, what can be defined as their own, as made by them? History, though here individual history, is not a set of events whose laws can be uncovered, but 'a phantom dim of past and future wrought'. The poem refuses not only Pope's idea that man is the true subject of human knowledge, as James Mays points out, but implicitly any strong form of historicism like Hegel's.

Although Coleridge was interested by the doctrine that *verum et factum convertuntur*, his notes on the *New Science* show that he paid less attention to Vico's principles than their applications. For instance, he did not comment on Vico's theory of poetic logic, as one would expect, but was intrigued by Vico's 'Discovery of the True Homer', which is a dazzling application of that theory.[111]

Coleridge's interest in Homer was lifelong. He pointed out in the *Philosophical Lectures* that Homer's writings were a kind of history of early Greece. Like most contemporary scholars and against Thucydides and

Herodotus, he thought Homer's poems were not written by a single person. He was even uncertain about the authorship of the *Iliad*: he wondered whether it was written by one poet or was a collection of different poems on the same subject by various poets, like Macpherson's *Ossian*. He could 'see no probability of Homer being a particular person' (*P Lects*, 1949, 87–9).

Given such antecedents, it is not surprising that he was excited by Vico's Homeric theory. Vico had anticipated Wolf, whose theories Coleridge claimed had been his own at college.[112] Whether his claim is true or not, such ideas were part of the late eighteenth-century and romantic attitude to primitive poetry. The difference is that Vico set them in a wider context, as a comparison with Wolf demonstrates. It was Vico's poetic logic and philosophy of history which justified his theory of primitive poetry.

Coleridge's latest conviction was that Homer was 'a mere synonyme with the Iliad'. Now he added a Vichian reason for it: men were all poets at that time. One man 'was perhaps a better poet than another, but he was a poet upon the same ground and with the same feelings' as the rest. The non-subjective character of the *Iliad* was demonstrated by the scarcity of adverbs in it (*TT* (*CC*) 7 Jul 1832). I am not certain, however, that Coleridge grasped Vico's reasons for the poetic character of the primitive mind and the concept of *universale fantastico* (imaginative universal or class concept) in particular. Besides, Coleridge had written of 'the absurdity of tracing the growth of poetic Genius by *ancestry*: as if Dante or Milton were *creatures* of *wandering Bards*' (*CN* III 3437, 1808–9). In other words, he found a loose application of the doctrine unconvincing.[113]

Another aspect of the *New Science* which intrigued the late Coleridge was the periodization of history. At first he accepted the division of history into an age of the gods, an age of the heroes and an age of men; to which hieroglyphic, symbolic and epistolary writing respectively belonged (*CN* IV 5232). But whereas Vico made it the basis of his cyclical interpretation of history and applied it to all the ancient peoples, Coleridge tried to apply it to Hebrew culture alone.[114]

Vico affirmed the uniqueness of Hebrew culture, which was chronologically the oldest, even though he did not derive the other cultures from it. After taking notes on the middle- and far-eastern peoples from Vico's Baroque learning, Coleridge made his own list of proofs for the primacy of Hebrew culture (*CN* IV 5205, 5207, 5232, May–Sept 1825). How little the matter had to do with history and how much with ethics is shown by the assertion that he did 'not care A Dam' for the Hieroglyphics or the Decypherer –. They are Stones, of which I cannot make my Bread, and for which I see no cause why I should make my *Wine* (whine)' (*CN* IV 5219, May 1825). It is not necessary to analyse Coleridge's attempts in detail;

the endeavours to demonstrate the primacy of Hebrew culture were understandable in Vico's time, but they were anachronistic in Coleridge's, though the tensions linked to their social and cultural implications were still significant. It will be remembered that the leading Egyptologists were French, and that Coleridge insisted on the primacy of Hebrew culture in *Lay Sermons*.[115]

Coleridge's Biblical preoccupations made him suspect that Vico inwardly considered Christianity as one of the various, possible religions. He found evidence for it in Vico's idea that any religion must keep its sacred texts secret in order to exist.[116] A debated problem like Vico's religiousness cannot be solved here; suffice it to remember that some of his doctrines, like the cyclical conception of history, are not Christian, and that the primacy of Hebrew culture is assumed rather than demonstrated in the *New Science*.[117]

The history to which Vico applied his cyclical scheme in greatest detail was neither Egyptian nor Hebrew: it was by an accurate description of Roman history that he illustrated the development of human society from the animal stage to splendour and decay. If not the clearest, it is the richest part of his work. Coleridge was struck by the originality of Vico's interpretation, and by his theory of class relations in particular. He argued that it was impossible for anyone of vigorous intellect to read Vico's

> *Literary* History . . . without something like a *revolution* in his mind – were it only from the connection of the *Heroic* History of Greece and Rome with the *Feudal* History of Modern Europe, after the disruption of the Western Empire – & (in perhaps a still livelier resemblance) with the state of Society in our present Colonies in the W. Indies. (*CL* V 470, 16 Jun 1825)

Coleridge drew a parallel between the relations of the Roman Plebeians with the Patricians and the social conditions of the English colonies, but when Henry Crabb Robinson asked him the reason for such inequality, he 'expatiated on history and on the influence of Christianity on society' without giving Robinson a clear answer.[118] It is not surprising that Coleridge eventually rejected even this aspect of Vico's philosophy: 'Man does not move in cycles, though Nature does. Man's course is like an arrow' (*TT* (*CC*) 15 May 1833).

Coleridge's late admiration for Vico was more political than philosophical. He recommended Vico should be read after Spinoza: Vico thought society tended to monarchy, Spinoza to democracy – a form of democracy which for Coleridge had been realized by the Quakers (*TT* (*CC*) 23 Apr 1832). Coleridge himself became increasingly closer to

Vico in this respect. His late, reactionary attitudes led him to believe that Europe tended to pure monarchy, that is, a government in which 'the Reason of the People shall become efficient in the apparent Will of the King'. The wise and the good were more and more disgusted 'with the representative form of government, brutalized as it is and will be by the predominance of democracy in England, France and Belgium'.[119]

The Garden of Boccaccio

The Garden of Boccaccio, which was Coleridge's longest remark on the Italian Renaissance in his late years, permits us to reconsider some crucial aspects of his ideas. It was composed in 1828, when Italian culture seemed far from his interests, and the perspective is not identical with the one underlying the 1818 lectures.[120] Stimulated by a drawing of Thomas Stothard entitled 'The Garden of Boccaccio' (plate V), the poet revisits his own intellectual life, from boyhood, 'in its own fancies lost', through youth, which 'Loved ere it loved', to manhood, 'musing what and whence is man'. The enigmatic definition of sentiment in adolescence, when he 'Loved ere it loved, and sought a form for love' is worth comparing with Augustine's, who described his first amorous feelings as follows: 'I was not yet in love, but I was in love with love . . . I sought some object to love, since I was thus in love with loving'. The passage from the *Confessions* need not be considered as a source of the line in the *Garden*, but as an interesting parallel in the light of Coleridge's affinity with the philosophy of love of Petrarch, for whom Augustine was the single most influential philosopher together with Cicero.[121]

Some images of the fabulous Middle Ages Coleridge haunted in his youth reappear in his mind; the last of them is a matron

> of sober mien,
> Yet radiant still and with no earthly sheen,
> Whom as a faery child my childhood woo'd
> Even in my dawn of thought – Philosophy;
> Though then unconscious of herself, pardie,
> She bore no other name than Poesy;
> And, like a gift from heaven, in lifeful glee,
> That had but newly left a mother's knee,
> Prattled and play'd with bird and plower, and stone,
> As if with elfin playfellows well known,
> And life reveal'd to innocence alone. (lines 46–56)

In the second part of the poem, in which the poet identifies himself with Boccaccio, the personal situation of the first part is transferred into an historical context. The poem thereby establishes a parallel between the poet's own intellectual development and the cultural development of modern Europe. The analogy between microcosm and macrocosm applied to history and the idea that ontogenesis repeats phylogenesis may have been suggested by Vico, whose philosophy is founded on such principles. The progression of both the individual and culture from poetry to philosophy, from metaphor to abstract discourse, also has a distinctive Vichian flavour.

The text illustrates the process in its early stage, when poetry and philosophy were still in harmony. The early Italian Renaissance was the late childhood of modern Europe, a golden age of fullness, as the Edenic atmosphere demonstrates. The erotic elements of the last section indicate, however, that Coleridge considered it as a childhood on the verge of adolescence; it can be assumed the balance was going to break.

Although the choice of Boccaccio as a symbol may be an accident prompted by Stothard's drawing, it is surprising in the light of Coleridge's former attitude to him. No doubt Boccaccio is a well-chosen symbol: he was a major writer and scholar, his culture was both Classical and medieval, and he celebrated love and eroticism in his works. However, the discrepancy between the scene portrayed in Stothard's work and the poem should not be overlooked. The poem contains some elements of the drawing – the fountain, the dance, the lovers –, but it combines them with other images and, above all, it portrays Boccaccio himself at work, that is, conceiving of the scene illustrated by Stothard. Coleridge's 'Garden of Boccaccio' is not the same as Stothard's, which is much closer to the image of Boccaccio common at the time: the additional elements give the scene a larger symbolic value. The implications of Coleridge's garden are not only erotic but also cultural and political.

The central problems to which Coleridge returned in the poem are the revival of learning and mythology. Boccaccio is represented as a scholar, holding a 'new-found roll' of Homer and a copy of 'Ovid's Holy Book of Love' (line 100), a syntagm of Boccaccio which struck Coleridge two decades before. In a note to the line, Coleridge specified he knew few better proofs 'of the overwhelming influence which the study of the Greek and Roman Classics exercised on the judgments, feelings, and imaginations' of European intellectuals in the early Renaissance than the passage containing the syntagm.[122] He argued it was almost impossible to conceive of their passion for Classical mythology: it was a kind of faith, as the frequent mixture of Christian and Classical figures showed (*CN* II 2670, Sept 1805).

Plate V: *The Garden of Boccaccio.*

Coleridge justified the adoption of Classical mythology in poetry as a device to embody the supernatural in fabulous human figures. On such a basis he sympathized with Petrarch's, Chaucer's and Spenser's use of mythology (*BL (CC)* II 75–6); otherwise, he was not convinced by the medieval and Renaissance allegoric interpretation of Classical mythology. The 'multum' which 'jacet sepultum' ('lies buried') under Boccaccio's definition of Ovid's *Ars amandi* as a 'holy book' was the tendency to paganism (*CM (CC)* I 544).

It is a common critical tenet to contrast Wordsworth's and Coleridge's suspicion of mythology to Hazlitt's, Shelley's and Keats' passion for it. Such an opposition, which is useful as a general view, can easily become too drastic. Certainly, Coleridge's enthusiasm for classical mythology is in no way comparable to that of Shelley and Keats; but Coleridge's objections, though significant, were not as severe as they seem. Even in the *Philosophical Lectures*, where he uttered his harshest indictments of Neoplatonic paganism, his judgement wavered, since he argued that the Greek Neoplatonists would have formed a Christian sect, had they lived in his time (1949, 295). His view of the relation between Scholasticism, Platonism and the Reformation was equally ambiguous.[123]

Coleridge's ideas were traditional and survived in the nineteenth century, when it was common to consider the Renaissance as a pagan age and the Reformation as a religious revival in opposition to it.[124] However, his religious uneasiness was somehow unfounded, since the combination of Christianity and classical mythology was more syncretic in the Middle Ages than in the Renaissance, when both traditions began to be historicized. The result was a clearer division of them, and not the paganization of Christianity which haunted him.[125]

Despite the fact that Coleridge justified mythology only so far as it anticipated or agreed with Christianity, he never dismissed the culture of the Renaissance, which remained a favourite period. What is most striking in *The Garden of Boccaccio* is the new, serene tone toward those aspects which upset him before. The tenderness with which the revival of learning, mythology and 'Ovidian' love are portrayed in the poem is far removed from the 'mythological pedantry' with which he had charged Boccaccio and other Renaissance poets in his lectures. His celebration of Florence as the crucible of a culture in which the Classical and the Christian world coexisted with mutual advantage had never been, nor would again be, so wholehearted.

Afterword

THE ITALIAN RENAISSANCE was a debated topic from the early eighteenth century onwards (as it had been, differently, before). All interpretations had political connotations which, in Coleridge's case, were explicit. The most influential studies of the Italian Renaissance in the early nineteenth century were Sismondi's *Histoire de républiques italiennes du moyen âge* and Roscoe's biographies of Lorenzo de' Medici and Leo X. Though they were both rooted in eighteenth-century historiography, they propounded quite different views of the age.

Sismondi's work is monumental, but the basic principles of his thesis are not difficult to summarize. He regarded liberty as the highest achievement of civilization, and thought that historical development depended more on law than culture and religion. The golden age of liberty was the age of the Italian communes. All that was admirable and valuable in modern Europe had been founded between the eleventh and the fourteenth centuries; the Medici, the Visconti, the Gonzaga and the Popes were usurpers and despots who destroyed the precious achievements of their ancestors. Sismondi did not deny the value of high-Renaissance art, but emphasized the contrast between it and the decay of political life. Henry Hallam's work on the Middle Ages, which was influential in England, repeated Sismondi's theses.[1]

Sismondi's view belongs to the eighteenth-century tradition, in which, however, the contrast between the free medieval communes and the despotic Renaissance cities was less marked. Voltaire described

Renaissance Florence as a new Athens, and the Medici as prototypes of the enlightened despot who patronizes the arts. In the wake of Renaissance historiography, he pointed out the contrast between intellectual splendour and political corruption.[2] Beside Voltaire, English historians developed the idea that the main cause, or at least the indispensable condition, of the Renaissance was the emergence of the middle class and commerce. The idea was supported by Paine, Burney, Robertson, Adam Smith, Gibbon, Goldsmith, Priestley, Russell and Thomas Warton. All of them drew parallels between the age of Pericles and the age of the Medici, and only some, like Hume and Gibbon, pointed out that the Medici were despots. The prevalent view of the Middle Ages was still not free from an anti-Catholic bias.[3] It was Gibbon who first made clear the role of the medieval communes, thereby introducing a different perspective into the debate.[4]

Before the discovery of the democratic medieval communes led to Sismondi, Roscoe brought forward a eulogistic interpretation of the Italian Renaissance which carried to extremes former ideas, but which was at odds with the traditional English view of the age as Machiavellian. The Medicis and even the notorious Leo X were for Roscoe patriots and enlightened patrons of culture; he rejected or played down the most disturbing episodes of Renaissance history, like the stories of the Borgias. Although Roscoe's history is by no means philosophical, he was the first in England to emphasize the role of Platonism in the Renaissance. Culture rather than economy, law or politics was the core of his Renaissance history, which is anti-mechanist and highlights the role of the individual. Nevertheless, Roscoe did not renounce the idea that the ultimate cause of the revival of learning was the political struggle of the preceding centuries. Roscoe enjoyed great popularity for a decade, but the colder reception of his work on Leo X in 1805 shows that contemporary interest was undergoing a change.[5]

I have introduced Roscoe, despite his limited originality, because he seems to have anticipated some of Coleridge's ideas.[6] In fact, Coleridge produced his own version of the myth of Renaissance Florence. His judgement on the mercantile class was ambiguous: he doubted wealth had increased the happiness of people, but recognised that 'all advances in civilization' were due to the industrial and trading classes. He compared the moral decadence since the seventeenth century with the greatness of Renaissance Florence (*C&S* (*CC*) 25; 64–5). Unlike contemporary politics, politics in the times 'shortly after the restoration of ancient literature' was characterized by a close 'intercourse with philosophy' (*LS* (*CC*) 172). Lorenzo, Pico, Ficino and Poliziano frequently debated metaphysical ideas, and the 'abstruse subjects of their discussion' was given great importance 'as the requisite qualifications of men placed by Providence as guides and governors of their fellow-creatures'.[7] Coleridge defined Cosimo and Lorenzo de' Medici as benefactors of their country at a time when, in the wake of Sismondi, they were generally considered as despots.[8] What Coleridge admired was the interchange between intellectuals and rulers: intellectuals provided power with a philosophical foundation; in return, rulers were patrons of culture.[9]

In short, Renaissance Florence was for Coleridge a sort of modern version of Plato's republic, a republic of the learned. This was his reply to the eighteenth-century liberal view of Florence as a new Periclean Athens. The contrast between the two interpretations became explicit when Sismondi and Thurot accused Roscoe of 'being led by his own political convictions and the constitution of his own country' to ignore the evils of Medicean despotism, and Roscoe in return accused Sismondi 'of being misled by his own love of republicanism'.[10] The episode took place in 1822; in the meantime, the younger generation of Romantics had accepted Sismondi's views. In Canto IV of *Childe Harold* (st. 48), Byron spoke of 'the Etrurian Athens' where 'was modern Luxury of Commerce born,/And buried Learning rose, redeem'd to a new morn'. In Hunt's opinion, Florence proved that a nation can be commercial and have true taste. Shelley's *Hellas* (ll. 60–3) and *Ode to Liberty* (st. IX) describe the rebirth of the Athenian spirit of Freedom in Florence.[11]

The symbolic role of Florence as a new Athens in Romantic England has neatly been summarized by Marilyn Butler. She sees Sismondi in opposition to Mme de Staël's *De l'Allemagne*, which would represent the Germanizing, conservative, authoritarian view of culture and society of which Coleridge was the English champion. The myth of the democratic communes would have been invented when Europe was threatened by the imperial tyranny of Napoleon. The later Romantics developed Sismondi's argument and the 'cult of the south' in opposition both to Napoleon and the northern, reactionary tendencies of Wordsworth, Coleridge and Southey.[12]

However, Marilyn Butler overlooks the fact that a similar contrast existed within the debate on Italian history, as the quarrel between Sismondi and Roscoe (whom she erroneously considers as an anticipation of Sismondi) shows. As a Genevan Swiss, Sismondi was motivated to depict the medieval free cities as models of democracy in opposition to Napoleon's imperial power; but such self-identification could not directly take place in England, itself the centre of an empire. Moreover, the cult of the small, free communes – which had also existed in northern Europe –

is not peculiar to the later Romantics, since it is akin to Wordsworth's view of society and his enthusiasm for Switzerland. They are both Rousseauist attitudes. How would this fit in with Butler's dichotomy of the first generation of Romantics as 'German', introverted and reactionary, and the second generation as 'Italian', extroverted and rebellious?

I think the matter can be restated as follows. The divergent political attitudes of the two generations of Romantics led to different interpretations of Italian history – Renaissance history in particular. Such approaches already existed in the eighteenth-century historiographic tradition, which was in its turn indebted to Renaissance historians.[13] In fact, the tension between social and metaphysical interests appears not only in fourteenth- versus fifteenth-century Italy, but also in pre-1450 versus post-1450 Florentine Humanism (I am obviously simplifying). The Plato of the former was the Socratic Plato who dealt with law, justice and the state; the Plato of the latter, of Ficino and his friends, was Plotinus's Plato, the metaphysician – which does not mean they did not have social interests.[14]

Romantic approaches led to various fictional images of Italy which had, among other things, a political meaning in reference to contemporary England. The south of Byron, Shelley and Peacock was, according to Marilyn Butler, a pagan land of liberty where human nature could develop in ways not repressed by civilization, and whose literature, like that of Greece, was liberal, extrovert and comic.[15] Despite the apparent clarity of the formulation, it seems to me that Greek taste in this sense fits Peacock and Byron but not Shelley, whose Greece was transcendental and had little to do with comicality and elegance.

Timothy Webb points out that Greek culture as Peacock understood it excluded the Dionysian, since it was an optimistic version of eighteenth- century epicurean Neoclassicism. Webb opposes Peacock's Greece, 'a remote, idealized, and happy world', to that of Byron, who was interested in modern Greece as a living nation.[16] Peacock's influence on Shelley was seminal, but the difference between their views of Greece, and conse- quently of the south, is remarkable. Shelley's attitude was summarized by Landor in *To Shelley*: 'He who beholds the skies of Italy/Sees ancient Rome reflected, sees beyond,/Into more glorious Hellas'. Shelley's image of the south was formed by combining Italian landscape and poetry and Greek culture:[17] but this metaphysical south of the Greek tragedians, and Dante and Calderón, is incompatible with Peacock's and Byron's.[18] Altogether, the word 'south' as a general term ought to be used cautiously. In many recent studies, southern culture has metonymically been identified with Hellenism, whereas the Italian experience of the Romantics has been underrated. However great their familiarity with

Greek culture, in reality they knew it in 'Italian translation', as it were: few of them visited Greece, whereas many of them spent a significant part of their lives in Italy.[19] Besides, a merely ideological discussion of the 'south' may induce students and scholars to believe that all they need to read in order to understand this interest of the Romantics is Derrida and Foucault rather than Dante and Ariosto.

If the definition of an image of the south common to all the younger Romantics is untenable, the idea of the north such a south is supposed to have countered is no less problematic. Public opinion in England associated metaphysics with Germany and disliked it for its obscurity, as it is evident in the reviews of Coleridge's *Lay Sermons* and *Biographia Literaria*. That is, Germany was viewed in a similar way with a mixture of attraction and suspicion. Byron cannot have made fun of the metaphysical tendencies of the north in general to provoke English readers, since his was the prevalent view in Great Britain.[20]

Byron saw a relation between metaphysical ambitions and social cant, to which he opposed Italian naturalness. However, I think Italian spontaneity had little to do with innate anti-metaphysical attitudes, but in large part depended on the backwardness of education. The vanity of English society, whose members claimed to be learned and were just silly, struck Foscolo and irritated Byron – who preferred no education at all (the renowned spontaneity) or the Catholic education he chose for Allegra.[21] The partiality of Byron's view of Italy is demonstrated by the fact that the German philosophy which met with resistance in England was easily assimilated in Italy, whose philosophic tradition, from the Florentine Platonism to Vico, was consonant with it. The anti-metaphysical strain in Italian literature, however popular in England, should not conceal the existence of a metaphysical tradition, of which some Romantics were aware.

Coleridge's ideal Italy was a garden in which nature and culture, sense and reason, poetry and philosophy, Classical and Christian culture achieved an enviable balance – a balance the younger Romantics never looked for, since they admired Italy as a pagan land. Coleridge himself never accomplished such a balance, as the predominance of the Christian element in his late thought demonstrates. He could only portray, as a symbol of that desired synthesis, Boccaccio sitting in the garden with a copy of Homer and Ovid's 'Holy Book of Love'. The political connotation of the garden emerges from the definition of Florence as 'once free' (line 73), and is reinforced by *Church and State*, in which contemporary Italy is described as a garden where one may find 'every gift of God – only not freedom'.[22] Boccaccio is an 'all enjoying and all-blending sage', the Renaissance polymath with whom Coleridge identified. The landscape is literary and, given the presence of Florence as the 'brightest star of star-bright Italy', the garden is also the ideal enclosure in which the 'literary clergy' described by Coleridge in *Church and State* would live, in harmony with political power. Coleridge's political works are above all concerned with education and the role culture ought to play in society – aspects which are central to the civic humanist tradition, as he knew through Petrarch.[23] It is a vision of the institutionalization of culture which the younger Romantics, in their distaste for institutions, would have found unpalatable. Far from the Pantisocratic isolation Coleridge had desired in his youth, his own life at Highgate could be seen as a vague reflection of the ideal portrayed in *The Garden of Boccaccio*. However coincidental Coleridge's choice of Boccaccio as a symbol may have been, it was not at odds with his views: Boccaccio the Humanist, unlike Dante and Tasso as the Romantics pictured them, stands for the attempt to arrive at a constructive compromise with the society he lived in.

The German element of Coleridge's culture can be overstated in a neat contrast to the younger 'Italian' Romantics, giving a distorted account of cultural history in early nineteenth-century England. His indictments of Renaissance Neoplatonism cannot be interpreted as the result of a specific anti-Italian attitude: they are in part based on Anglican anti-Roman rhetoric, and in part due to his general attitude to pantheism. His indecision about the paganism of Renaissance culture shows that he was not certain of it: there were Boccaccio, Ariosto and Pulci, but there were Dante, Petrarch and Michelangelo. It is noteworthy that his last extended remark on Italian culture, *The Garden of Boccaccio*, was a sympathetic one.

Even if the younger generation of Romantics used their fictional image of the south to oppose the conservatism of their elders and identified it as 'German', a cultural dichotomy did not exist in reality. Coleridge was not the English counterpart of Mme de Staël, the champion of a cultural project which opposed the north to the south, and which extolled German above any other tradition. He did not oppose German to Italian culture, but envisaged their combination. He wrote in 1815:

> Were I forced into exile, or if, without a perforce, I could take with me those whom I most love and regard, I should wish to pass my summers at Zurich, and the remaining eight months alternately at Rome and in Florence, so to join as much as I could German depth, Swiss ingenuity, and the ideal genius of Italy. (*CL* IV 569)

The different view of Italy each of the major Romantics held should not conceal the most important point for a literary history of the period: that their interest was decisively stimulated by the presence of Italian culture in the English Renaissance, of which their poetry intended to be a revival. It is frequently repeated that Romanticism is an invention which postdates the fact; but as early as 1820 Coleridge wrote of the

> re-establishment of the Romantic and Italian School in Germany and G. Britain by the genius of Wieland, Goethe, Tieck, Southey, Scott, and Byron among the poets, and the Lectures of Coleridge, Schlegel, Campbell and others among the Critics. (*IS* 158)

The note is not unique, and the ideal combination of English, German and Italian culture underlies all Coleridge's lectures. Therefore, as far as *Italy* is concerned, his theory and the younger Romantics' practice are not opposed but complementary: as in the Renaissance, a scholarly and a poetic interest complete each other. Even Byron, who in many respects was influenced by the eighteenth-century Anglo-French tradition, is not an exception: his fabulous image of Italy was formed on Italian poetry and history (the Italian root), the Elizabethans and Otway (the English root), Mme de Staël, Schiller and Anne Radcliffe (the 'German', Gothic root). Such complementarity can also be traced in the political opinions of the major Romantics. A misinterpreted aspect of Byron's and Shelley's south is their admiration for Classical Athens, which is frequently quoted in support of the view of them as liberal. However, their admiration was ambiguous, since the Athens of Pericles (whom Shelley rarely mentioned) is not the same as Plato's (who is everywhere in Shelley's works).[24] Plato's republic can hardly be considered liberal, so that even in this case the ideas of the younger and the elder Romantics seem complementary rather than opposite: Coleridge's statesman's manual was the Bible, Shelley's was Plato's *Republic* – both autocratic models.

Coleridge and Shelley are two poles of the same world, two extremes of the same context, and this should justify the use of Romanticism as a common category for both. There is no need to resort to an improbable spirit of the age, like Thomas McFarland, or to break Romanticism up into unrelated Romanticisms, like Marilyn Butler. The ideas of state, culture and the social role of the poet as the major Romantics conceived them can be inscribed into the same intellectual horizon, though at different points on it: and this is a sufficient reason to preserve the term Romanticism as a common category for them all.

But fortunately Romantic interest in Italy cannot be reduced to its ideological implications, however important they are. This study was intended to show that Italian culture did contribute something substantial to Coleridge's intellectual life. His Italy cannot be compared to Byron's and Shelley's in terms of poetry, but intellectually it is no less fascinating.

Notes

Introduction

1   *The Norton Anthology of English Literature*, ed. M. H. Abrams, Norton: New York and London, 1962 (5th edn, rpt. 1986), vol. II, p. 329.

2   'First and Last Romantics', *Studies in Romanticism*, IX (1970) (rpt. in his *The Ringers in the Tower. Studies in the Romantic Tradition*, Chicago UP: Chicago & London, 1971, p. 226).

3   'The English in Italy' (Oct 1826), *The Mary Shelley Reader*, eds. B. T. Bennett and C. E. Robinson, OUP: New York and London, 1990, pp. 341–2. How much the hostility to France in Napoleon's time was felt appears from Coleridge's fanciful anecdote of his escape from Rome in 1806. He claimed he had to flee from Italy owing to his Francophobic reputation (*CL* II 1174–7 (Aug 1806); *BL* (*CC*) I 216; *L Lects* (*CC*) II 13–14).

4   A map of Coleridge's travels through Italy appears in *CN* II Notes, plates II and III.

5   A. Mozzillo (ed.), *Viaggiatori stranieri nel Sud*, Edizioni di Comunità: Milano 1964, pp. 9–13. The introduction to the book, a valuable anthology of travellers in the south of Italy, is the best study available on the subject.

6   Mozzillo, ibid., pp. 12, 40–5, 47. On Coleridge's view of roads and inns in the south, see *CN* II 2744 (Nov–Dec 1805). Coleridge had a good knowledge of travel literature. He found in Leckie's library in Malta John Moore's *A View of Society and Manners in Italy with anecdotes relating to some eminent character* (6th edn 1795), from which he copied out the stories of the Foscaris and Marino Faliero (*CN* II 2713, 2714 (Oct–Nov 1805); Sultana (1969) 377). He knew Sharp's vitriolic travel book on Italy and held both Sharpian and Moorist travellers in low regard. He found the latter more entertaining, but justified the former in part (*CN* II 2719 (Nov–Dec 1805)). Sterne's *Sentimental Journey* was 'poor sickly stuff' [*TT* (*CC*) 17 Aug 1833]. In Malta he perused Patrick Brydone's *Tour through Sicily and Malta* and Henry Swinburne's *Travels in the Two Sicilies* (Sultana (1969) 197; Coffman xxii). On Swinburne, who wrote one of the less erudite and most valuable guides of his time, see Mozzillo, ibid., pp. 23, 26.

Other works on Italy Coleridge may have read are: Addison's *Letters from Italy*, in *The Poetical Works of Joseph Addison* (Edinburgh 1793); Gray's letters from Italy in *The Works of Thomas Gray* (London 1814); Marianna Starke's popular *Travels on the Continent* (London 1820) (Coffman 2, 91, 201).

7   See Mozzillo, ibid., pp. 34–7. Thomas Jones (1743–1803), a Welsh artist, recorded that the Romans used to arrange English visitors into three classes: artists, 'mezzi cavalieri' (those who lived 'independently of any profession' but were not rich), and 'Cavalieri or Milordi' (D. Sutton, 'Aspects of British Collecting, Part II', *Apollo*, NS CXVI, No 250, Dec 1982, pp. 405–6).

8   On the origins of Romantic travel, see G. B. Parks, 'The Turn to the Romantic in the Travel Literature of the Eighteenth Century', *Modern Language Quarterly*, XXV (1964), 22–33. Coleridge read Francesco Ferrara, *Storia generale dell'Etna* (Catania 1793), and was impressed by Greenough's description of the volcano (*CN* II 1864, 1866 (Jan–Feb 1804)). Another source for his interest was Henry Swinburne, who described his ascent of Etna from Nicolosi in Romantic tones (Mozzillo, *Viaggiatori stranieri nel Sud*, pp. 103–9). Coleridge set *The Mad Monk* (1800) on Mt Etna; the sublimity of southern landscape had been celebrated before the Romantics by Ann Radcliffe and Patrick Brydone. On Coleridge's ascent of Etna, see *CN* II 2170–7 (Aug 1804); *CL* II 1157 (Dec 1804). He later referred to the volcano to illustrate diverse concepts (see e.g. *CL* III 482 (Apr 1814); *CM* (*CC*) I 421 (1826–9); N 49.8 f11 and 11v (Nov 1830)). The places whose natural beauty aroused his enthusiasm were Taormina and the region between Taormina and Messina (*CN* II 2688, 2696 (Oct 1805)), Valverde near Catania (*CN* II 2682 (Sept–Oct 1805)), Mount Vesuvius (*CN* II 2748 (Nov–Dec 1805)), the hilly landscape and the vineyards of Umbria and the Marmore waterfall near Terni (*CN* II 2848, 2849 (May 1806)).

9   Mozzillo, ibid., pp. 18–19. This does not mean Coleridge was indifferent to poetic celebrations of Italy. Henry Crabb Robinson reported that he repeated Goethe's *Kennst du das Land* 'with tears in his eyes' (*CRB* I 124). For a fragment of his translation of Goethe's poem, see *PW* (*CC*), poem No 582.

10   Although I often refer to Italy in general, it must not be forgotten that Italy was a cultural and geographic expression but not a political expression in Coleridge's time. Therefore, the influence of the Roman Church on politics was uneven: it was stronger in the Papal State and the Two Sicilies, whereas it became weaker in the north, first in the wake of eighteenth-century Enlightenment (in Tuscany, Parma, and the Austrian territories), and later as a consequence of liberalism, which theorized the separation between Church and state (as in Piedmont). Similar attempts were made in the south, but they did not lead to significant practical results, probably because of the backwardness of the region and its monarchs.

11   On works and faith, *CN* II 2206 (Oct 1804), II 2434 (Feb 1805); on miracles and saints, *CN* III 3779, 3868 (1810); *CM* (*CC*) I 47–8; on charity, *Friend* (*CC*) I 283; on Purgatory, *MC* 327. He attended the ceremony of beatification of Francesco di Geronimo in Rome (*CN* II 2845 (May 1806)). Transubstantiation was to him a special case: see *CN* III 3868 (Jun 1810); *AR* (*CC*) 189–90; *CM* (*CC*) I 313–14.

12   On the threats of clergy, *CN* II 2229, 2216; *Friend* (*CC*) I 284; on ignorance, N

10.11 f22v (1828), *C&S* (*CC*) 136; *LS* (*CC*) 6; *CM* (*CC*) I 845, I 313–14; *TT* (*CC*)
24 Jul 1831; on monastic orders, *CN* II 2854 (1806), II 3065 (May 1807); on
processions, *CN* II 2561 (1805); *LS* (*CC*) 64–5; on wisdom and pilgrimages, *CN*
II 2664 (Sept 1805); *Friend* (*CC*) I 56; on faith and reason, *CM* (*CC*) I 203; on
ancient paganism, *CN* II 2561, 2378 (1805). Few English intellectuals realized
that the supposed irrationality of Roman Catholicism was at odds with the
existence of the Scholastic tradition. Coleridge believed that 'the Council of
Trent made the Papists what they are', and that all the great English Schoolmen
opposed the temporal power of the Roman Church (*TT* (*CC*) 27 Apr 1823;
4 May 1833).

13 See also *Friend* (*CC*) I 566. This view did not apply to northern Catholics, whom
he considered as hardly comparable to Mediterranean ones (N Q. f47 (1833)).
He thought the Irish were the worst of all, but his reason for thinking so was not
merely religious.

The experience of Italian paganism influenced Coleridge's view of the origins
of drama. He considered the Italian representations for Christmas, which recall
the Mysteries, as examples of the possible earliest forms of drama. Such representations showed the persistence of polytheistic elements in Italian culture. The
example he gave was an improvized dialogue between a mountebank and a
spectator he saw in Naples which struck him for its Priapesque character
(*L Lects* (*CC*) I 49–51, 54; *CN* II 2717 (1805)). Sir William Hamilton, the
British ambassador to Naples, had made much of similar ideas in a pamphlet
which influenced Richard Payne Knight and the Romantics at Marlow (Butler
(1981) 130–2).

14 On the *Index, TT* (*CC*) 6 Aug 1831; *Friend* (*CC*) I 74. On the Irish question, see
CM (*CC*) I 732–3; *CRB* I 19; *Cormorant* II 456–7; *C&S* (*CC*) xxxv–xxxix, xlii–li.

15 *Lects 1795* (*CC*) 89; *LS* (*CC*) 131 ff.; *CM* (*CC*) I 831–2 (1823). His final view
appeared in *Church and State*, a part of which is devoted to the 'Church of the
Antichrist' (*CC* 129–45). His interest is evident from the number of Italian
books on the subject he bought or read: Domenico Bernini (fl. 1800–1825),
Istoria di tutte l'eresie (Venice 1745) (*CN* III 3898), Antonino Diana
(1585–1663), *De sacramento matrimonii* (Venice 1698) (*CN* II 2435 (Feb 1805)),
Antonio Pilati di Tassullo (1733–1802), *Di una riforma d'Italia* (Venice 1767)
(*CN* IV 5468 (1826); *C&S* (*CC*) 80–1, 120–3), Girolamo Vincenzo Spanzotti
(1741–1812), *Disordini morali e politici della Corte di Roma* (2nd edn, Torino
1801) (N 40.35 f16 ff. (Jul 1828); *C&S* (*CC*) 129, 136–9).

16 *CN* III 4145 (Apr 1812). Vittorio Barzoni, the author of *Rivoluzioni della
repubblica Veneta* (Valletta 1804) whom he met in Malta, stimulated his interest
in Venetian history (*CN* II 2677 (Sept–Nov 1805); App D); see also *C&S* (*CC*) 86.

17 On Genoa, see *Watchman* (*CC*) 246–7, 325–6, 359–67; *CN* I 206 (1796–7);
CRD I 167 (1811), where he criticized Bentham's censure of the laws on usury,
which he regarded as a valid deterrent: 'Genoa fell by becoming a people of
money–lenders instead of merchants.' On the south, *Watchman* (*CC*) 74, 101,
183; *EOT* (*CC*) I 144. On Italy in general, see *EOT* (*CC*) I 23–6 (1798), III 60–3
(1800).

18 On the north of Italy, see *Watchman* (*CC*) 297; *CN* III 3752 (1810); *TT* (*CC*) 11
Apr 1833; N F°187 f80v (2 Mar 1832); N 54.16 f18 (1833 or 1834); *Cormorant*

II 398. After his return from Italy, he wrote comments and articles on the south, on which he said he had been working for nine months (see *CL* II 1164 (2 Feb 1805), 1165 (30 Apr 1805), 1181 (16 Sept 1806); *CL* III 238 (9 Oct 1809)).

19 *TT (CC)* 16 Apr 1834; *CL* II 1157 (1804); *Friend (CC)* I 260–1; *EOT (CC)* II 281 n.

20 *CN* II 2163, 2229, 2230 (1804); *CL* II 1150–56 (1804). On justice, *CN* II 2261; *Friend (CC)* I 261. On taxation, *CN* II 2231 (1804); *TT (CC)* 16 Apr 1834. On the government, *C Talker* 210.

21 *CN* II 2324 (Dec 1804); *CM (CC)* I 305; *TT (CC)* 16 Apr 1834. A constitution modelled on the British was introduced in Sicily in 1812, but it was abolished – with Castlereagh's approval – after the fall of Napoleon (Brand (1957) 197, 200). The experience of Sicily changed Coleridge's view of revolutionary dangers in England. With reference to England in 1793–6, he wrote: 'I who had been travelling in Sicily and Italy, countries where there were real grounds for the fear (of a revolution), was deeply impressed with the difference' (*TT (CC)* 8 Jun 1833).

22 *CN* II 2162 (Aug–Nov 1804). Cf. *CN* II 2677; *CL* II 1060 (1804); *Friend (CC)* I 564, 571; *EOT (CC)* III 86 (1804). On English interests in the region, see Brand (1957) 196–7.

23 *CN* IV 4866 (Jan 1822); 5412 (Jul 1826). Coleridge compared the character of the Spaniards with the Neapolitans to point out the greater sense of dignity of the former, though they lived in similar political conditions (*EOT (CC)* II 97–8). He planned a sonnet on the 1821 insurrection in Naples (*CN* IV 4801 (Feb 1821)).

24 Although Hazlitt's familiarity with Italian culture was, excluding painting, inferior to the average, his *Notes of a Journey through France and Italy* show that a pinch of common sense helped to get over commonplaces which few travellers were able to avoid. He noted it had become nonsense to talk of banditti, and that travel was safe as far south as Naples (*The Complete Works of William Hazlitt*, ed. P. P. Howe, 21 vols., Dent: London and Toronto, 1932, vol. X, pp. 248, 256). Courtesans, 'from which one cannot separate the name of Italy even in idea', were not more numerous than in London (p. 250). Generalizations about Italian laziness were unfounded, since the Po plain was as well cultivated as the best parts of the English country (pp. 200, 275–6). Though he blamed the Roman Church, he appreciated the behaviour of priests in Rome, who were never polemic with Protestants (pp. 214–16, 261).

25 Hunt moved to Italy to set up a new journal with the assistance of Shelley and Byron (*The Autobiography of Leigh Hunt*, ed. J. Morpurgo, Cresset Press: London 1949, p. 289). He set off with his family in 1821 and spent four years abroad. His experience of Italy, as told in his *Autobiography*, was genuine and reasonable in comparison to many other travellers. Cultural reminiscences are frequent but not obsessive, and his censure of some detestable aspect of Italian politics and society never turns into an invective. At first he found Italy as he expected it (ibid., p. 311). Whereas travellers often saw in antiquities decay and death, Hunt was struck by the new look many Italian houses had despite their age (p. 334). The most unhappy part of his sojourn was the last, when he resided at Maiano, a place full of reminiscences (Boccaccio, Michelangelo) (pp. 370–2). He eventually got tired of harsh landscapes and cold winters, and returned to

England (p. 376). Scholarly attitudes to Italy, like Ruskin's, are more characteristic of the Victorian than the Romantic age.

26 Byron's observations on Italian life are well known and too numerous to be quoted here. The most comprehensive example is the letter he wrote to John Murray on 21 Feb 1820 (*BL&J* VII 42–3), but many other letters between the late 1816 and 1820 are rich in comments. Thereafter his remarks became rarer. On Shelley's caustic observations, see *SL* 58, 60, 69, 316–17, 323, 363. The only positive remark on Italian women appears at p. 92 (6 Apr 1819).

27 P. W. Martin, *Byron. A Poet before His Public*, CUP 1982, p. 183.

28 On account of its cheapness, Coleridge wished Sicily could become British, so he could settle and live there, which would have solved his insoluble financial problems (*CL* II 1059–60 (8 Feb 1804)). A major reason for Landor's residence in Italy was financial. He did not have contacts with Italians, whom he despised, though he liked to converse with Tuscan country folk (M. Elwin, *Landor. A Replevin*, Macdonald: London 1958, p. 216). Examples of this kind are numerous. It is interesting to compare the Romantic with the early eighteenth–century view of Italians. Addison found them more silent, sober, ceremonious and reserved than the French. The Venetians, though they went crazy for some days during carnival, were naturally grave (*Remarks on Several Parts of Italy, &c., In the Years 1701, 1702, 1703*, in *Works*, London 1741, vol. II, pp. 15, 31). Horace Walpole thought that vices varied in form only: England had elections, drinking and whoring, Florence had Jesuits, Cicisbeos, Corydon and Alexis (i.e. homosexuals). The Florentines were not as mad as the English; Italian faults were national, English faults individual. The incidents of a day in London would supply Italy for a year (*The Letters of Horace Walpole*, ed. Mrs P. Toynbee, Clarendon Press: Oxford 1903–25, vol. I, p. 47, Florence, 24 Jan 1740). Walpole found Florentine people moderate in behaviour and cool in politics: in short the reverse of the English, who were generally mad (ibid., pp. 83–4, 25 Sept 1740).

29 But as John Ash and Louis Turner argue, when the tourist travels in poorer countries, he takes up an aristocratic status anyway (*The Golden Hordes. International Tourism and the Pleasure Periphery*, Constable: London 1975, p. 50).

30 Although Wordsworth's familiarity with Italy was inferior to the average – he did not make a proper tour until 1837 – he was one of the very few who realised the unity of Alpine culture after his pedestrian tour in 1790. His interest in mountains and lakes helped him with the discovery, whose epitome is the description of his unintentional crossing of the Simplon Pass in *The Prelude* (1805, bk. VI, ll. 488–591). In *Descriptive Sketches* (line 77) the scene moved abruptly from the French side of the Alps to Como. Most travellers felt the Alps were merely a border, which is culturally incorrect. Wordsworth's mental map of Europe did not oppose the north to the south, but Lake Districts as images of nature (Cumberland, Switzerland and North Italy) to the city (Cambridge, London and Paris).

31 In *A Philosophical View of Reform* (1819–20), Shelley expressed admiration for Germany, which possessed passionate poetry, deep religious sentiment (though distorted), a flexible language, a subtle and deep philosophy (though mixed with errors), and flourishing plastic arts (*SCW* VII 15). German philosophy only

saw the silver side of things, but it was better than French, 'which only saw the narrow edge of it' (*SL* 266 (18 Feb 1821); see also p. 278 (? Spring 1821)). On Shelley and Goethe, see T. Webb, *The Violet in the Crucible. Shelley and Translation*, Clarendon Press: Oxford 1976, chs. IV and V.

32   See H. Weisinger, 'The English Origins of the Sociological Interpretation of the Renaissance', *Journal of the History of Ideas*, XI (1950), p. 328; and Hale (1954) 80.

33   On Shelley's and Byron's Dante, see Ellis; and my chapter II below. Timothy Webb reminds us that Shelley's admiration for Greece did not prevent him from criticizing some aspects of its culture, such as the subordination of women (*Shelley: A Voice not Understood*, Manchester UP: Manchester 1977, p. 194). He resorted to Dante's and Petrarch's image of the women, whose Christian sources he does not seem to have considered at all.

Coleridge and Italian Lyric Poetry

1   Neither Boileau nor Preston first regulated the composition of the sonnet – an idea Coleridge found in Preston's preface to his love poems (*Poetical Works*, 2 vols., Dublin 1793, I, p. 267).

2   *PW* (EHC) I 1139. Petrarch was frequently blamed for his conceits, that is, the artificiality of his sentiment. The idea was even shared by Preston, who found in Petrarch's Platonism the reason for his obscurity (*Poetical Works*, I, pp. 262–3).

3   Coleridge quoted a sonnet on the sonnet of the Italianizing Anna Seward, whose style resembled 'racked and tortured Prose' more than poetry (*PW* (EHC) II 1140). Hostility to the Italian sonnet in English was common: Samuel Johnson, Charlotte Smith, Erasmus Darwin, George Steevens, later Walter Savage Landor and others, agreed on the point (Havens 521–3; 535; cf. Brand (1957) 95).

4   Raymond Dexter Havens' bibliography of sonnets published in the eighteenth century provides a statistical view of the situation (Havens 685–97). Sonnets published between 1700 and 1770 are listed in a page and a half, whereas sonnets published after 1770 fill ten pages.

5   Milton may have contributed to the fortune of Petrarch's sonnets before the full rediscovery of the Elizabethan poets thanks to the structure of his own sonnet which, though original, is more like the Petrarchan than the Shakespearian sonnet. Elizabethan sonnets were usually neglected (Havens 480). A more correct evaluation of both early Italian and English sonnets was a result of the process we are analysing.

6   Marshall 124. Susannah Dobson's translation enjoyed seven editions by 1805. Marshall's study, though arid, is still the single richest source of information on its subject.

7   The most sensational point of de Sade's biography was his identification of Laura as an ancestor of his. Petrarch became the first specimen of the Romantic hero exemplified later in different forms by Dante and Tasso (and Byron), even if writers like Horace Walpole, James Beattie and Alexander Tytler objected to de Sade's theses. Tytler is the author of an *Essay on the Life and Character of Petrarch* (1784). Coleridge may have read or heard of it from Charles Lamb,

who quoted it in a letter to Coleridge on 8 November 1796 (*The Letters of Charles and Mary Lamb* (1796–1817), ed. E. W. Marrs, Jr, 3 vols., Cornell UP, Ithaca & London, 1975, vol. I, p. 60). However, it must be emphasized that the legend of Petrarch's life was not invented in the Romantic age. Biographic interest developed in the Renaissance, when the *imitatio vitae* was almost as important as the *imitatio stili* (L. Baldacci, *Il Petrarchismo italiano nel Cinquecento*, Liviana: Padova 1974, pp. 50–1).

8   Havens 486. Some sonnets of Petrarch were included in the standard exercises of translation selected by Agostino Isola, the teacher of Italian and Spanish at Cambridge since 1764. William Hayley, Thomas James Mathias and William Wordsworth read Italian with him.

9   The last tercet of 'Solo et pensoso' is an example of Preston's flattening translations: 'Yet not a path so desolate is found,/But love is there, to drink my vital blood,/And mem'ry there, to goad the slumb'ring woes.' (*Poetical Works*, vol. I, p. 269). The original goes: 'Ma pur sí aspre vie né sí selvagge/cercar non so ch'Amor non venga sempre/ragionando meco, et io co llui'.
    Mary Robinson is another Petrarchizing sonneteer Coleridge admired. According to Havens (689), of her seventy-one sonnets forty-six are Petrarchan, five Shakespearean and twenty irregular. (Havens classifies as Petrarchan only the rhyme schemes ABBA ABBA CDE CDE, or CDC DCD, although different arrangements appear in Petrarch.)

10 Smith's poems enjoyed eleven English editions and were reprinted in America (Havens 503). Marshall (136–7) observes that 'a number of [her] original productions . . . can hardly be distinguished from the translations.'

11 Quoted by Havens 511–12.

12 Donald H. Reiman believes that Bowles' sonnets 'embody almost every variety of sentimentality, faulty diction, awkwardly inverted word order, overobvious alliteration, and corrupted formal structure that has ever been attributed to late eighteenth–century poetry' (Introduction to Bowles, *Fourteen Sonnets and Other Poems*, Garland Press: New York & London 1978, p. vii). Reiman argues that the reason for Coleridge's admiration was due to Bowles' theme – landscape – rather than his syntax. Anna Seward was one of the most prolific sonneteers of the time. Despite her frequent references to Petrarch, she disapproved of Petrarch's as well as Shakespeare's and Spenser's conceits (Havens 501 n. 1).

13 Coleridge's first published poem, *The Abode of Love*, appeared in *The World*, the Della Cruscan magazine, in 1790 (*PW* (*CC*), editorial commentary to poem No. 20). The magazine was edited by the second Della Cruscan group, which must be distinguished from the original one that contributed to the *Florence Miscellany* (1785). The Della Cruscans, who anticipated the Romantics in their enthusiasm for anything Italian, experimented with several stanzaic and metrical forms including the sonnet. Petrarch was one of their favourite Italian poets, and attracted in particular William Parsons and Bertie Greatheed. Although they have often been abused, Edward E. Bostetter points out that 'the characteristics for which the Della Cruscans were attacked were in great part simply characteristics common to the sentimental poetry of the period', and that 'all the major Romantics in their youth wrote poems not much different from the poetry attacked by Gifford' ('The Original Della Cruscans and the Florence Miscellany',

Huntington Library Quarterly, XIX, No 3 1956, p. 298). Public hostility toward them may have been politically motivated.

14 Lamb's, Lloyd's and Southey's sonnets were not influenced by Petrarch, although Lloyd, whose sonnets have a Petrarchizing structure (Havens 518), included the translation of eight sonnets of Petrarch in his *Poems on Various Subjects* (1795) (F. J.-L. Mouret, *Les traducteurs anglais de Pétrarque 1754–1798*, Didier: Paris 1976, pp. 222–3). Lamb's attitude to Petrarch was critical: he claimed Petrarch had taught him to love creatures more than their Creator (*Cormorant* II 422).

15 Mays points out that Coleridge's sonnet *To the River Otter*, for example, recalls Bowles' on rivers, especially *To the River Itchen*; but Bowles' partake in their turn-of-an eighteenth-century 'fashion for sonnets on the subjects of rivers and streams . . . associated with Collins.' Thomas Warton, Thomas Brydges and Charlotte Smith wrote sonnets on the subject (*PW (CC)* editorial note No 140).

16 The general idea of the *Sonnets on Eminent Characters*, published in the *Morning Chronicle* in December 1794 and January 1795, is probably derived from the tradition of Milton's sonnet to Cromwell, but the sonnets belong in all other respects to the Bowles and Della Cruscan school. The *Sonnets on Various Authors*, a pamphlet Coleridge introduced and edited in the autumn of 1796, show his enthusiasm for Bowles, whose sonnets were included in the selection. Southey also wrote political sonnets.

17 Laura appears in *On a Lady Weeping*, an imitation of Nicolaus Archius' *De Lacrimis Puellae*, which is in its turn an imitation of Ariosto ('LOVELY gems of radiance meek/Trembling down my Laura's cheek') (*PW (EHC)* I 17 (?1790); and *PW (CC)* editorial note No 46); in the first–known manuscript of *Sonnet: to an Old Man in the Snow (with Samuel Favell)*, l. 9 (later replaced by 'Sara') (*PW (CC)*, editorial note No 88); in sonnet XI on Eminent Characters, *To Richard Brinsley Sheridan* ('And sweet thy voice, as when o'er LAURA's bier/Sad Music trembled thro' Vauclusa's glade') (*PW (EHC)* I 88); in *Lines on the Portrait of a Lady*, l. 15 (*PW (CC)* poem No 126 (Feb–Mar 1796?)); and in *The Snow-Drop*, lines 5, 32 and 53 (*PW (EHC)* I 356–8 (1800)), even if Mary Robinson, one of whose pseudonyms was Laura Maria, is probably meant here, since she inspired Coleridge's poem (*PW (CC)* editorial note No 165). In 1796 Coleridge advised Southey to substitute Petrarch and Vaucluse for Rousseau and Ermenonville in a sonnet which was intended to be Southey's inscription for Rousseau's cenotaph at Ermenonville (*CL* I 244–5). 'That Petrarch was often in the sonneteers' minds – writes Marshall – is proved by innumerable references to him and Laura' (Marshall 340).

18 For the early statement, see *PW (EHC)* II 1139; for the late article, P. M. Zall, 'Coleridge and "Sonnets from Various Authors"', *Cornell Library Journal*, II (spring 1967), p. 62. A sonnet composed of eleven lines from *Youth and Age* and of three nonsense lines exemplified Coleridge's ideas.

19 It is noteworthy that even William Roscoe, who did more than anybody else to popularize Italian culture in England in the last decade of the century, had reservations about the sonnet. He argued that its structure was so rigid that it limited the free development of thought, and made passion the most common subject of sonneteers (*Life of Lorenzo de' Medici*, London 1797 (3rd edn), pt. I, pp. 272–3).

20 See Shaffer (1975) 28–30.

21 *Cormorant* I 152–3.

22 See *CL* I 453–4 (4 Jan 1799): 'I owe it to my industry that I can read old German, & even the old low-german, better than most of even the educated Natives – it has greatly enlarged my knowledge of the English language.'

23 On Dante and Boccaccio, see ch. III. Boccaccio is the source of the first Italian sentence Coleridge transcribed in his journal on 10 November, 1803 (*CN* I 1649).

24 *CL* II 1059 (8 Feb 1804). William Wordsworth's first approach to Italian literature may date from his boyhood, since he left a copy of Hoole's translation of Tasso as a farewell presentation to the Hawkshead library in 1787 (B. R. Schneider, *Wordsworth's Cambridge Education*, CUP 1957, p. 103). At Cambridge he paid more attention to Spanish and Italian, which he read with Agostino Isola, than to the obligatory subjects. Isola introduced him to Italian epics (Ariosto, Tasso), and lyric poetry (especially sixteenth-century lyric and Metastasio) (see Sturrock (1984–5)). William had a copy of the *Orlando Furioso* with him on his tour of the Alps in 1790 (Sturrock (1984–5) 806). The Prelude testifies to his early knowledge of Ariosto and Tasso (1805; bk. IX, lines 454–6). He decided to improve his Italian in 1794, and in 1795–6 he and Dorothy were studying it eagerly (Sturrock (1984–5) 806). In March 1796 they were reading Ariosto, Machiavelli, Boccaccio, and Enrico Caterino Davila in the original (*Cormorant* I 439; and 201 n. 23). In 1802–3 Wordsworth translated Ariosto, 'completing as much as a hundred lines a day' (Sturrock (1984–5) 808 n. 43).

25 *CN* I 1269. On Coleridge's knowledge of the Italian language, see my Appendix.

26 E. L. Griggs, introduction to letter to Thomas Poole, 7 Sept 1801 (*CL* II 755). Thomas Wedgwood refused Coleridge as a companion on his tour of the Continent because of his bad health and his 'ignorance of French and Italian' (*CL* II 936 (12 Mar 1803)).

27 Madeira, the Azores and the Canary Islands are mentioned *CL* II 719, 726, 739, 761, 889, 903, 906, 919, 965, 1021, 1035, 1041, 1043, 1049; Spain and Portugal, 896, 922, 924, 938; France, 786, 922, 924, 955; Italy appears first 889, then 901, 913, 919, 924, 928, 939, 1049. He finally decided 'to go to Malta & thence to Sicily' (*CL* II 1050 (31 Jan 1804)). On Italy, see also *CL* II 1059, 1065, 1067, 1084, 1086.

28 *Opera quae extant omnia*, 4 vols., Basel 1554. The volumes remained at Keswick when he left for Malta, even though he intended to return them (*CL* IV 655 (16 Jul 1816)). In 1812 he reassured Mrs Sotheby he would return them soon (*CL* III 364), but the following year he was still asking his wife for them (*CL* III 431). Sotheby received his volumes back in 1816.

29 An edition whose small type is uninviting (*Cormorant* I 444). Besides, it is full of blunders, as he noted in 1808: 'Editio hæc innumeris mendis scatet – et erratis deformatur, singulis fere paginis, quæ omnem sensum prorsus adimant – præsertim in poematibus' (*CN* III 3360).

30 The title is given in *Cormorant* II 425. Coleridge purchased a copy of Petrarch's Latin writings, that is vols. I–III (in one) of the folio edition he had borrowed from Sotheby (*Cormorant* II 424). In 1819 Henry Francis Cary presented Coleridge with another edition of Petrarch, *Il Petrarca di nuovo ristampato* (Venice 1651) (C. C. Seronsy, 'More Coleridge Marginalia', *Studies in Philology*,

LII, No 3, Jul 1955, pp. 497–8). On Coleridge's editions of Petrarch, see Coffman 161–2.

31 The Roman cipher indicates the number of the poem in the edition I have used (see bibliography). On the Romantic fortune of 'Solo et pensoso', see *Le Rime*, eds. G. Carducci and S. Ferrari, Sansoni: Firenze 1899 (rpt. 1965), p. 53.

32 Other poems he marked, the sonnet 'Quanto piú m'avicino' (XXXII), which echoes 'Voi ch'ascoltate', and the *canzone* 'Sí è debile il filo' (XXXVII), deal with the vanity of human hopes and the transitoriness of things. The only political poem he noted was 'O aspectata in ciel' (XXVIII), the *canzone* to Giacomo Colonna for the Crusade. Coleridge seems to have ignored Petrarch's 'patriotic' poems like 'Italia mia' which were popular with other Romantics (for instance, Shelley was particularly fond of 'Italia mia') (Brand (1957) 96–7).

33 Petrarch argues in the first poem that he would follow Laura, who is dead, but Love advises him to renounce his intention and to write on her instead. Writing as a late consolation is also the subject of the sonnet 'Se la mia vita' (XII), which Coleridge admired.

34 He marked lines 17–19, 54–6, 76–7. He found lines 87–8, 'poser in dubbio a cui/devesse il pregio di piú laude darsi', 'rather flatly worded' (*MC* 26).

35 Another proto-Baroque *canzone* Coleridge found pleasing in sound is 'Nel dolce tempo' (XXIII), in which Petrarch sees himself turned into a laurel, a swan, a stone, a fountain, and a deer. He found the thoughts ridiculous – although he overlooked the proverbial 'perché cantando il duol si disacerba' (line 4), 'because grief attenuates in singing'. I think it was such metamorphic imagery that reminded him of Herbert, even though Henry Nelson Coleridge could not find any exact imitation in George Herbert (*MC* 25). Coleridge would later repeat such an attitude to Italian Baroque poetry, that is, he would find it rich in sound and poor in thought.

36 G. M. Ridenour, 'Source and Allusion in Some Poems of Coleridge', *Studies in Philology*, LX (1963), p. 76. Some poems of Guinizelli, Buonagiunta da Lucca, Guittone d'Arezzo and Cavalcanti were included in the notes of H. F. Cary's translation of Dante's *Purgatorio*, which Coleridge read in 1817 (King (1925) 186 n. 2).

37 *PW* (EHC) I 332 n. I reproduce with small graphic variants the translation given by *CN* III 4178 n:

You peruse the causeless cares that once in my tender youth my humble pen poured forth. You read here of tears and how the quivered boy wounded me, a boy, with piercing barb. Advancing time devours all things by degrees, and as we live we die, and as we rest we are hurled onward. For if I am compared with myself I shall not seem the same. My face is changed, my ways are changed, I have a new kind of understanding, my voice sounds otherwise – With cold heart now I pity hot Lovers, and am ashamed that I myself burned. The peaceful mind shudders at past tumults, and reading again thinks that some other wrote those words.

The passages on death in life (lines 44–5) and past passion (lines 64–5) were transcribed in capitals by Coleridge. I think the motto is more than an apology to the Wordsworths, who disapproved of his passion for Sara Hutchinson, as Ernest Hartley Coleridge maintained (T. M. Raysor, 'Coleridge and "Asra"', *Studies in Philology*, XXVI, Jul 1929, pp. 308–9).

38 Anacreon and Catullus seem to have been his favourites among the latter, if we consider poems as *An Ode in the Manner of Anacreon* (*PW* (EHC) I 33–4 (1792)), *An Extempore* (*PW* (*CC*) No 58 (Jun 1793)), or adaptations like *To a Painter* (*PW* (*CC*) No 62 (Oct–Nov 1791?, rev. Aug 1793?)), as well as his assertions in chapter XVI of *Biographia*. Such preferences are surprising, since he blamed other writers whose eroticism was less overt than Anacreon's and Catullus's.

39 See *Familiarum rerum libri*, IV, 1 (the date is uncertain: between 1336 and 1352–3), in which he tells that while he was admiring the vast landscape from the top of Mt Ventoux, he accidentally opened Augustine's *Confessions*, a book he always carried, and read a warning against those who travel and admire the external world and ignore themselves. Petrarch continues: 'librum clausi, iratus michimet quod nunc etiam terrestria mirarer' (*Prose* 840).

40 See for instance *Secretum* (*Prose* 32–8, and 214). The quotation is from R. Amaturo, *Petrarca*, Laterza: Bari 1971 (rpt. 1974), p. 117. If not otherwise indicated, translation is mine.

41 Sapegno (1963) 252. Hesitation may partly be due to the fact that he combined the Provençal tradition, in which sexual fulfilment is not excluded, with the *stilnovo*, whose view of the woman as a symbol of the divine radically excludes sexuality.

42 U. Bosco, *Francesco Petrarca*, Laterza: Bari 1946 (rpt. 1961), p. 26.

43 Sapegno (1963) 254.

44 F. Montanari, *Studi sul Canzoniere del Petrarca* (2nd edn), Editrice Studium: Roma 1972, pp. 53–4.

45 Ibid., pp. 56–7.

46 Ibid., p. 57. Dante's descriptions are often more realistic and crudely detailed than Petrarch's.

47 On Petrarch's language of poetry, see Gianfranco Contini, 'Preliminari sulla lingua del Petrarca', the introduction to the edition of the *Canzoniere* used here.

48 L. S. Lockridge, *Coleridge the Moralist*, Cornell UP: Ithaca and London 1977, p. 81.

49 *PW* (EHC) I 485 (?1830). Much earlier he had written that 'All thoughts, all passions, all delights,/Whatever stirs this mortal frame,/All are but ministers of Love,/And feed his sacred flame' (*Love*, lines 1–4, *PW* (EHC) I 330 (1799)).

50 In Coleridge's words: 'The best, the truly lovely, in each & all is God. Therefore the truly Beloved is the symbol of God to whomever it is truly beloved by!' (*CN* II 2540 (Apr 1805))

51 See below on Coleridge's response to Dante's and Shakespeare's lyric poetry.

52 'Either therefore we must brutalize our notions with Pope 'Lo̶v̶eust thro' some gentle Strainers well refin'd Is gentle Love & charms all womankind' – or dissolve & thaw away all bonds of morality by the inevitable Shocks of an irresistible Sensibility with Sterne' (*CN* III 3562 (Jul–Sept 1809)).

53 *CN* III 3562 n. The *Notebooks* editor does not give the date of the entry. In any event, the subject was discussed in *The Friend* Nos 9, 21 and 23 ((*CC*) II 125–6, 295, 313–14). It is worth pointing out that Coleridge read and annotated Petrarch's Latin writings between September 1808 and November 1809 (see ch. IV). Kant is quoted from *Metaphysik der Sitten*, *Sämmtliche Werke*, ed. G. Hartenstein, Voss: Leipzig 1867–8, vol. VII, p. 205.

54 Fichte's philosophy, which Coleridge defined as a 'crude egoismus, a boastful and hyperstoic hostility to NATURE' (*BL (CC)* I 158–9), can be regarded in this respect as a paroxysmal version of Kant. What Coleridge says about Kant on duty is equally valid for Wordsworth, whose ethic became Stoic in the early nineteenth century (cf. his *Ode to Duty*).

Wordsworth is by nature incapable of being in Love, tho' no man more tenderly attached – hence he ridicules the existence of any other passion, than a compound of Lust with Esteem & Friendship, confined to one Object, first by accidents of Association, and permanently, by the force of Habit & a sense of Duty. Now this will do very well – it will suffice to make a good Husband – it may even be desirable (if the largest sum of easy & pleasurable sensations in this Life be the right aim & end of human Wisdom) . . . but still is not *Love* (*CL* III 305 (12 Mar 1811)).

55 See J. C. C. Mays, 'Coleridge's "Love": "All He Can Manage, More than He Could"', in *Coleridge's Visionary Languages*, Boydell Press: Woodbridge 1993, pp. 49–66.

56 I find it difficult to agree with Graham Davidson, who in his valuable *Coleridge's Career* (Macmillan: London 1990, pp. 132–51) would have us believe that Coleridge's failure with Sara Hutchinson was nearly a spontaneous moral decision of his rather than a true failure. Coleridge never 'disciplined himself to give up his natural hopes of Sara' (ibid., pp. 138–9). On the contrary, he wrote: 'O who has deeply felt, deeply, deeply! & not fretted & grown impatient at the inadequacy <of Words to Feeling,> of the symbol to the Being? . . . O what then are Words but articulated Sighs of a Prisoner heard from his Dungeon! powerful only as they express their utter impotence!' (*CN* II 2998 (Feb 1807)) The passage highlights the insufficiency of a mere intellectual solution to his sentimental problems.

57 *PW (EHC)* I 361–2. *To a Painter* (*PW (CC)* No 62 (Oct–Nov 1791? rev. Aug 1793)) contains descriptive imagery which seems Petrarchesque, but the poem is an adaptation of Anacreon; *Sonnet: to a Lady* (*PW (CC)* No 159 and editorial note (1799?)) seems either not by Coleridge or a mock–sonnet of the 'Nehemiah Higginbottom' group. *Alcæus to Sappho*, written between October of 1798 and January of 1799 (*PW (CC)* editorial note No 192), makes use of Petrarchesque imagery, but it is a reworking of a poem by Wordsworth, so that it does not testify to a genuine interest in Petrarchan style and imagery.

58 See for example *The Kiss and the Blush* (*PW (CC)* No 330 (Apr 1803?)), *Written at Coleorton* (*PW (CC)* No 396 (Dec 1806)), *Those Eyes of Deep & Most Expressive Blue* (*PW (CC)* No 397 (before Dec 1806)), *Thou and I* (*PW (CC)* No 612 (1820s)).

59 See for example *An Anagram of Mary Morgan's Face*: 'The Blue, the rosy Red, the Black, the White' which 'charm our sight/In Woman's Face' do not respectively refer to her eyes, her lips, her hair and her teeth, as one might expect, but are mixed up, so that the lips are white, the nose blue, and hair red (*PW (CC)* No 430 (1807? 1808?)). The rhyme scheme is also burlesque (aabb ccdd eeffff). Mock-Petrarchism was not new in his poetry, as the *Epigram on my Godmother's Beard* (1791 or 1792), and the *Sonnet to a Lady* show (*PW (CC)* No 37 and 159).

60 *PW (EHC)* I 391 (1804); II 1010 (n.d.). The latter fragment was found on a fly-leaf of Benedetto Menzini's *Poesie* (2 vols., Nizza 1782) (*PW (EHC)* II 1010;

Cormorant II 386; Coffman 141); see *PW (CC)*, editorial note to the poem. Although the exchange of hearts is corporeally impossible, Coleridge seems to imply the contrary in 'Two wedded hearts, if ere were such' (*PW* (EHC) II 1003 (1808)).

61 The idea is expressed in *Phantom* (1805), *To a Lady* (?1811), *Reason for Love's Blindness* (?1811), *Éro͂s aeì làle͂thros hetaïros* (1826), and perhaps most clearly in the fragment 'THE Body,/Eternal Shadow of the finite Soul,/The Soul's self-symbol, its image of itself./Its own yet not itself' (*PW* (EHC) II 1001 (n.d.)).

62 *Apostrophe to Beauty in Malta* (*PW (CC)* No 336 (May–Jun 1805)). The *CC* editor translates the Italian as follows: 'in charming mortal spoils/A most beautiful soul.'

63 *Donne by the Filter* (*PW (CC)* No 652), adaptations from Donne's poems composed in 1830, testifies to his interest in wit, although its tone is ironic.

64 *Separation* (?1805), the sonnet *Farewell to Love* (1806), *Recollections of Love* (1807), *Lines Written in Dejection, May 1810* (*PW (CC)* No 464), *Extempore lines in Notebook 28* (*PW (CC)* No 584), *Love's Burial-Place* (1828), *Love and Friendship Opposite* (?1830). Max F. Schulz describes *Recollections of Love* as Coleridge's 'last unqualified expression of faith in the permanence of the love–sentiment' ('The Wry Vision of Coleridge's Love Poetry', *The Personalist*, XVL, 1964, p. 223).

65 'The sweet hills where I left myself, when I departed from the place I can never depart from, are before me as I go, and still behind me is that sweet burden Love has entrusted to me. Within myself I am often amazed at myself, for I still go and yet have not moved from the sweet yoke that I have shaken off in vain many times, but the farther I go from it the closer I come. As a hart struck by an arrow, with the poisoned steel within its side, flees and feels more pain the faster it runs, so I, with that arrow in my left side which destroys me and at the same time delights me, am tormented by sorrow and weary myself with fleeing.

Tr. Robert M. Durling, *Petrarch's Lyric Poems. The 'Rime Sparse' and Other Lyrics*, Harvard UP: Cambridge (Mass.) and London, 1976.

66 English interest in Petrarch attained its height in the first two decades of the new century. Four anthologies made most of Italian lyric poetry available to English readers about 1800: Nardini and Buonaiuti's *Saggi di prose e poesie* (1796–8), Giovanni Battista Cassano's *Fiore della poesia italiana del secolo XVIII* (1802), Thomas J. Mathias' *Componimenti lirici de' più illustri poeti d'Italia* (3 vols. in 1802, and another three in 1808), and Antonio Montucci's *Italian Extracts* (1806) (Marshall 324). Petrarch enjoyed separate editions (Marshall 323, 337–8), and numerous versions appeared in literary journals (Brand (1957) 98–9). Capell Lofft's *Laura, or an Anthology of Sonnets (on the Petrarchan Model) and elegiac Quatorzains, English, Italian, Spanish, Portuguese, French, and German . . .* (5 vols., 1814) is the monument to Romantic enthusiasm for the sonnet (*DNB*). Besides, critical debate on Petrarch was lively in the wake of de Sade's and Susannah Dobson's studies (Brand (1957) 94–5, 100–101).

67 See *CN* I 998 and n. (Sept–Oct 1801); I 1003 and n. (Nov 1801); *CL* II 707 (16 Mar 1801).

68 Its rhyme scheme (abbcdadc) may also have stimulated his curiosity (*CN* II 2116). There is an earlier reference to Italian metrics, but it does not testify to a

genuine knowledge. He wrote to Wordsworth in December 1798 about modern reading of Classical poetry, which does not reproduce quantity, even though we are aware of its existence. The result is 'an effect produced in the brain similar to harmony without passing through the ear–hole. The same words, with different meanings, rhyming in Italian, is a close analogy' (*CL* I 450). He was studying German metrics at the time, and may have come across the idea in some book or journal.

69   The quote is from Elwert (1973) 2. Coleridge noted pentasyllables ('Scendi propizia'), double pentasyllables ('Come il candore D'intatta neve'), seven-syllable lines ('Siam passeggier erranti'), hendecasyllables ('Del gran padre Ocean lo speco angusto') (*CN* II 2224 *f*20). He observed that the seven-syllable line was the common metre of operatic arias, but he failed to understand that the number of syllables is variable. There can be six, seven, eight and even nine syllables depending on the accent of the last word in the line. The only characteristic of Italian verse he seems to have been aware of is synalephe, as his notation on the following line shows (*CN* II 2224 *f*20):

˘   —   ˘   —   ˘ ˘ ˘   — ˘   —

Del gran padre Ocean lo speco angusto

70   On Metastasio, see below; he probably heard Fioravanti's *Le cantatrici villane* (*CN* II 2201) and works by Guglielmi and Nasolini in September (*CN* II 2185 (Aug–Sept 1804)). His sources include some untraced librettoes. By October 1804 he collected eighteen arias (*CN* II 2224 *f*21).

71   *Cormorant* II 459; Coffman 179. Coleridge's volume is dated Venice 1594.

72   The Italian Alexandrine, which was twice introduced from French with unexciting results, consists of fourteen syllables, since another extra-syllable is counted before the caesura – the line is also called a double seven-syllable line. The note brings new evidence for Coleridge's interest in Italian metrics as well as the limits of his knowledge.

73   Elision is usually marked by an apostrophe in printed texts from the Renaissance onwards (Elwert (1973) 33). Coleridge wrote: 'What indeed can be more incongruous than to admit that in one instance a Vowel shall not be pronounced at all, that in another a Vowel shall be distinctly pronounced, and yet the latter is to count for as a complete nothing as the actually non–existent former?' (*IS* 155) In Petrarch's 'Voi ch'ascoltate in rime sparse il suono', he would have found acceptable 'ch'ascoltate', the elision of 'che ascoltate', whereas he would have disapproved of 'Voi' as monosyllabic (synaeresis in the bisyllabic 'vo/i'), and the synalephe in 'sparse il', which turns the two syllables '–se il' into one.

74   Elwert (1973) 6–7.

75   Coleridge might be referring to compound metres like the double pentasyllable he had transcribed. A proper union of different lines is impossible in Italian, as Elwert points out ((1973) 43): 'In Italian poetry each line is metrically an independent element. Synaphea, that is, the union of a line with the following one, as in Latin poetry, is unknown. Experiments of this kind, like Pascoli's, are imitations of Latin poetry'.

76   *MC* 338, marginal note on Scott's *Quentin Durward* (after 1823).

77   Henry Nelson Coleridge in *Quarterly Review* (1834) (*CH* 623).

78 See R. Fiske, *English Theatre Music in the Eighteenth Century*, OUP: London 1973; F. C. Petty, *Italian Opera in London: 1760–1800*, UMI Research Press: Ann Arbor (Mich.) 1980; Brand (1957) ch. 12.

79 See H. Rossiter Smith, 'Wordsworth and His Italian Studies', *Notes & Queries*, CXCVIII, No 6 (Jun 1953), p. 248. His translations of a cantata and five ariettas from Metastasio were published in the *Morning Post* in the autumn of 1803. See Wordsworth, *Poems, in Two Volumes, and Other Poems 1800–1807*, ed. J. Curtis, Cornell UP: Ithaca (N. Y.), 1983, pp. 589–93. See also *EOT (CC)* III, App. D.

80 Brand (1957) 102.

81 *CL* I 79 (7 Apr 1794). See Barry 139–40. On Coleridge's association with Charles Hague, who set to music some of his poems, *CL* I 51–2 (7 Feb 1793). On his first musical experiences in London, *CL* I 31 (14 Feb 1792). See also Introduction to *PW (CC)*, pt. V (Drama).

82 See *CL* II 789 (24 Feb 1802).

83 See *CN* II 2184 (Aug–Sept 1804), II 3190 n., and *CN* III 3404 f25 (Oct 1808). Another singer he admired was Angelica Catalani (1780–1849), whom he met in London in 1811, according to Donald Sultana (Introduction to *New Approaches to Coleridge: Biographical and Critical Essays*, Vision: London 1981, p. 15; see also *L Lects (CC)* I 353 n. However, *EOT (CC)* II 196 n. 2 is correct as regards this reference). Coleridge referred to her whenever he needed to mention a singer (*L Lects (CC)* I 353 (1811); 'On the Principles of Genial Criticism', *BL* (1907) II 231, and E. C. Knowlton, 'A Coleridge Allusion to Angelica Catalani (1780–1849)', *Notes & Queries*, XXV, No 3 (June 1978), p. 221). On Catalani in England, see T. Fenner, *Leigh Hunt and Opera Criticism. The 'Examiner' Years 1808–1821*, Univ. of Kansas Press: Lawrence, Manhattan and Wichita, 1972, pp. 19–20; 159–62. The Shelleys, who attended the opera in London on the recommendation of Hunt and Peacock, found the quality of the performances in Italy inferior to England (ibid., p. 39).

84 *CN* II 2224 f21 (Oct 1804). Kevin Barry (173) points out that the central principle of Tartini's harmonic system was 'the reduction of *la moltiplicata alla Unita*', which recalls Coleridge's principle of beauty as multëity in unity. Tartini's third sound was mentioned as an example of dialectic synthesis in *CN* IV 4522 (Apr 1819) (see also *P Lects* (1949) 407 n. 19).

85 See *CL* II 789 (24 Feb 1802) and *IS* 214 (N 52.6 f5–6 (1833)). Coleridge's limited knowledge of music may include Charles Burney's *General History of Music*, whose vol. II he borrowed from the Bristol library in 1797 (G. Whalley, 'The Bristol Library Borrowings of Southey and Coleridge, 1793–8', *Library*, IV, Sept 1949, p. 124).

86 The structure of Cimarosa's work is not the same as Metastasio's, since *opera seria* changed in almost every respect in the second half of the century. See G. Pestelli, *L'età di Mozart e di Beethoven*, vol. VI of *Storia della musica*, EDT: Torino 1979 (rpt. 1980), pp. 76–7.

87 On Cimarosa's harmony, *BL (CC)* I 117–18; on music and the mind, *Friend (CC)* I 129–30, *L Lects (CC)* I 221; for the late references, *IS* 156 (after 1820); *TT (CC)* 1 Jul 1833. Coleridge had heard some of Palestrina's madrigals in Rome (*TT (CC)* II 244 n.).

88 Pestelli, ibid., p. 265.

89 Metastasio, *Opere*, XII vols., London (Leghorn) 1782–3. Vol. V is inscribed by S. T. Coleridge. Annotations in ink and pencil in his handwriting appear on vols. I, VII and XII. The volumes are probably the hitherto unknown source of his transcriptions from Metastasio. They were owned by Mr Brian Lake (London), who kindly allowed me to read the unpublished annotations. They are now in the Coleridge Collection, Victoria College Library, Toronto. For the edition of Metastasio's works Coleridge may have read in Malta, Coffman 142.

90 *CN* III 4106. Coleridge marked numerous passages and arias in vol. I (e.g. in *Artaserse*). Other volumes contain marks and crosses in pencil and translated words. Metastasio's *Semiramide* (*Opere*, vol. VII) contains a note on love. Coleridge found it intolerable that the main character, Ircano, insisted on wooing a woman who despised him. Did he want her body?

91 Hazlitt was not enthusiastic about opera as a form of art. When he reviewed some performances about 1818, he criticized melodrama according to eighteenth-century principles – it was unnatural, effeminate, immoral, and the predominance of music over words was excessive (see Fenner, *Leigh Hunt and Opera Criticism*, p. 180 ff.). Fenner thinks Hazlitt 'does not penetrate much beneath the surface of music, yet he shows a genuine response to song' (p. 184). Hunt's attitude to music was literary, as he did not have any technical knowledge of it (p. 190). He began the study of Italian in 1805 and improved it in gaol (p. 304 n. 42). He disliked librettoes and held Metastasio in low regard (pp. 193–4). His initial response to Rossini was negative, but he later praised some aspects of his works (p. 213).

92 The characterisation of Abel in *La morte d'Abel* (*Opere*, vol. VII) was equally unlikely. Abel sings an air in which he describes his control over his herd, and Coleridge noted it was a bad example. Abel was the epitome of pastoral life, in which the sense of property was weak. Cain represents the city and property, and therefore evil, avarice, murder.

93 Metastasio is quoted from *Tutte le opere*, ed. B. Brunelli, Mondadori: Milano 1943–54, vol. II, p. 975. With reference to the present discussion, see especially pp. 982–4, 986. Metastasio, who wrote the *Estratto* as a defence of his own poetics, specified that the ignorance of the distinction between copy and imitation was the basis of the charge of unlikelihood against melodrama (ibid., pp. 994–5). The treatise, completed in 1773, was published posthumously in 1780–2. Coleridge's long annotations, to chs. I and II in particular, appear in vol. XII of his edition.

94 *L Lects* (*CC*) I 52–3 (1808). He compared a character of *La morte d'Abel* to Iago, although he found the comparison almost blasphemous (marginal note in Metastasio, *Opere*, vol. VII).

95 He found the observations in Voltaire and August Wilhelm Schlegel, although the idea that modern opera was a reproduction of Greek tragedy had been the core of the aesthetics of the Camerata de' Bardi, which invented it. In his *Estratto dell'arte poetica d'Aristotile*, Metastasio drew innumerable comparisons between Classical theatre and melodrama.

96 *L Lects* (*CC*) II 118 (1818). Another note shows that Shakespeare was always at the back of Coleridge's mind whenever he meditated upon theatre. The finest passages of Sebastiano Nasolini's *La morte di Cleopatra* and of Gaetano Andreozzi's *Amleto*

were affecting but unnatural. His conclusion was that 'we are adapting all to the Vulgar, instead of raising up the Vulgar to the best' (*CN* II 2339 (Dec 1804)). Shakespeare was the implicit standard by which he judged them.

97 I do not think he was referring to Goldoni or Gozzi here. Like most Romantics, Coleridge preferred Carlo Gozzi to Goldoni. He tried to acquire Gozzi's works and eventually got hold of them in 1817, when he planned a play based on Gozzi to solve his financial problems (*CL* IV 597 (1815); IV 633; IV 635; IV 656 (1816); IV 733 (1817)). Though not a genius, Gozzi was 'a delightful fellow'. Coleridge thought, perhaps under the influence of the Elizabethan tradition, that Italian theatre provided many excellent situations which could be used for new plays. Gozzi's dramatic fables adapted to an English setting would supersede Goldoni and the *comedie larmoyante* (*CL* IV 940–1 (6 May 1819)). For his copies of Goldoni's and Gozzi's works, Coffman 90–1. Another Italian playwright Coleridge knew was Tommaso Garzoni da Bagnocavallo (1549–89), whose *Opere* (Venice 1637) he owned and inscribed (29 Dec 1807) (Coffman 86).

98 *CN* II 2625 (?Jul–Oct 1805). *Il rossignuol cantante* goes as follows:

Sovra l'orlo d'un rio lucido e netto
Il canto soavissimo sciogliea
Musico rossignuol, ch'aver parea
E mille voci e mille augelli in petto.
Eco, che d'ascoltarlo avea diletto,
Le note intere al suo cantar rendea:
Ed ei vie piú garria, che lei credea
Vago, che l'emulasse, altro augelletto.
Ma mentre che tenor del bel concento
Raddoppiava piú dolce, a caso scorse
L'imagin sua nel fuggitivo argento.
Riser le ninfe, ed ei ch'allor s'accorse
Schernito esser dall'acque, anzi dal vento,
A celarsi tra rami in fretta corse.

99
Apre l'uomo infelice, allor che nasce
in questa vita di miserie piena,
pria ch'al sol, gli occhi al pianto, e, nato a pena
va prigionier tra le tenaci fasce.
Fanciullo, poi che non piú il latte pasce,
sotto rigida sferza i giorni mena;
indi, in età piú ferma e serena,
tra Fortuna e Amor more e rinasce.
Quante poscia sostien, tristo e mendico,
fatiche e morti, infin che curvo e lasso
appoggia a debil legno il fianco antico?
Chiude alfin le sue spoglie angusto sasso,
ratto cosí, che sospirando io dico:
'Da la cuna a la tomba è un breve passo!'

Unhappy man when he is born into this life full of miseries opens his eyes to weeping rather than to the Sun; and, scarcely born, is made the prisoner of constricting swaddling–bands. Next, as a boy whose food is no longer milk, he spends his days beneath the severe rod. Then in an age more sure and more serene, he dies and is reborn between love and fortune. Later, sad and poor, how many labours and deaths does he endure, until, bent and weary, he supports his ancient body with a weak staff? At last a narrow stone seals in his remains so swiftly that sighing I say: From the cradle to the grave is but a short step.

(*CN* II 2625 n.)

100 He might not have understood the word properly, since his paraphrase focused on the metereologic meaning of the word. Besides, his two attempts to rephrase the line show that Italian versification was still obscure to him: his lines are dodecasyllables, whereas the original is in hendecasyllable.

101   Sotto caliginose ombre profonde
        Di luce inaccessibile sepolti
        Tra nembi di silenzio oscuri e folti
        L'eterna mente i suoi segreti asconde.
              E s'altri spia per queste nebbie immonde
        I suoi giudizi in nero velo avvolti
        Gli umani ingegni temerari e stolti
        Col lampo abbaglia, e col suo tuon confonde.
              O invisibile Sol, ch'a noi ti celi
        Dentro abisso luminoso e fosco
        E di tuoi propri rai te stesso veli;
              Argo mi fai, dov'io son cieco e losco,
        Ne la mia notte il tuo splendor reveli;
        Quanto t'intendo men, piú ti conosco.

Beneath deep gloomy shadow 'buried in light inaccessible', amongst 'thick and obscure storm–clouds of silence', the eternal Mind conceals his secrets. And if anyone spies out through these impure mists his judgements, wrapped in a black veil, he dazzles with is lightning and stuns with his thunder that rash and foolish human intelligence. Oh invisible Sun, who dost conceal thyself from us within a 'luminous dark' abyss, and dost veil thyself with thine own rays; make me another Argos, blind and ignorant though I be, in my night reveal thy splendour; the less I understand thee, the more I know thee.

(*CN* II 2625 n.)

102 The sonnet tries to represent the intellectual inaccessibility of God by antitheses and oxymora, both traditional devices to define the divine. The antithesis 'dark light' is the central one in the sonnet. Coleridge disliked the basic principle on which the poem is constructed: accumulation. The sonnet is not a masterpiece, but repetitions in themselves are not responsible for it. Lines are piled up like clouds varying on the same image: the sun buried under its own light. Coleridge thought that lines 1 and 3 were superfluous, that 'oscuri' (line 3) was a useless repetition, that 'asconde' after 'buried in light inaccessible' was predictable (line 4), so that 'one steps into a hole when one is expecting to place the foot on a stair higher.' Interestingly, he referred to this flaw, that is, frustrated expectation, in ch. XVIII of *Biographia*, in which he discussed the effects of metre (*CC* II 66).

103 There was a copy of *La lira* (Venezia 1674) in Southey's library (Coffman 137).

104 See G. Getto, *Barocco in prosa e in poesia*, Rizzoli: Milano 1969, p. 41.

105 See Edoardo Taddeo, *Studi sul Marino*, Sandron: Firenze 1971, p 137. 'Sotto caliginose ombre profonde' seems to have been inspired by another stanza of Magno's *Deus* (ibid., pp. 138–9).

106 Donald Sultana states that 'It was on his translations from the Italian that Coleridge appears to have lectured his visitors' in Malta and Sicily (Sultana (1969) 351 and nn.).

107 *CN* II 2625: his analysis of Marino's poems 'may perhaps hereafter be serviceable in giving Hartley or Derwent a gode and a guide to the close Hunt of Good Sense, & fineness and steadiness to the right Scent'. On Coleridge's lessons of Italian to Sara in 1808 and afterwards, *PW* (*CC*) No 439, editorial note, and *Minnow* 12.

108 *PW* (EHC) I 392–3. I have changed EHC's text in two places: 'there' for 'these' at line 12 (see *CN* III 3377 n.), and the italics of '*my*' instead of '*thou*' (line 14) as in *CN*.

109 On Petrarch's and Marino's antithesis, see Elwert (1967) 61.

110 See Elwert (1967) 29.

111 Getto, *Barocco in prosa e in poesia*, p. 32. However, the Baroque image of women is more varied in extension, as it were, than the Petrarchist image, since women of every aesthetic and social condition appear in seventeenth–century poetry.

112 Love is consequently 'the contact of two skins, . . . but also devoid of brutal violence and smutty vulgarity. . . . Love seems the prevailing occupation, the main thought of an elegant and luxurious life, and itself seems to become a form of exquisite luxury. It is the only conceivable activity in this world of immovable decorative splendour' (ibid., p. 55).

113 Figures of position, like asyndeton, polysyndeton, zeugma, parallelism, antithesis etc., dominate Petrarch's style, whereas tropes, like metaphor and metonymy, are relatively unimportant. Marino and the Marinists reversed the relation: tropes prevail in their style (Elwert (1967) 54–7). See also Mirollo, *The Poet of the Marvelous: Giambattista Marino*, pp. 153–6; and A. Asor Rosa, *La lirica del Seicento*, Laterza: Bari 1975, p. 145. Tasso was the model of the new attitude to Petrarch (Getto, *Barocco in prosa e in poesia*, p. 65).

114 Mirollo indicates a sonnet of Angelo Di Costanzo as well as an intermediary French source (ibid., pp. 188–90). Di Costanzo's sonnet is in turn derived from a sonnet of Cariteo, a fifteenth–century Petrarchist.

115 However, we should not forget that 'the poems of Marino and his followers on amorous pleasure, kisses etc., are not love poems, but the seventeenth-century equivalent to Petrarchist theoretical *canzoni*, in which the nature of love is discussed' (Elwert (1967) 30).

116 Marino was an enthusiastic amateur of music, and his poems were in their turn admired by contemporary musicians (Elwert (1967) 197 and n. 32).

117 Marshall 336–7. William Collier was Marino's champion in Coleridge's time. Leigh Hunt provides an example of the prevailing attitude to Marino in the early nineteenth century. He thought Marino corrupted Italian poetry, even if he possessed real poetic fancy (intr. to Hunt (1956) 44). Marino 'carried every folly in verse to an extreme' ('Epithalamius' (1841), Hunt (1956) 495). On the contrary Henry Francis Cary, the translator of Dante, considered Marino's *L'Adone*, which he read in 1801, as unjustly neglected (*Cary M* I 204).

118 Interestingly, Marino did not remind Coleridge of Crashaw, whose version of Marino's *Sospetto d'Erode* he knew (*CN* III 4098 (May–Aug 1811)).

119 Elwert (1967) 102. Chiabrera has several points in common with Marino: his intention to surprise the reader, his hedonism, his courtly and sensual view of love and women, his taste for jewelry and precious materials, for pastoral fiction and mythology, etc. There are, however, evident differences: conceits, hyperboles and antitheses are rare in his writings; he avoided extravagant and ugly subjects; he renewed the aristocratic poetic style of the sixteenth century by adding Latinisms and neologisms, thereby making it even more refined – conversely, Marino did not exclude technical and popular terms.

120 The former, also called 'Anacreontic canzonetta', is characterized by short lines and stanzas. It was prompted by the Pléiade, and dominated Italian lyric poetry in the seventeenth and eighteenth centuries. Besides, Chiabrera invented an Italian adaptation for the Horatian and the Pindaric ode (Elwert (1973) 154–60, 182–93). Although his odes were influential, nowadays the *canzonetta melica* is regarded as his most valuable invention. It must be emphasized that the *canzone* and the ode are not the same form in Italian: the former was imitated from the Provençal in the thirteenth century; the latter first appeared in the sixteenth century as an imitation of the Classics. Sometimes the *canzone* is improperly called 'ode' in English translations.

121 *CN* II 2365 (Dec 1804); and III 3318 n. Coleridge's annotated edition of Chiabrera's works (vols. I–III of 5, Venezia 1782) is lost (*CM* (*CC*) II 23); place and time of the purchase are unknown. Wordsworth owned a complete copy of the same edition (Coffman 49).

122 A dodecasyllable would also be the result of another correction he propounded for stanza 4 of Chiabrera's ode on Columbus (*CN* III 3318). Besides, he sketched an eleven–line stanza.

123 The translations appeared in *The Friend* between December 1809 and February 1810. Coleridge must have found the story of Columbus attractive, since he even purchased Ubertino Carrara's (1640–1715) obscure *Columbus, carmen epicum* (1715) in 1806 (*Cormorant* II 213). The passages from Chiabrera appeared in *Friend* (*CC*) I 65–6 (1818) (transcribed *CN* III 3578 (Jul–Sept 1809)); and 480 (1818).

124 *Friend* (*CC*) II 248–9, 269–70, 334–46. Coleridge quoted Chiabrera in two letters (*CL* III 264 (22 Dec 1809); III 313 (26 Mar 1811)).

125 Milton's *On Shakespeare* is quoted at the end of Wordsworth's *Essays upon Epitaphs* (*Friend* (*CC*) II 346). Wordsworth's admiration for other anti-Marinist poets like Vincenzo da Filicaia belongs to the same context (see *Siege of Vienna Raised by John Sobieski February, 1816, WPW* III 150).

126 Marshall 329. Baroque poets like Chiabrera, Guidi and Filicaia were among Mathias' favourites, and influenced his style. Ugo Foscolo criticized his translations for their bombast (E. R. Vincent, *Ugo Foscolo. An Italian in Regency England*, CUP 1953, p. 179).

127 See *PW* (*CC*) poem No 453, editorial note. Lines 19–25 of Coleridge's text are very close to Wordsworth's lines 8–13 (*WPW* IV 251; *Friend* (*CC*) II 184). As late as 1835, Wordsworth still had Chiabrera in mind when he composed *Written after the Death of Charles Lamb* (*WPW* IV 458). Chiabrera is mentioned

in *Musings near Aquapendente April, 1837*, in *Memorials of a Tour in Italy, 1837*, l. 232 ff. (*WPW* III 209).

128 *Friend* (*CC*) II 342. In any event, Wordsworth preferred it to Pope's epitaphs, which he criticized in his second essay *Upon Epitaphs* (*W Prose* II 76 ff.).

129 Three English editions (1763, 1774 and 1778) and a translation (by William Grove, the fourth in English literature, 1782) of the *Pastor fido* appeared in the second half of the eighteenth century (Marshall 118). They were followed by new critical evaluations. Ginguené dealt with Guarini in his *Histoire littéraire d'Italie*, and the Schlegel brothers expressed admiration for *Il pastor fido*. August Wilhelm considered its combination of Classical and modern elements as perfect; Friedrich extolled it in 1800, although he later expressed reservations about its style (see N. J. Perella, *The Critical Fortune of Battista Guarini's 'Il Pastor Fido'*, Olschki: Firenze 1973, pp. 140–3).

130 In September 1806 he transcribed two madrigals of Guarini from a volume (Amsterdam 1663) he may have acquired in Italy (*CN* II 2871, 2872). He later asked his wife to send him the volume 'for the sake of the minor poems' (*CL* III 393 (24 Apr 1812)), one of which, *Dialogo. Fede, Speranza, Carità* he translated in 1815. The last excerpt dates from 1817 (*CN* III 4354).

131 Coleridge's version is close enough to the original text. He turned Guarini's tercets into quatrains, so that he was often compelled to expand the original, whose meaning is nonetheless always preserved. The allegorism of Guarini's poem might underlie the general plan for *Love, Hope, and Patience in Education* (*PW* (EHC) I 481–2 (1829)), although there are no direct borrowings. Angela G. Dorenkamp argues that the poem 'in many ways ... is a summation of (Coleridge's) late poetry' ('Hope at Highgate: The Late Poetry of S. T. Coleridge', *Barat Review*, VI, 1971, p. 61). On the problem of faith, see J. R. Barth, *Coleridge and Christian Doctrine*, Harvard UP: Cambridge (Mass.) 1969, pp. 32–3 and 82. Coleridge's view of faith was a compromise between Catholicism, in which it is compounded of hope and love, and Protestantism, in which faith is a single act of will.

    On Coleridge's lessons of Italian, see *Minnow* 12 (3 Aug 1810). Mrs Coleridge wrote that 'Sara has read through a little book of Poems in that Language, many of which she can now repeat, and we are trying the PASTOR FIDO.' It seems likely that the 'little book' was the volume of Guarini's poems.

132 *CN* III 3379. He had evidently read Guarini's non–sacred poems in the meantime.

133 Alberto Asor Rosa argues that in the *Pastor fido* 'everything hinges on the idea of material pleasure, an idea that may be – and in fact is – very refined. However, this leads up to that vulgarisation of the philosophy of love which will be fundamental to nearly all Baroque poets in the seventeenth century' (*La lirica del Seicento*, p. 4). Asor Rosa considers Guarini's role in the transition as decisive.

134 E. Bonora, 'Il Classicismo dal Bembo al Guarini', in *Storia della letteratura italiana*, eds. E. Cecchi and N. Sapegno, vol. IV: *Il Cinquecento*, Garzanti: Milano 1966, p. 637.

135 The word [Still] (line 4) is deleted in the original.

136 Coleridge may have found some reference to Ovid's story of Pyramus and Thisbe, which is echoed in the stanzas (*CN* III 3379 n.), in Guarini or Marino. Ovid was a major source of Marino.

137 The link of these notes with the 'Soother of Absence' is evident. They are surrounded by other entries on Sara and poetic sketches (*CN* III 3374, 3375, 3376, 3380, 3383, 3385 (all Sept 1808)).

138 'Italy's characteristic is that Renaissance poetry does mean Petrarchesque poetry . . . The repertoire of metrical forms is that of Petrarch as Bembo had made it prescriptive: *canzone, sestina*, sonnet, madrigal and ballad. The language of poetry, an aristocratic variant of literary language, already preexists and is also due to Petrarch . . . Love remains the main theme: not any longer in Petrarch's courtly and troubadoric manner, but changed by fashionable Platonism thanks to Bembo . . . Such noble and aristocratic poetry . . . tends to become increasingly refined . . . [and to] a more esoteric hermetism.'
There were two main ways of revolting against Petrarchism: Marino's and Chiabrera's (Elwert (1967) 130–2). See also Asor Rosa, ibid., p. 141. Edoardo Taddeo eloquently summarized the difference between Mannerist and Baroque poetry: 'on the one hand, the cult of technical difficulty as perfection, a mysticism of form; on the other, the discovery of the new world of analogy as the joyful union of intellect and sense perception' (*Il manierismo letterario e i lirici veneziani del tardo Cinquecento*, Bulzoni: Roma 1974, p. 64).

139 Coleridge knew other Italian Baroque poets, but they did not intrigue him so much as Marino and Chiabrera. Lorenzo Lippi's (1606–64) *Il Malmantile riacquistato* was included in a list of books he intended to buy in February 1808 (*CN* III 3276); he purchased Francesco Baldovini's (1634–1716) *Lamento di Cecco da Varlungo* in Florence in 1806. Although the former is a mock–heroic poem and the latter an *idillio rusticano* (rustic idyll), both are written in the Florentine vernacular. Coleridge's interest may have been chiefly linguistic, as his marginalia to Baldovini's poem show (*CM* (*CC*) I 206–10). The *Lamento di Cecco da Varlungo* was translated into English by John Hunter as *Cecco's Complaint* in 1800. The metre of the original, *ottava rima*, was preserved in the English version, and it is perhaps the most valuable use of the stanza in English before 1811, together with Huggins' version of Ariosto (Marshall 326–7). On Coleridge and Salvator Rosa, see ch. II. Coleridge inscribed a copy of Tassoni's mock–heroic poem *La secchia rapita* which was in Green's library (Coffman 212). There was a copy of Francesco Redi's (1626–98) *Bacco in Toscana* in Wordsworth's library (Coffman 172–3). On Coleridge's copy of Menzini's poems, see n. 60.

140 *CN* II 2599 (May–Aug 1805). Significantly, the same passage in *Biographia* includes 'lovely damsels, cruel as fair, nymphs, naiads, and goddesses' as examples of Petrarchist images (*(CC)* II 33).

141 See *CN* II 2599. The Italian lines mean: 'that the clear wave,/And the shade no less dear'. The pun is not confined to these lines but continues into the following one: 'che l'onda chiara,/E l'ombra non men cara/A schERzARE, e cantAR pER suoi boschetti'.

142 See for example 'Hor lieve ape foss'io, che tanto andrei'. The following madrigal of Strozzi is worth quoting as a paroxysmal version of Petrarch's 'Erano i capei d'oro a l'aura sparsi' (*Canz.* XC): 'Ne' RAggi AmOR del mio bel sole assiso/con lui schERza e con lORO,/e con l'ÔRA e con l'ORO del bel viso;/sì con sì dolce RIso/a sì dolce schERzAR l'anima invita,/ch'io pUR tROvo in vita e spiRO, e

spERO/non pERIR mai, se del piacER non pÉRO.' Alliteration of 'l', which is a liquid consonant as 'r', should be considered. The *Notebooks* editor indicates a marginal note on Donne's poems concerning paronomasy in Henry King's elegy *To the Memory of Donne* (*CN* III 3762 n.).

143 Cf. especially Lecture VII of the 1811–12 course on Shakespeare and Milton (*L Lects* (*CC*) I 303–21). Though Coleridge never justified Shakespeare's puns completely, he was more tolerant than many former critics, for example Samuel Johnson (*L Lects* (*CC*) I 292–3). He observed that Renaissance taste for punning may have been due to Scholasticism and the revival of letters, both of which made frequent use of such devices (*L Lects* (*CC*) I 312; II 496–7).

144 Leonard Forster reminds us that, 'for the young Alexander Pope petrarchism was something charming but entirely unreal'. John Gay made sport of it in *The Beggar's Opera*; Jonathan Swift considered it as 'a sham to be unmasked: "Celia shits" (*The Lady's Dressing Room*, 1730)'; Lessing depicted it as 'the language of insincere court compliment' (*The Icy Fire. Five Studies in European Petrarchism*, CUP 1969, pp. 57–8).

145 Warton 648 and 635.

146 William Roscoe, *The Life of Lorenzo de' Medici*, 2 vols., London 1797 (3rd edn), p. 276.

147 'That this conviction is well founded is proved in no unequivocal manner, by the innumerable throng of writers who have imitated the manner of Bembo; and who, availing themselves of the example of this scholastic style of composition, have inundated Italy with writings which seldom exhibit any distinction either of character or of merit. That the introduction of this manner of writing was fatal to the higher productions of genius cannot be doubted. Internal worth was sacrificed to external ornament. The vehicle was gilt and polished to the highest degree, but it contained nothing of any value; and the whole attention of these writers was employed, not in discovering what should be said, but how it should be said.'

(*The Life and Pontificate of Leo the Tenth*, 6 vols., London 1806 (2nd edn), vol. III, p. 279).

148 See Brand (1957) 103–7; and Marshall 140–1.

149 Roscoe, ibid., p. 306.

150 Brand (1957) 107. Brand points out that, 'By the end of the 1820s the number of translations, imitations and critical appreciations of the Italian lyric has considerably diminished. Its popularity after 1815 was a heritage of the Roscoe-Mathias generation, which the next generation looked upon affectionately but did little to preserve'.

151 He said for example of Michael Drayton's sonnets: they 'are not *metrically* Sonnets; but poems in 14 lines – and it would be difficult to point out a good one' (*CM* (*CC*) I 57). The negative view was repeated in *Biographia* ((*CC*) II 94). Cf. Wordsworth's judgement: 'These sonnets seem to me not worth reading – flat, far-fetch'd conceits, with scarcely a single natural thought throughout the whole' (quoted *CM* (*CC*) I 40).

152 He praised Wordsworth's language and sentiment for being as pure as Samuel Daniel's, although Wordsworth's 'sinewy strength and originality of single lines and paragraphs' surpassed Daniel's (*BL* (*CC*) II 146–8).

153   Coleridge had left some space in his notebooks for a collection of Italian poems (*CN* III Notes, editor's introduction, p. xxv).

154   The structure of the early madrigal, like Petrarch's or Sacchetti's, is less varied than in the sixteenth century, when it was influenced by music. The musical fortune of the madrigal in the sixteenth and seventeenth centuries is well known (see Elwert (1973) 134–6). On the madrigal in sixteenth–century poetics, see M. Ariani, introduction to G. B. Strozzi il Vecchio, *Madrigali inediti*, Argalia: Urbino 1975, pp. XVI and XLVII.

155   Ariani, ibid., pp. VIII–XI. Ariani's essay is the main source of my discussion. Strozzi's vocabulary, for example, is Petrarchistic and not 'polluted' by Dantesque elements, but the use he made of it was often anti–Petrarchan (ibid., p. CXX).

156   L. Baldacci (ed.), *Lirici del Cinquecento*, Longanesi: Milano 1957 (2nd edn, rpt. 1984), pp. 314–15.

157   Ariani, ibid., p. CXXII.

158   Ibid., p. CXLI.

159   Ibid., p. CXLVIII. Natalino Sapegno argues that 'longing for idyllic escape and . . . anxiety about death stem from the same root and testify in different ways that the moral and rational balance of the early Renaissance was breaking and dissolving, and that a different spirituality, more uneasy, avid and sensuous, was replacing it' (*Antologia storica della poesia lirica italiana nei secoli XVI e XVII*, ERI: Torino 1964, p. 80). Though Coleridge focused on the serious side of Petrarchism, he was curious of the so-called anti-Petrarchism. He owned and annotated a three-volume anthology of burlesque works which included sixteenth-century poets like Berni and Maura (Coffman 155).

160   Coleridge wrote to Wordsworth immediately before leaving for Malta: 'buy me . . . Dante & a Dictionary' (*CL* II 1059 (8 Feb 1804)). He also received Sir George Beaumont's copy of the *Divine Comedy* (*CM* (*CC*) II 132). A note he made in 1805 ('Dante, Ariosto, Giordano Bruno [shall] be my Italy', *CN* II 2598) shows he had been reading Dante presumably in the original. In Rome he became acquainted with Michele Arcangelo Migliarini, an artist who recited and discussed Dante with him (C. P. Darcy, 'Coleridge and the Italian Artist, Migliarini', *Notes & Queries*, XXIII, No 3, Mar 1976, p. 105). Coleridge bought his complete edition of Dante's works probably in Italy (*Opere*, col comento del M. R. P. Pompeo Venturi, 5 vols., Gatti, Venezia 1793) (*CN* II 3014 n.).

161   'Death first of all – eats of the Tree of Life/& becomes immortal describe the frightful metamorphosis/weds the Hamadryad of the Tree/their Progeny – in the manner of Dante' (*CN* II 2919 (Oct–Nov 1806)). However, no marginal notes on Dante's poem are extant, so that the lectures he gave in the following decade are the only source for his opinions of the *Comedy*. As George Whalley points out, 'If we assume that the more important the book the more copious the notes, we often find the emphasis inverted.' There are, for example, no surviving marginalia on Bacon, Cudworth, Bruno, Vico, Augustine, Origen, Aquinas, Davy etc. (*CM* (*CC*) I lxiii). See my ch. III on Dante in Coleridge's lectures.

162   It was probably composed at the beginning of the exile, that is, about 1302. It became a favourite with nineteenth–century scholars thanks to its subject.

163   See G. Contini, editor of Dante's *Rime*, Einaudi: Torino 1946 (rpt. 1987), pp. 172–3.

164 *Dante's Style in His Lyric Poetry*, CUP 1971, p. 141. Boyde emphasizes that 'Dante *became* a metaphoric poet' in the *Comedy*; 'he did not begin as one' (p. 130).

165 Contini, ibid., p. 175.

166 Boyde, ibid., p. 148. The obscurity which Coleridge found impenetrable is due to the three women being probably allegories of *jus divinum et naturale, jus gentium* and *jus humanum* (Contini, ibid., p. 172).

167 Contini, ibid., p. 71.

168 Ibid., p. 58.

169 Kenelm Foster and Patrick Boyde point out that 'Tre donne' and 'Doglia mi reca' are 'the summit of Dante's achievement in ethical poetry prior to the Comedy' (*Dante's Lyric Poetry*, 2 vols., Clarendon Press: Oxford 1967, vol. II, p. 296). Coleridge used to associate Dante's *canzone* 'Voi che 'ntendendo il terzo ciel movete' (*Convivio*, II) with Wordsworth's *Intimations of Immortality* on the grounds of their philosophic complexity (*Friend* (*CC*) I 510–11; *BL* (*CC*) II 147). Coleridge adapted from the *Convivio* a Pythagorean definition of love and beauty according to which 'Nella beltà si fa uno di più' ('In Beauty the Many is made one') (*CN* II 3201 (1807–8)). As the editor's note points out, the original passage does not refer to beauty but to friendship ('Ne l'amistà si fa uno di più', *Convivio*, IV, i). The concept also appears in 'Doglia mi reca', line 14; Contini indicates it was a *stilnovo* commonplace (ibid., p. 184).

170 For instance, it is well known that the *Vita Nuova* was 'discovered' by Shelley, whose enthusiasm for it was unusual in his time.

171 *CM* (*CC*) I 41. The word {laboriousness} is deleted in the original.

172 *CM* (*CC*) I 43. The note deals with love in Shakespeare's sonnets, which he regarded as ideal and chaste. Petrarch was obviously less disturbing in this respect.

173 *CN* II 2428. Cf. *CN* III 3303 (1808–10): 'Every single thought, every image, every perception, was no sooner itself, than it became *you* (i.e., Sara Hutchinson) by some wish that you saw it & felt it . . . some way or other it always became a symbol of *you* – I played with them, as with *your shadow* – as Shakespeare has so profoundly expressed it in his Sonnets'.

174 It is sufficient to mention as examples the Petrarchist description of Lucrece (lines 386–7, 400–407, 419–20), conceits like 'My love to love is love but to disgrace it,/For I have heard, it is a life in death,/That laughs and weeps, and all but with a breath' (*Venus and Adonis*, lines 412–14), and the extravagant sexual innuendo of lines like 'I'll be a park, and thou shalt be my deer' (ibid., line 231). Two points recall the poems of Marino discussed before: the image 'blinded with a greater light' (*Lucrece*, line 375); and two stanzas in the same poem (lines 736–49), which are structurally like Marino's *Alla sua amica*, that is, made up of binary parallelisms. For Coleridge on *Romeo and Juliet*, see my section on Strozzi above.

175 M. Praz, *Mnemosyne: The Parallel between Literature and the Visual Arts*, The National Gallery of Art: Washington D.C. 1970; OUP: London, p. 105. Another evident analogy between Shakespeare's poems and Marino's is their frequent use of antitheses. See Douglas Bush, *Mythology and the Renaissance Tradition in English Poetry*, Univ. of Minnesota Press, 1932 (rpt. Norton: New York 1963, p. 141).

176 *BL* (*CC*) II 30. Coleridge emphasized that the clarity of thought depends on language, as the fact that philosophical mistakes are often due to linguistic equivocations demonstrates (*BL* (*CC*) II 31). He believed that one of the greatest merits of Cary's version of Dante was its linguistic purity, as he wrote him: 'I may be thought to appreciate this merit too highly; but you may have seen, what I said in defence of it in the Literary Life' (*CL* IV 781 (6 Nov 1817)).

177 However, the editor quotes a passage which seems close to Coleridge's statement. It is a section in which Dante deals with *decorum*, that is, the appropriateness of style to its subject–matter, according to which tragedy needs 'vulgare illustre', comedy 'mediocre', and elegy 'humile' (*De vulgari eloquentia*, II, iv). Though Dante theoretically accepted the classical threefold division of style (*gravis, mediocris* and *humilis*), he mixed them up in the *Divine Comedy*, thereby throwing the division overboard. Coleridge blamed 'Southey, W. Scott &c' for the impurity of their language in a marginal note on Southey's *Joan of Arc* in which Dante is mentioned (*BL* (*CC*) II 30 n. 2).

178 *BL* (*CC*) II 56. Dante wrote: 'Itaque adepti quod querebamus, dicimus illustre, cardinale, aulicum et curiale vulgare in Latio, quod omnis latie civitatis est et nullius esse videtur, et quo municipalia vulgaria omnia Latinorum mensurantur et ponderantur et comparantur' (*De vulgari eloquentia*, I, xvi). Dante argued that such common language does not exist in everyday speech, but is artificially derived by poets from it and other sources. What he means by 'vulgare illustre' is the language of poetry introduced by the Sicilian school and refined by the *Stilnovo*.

179 L. Forster points out that 'in the light of petrarchism the conceits of Ovid, and the newly discovered Anacreon . . . and the Greek Anthology . . . acquired new meaning and relevance' (*The Icy Fire*, p. 33).

The Fine Arts

1 C. Woodring, 'What Coleridge Thought of Pictures', in *Images of Romanticism. Verbal and Visual Affinities*, eds. K. Kroeber and W. Walling, Yale UP: New Haven and London 1978, 91–106; K. Barry, *Language, Music and the Sign. A Study in Aesthetics, Poetics and Poetic Practice from Collins to Coleridge*, CUP 1987, pp. 134–77.

2 Beaumont's bequest to the National Gallery includes paintings by Jan Both, Sébastien Bourdon, Canaletto, Claude, N. Poussin, Rembrandt, Reynolds, Rubens, Benjamin West, David Wilkie, Richard Wilson ('*Noble and Patriotic*'. *The Beaumont Gift, 1828*, The National Gallery of London, 3 Feb–3 May 1988, National Gallery Publications, 1988). Beaumont was one of Wordsworth's best friends: his first collected poems were dedicated to Beaumont, who in his turn made drawings to illustrate them (F. Blanshard, *Portraits of Wordsworth*, Allen & Unwin: London 1959, p. 41).

3 Woodring, 'What Coleridge Thought of Pictures', p. 92, points out the collection of Lord Ashburnham, and the collection later purchased from J. J. Angerstein for the National Gallery which included works by Titian, Correggio, Sebastiano del Piombo, both Poussins, Claude, Rubens, Rembrandt, Van Dyck and Cuyp.

4   In Rome Coleridge also met the English painter George Augustus Wallis and his son Trajan, with whom he visited the Roman *campagna* (*Cormorant* I 447; *CL* II 1172–3 (17 Jun 1806); and *CN* II 2795). On the Wallises, see W. H. Gerdts, 'Washington Allston and the German Romantic Classicists in Rome', *Art Quarterly*, XXXII, No 2 (1969), p. 184. Thomas Russell of Exeter, who was studying art in Rome, accompanied Coleridge on his visit to Pisa in June 1806 (*TT* (*CC*) 25 Jun 1830 n. 1). Coleridge's friends were not all German and English: we know he was acquainted with the Italian painter Michele Arcangelo Migliarini (*c.* 1785–1865), with whom he discussed Shakespeare and Dante (see C. P. Darcy, 'Coleridge and the Italian Artist, Migliarini', *Notes & Queries* XXIII, No 3, Mar 1976, 104–5). Besides, Coleridge made use of G. A. Vasi's guide to Rome, Pietro Rossini's *Il mercurio errante delle grandezze di Roma* (Roma 1750), and later of a guide to the Uffizi (Firenze 1804) (Coffman 222, 179, 80).

5   See Gerdts, 'Washington Allston and the German Romantic Classicists in Rome', pp. 167, 173–4, 177–8, 183–4, 189–92. Gerdts attributes to Alexander von Humboldt the theoretical principle of landscape painting of the circle. Since such essentialist ideas are typical of the Romantic attitude to nature, they may well have come to Allston from Coleridge (ibid., p. 189). On Allston, see also *CN* II 2794 n.

6   Samuel Rogers owned some early Italian paintings which William Young Ottley (1771–1836) had passed on to him (D. Sutton, 'Aspects of British Collecting, Part IV', *Apollo*, NS CXXIII, No 282 (Aug 1985), p. 85). On Ottley, an important collector and probably the most original English interpreter of early Italian art in his time, see G. Previtali, *La fortuna dei primitivi da Vasari ai neoclassici*, Einaudi: Torino 1964, pp. 182–4. Early Italian paintings were part of Lord Bristol's collection in Rome (B. Ford, 'The Earl–Bishop. An Eccentric and Capricious Patron of the Arts', *Apollo*, NS XCIX, No 148, Jun 1974, 426–34). Charles and Eliza Aders owned an important collection of early Northern painters (Van Eyck, Van Leyden, Memling, and a number of German renaissance items) but also some early Italians. Coleridge became acquainted with the Aders in 1812 and was often at their receptions, where he met the Lambs, Henry Crabb Robinson, Blake, Thomas Campbell, John Flaxman, Landor, Samuel Rogers, the Wordsworths (see *The Letters of Charles and Mary Lamb*, vol. III, pp. 109–10 n. 3; *Blake Records*, ed. G. E. Bentley, Jr, Clarendon Press: Oxford 1969, p. 310 n. 1; Woodring, 'What Coleridge Thought of Pictures', p. 101). For the other major British collections of early Italian painting, see Previtali, ibid., pp. 222–9, 245–8.

7   The role of the Pisan frescoes in the development of Italian painting was even overrated; Ottley was the first who clearly realized that they were not so important as the frescoes at Assisi (Previtali, ibid., p. 183). On Beckford, see Marshall 168–9 n. Smollett was struck by the expressiveness and variety of the Pisan frescoes (*Travels through France and Italy*, ed. F. Felsenstein, OUP: Oxford 1979, pp. 224–5). On Marianna Starke's lines to the Pisan frescoes, which she however praised as a promise more than for their intrinsic value, see Hale (1954) 120–1. Leigh Hunt describes the frescoes in detail in his *Autobiography* (pp. 340–4). Keats saw Carlo Lasinio's engraving of the *Triumph of Death* in Haydon's studio in December 1818. The work is, together with *Romeo and Juliet*,

the main source of *The Eve of St Agnes*. Keats found the fresco grotesque but finer than any accomplished work he had seen, because it left much room for the imagination (R. Gittings, *John Keats*, Heinemann: London 1968, pp. 279–81). On Ruskin's discovery, see all his letters from Pisa in *Ruskin in Italy. Letters to His Parents 1845*, ed. H. I. Shapiro, Clarendon Press: Oxford 1972. Finally, it is well known that the Pisan frescoes played a significant role in the formation of several Pre–Raphaelites.

8   Giotto's importance had obviously been noted long before Vasari, beginning with Dante, Boccaccio, Sacchetti and Villani. See M. Baxandall, *Giotto and the Orators*, Clarendon Press: Oxford 1971.

9   On the frescoes in the Camposanto at Pisa, see M. Meiss, *Painting in Florence and Siena after the Black Death*, Princeton UP: Princeton (N. J.) 1951 (rpt. Harper: New York, Evanston and London, 1964); P. Toesca, *Il Trecento*, UTET: Torino 1951; F. Antal, *Florentine Painting and Its Social Background*, K. Paul: London 1947; R. Longhi, *Opere complete*, vol. VI: *Lavori in Valpadana*, Sansoni: Firenze 1973; L. Bellosi, *Buffalmacco e il Trionfo della Morte*, Einaudi: Torino 1974; G. Previtali, *Giotto e la sua bottega*, Fabbri: Milano 1967. On Coleridge and the frescoes, see E. S. Shaffer, '"Infernal Dreams" and Romantic Art Criticism: Coleridge on the Campo Santo, Pisa', *The Wordsworth Circle*, XX (1989), 9–19, and 'Coleridge and the Object of Art', *The Wordsworth Circle*, XXIV (1993), 117–28.

10   Coleridge's silence about Michelangelo's poems is all the more surprising considering Wordsworth's and Southey's interest in them. In 1805 Richard Duppa asked Wordsworth and Southey to translate some poems of Michelangelo for his biography of the artist which was published in 1806 (K. Curry, 'Uncollected Translations of Michaelangelo by Wordsworth and Southey', *Review of English Studies*, XIV, 1938, 193–9). Two translations, a revision of an 1805 draft and a new one, were included in *Memorials of a Tour in Italy, 1837*. Wordsworth found Michelangelo's texts difficult, and wrote that Michelangelo and Dante show that the effeminacy of Italian is not connatural to the language (Rossiter Smith, 'Wordsworth and his Italian Studies', 249–50; and S. Rossi, 'Wordsworth e l'Italia', *Letterature moderne*, IV, No 5, Sept–Oct 1953, pp. 542–3). On Duppa's biography, a compilation which was nonetheless popular, see Marshall 300–1, 334–5; and G. Melchiori, *Michelangelo nel Settecento inglese*, Edizioni di Storia e Letteratura: Roma 1950, p. 75. See also S. Curran, *Poetic Form and British Romanticism*, OUP: New York 1986, p. 45.

11   Before visiting Italy, Coleridge saw some of Michelangelo's works in Beireis's collection (*CL* I 522 (6 Jul 1799)); he saw works by Raphael at Oakover (*CL* I 231 (22 Aug 1796)) and in Beireis's collection, where he was struck by the 'St Helena dreaming the vision of the Cross, designed by Raphael and painted by Paul Veronese' (*CL* II 1110 (28 Mar 1804)). I find Jack Stillinger's suggestion that Kubla's 'pleasure dome' might echo Michelangelo's words about St Peter's dome groundless ('"Kubla Khan"' and Michelangelo's Glorious Boast', *English Language Notes*, XXIII, No 1, Sept 1985, 38–42). The only book known to Coleridge which mentions Michelangelo's words was John Moore's *A View of Society and Manners in Italy*, which he read in Malta. Raphael is mentioned in *To a Painter* (*PW (CC)* No 62 (Oct–Nov 1791?; rev. Aug 1793?)).

12   *L Lects* (*CC*) II 59–60; *P Lects* (1949) 167, 193; *CL* V 15. He believed that 'Michael Angelo and Raphael fed their imaginations highly' with the frescoes in the Camposanto at Pisa (*TT* (*CC*) 25 Jun 1830), an opinion Leigh Hunt shared (*Autobiography*, p. 343). John Ruskin thought the Pisan *Last Judgement* was the source of Michelangelo's (*The Works of John Ruskin*, eds. E. T. Cook and Alexander Wedderburn, Allen: London; Longman, Green and Co.: New York, 1903–12, vol. IV: *Modern Painters*, pt. III, sec. II, ch. III, p. 275 n. 4); he noticed the similarity between the Pisan and Michelangelo's Christ (ibid.; see also *Works* vol. XII, p. 226, 1847; and p. 147, 1854), which modern criticism has confirmed (see P. De Vecchi, 'Michelangelo's Last Judgement', in *The Sistine Chapel: Michelangelo Rediscovered*, Muller, Blond & White: London 1986, p. 182).

13   *CN* III 3827 (1810); *CL* III 520–21 (1814); *L Lects* (*CC*) I 221.

14   *CN* II 2828. The figure of Michelangelo's to which Coleridge referred has not been identified (*CN* II 2828 n.). John Opie (1761–1807) and Mme Lebrun (1755–1842) were fashionable portraitists in Coleridge's time. Hazlitt and Shelley did not share Coleridge's admiration for the *Last Judgement*. The former was uncertain about it: the figures at the bottom were 'hideous, vulgar caricatures of demons and cardinals, and the whole is a mass of extravagance and confusion' (*Notes of a Journey through France and Italy, Complete Works*, vol. X, p. 241). Shelley liked the study of the *Last Judgement* in the Gallery in Naples, but found the finished work 'a kind of Titus Andronicus in painting' (*SL* 79 (29 Feb 1819)). Shelley's is the funniest among the negative responses to Michelangelo's frescoes in the Sistine Chapel I have met: 'Jesus Christ is like an angry pot–boy & God like an old alehouse–keeper looking out of window' (*SL* 111 (*c.* 20 Aug 1819)). Interestingly, John Ruskin deals with Michelangelo's *Last Judgement* in *Modern Painters*, ch. III, 'Of Imagination Penetrative', to exemplify his concepts of imagination and fancy. He quotes and commends Hunt's Imagination and Fancy but not Coleridge, although Hunt's essay is based on Coleridge's theory.

15   *CN* III 4397 (10 Mar 1818). The fact that this note is an abridgement of Schelling's *Ueber das Verhältniss der bildenden Künste zu der Natur* does not mean that Coleridge had not formerly developed similar ideas, as his comments on Michelangelo's and Raphael's idealism show. Such concepts were widespread in the Renaissance: for example, Michelangelo regarded imitation as an exhibition of the idea in the artist's mind, and artistic creation as analogous to *natura naturans* rather than as a mirror of *natura naturata* (D. Summers, *Michelangelo and the Language of Art*, Princeton UP: Princeton (N. J.), 1981, pp. 280, 286–7). The parallel between artistic and divine creation is characteristic of Renaissance art theory from Alberti to Leonardo, Michelangelo, Dürer and many others. On Renaissance theories of imitation, J. Bialostocki, 'The Renaissance Concept of Nature and Antiquity', in *The Renaissance and Mannerism. Studies in Western Art*, Acts of the Twentieth International Congress of the History of Art, vol. II, Princeton UP: Princeton (N. J.), 1963, 19–30.

16   Coleridge maintained that years of physiognomic studies are not necessary to understand that there is a relation between the form of the head and its capacities. Raphael, Michelangelo or Van Dyck would have never painted an

imaginary Plato or Shakespeare with a narrow forehead (N Q.19 f24 (after 1829)). The consonance of soul and body was the general principle of the physiognomic theories which belonged to the background of all painters in the Renaissance (see Summers, ibid., pp. 340–1).

17   *L Lects (CC)* II 333. Paget Toynbee (*Dante Studies*, Clarendon Press: Oxford 1921, pp. 135–6) points out that the story of a copy of the *Divine Comedy* illustrated by Michelangelo can be traced back to a note in Giovanni Bottari's (1689–1775) edition of Vasari's works. The story was reported by the *Annual Register* in 1764 and 'played an important part in directing the attention of English artists to the *Commedia* as a subject for illustration'. For another parallelism between Shakespeare and Michelangelo, *TT (CC)* 5 Jul 1834.

18   *CN* III 4227 and n. (1814). The dialogue between Coleridge and Wordsworth is reported in *CRB* I 214–15 (1817). Wordsworth insinuated that Coleridge would not have praised those Madonnas, had he not known they were by Raphael. It is curious to compare Coleridge's to André Chastel's idea that 'Raphael had developed a singular skill in the art of enlivening the composition by the characters' *glances*. . . . The sublimity of some of his Madonnas derives from this sort of magnetism of the figures' ('Amor sacro e amor profano nell'arte e nel pensiero di Raffaello', in *Raffaello a Roma. Il Convegno del 1983*, Elefante: Roma 1986, p. 9). On the implications of the English eighteenth-century attitude to Raphael, see C. G. Argan's excellent 'Raffaello e la critica', in *Raffaello a Roma. Il Convegno del 1983*, pp. 385–93.

19   *CL* VI 588 (15 Jul 1826); *CL* II 1110 (28 Mar 1804). He noticed that Parmigianino's *Holy Family* in the Uffizi was the source of Reynolds' *Puck* and *Muscipula (CN* II 2853 (Jun 1806)), and that stanza XV of Milton's *Ode on the Morning of Christ's Nativity* would have been an excellent subject for a fresco in Parmigianino's or Allston's style (*MC* 183–4 (after 1823)). Cellini's *Life* appears in a list of books Coleridge intended to acquire in 1808 (*CN* III 3276); he mentioned it later as one of 'the best attempted stories of Ghosts and visions' (*L Lects (CC)* II 138).

20   *L Lects (CC)* I 349. Coleridge saw some 'first–rates of Raphael and Titian' at Oakover in 1799 (*CL* I 231). He later wrote (*CL* II 960 (1 Aug 1803)): 'Young Hazlitt has taken masterly portraits of me & Wordsworth, very much in the manner of Titian's Portraits'. He visited Lord Bristol's collection in Rome and was struck by two copies from Titian, one of them by Salvatore Mazzarese (1755–1847) (*CN* II 2840 (May 1806)). A French imitation of Titian was instead an example of French grossness (the imitation was in effect by Horace Hone) (*TT (CC)* 29 Jun 1833). He mentioned Titian with Raphael and Rubens as one of the three greatest painters (*C Talker* 174), and thought Allston's chiaroscuro and colours had something in common with the Venetian school (*CL* IV 795 (1817); *C Talker* 183). He may have been echoing his German friends in Rome, who referred to Allston as 'the American Titian' (Gerdts, 'Washington Allston and the German Romantic Classicists in Rome', p. 183). For other references, see *BL (CC)* I 192; *L Lects (CC)* I 347 (1811); *P Lects* (1949), 178–9, 387; *CN* III 4227 (1814); *CL* IV 759. On Titian's influence on contemporary English painting see Brand (1957) 144–5. For Reynolds' view of the Venetian School, see *Discourses on Art*, Collier: New York 1961, pp. 60,

63–4, 172. On Tintoretto, Veronese and the Bassanos, *CN* III 4227 (1814); *CN* I 663 (1800–3); *CL* II 1110 (1804); *CN* III 4227; *CL* IV 795 (1817); *CN* IV 5290 (1825–6). On Correggio, to whom Coleridge paid lip-service, *CL* I 522 (1799); *CL* V 289 (8 Aug 1823).

21   *CL* IV 569, (25) May 1815. He probably saw Caravaggio's *Beheading of St John* in Malta (*CN* II 2101 and n. (May 1804)); on Caravaggio and Spagnoletto see also *EOT* (*CC*) II 429–30 (1816), and *C&S* (*CC*) 151. The '*Academic* School of the Carracci' is mentioned *SM* (*CC*) 103–4 n. 3, and *CL* IV 759 (28 Jul 1817). The analogy between the poetic of Giambattista Marino and Annibale Carracci is pointed out by G. C. Argan, and B. Contardi, *Da Leonardo a Canova*, vol. IV of *Storia dell'arte classica e italiana*, diretta da G. C. Argan, Sansoni: Firenze 1983, p. 259.

22   Some of these painters – for example Carlo Dolci – had been popular in the eighteenth century. He saw them at Corsham (*CN* III 4227 and n. (1814)) and Burleigh House (*CN* III 3995 (1810)). 'Carlo Dolce's representations of our Saviour are pretty, to be sure; but they are too smooth to please me. His Christs are always in sugar candy' (*TT* (*CC*) 24 Jul 1831; see also *C Talker* 308).

23   For Horace Walpole's and Lady Morgan's comparison between Shakespeare and Salvator, see L. Salerno, *Salvator Rosa*, Edizioni per il Club del Libro: Milano 1963, pp. 78 and 81. Lady Morgan found that Milton and Salvator 'in genius, character, and political views, bore no faint resemblance to each other' (*The Life and Times of Salvator Rosa*, London 1855, p. 71). On eighteenth-century views, see E. W. Manwaring, *Italian Landscape in Eighteenth Century England*, OUP: New York 1925 (rpt. Frank Cass: London 1965), pp. 44–9. Ruskin went so far as to see in Salvator the last signs of spiritual life in Europe (ibid., p. 49).

24   *CN* I 1207 (1802); I 1495 (1803); II 1899 (1804). Coleridge wrote that beauty depended on the correspondence between unconscious thoughts and perceived forms. The intrusion of fantastic or arbitrary elements disturbed such a delicate balance and produced the sublime: 'This might be abundantly exemplified and illustrated from the paintings of Salvator Rosa' ('Fragment of an Essay on Beauty', *BL* (1907) II 250). He also read Salvator's poems, from which he quoted some lines on the abundance of asses in contemporary cultural life (see *CN* III 4258 and n. (Aug–Sept 1815); *BL* (*CC*) I 167; on his copy of Salvator's satires, see Coffman 178).

25   Denis Sutton points out that 'the British connection with Piranesi was a notable feature of Roman Art life'; Piranesi had English patrons and designed the Egyptian decorations of the *Caffè degli Inglesi* in Rome ('Aspects of British Collecting, Part II', *Apollo*, NS CXVI, No 250, Dec 1982, p. 409).

26   *Confessions of an English Opium-Eater*, in *The Collected Writings of Thomas de Quincey*, ed. D. Masson, London 1896–7, vol. III, pp. 438–9. What Coleridge is reported to have called *Dreams* correspond to Piranesi's *Carceri d'invenzione* or *Capricci*. It is not known whether the *Dreams* are the 'Folios' for Wordsworth mentioned by Coleridge in a letter to Sara Hutchinson accompanying Chapman's *Homer* (*CM* (*CC*) II 1118 and n. (Feb 1808)). The passage has stimulated several scholars: A. Hayter, *Opium and the Romantic Imagination*, Faber and Faber: London 1968 (rpt. 1969), p. 93 ff., who links it to opium–taking; J. Beer, *Coleridge's Poetic Intelligence*, Macmillan: London and

Basingstoke 1977, pp. 276–7; D. Jasper, *Coleridge as a Poet and Religious Thinker*, Macmillan: London and Basingstoke 1985, pp. 1–2; Arden Reed's vaporous comments in *Romantic Weather*, p. 209 ff.; E. S. Shaffer, 'Coleridge and the Object of Art', *The Wordsworth Circle*, XXIV (1993), 118–23. Other Coleridgean references to Piranesi, *CL* III 541 (3 Nov 1814); *CN* IV 5163 (1824).

27   *CM* (*CC*) I 627. The anecdotes on the Italian painters he related in his lectures may have been taken from secondary sources like Roscoe or Reynolds. The anecdote on Michelangelo in *CN* II 2792 (1806) appears in Roscoe's *Life of Lorenzo*, ch. IX, p. 206, n. (b); see also *P Lects* (1949) 178–9 and 413 n. 9. A copy of a French translation of Vasari was in Green's library (*CM* (*CC*) I 627 n.).

28   'On the Principles of Genial Criticism', *BL* (1907) II 226; *CN* III 4157 n.; *C&S* (*CC*) 82.

29   Brand (1957) 159.

30   *L Lects* (*CC*) I 348–9. Although there is a grain of truth in his remark, it makes Raphael and Titian more 'Gothic' than they are – as for example Raphael's Madonnas or Titian's portraits can show. The comparison and the examples derive from August Wilhelm Schlegel's *Vorlesungen über dramatische Kunst und Literatur*, I i, and II ii; the original source is Schiller's 'Ueber naive und sentimentalische Dichtung' (see *L Lects* (*CC*) I 348–9 nn.).

31   He wondered what the architectural 'genius of Italy' might have done in an environment like Hamburg, which he found ugly as it was (*CL* I 432 (26 Oct 1798); *Friend* (*CC*) II 212; *BL* (*CC*) II 178). He was indifferent to Baroque architecture, and compared it unfavourably with Classical remains in Syracuse (*CN* II 2244 (5 Nov 1804)). Architecture made him reflect on the sense of magnitude, which in his opinion did not depend on the absolute size but on the comparative size of the components in relation to the whole (N 51.15 f10 (1833)).

32   *Histoire* IV 177; see also 178–9. On S. Paolo fuori le mura see J. White, *Art and Architecture in Italy 1250 to 1400*, Penguin: Harmondsworth 1966, pp. 62, 94; A. Smart, *The Dawn of Italian Painting 1250–1400*, Phaidon: Oxford 1978, p. 22. For restorations and additions to the church from 1300 to 1800, see M. Fagiolo, and M. L. Madonna, (eds.), *Roma 1300–1875: La città degli anni santi*, Mondadori: Milano 1985, pp. 71–2, 84, 201, 209, 226, 235, 254–5, 300, 321, 334. Soon after the foundation, S. Paolo was the most important religious building in Rome with S. Peter's. The Byzantine bronze doors were ordered in 1070; the cloister was built between 1193 and 1228, the apse mosaic between 1218 and 1227 (R. Krautheimer, *Rome. Profile of a City, 312–1308*, Princeton UP: Princeton, N. J., 1980, pp. 42–3, 175–6, 179). The church still contains Arnolfo di Cambio's important tabernacle (1285).

33   *L Lects* (*CC*) I 347; 'On Poesy or Art', *BL* (1907) II 260–1.

34   *CL* IV 569 ((25) May 1815); *L Lects* (*CC*) II 60. On his hostility to Baroque sculpture, see also his comments on Roubilliac's *Newton* at Cambridge (*CN* I 822 (4–7 Oct 1800)). Coleridge mocked those who were not able to perceive the symbolic character of Michelangelo's art, like two (obviously) French visitors who interpreted the horns of *Moses* as signs of cuckoldism (*BL* (*CC*) II 116–17). See also *CN* I 1352 (1803), and *Friend* (*CC*) I 320–1. Shelley provides again an interesting counterpoint: he found Michelangelo's *Moses* distorted, monstrous

and detestable (*SL* 80 (25 Feb 1819)). It is not certain that Coleridge met Canova in Rome, as he claimed (*CL* III 352 (7 Dec 1811); *CN* II 2811; Sultana (1969) 393).

35 Coleridge was first struck by the bad conditions of Daniele da Volterra's *Descent from the Cross* (*CN* II 2759 (31 Dec 1805)). After visiting the Sistine Chapel, he was again hurt at the idea of the frailty of frescoes, and even planned a poem on the topic (*CN* II 2813 (Mar–Apr 1806)). The observation was repeated in the lectures (*L Lects* (*CC*) I 76–7; I 208; *CN* III 3286 (Mar 1808)). Complaints about the conditions of frescoes were not unusual: see Hazlitt, *Notes of a Journey through France and Italy, Complete Works*, vol. X, pp. 237, 240; and Goethe, *Italienische Reise*, Berliner Ausgabe, vol. XIV, pp. 294–5.

36 *BL* (1907) II 221; also 'On Poesy or Art', *BL* (1907) II 255.

37 *BL* (*CC*) I 85. He found in Italian Renaissance painting the application of many congenial principles, like the idea of beauty as '*il più nell'uno* – Multitude in unity' (*TT* (*CC*) 27 Dec 1831). The source of the definition is St Francis of Sales; see also 'On the Principles of Genial Criticism', *BL* (1907) II 230, 232. St Francis was repeating a Renaissance commonplace, so that Henry Nelson Coleridge's attribution of the definition to the 'Roman school of painting' was not arbitrary (*TT* (*CC*) II 154). Coleridge was aware of the fact that the conception of beauty as *concinnitas* was at odds with the idea of beauty as intuition or illumination. He solved the problem by saying that the relation of the parts to the whole is immediately intuited, so as to exclude any possibility of measurement ('On the Principles of Genial Criticism', *BL* (1907) II 239, 243). His aim was to oppose the analytic taste for details. On the topic, see E. Panofsky, *Idea, A Concept in Art Theory*, Teubner: Leipzig 1924 (tr. J. J. S. Peake, Univ. of South Carolina Press: Columbia 1968, p. 29).

38 'On Poesy or Art', *BL* (1907) II 258; *CN* IV 4630 (1819–20); IV 5088 (Dec 1823); *TT* (*CC*) II 244 n. (6 Jul 1833); N 52.11 f10v (1833). On the idea, Erwin Panofsky's *Idea* is still helpful; on the idea in Florentine Neoplatonism, see Argan, and Contardi, *Storia dell'arte classica e italiana*, vol. III, p. 255.

39 *IS* 215–16; *CN* IV 4832 (1821); IV 5290 (1825–6); IV 5447 (Sept 1826). Coleridge's 'structuralism' is emphasized by Barry 169–70. On the Romantic conception of colour, see Heffernan (1985) 149–57.

40 N Q.12 f15v (after 1829); N Q.13 f16 and 17 (after 1829).

41 Reynolds, *Discourses*, p. 129. He continued: 'There are, however, other intellectual qualities and dispositions which the Painter can satisfy and affect as powerfully as the Poet; among these we may reckon our love of novelty, variety, and contrast' (ibid., p. 130). Reynolds' attitude to novelty is as ambiguous as Coleridge's, who believed there was no progress in art: 'The Arts and the Muses both spring forth in the youth of nations . . . all-armed; manual dexterity may be improved indeed by practice' (*TT* (*CC*) 25 Jun 1830). Allston also ranked poetry over painting, if the anecdote Coleridge was fond of relating is reliable (*L Lects* (*CC*) I 207; *CN* II 2794 n.; III 3827 (Mar 1808)).

42 Heffernan (1985) 41–2. There is a Neoplatonic echo in Shelley's view of matter as 'resistance'. Shelley preferred Classical to medieval and Renaissance art (*SL* 321–2 (8 Aug 1821)). He liked Raphael, Titian, Guido and the Carraccis (*SL* 81 (25 Feb 1819)), but his important artistic experiences were Pompeii,

Paestum and Classical Rome (*SL* 71, 79 (1819)). He considered St Paul's as superior to St Peter's, and both as inferior to the Pantheon. However, he admired St Peter's square and the fountains in Rome (*SL* 87–8 (23 Mar 1819)). Shelley took long notes on Classical sculpture and paid little attention to painting. His response to Michelangelo is emblematic: although he acknowledged his technical skill, he was repelled by his vision. Michelangelo's Bacchus was Bacchus seen by a Catholic, that is, a brutal, obtuse, disgusting figure. It had nothing of the Greek Bacchus (*SCW* VI 329).

The fine arts were a secondary aspect of Byron's experience of Italy, though he expressed great admiration for cities like Venice and Rome (*BL&J* V 129, 221). His taste was neoclassical and influenced by fashion: the Venetians, Guido and Canova were his favourite artists (*BL&J* VII 45; *Don Juan* XIV st. 40; *BPW* II 123; *Childe Harold* Canto IV st. 55; *Beppo* st. 46). However, he abhorred all religious pictures and disliked painting 'unless it reminds me of something I have seen or think it possible to see'. Painting was the most artificial art, '& that by which the nonsense of mankind is the most imposed upon. – I never yet saw the picture – or the statue – which came within a league of my conception or expectation' (*BL&J* V 213). It is noteworthy that canto IV of *Childe Harold* includes a long celebration of Classical Rome but does not mention the Renaissance. On Byron, Shelley and Italian art, see H. Barrows, 'Convention and Novelty in the Romantic Generation's Experience of Italy', *Bulletin of the New York Public Library*, LXVII, No 6 (Jun 1963), 360–75.

43   Heffernan (1985) 233–5.
44   V. A. Burd, 'Background to *Modern Painters*: The Tradition and the Turner Controversy', *PMLA*, LXXIV (1959), p. 258.
45   Heffernan (1985) 233–5.
46   J. A. W. Heffernan, 'The English Romantic Perception of Color', in *Images of Romanticism. Visual and Verbal Affinities*, eds. K. Kroeber and W. Walling, Yale UP: New Haven and London 1978, p. 138. See also Heffernan (1985) 148–57.
47   *BL* (*CC*) II 35–6. Reynolds appreciated Salvator's painting, of which he emphasized the *decorum* – the fitness of style to its subject matter. He thought Salvator's was one of the few examples of poetical landscape painting thanks to its wholeness and visionary power (*Discourses*, pp. 78, 225–6). Coleridge quoted Reynolds also in 'On Poesy or Art' (*CN* III 4397). A part of the passage from James Harris reported in n. 2 by the *CC* editor (p. 36) is quoted by Reynolds (*Discourses*, p. 243).
48   *CL* III 352 (7 Dec 1811); 'On the Principles of Genial Criticism', *BL* (1907) II 234.
49   Reynolds, *Discourses*, pp. 66, 55; see also pp. 44 and 60. Cf. Johnson on the metaphysical poets: 'Sublimity is produced by aggregation, and littleness by dispersion. Great thoughts are always general, and consist in positions not limited by exceptions, and in descriptions not descending to minuteness.' (*Life of Cowley, Lives of the English Poets*, ed. G. Birkbeck Hill, 3 vols., Clarendon Press: Oxford 1905, vol. I, p. 21).
50   *Discourses*, pp. 20, 57–8. Reynolds's idea that history painting should be called poetical painting is paralled by Lomazzo's, who in turn may have recalled Philostratus' definition (R. W. Lee, *Ut Pictura Poesis: The Humanistic Theory of*

Painting, Norton: New York 1967, p. 18 n. 75). Though it was not completely clear what it meant to call a painter 'poetical', both poets and painters 'clearly saw that besides taking its subject matter from poetry, painting could mediate between spirit and matter, and could thus transcend the mere copying of natural objects' (Heffernan (1985) 43–4). On Coleridge and history painting, see also *C&S* (*CC*) 151; N 50.6 f.3 (15 Feb 1831).

51   Heffernan (1985) 37–8, 44.

52   Burd, 'Background to *Modern Painters*', p. 259.

53   D. B. Brown, 'Sir George Beaumont as a Collector and Connoisseur. The Taste of the Golden Age', in *'Noble and Patriotic'. The Beaumont Gift, 1828*, pp. 27–8.

54   Heffernan (1985) 233; *C Talker* 317. Procter's judgement is based on the fact that Coleridge discussed a mediocre picture as if it was Raphael's, so that it 'became transfigured, sublimated, by the speaker's imagination, which far excelled both the picture and its author'.

55   Barry 138–9. Barry seems to have undervalued certain aspects of Coleridge's interest, like his early interest in the opera and in the settings of his own poems.

56   Abrams and Kevin Barry ascribe to Romantic aesthetics the substitution of music for painting as the ideal model for poetry. This is correct in regard to the theory of poetry, but it is incomplete. The relationship between poetry and music was changed decisively by Baroque aesthetics. The epitome of the new attitude is Bach's *Wohltemperiertes Klavier* (vol. I, 1722; vol. II, 1744) (which in modern English would be *The Well-Tempered Keyboard*). As yet, the human voice had always been the centre round which musical theory was organized. Bach's theoretical work, which is the pinnacle of decades of musical experiments, not only affirmed the independence of instrumental from vocal music: it set intrumental music as the centre to which vocal music itself was subordinated. Poetry was also subordinated to music in the opera, which flourished in the seventeenth century. The inferiority of the human voice implicitly meant that music was now ahead of poetry, and that it was in a way its model. Though theoretical awareness of the new relationship between the two arts dates from much later, the premises are Baroque.

Moreover, I prefer a general view of the relationship among the arts in Romanticism like Heffernan's. He speaks of a triangulation among the arts, since Romantic admiration for music was not incompatible with admiration for painting. The idea of *Gesamtkunstwerk* seems to me to be innate in Romantic aesthetics and its tendency to abolish the distinctions among genres and among the arts.

57   *CN* II 2728 (Nov–Dec 1805). Cf. Reynolds, *Discourses*, p. 132:
The writers of every age and country, where taste has begun to decline, paint and adorn every object they touch; they are always on the stretch; never deviate or sink a moment from the pompous and the brilliant. Lucan, Statius, and Claudian, (as a learned critick has observed,) are examples of this bad taste and want of judgment; they never soften their tones, or condescend to be natural: all is exaggeration and perpetual splendour.

58   K. Popper, *Logica della scoperta scientifica*, Einaudi: Torino 1970 (orig. edn Vienna 1934), pp. 277 and 306.

59   See above ch. I, n. 93 in particular. The marginalia are in pencil and very
      difficult to read, since they are almost faded. An additional difficulty is that the
      notes at the very margin of the pages were trimmed when the volumes were
      rebound.

60   For instance, he praised the 'almost faultless position and choice of words, in Mr
      Pope's *original* compositions' in *Biographia* (*(CC)* I 39 n.), whereas he had
      severely criticised him a decade before (*CN* II 2826 (*c.* Mar 1806)). Another
      consequence was his return to the rhyming couplet in his late poetry, which is
      insufficient to interpret as the result of an ideological involution.

Italy and Modern European Literature

1   In 1800 he proposed to Southey a plan for a history of poetry in which the
      Italian Renaissance appeared after the Greek and Roman period and before the
      Spanish and English Renaissance. Coleridge's contribution would have been an
      essay on recent German poetry (*CL* I 575). Nine years later, the prospectus of
      The Friend included among its main subjects 'Information of the present State
      and past history of Swedish, Danish, German, and Italian Literature' (*(CC)* II
      18). The 1812 course of lectures proposed to analyse 'the Drama of the Greek,
      French, Italian, and Spanish Stage, chiefly with reference to the Works of
      Shakespeare' (*CL* III 390 (24 Apr 1812)).

2   *CN* I 170 (1796). A reference to Dante's Hell in a passage on slave trade in the
      Watchman probably derives from his reading of Henry Boyd's translation of the
      Divine Comedy which Southey borrowed from the Bristol Library in 1794
      (*Watchman* (*CC*) 133; and see *Lects 1795* (*CC*) 237). On Southey's and
      Coleridge's borrowings, Whalley, 'The Bristol Library Borrowings of Southey
      and Coleridge, 1793–8', pp. 118, 123. A note on Dante appeared in the
      Anthologia Hibernica, which he borrowed in Mar–Apr 1796 (Lowes 567 n. 100).
      Lamb mentioned Dante in some letters to Coleridge in 1796 (Toynbee (1909)
      I 535; *Cormorant* II 239).

3   The first who noted the similarities between Dante and the *Ancient Mariner* was
      F. Olivero, 'Dante e Coleridge', *Giornale Dantesco*, XV, No 5 (1908). Lowes 217
      and n., 287–8 and n., analyses the matter in detail; his suggestion that Coleridge
      might have read the original text at least in part at an early date (Lowes 525–8)
      is to my knowledge unfounded. See also Norman Fruman's reservations about
      Lowes (*The Damaged Archangel*, p. 549 n. 28), and W. P. Friedrich's about
      Olivero (*Dante's Fame Abroad*, Univ. of North Carolina Press, 1950, p. 243).
      A. A. Mendilow, 'Symbolism in Coleridge and the Dantesque Element in The
      Ancient Mariner', *Scripta Hierosolymitana* (1955), 25–81, points out many
      parallel images in the *Divine Comedy* and the *Ancient Mariner*, but only the
      analogy between Mastro Adamo's (*Inf.* XXX) and the Mariner's thirst is
      convincing (p. 72). Analogies between Dante's Ulysses and the *Mariner* are
      suggested by I. H. Chayes, 'A Coleridgean Reading of "The Ancient Mariner"',
      pp. 88, 98; and M. Bodkin, *Archetypal Patterns in Poetry*, pp. 44–6. G. Wilson
      Knight, *The Starlit Dome*, discusses *Christabel*, the *Ancient Mariner* and *Kubla
      Khan* as a Coleridgean *Divine Comedy*. Recent studies include Haase, 'Coleridge

and Henry Boyd's Translation of Dante's *Inferno*'; Greer, 'Coleridge and Dante: Kinship in Xanadu'; Reed, *Romantic Weather*, pp. 154–5.

4   In *The Destiny of Nations*, lines 183–94, Coleridge describes the Virgin led by her angel-guide on a mountain; a Pilgrim-man is also mentioned. Another possible Dantesque echo is in *Fire, Famine and Slaughter* (*PW* (EHC) I 237, lines 5–15), even if the witches of *Macbeth* are a more probable source. Dante is referred to in the *Apologetic Preface to Fire, Famine and Slaughters* (*PW* (EHC) II 1100; and *CC*, commentary to poem No 167) probably composed in 1815, where he wonders whether Dante really wished the characters of his poem suffered the torments he described. Heffernan ((1985) 112) finds Dantesque echoes in the images of frost in *Frost at Midnight*. The moral degeneration of Lewis' monk reminded Coleridge of the characters in Dante's Hell (review of *The Monk* (1797), *MC* 372).

5   On Coleridge and Dante's minor works, see chs. I and IV. Other references to Dante: *CN* I 413 (May 1799); I 1373 (May–Jul 1803).

6   *CL* III 364 (6 Feb 1812). For the early references to Dante, see *L Lects* (*CC*) I 229; 431; 492; 511; 516.

7   Cary studied Italian at the university as an optional subject, though he had read it for at least a year before going to Oxford (King (1925) 35–8, 47, 55. King's work is still the most complete source on Cary). Cary's interest in Dante developed early, since in 1792 he defended him against Anna Seward's strictures. Five years later he began his translation, which he completed in 1812 (King (1925) 57–60, 78, 97).

8   King (1925) 100–2. The *Edinburgh Review*, which had praised Boyd's version in 1803, ignored Cary's *Inferno*, which appeared in 1805–6; the *Literary Journal* preferred Boyd's to Cary's Dante (King (1925) 89–90). The 1814 edition appeared at Cary's own expense, since he could find no publisher interested in his translation (King (1925) 101).

9   King (1925) 111–12; see also *Cary M* ii 18–19. Samuel Rogers claimed that Thomas Moore had mentioned Cary's version to him; and that he mentioned it to Wordsworth, and Wordsworth in his turn to Coleridge (King (1925) 115–16; *CM* (*CC*) II 133). However, there is no reason to believe that the episode related by Cary's son is false. H. F. Cary himself acknowledged his debt to Coleridge in the preface to the 1819 edition (King (1925) 116 n.). The indifference with which Cary's translation was first received consoled Coleridge for the failure of his *Wallenstein* (*Friend* (*CC*) I 429).

10 See G. F. Cunningham, *The Divine Comedy in English. A Critical Bibliography 1782–1900*, Oliver and Bush: Edinburgh and London, 1965. Boyd's translation is longer than the original because he intended to improve on it according to eighteenth-century standards. The other versions available in 1817 were all partial: Rogers (1782) – the first to translate more than a canto, Nathaniel Howard (1807) and Joseph Hume (1812) had translated the *Inferno* only.

11 *CL* IV 781 (6 Nov 1817). Cf. *CL* IV 779 (29 Oct 1817): 'In itself the Metre is, compared to any English Poem . . . the most varied and harmonious to my ear of any since Milton – and yet the effect is so Dantesque that to those, who should compare it only with other English Poems, it would . . . have the same effect as the Terza Rima has compared with other Italian Metres.' On Cary's style, see King (1925) 300–6; Havens 354–6.

12　For Coleridge's marginalia, see *CM (CC)* II 133–38; *CN* IV 5043 (1823); his letters to Taylor and Hessey, *CL* IV 804; 823–4; 827; 834–5 (all 1818).

13　King (1925) 115, 117–18; and *Cary M* ii 27–8. The new edition included a longer commentary and a 'Life of Dante' (King (1925) 119). See also T. L. Cooksey, 'Dante's England 1818: The Contributions of Cary, Coleridge, and Foscolo to the British Reception of Dante', *Papers on Language and Literature*, XX, No 4 (fall 1984), 355–81. In 1823 Coleridge tried to persuade Cary to translate and edit 'a Volume or two of Italian scraps, from Dante downwards' for Taylor and Hessey (*CL* V 302).

14　Ellis 252 n. 22. John Taaffe was the author of an English commentary on the *Divine Comedy* (1822). On Cary's Dante in nineteenth-century England, see Cunningham, *The Divine Comedy in English*, p. 20.

15　On Shelley's translation of Dante, see Webb, *The Violet in the Crucible*. Shelley read Cary's *Dante* in 1817 (p. 282). His version of Dante is not Miltonic and is characterized by *terza rima*. He complained of Cary's Miltonisms, but the insuperable problem is that a Dantesque language does not exist in English. Pound's translation of Cavalcanti provides an interesting analogy.

16　Coleridge's plans for his criticism of Dante were laborious. In 1816 he expressed the desire to review old authors in couples, one of which was Dante and Milton (*CL* IV 648). He put it into practice on 27 February, 1818, when he gave the first of his Dante lectures. The original prospectus had promised a lecture on Dante, Donne and Milton, but the announcements in the newspapers had reduced it already to Dante and Milton (*L Lects (CC)* II 184–5). However, he did not abandon the original plan, since he later wrote Cary he intended to publish an essay on them (*CL* IV 827 (2 Feb 1818)). Neither notes nor reports are extant, so it is not known whether and to what extent he compared Dante and Milton. Henry Crabb Robinson noted that it was one of his best lectures: 'He digressed less than usually, and really gave information and ideas about the poets he professed to criticise' (*CRB* I 220 (27 Feb 1818)). It is possible that the notes for this successful lecture were reworked for the other one on Dante he gave on 11 March 1819, as R. A. Foakes argues (*L Lects (CC)* II 184–5). Comparisons between Dante and Milton were also drawn in 1819.

17　Hallam made the same point and argued that few German scholars like Tennemann and very few Englishmen, one of whom was Coleridge, knew Scholastic philosophy (Hallam II 485–6 and nn.). Beatrice Corrigan points out that Hallam's book 'became one of the most frequently quoted authorities on the Italian poets' (Corrigan 13), despite (or thanks to) its simplicity. As far as Italian literature is concerned, Hallam's sources were Muratori, St Marc, Denina, and above all Sismondi (Hallam I 218–19 n.).

18　See E. P. Vincent, 'Fortuna di Dante in Inghilterra', in *Enciclopedia dantesca*, Istituto della Enciclopedia Italiana: Roma 1970–8, vol. III, p. 446. For Roscoe, see *Life of Leo X*, vol. III, pp. 196–9; for Shelley, Ellis 17 ff.

19　Coleridge read the manuscript of Rossetti's commentary on the *Comedy* which was published in 1826–7. He was later given a copy of *Sullo spirito antipapale che produsse la Riforma* (1832) (*CL* V 403 (14 Dec 1824); V 431 (May 1825)).

20　See Ellis 21–2. Cary criticized Venturi, even though he acknowledged the value of his scholarship ('Life of Dante', in *The Divine Comedy*, OUP: London 1910, rpt. 1950, pp. xxxviii–xxxix). According to C. P. Brand, the idea of Dante as a patriot was 'spread in England by a small band of Italian political exiles of the first decade of the nineteenth century . . . – Foscolo, Rossetti, Berchet, Panizzi, Mazzini and others.' ('Dante and the English Poets', in *The Mind of Dante*, ed. U. Limentani, CUP 1985, p. 164). But they in their turn were influenced by the English poets, foremost by Byron.

21 Hallam provided the information for this section: see for example Hallam I 259 ff.; and notes in *CN* III 4498 and *L Lects (CC)* II 400–401. Hallam drew on Sismondi, who dealt with the subject extensively (see e.g. *Histoire* III 245 ff.).

22 See Hallam II 450–70; F. Schlegel, *Geschichte*, Lectures VI, VII and VIII.

23 *Geschichte* 210.

24 Schelling, 'Ueber Dante in philosophischer Beziehung', *Sämmtliche Werke*, Cotta: Stuttgart and Augsburg, 1859, vol. VI (1802–3), p. 155. Schlegel, *Geschichte* 211.

25 See S. Zecchi, *La fondazione utopica dell'arte. Kant Schiller Schelling*, Unicopli: Milano 1984, p. 193. Zecchi points out that 'the difference between the two mythologies plays in Schelling the same role as the distinction between the "naive" and the "sentimental" in Schiller' (ibid., p. 194). Coleridge did not read Schelling's work, which remained manuscript for a long time. Cf. also *LS (CC)* 62.

26 *Geschichte* 214; see also *Wissenschaft der Europäischen Literatur. Vorlesungen, Aufsätze und Fragmente aus der Zeit von 1795–1804* (*Kritische Ausgabe* XI 149–50), where Friedrich argues that such a combination of poetry and philosophy had not been possible before because in the Classical world they were very much separated. However, the union of all human knowledge is superior to the capacity of any mind, so that even Dante achieved it occasionally. August Wilhelm thought instead that 'Bei Dante . . . hat sich Philosophie und Poesie wahrhaft durchdrungen' (*Geschichte der romantischen Literatur*, ed. E. Lohner, Kohlhammer: Stuttgart 1965, p. 178). Friedrich's interest in Dante began and developed through his brother about 1791, when he published his first article on the Italian poet. The other main sources of his criticism of Dante are Mazzoni and Tiraboschi (*Kritische Ausgabe* XI 320, n. 324; 321, n. 329). For other comments of F. Schlegel's on Dante, see *Gespräch über die Poesie* (*Kritische Ausgabe* II) and especially *Fragmente zur Poesie und Literatur* (*Kritische Ausgabe* XVI).

27 The subject is very important, since it involves Coleridge's conception of epic, the Bible, and their interaction. He defined the Old Testament as 'a *Divina Commedia* of a superhuman . . . Ventriloquist' (*CIS* 53). See Shaffer (1975), especially pp. 34–44, 52–5, 62–3.

28 The best study of Byron's, Shelley's and the Byronic Dante are Ellis, *Dante and English Poetry*, and Pite, *The Circle of Our Vision*. It should not be expected that other philosophical English critics followed Coleridge's pattern: Carlyle's 'The Hero as Poet' is a digest of Byronic and Shelleyan attitudes to Dante (Ellis 62–5). Coleridge thought that poets like Homer, the Greek tragedians, Dante, Shakespeare and Milton, who moved 'in the sphere of religion', deserved a philosophical criticism (*MC* 170).

29 Hallam (II 506) writes that Dante was read in Italian universities more for his

philosophy than for his poetry, but he does not mention John of Ravenna as Coleridge did. John of Ravenna was referred to in *P Lects*, so that Kathleen Coburn indicated Tennemann as a possible source. However, it must be pointed out that Coleridge knew Petrarch's letters, in which Giovanni da Ravenna, Petrarch's pupil, appears frequently. Coleridge knew also Boccaccio's *Trattatello in laude di Dante*, which emphasizes Dante's learning. See ch. IV below for more detail.

30   The same opinion was expressed by Schelling ('Ueber Dante in philosophischer Beziehung', pp. 156–7). Gilson argues that Dante is 'a moralist and reformer who arms himself with all the theses required for his work of reformer and by his moral philosophy', and that his poem is not a system but 'the dialectical and lyrical expression of all his loyalties' (*Dante the Philosopher*, tr. D. Moore, Sheed & Ward: London 1948, pp. 276, 281).

31   The presence of Scholastic philosophy and language in Dante reinforced his idea that the Schoolmen made the European languages what they are (*TT (CC)* 31 Mar 1830).

32   Coleridge's source was first noticed by A. C. Dunstan, 'The German Influence on Coleridge', *Modern Language Review*, XVII, No 3 (Jul 1922), pp. 274–5. See also the notes in *CN* and *L Lects (CC)*. Schiller is the ultimate source of the distinctions between Classical and modern art made by Schelling and the Schlegels. Dante, Chaucer, Shakespeare and Jonson were mentioned in a note for a planned essay on the passions as the best sources (*IS* 68). In 1803 Coleridge had compared Dante's and Chaucer's sense of humour with the humour of the Classics, who hardly possessed any (*CL* II 951). Shelley disagreed with such views: he argued in the preface to *Prometheus Unbound* that images from the operations of the human mind were common in Greek poetry, whereas they were occasional in modern poetry, as in Dante and Shakespeare.

33   *CN* III 4498. The example he gave to illustrate this capacity was the description of the Stygian Lake (*Inf.* VII 120–30). His reference to the Francesca and Ugolino episodes – the standard illustrations of the concept at the time – belongs to this context. Hazlitt's view is worth comparing with Coleridge's:

The immediate objects he [Dante] presents to the mind, are not much in themselves; – they generally want grandeur, beauty and order; but they become everything by the force of the character which he impresses on them. His mind lends its own power to the objects which it contemplates, instead of borrowing it from them. He takes advantage even of the nakedness and dreary vacuity of his subject.

Review of Sismondi's *Literature of the South of Europe*, in the *Edinburgh Review* (Jun 1815), quoted from Toynbee (1909) II 176; repeated in *Lectures on the English Poets* (1818). Beatrice Corrigan argues that the essay, which is perceptive and defends Dante from Sismondi's old-fashioned strictures, 'marks an important development in Italian studies in England'. Sismondi's work and Ginguené's *Histoire littéraire d'Italie* (1811–16) were widely read and influential in England (Corrigan 10). Heffernan points out the analogy between Hazlitt's criticism of Dante and Turner, who according to Hazlitt were able to give reality to airy nothing (Heffernan (1985) 164–5).

34   The comparison between Dante and Milton, the authors of the greatest Catholic

and Protestant epics, became commonplace in the nineteenth century. See I. Samuel, *Dante and Milton. The 'Commedia' and 'Paradise Lost'*, Cornell UP: Ithaca (New York) 1966, p. 31; Ellis 49; and E. T. McLaughlin, 'Coleridge and Milton', *Studies in Philology*, LXI (1964), p. 561 (and also pp. 546–7; 563). The comparison appears in Cary's notes to Canto XXXIV. Lessing remarked that Milton alone could represent the devil without making him physically ugly. Pound and Eliot preferred Dante's graphic precision to Milton's vagueness, but they also found Milton's Satan more convincing than Dante's. For other comparisons between Dante, Donne and Milton, and between Dante and Jeremy Taylor, see *MC* 184 and *C 17th C* 259.

35   He wondered whether Dante had gained inspiration from Giotto's representation of the otherworld or vice versa (*TT* (*CC*) 25 Jun 1830). Cary maintained that Dante and Giotto were friends ('Life of Dante', p. xxvii). On Coleridge and Giotto see my ch. II.

36   *TT* (*CC*) 31 Mar and 6 Aug 1832; for the reference to *Biographia*, see *BL* (*CC*) II 21. In 1812 Coleridge argued that Shakespeare's picturesqueness was only equalled by Dante and Milton; another report gives 'Pindar' instead of Milton, which seems more probable considering the passage quoted below, and that he regarded Milton as a musical poet (see *L Lects* (*CC*) I 361; and McLaughlin, 'Coleridge and Milton', p. 563). He argued that the scene of Lear's madness was visually more powerful than any a Michelangelo inspired by Dante might have painted (*L Lects* (*CC*) II 333 (1819)). In the lecture on Dante, he specified that Dante was 'Picturesque beyond all, modern and ancient – more in the stern style of Pindar than any other'. He quoted two vivid passages from *Inferno* in support of his view, the one portraying Charon (III 94–108) and the other Pluto (VII 1–15) (*CN* III 4498).

37   Coleridge used the concept in other lectures (see my ch. II). He does not seem to have known Schelling's idea, recalled by A. W. Schlegel in his *Geschichte der romantischen Literatur* (p. 180), that the *Inferno* is plastic, the *Purgatorio* picturesque and the *Paradiso* musical. Schlegel thought, however, that the three elements were contained in each part (e.g., the *Inf.* was full of dissonances and chiaroscuro contrasts).

38   See Friedrich, *Dante's Fame Abroad*, p. 234. Friedrich points out that the comparison had first been made by Bodmer and Moutonnet de Clairfons (ibid., p. 382 n.). For the comparison between Classical and modern architecture, see my ch. II. Comments on Gothic architecture appear in Hallam II 419–21.

39   A. Vallone, *La critica dantesca nel Settecento ed altri saggi danteschi*, Olschki: Firenze 1961, p. 13. Hallam, who thought Dante's extraordinary command of language produced abuses and obscurity, suggested that if 'Petrarch, Bembo, and a few more, had not aimed rather at purity than copiousness, the phrases which now appear barbarous, and are at least obsolete, might have been fixed by use in poetical language' (Hallam II 505).

40   Warton 789–90. In Warton's summary of the *Divine Comedy* (pp. 779–91), the *Inferno* was given more space than the other two parts (the *Paradiso* is condensed in a paragraph). He emphasized that the poem, though powerful, is too often abstruse and indecent: 'Rude and early poets describe every thing' (p. 787). Consequently, it is often ridiculous. 'The truth is, Dante's poem is a

satirical history of his own time' (p. 790). The selected passages include the
beginning of *Inf.* III, the Francesca, Ugolino and Gerione episodes.

41   *The Pentameron and Other Imaginary Coversations*, ed. H. Ellis, Walter Scott:
London, n.d., p. 50. Like most of his contemporaries, Landor preferred the
Inferno to the other parts of the *Divine Comedy*, and in the *Inferno* the episodes of
Francesca and Ugolino in particular (ibid., pp. 17–20). He disliked allegory,
both in Dante and Spenser, but could not appreciate Dante when he was too
realistic. Ugolino's story shows that 'Dante is the great master of the disgusting'
(ibid., p. 49). Some passages of the *Paradiso* were in his opinion superior to
Paradise Regained, but on the whole *Paradise Lost* was the most perfect long
poem (letter to John Forster, 1850; *Landor as Critic*, ed. C. L. Proudfit,
Routledge and K. Paul: London and Henley 1979, p. 89). Surprisingly, Landor
found Dante's harsh temper distasteful (see e.g. *Pentameron*, pp. 6–7). With
reference to Dante's invectives, Landor's Petrarch states that the *Inferno* is 'the
most immoral and impious book that ever was written' (*Pentameron*, p. 19).
Landor objected to the structure of Dante's poem which was neither an epic nor
a tragedy: 'there are nowhere two whole cantos in Dante which will bear a
sustained and close comparison with the very worst book of the *Odyssea* or the
Æneid' (ibid., p. 25). He thought, however, that something purely Greek could
be found in Dante (*Poems*, ed. G. Grigson, Centaur: London 1964, p. 94 n. 1).

42   *Dante's Divine Comedy. The Book and Its Story*, G. Newnes: London, n.d., p. 52.
The introduction, 'Dante's Life and Genius', is a biographical approach to Dante,
whose life and temper are discussed more than his poetry. Dante was bigoted
and intolerant though a great poet at times. The allegorical meaning is held to be
unimportant for the reader (ibid., p. 38). Many passages are impious or absurd
in Hunt's opinion, e.g. *Inf.* III 1–6 (ibid., p. 46). In the light of modern science,
Dante's vision seems 'no better than the dream of an hypochondriacal savage'
(ibid., p. 47). Hunt's two favourite episodes are Francesca and Ugolino (ibid.,
p. 54). Homer and Shakespeare are superior to Dante in all respects (ibid.,
pp. 57–8). Compared to them, Dante was 'a gratuitous logician, a preposterous
politician, a cruel theologian' (ibid., p. 60). Hunt repeated his view of Dante in
other works (see for example *Autobiography*, p. 445). However, Hunt's role in
popularizing Italian literature must not be undervalued. He made use of Italian
material in his own poetry, and the best-known example is his *Story of Rimini*,
an expansion of the Francesca episode which sold well. Hunt himself later
acknowledged the faults and the weakness of his poem (*Autobiography*,
pp. 257–8). The *Stories from the Italian Poets* (1846), of which *Dante's Divine
Comedy* is a section, contain translations, criticism, prose summaries, and
enjoyed great fortune in England and in the United States thanks to their simple
style (intr. to Hunt (1956) 28). See also R. W. King, 'Italian Influence on English
Scholarship and Literature during the 'Romantic Revival'', *Modern Language
Review*, XXI (1926), pp. 32–3.

43   The longest reference is the fragment of the *Paradiso* (I 88–90) quoted as a
conclusion to *C&S*, which is included in his poems as *Reason* (*PW* (EHC) I 487).
Reason is described as clear vision, and as such opposed to the misty perception
of the senses. Coleridge invites the reader, puzzled like Dante at the beginning
of Paradise, to abandon his 'falso imaginar' ('false imagination') if he wants to

enter a different reality. The same lines had been quoted with reference to religious faith in 1820–21 (*CN* IV 4786). On *Reason* see E. Kessler, *Coleridge's Metaphors of Being*, Princeton UP: Princeton (N. J.) 1979, pp. 43–5, who argues that in Coleridge's vision the essence maintains some link with its phenomenal body, so that he denies Dante's unmediated *visio intellectualis* of pure light; and Reed, *Romantic Weather*, pp. 83–90.

44　For these lectures see *L Lects* (*CC*) and *CN* III 4378–4379; 4383–4384 and nn. (1818). The same subject was discussed in *P Lects*, Lecture VIII. Coleridge's anthropology was based on Kant, Richard and Blumenbach, although in the lectures he mainly drew on F. Schlegel. Coleridge thought southern Italians belonged to the same racial branch as the Greeks and Macedonians, while he grouped northern Italians with the Celts (*CN* IV 4548 (Jun 1819); *TT* (*CC*) 24 Feb 1827). On the Celtic races, see *P Lects* (1949) 430 n. 11.

45　On the subject, see my Appendix.

46　Coleridge transcribed his first sentence of Italian from Boccaccio's *Genealogia degli dei* in 1803 (*CN* I 1649, 1653). He was probably reading Giuseppe Betussi's Italian translation of *De genealogia deorum* (first published Venice 1545) (Wright 337). The provenance of the book is uncertain (*Cormorant* I 445–6); a copy was in Green's library (*Cormorant* I 204 n. 44; *CN* II 2737 n.), and another (Venice 1588) in Wordsworth's (Coffman 27). In 1800 Coleridge had mentioned Boccaccio's 'fatal Stories' (*CN* I 687), which he read in the original in Malta and Italy (*CN* II 2692 (Oct 1805)), where he may have bought his edition of Boccaccio's works (ed. Lorenzo Ciccarelli, vols. I–IV of 6, Naples 1723).

47　F. Schlegel, *Wissenschaft der Europäischen Literatur* (*Kritische Ausgabe* XI), p. 151. See also 'Nachricht von den poetischen Werken Johannes Boccaccio' (1801) (*Kritische Ausgabe* II 393–6), in which he developed his theory of the *novella*.

48　*L Lects* (*CC*) II 233; 238–9. The problem is of course complex; a good introduction is M. Croll, 'The Baroque Style in Prose', orig. publ. 1929, now in *Style, Rhetoric, and Rhythm*, ed. J. M. Patrick, Princeton UP: Princeton (N. J.) 1966. On Coleridge's response to Ciceronianism, see my ch. IV.

49　For instance, Baretti and Johnson expressed such an opinion (see N. Jonard, 'Giuseppe Baretti e la critica johnsoniana', in *Problemi di lingua e letteratura italiana del Settecento*, Steiner: Wiesbaden 1965, p. 282).

50　Wright 359–60. In 1805 Coleridge noted: 'Of the Italian language in Machiavelli & Boccacio/wherein better, wherein worse than the Latin. Of the present Gallicism and uniformity of construction throughout Europe, & its effects' (*CN* II 2512). The model of Machiavelli's prose was Tacitus; of Boccaccio's, Cicero.

51　*L Lects* (*CC*) II 92. An interesting observation he made on the *Decameron* was that he found its *cornice*, its frame, less achieved than Chaucer's: 'When you reflect that the company in the Decameron have retired to a place of safety from the raging of a pestilence, their mirth provokes a sense of their unfeelingness' (*L Lects* (*CC*) II 105).

52　'I dare affirm them far more interesting than the Decamerone itself – and if less amusing, yet . . . more entertaining' (*CL* III 529 (10 Sept 1814)). See also *CL* (*CC*) IV 570, 592 (1815). It is not clear whether the 'Prose Works' he mentioned to Murray included Boccaccio's Latin writings and metrical romances or not. His observation on the 'almost neglected Romances' does not clarify the point. The comparison between Boccaccio and Cervantes appears in other critics. F. Schlegel often mentioned them together: '*Boccaz* Vorgänger und Ergänzung des *Cervantes*' (*Fragmente zur Poesie und Litteratur, Kritische Ausgabe* XVI, (IX 799)).

53　Attitudes ranged from Sismondi's, who held them in low regard (*Histoire* VI 154 ff.; and *South* I 299); to Hazlitt's, who knew little or nothing about them; to Landor's, who paid little attention to them, though he liked *Fiammetta*, which inspired some of his works (Wright 360; 348–9); to Hunt's, who read and appreciated most of them, even though he thought Boccaccio 'great and poetical–natured, but no great poet' (Wright 352; *The World of Books and Other Essays*, Gay & Bird: London 1819, p. 46); to F. Schlegel's, who regarded *Ninfale fiesolano* as the work, together with some tales in *Decameron*, in which Boccaccio's personality emerged most clearly, and *Fiammetta* as superior even to *Decameron* ('Nachricht von den poetischen Werken des Johannes Boccaccio', *Kritische Ausgabe* II 395; *Fragmente zur Poesie und Litteratur, Kritische Ausgabe* XVI 579 n. 731). Coleridge's interest is historically grounded if we remember these works are the archetypes of several genres which flourished in the Renaissance, when they were popular. See V. Branca, intr. to *Amorosa visione*, in Boccaccio, *Tutte le opere*, Mondadori: Milano 1967–, vol. III, and E. M. W. Tillyard, *The English Epic and Its Background*, Chatto and Windus: London 1968 (first publ. 1954), p. 194 ff. On Boccaccio's minor works before 1800, Wright 44–112.

54　See Branca (1964) 62.

55　*SL* 121–2 (27 Sept 1819). He continued in the same letter: 'I think him – not equal certainly either to Dante or Petrarch – but far superior to Tasso and Ariosto, the children of a later and colder day.' On Shelley and Boccaccio, see Brand (1957) 110; Wright 336. Hunt stimulated Shelley's interest in Boccaccio. Shelley admired the vitality of Boccaccio, and sympathized with Boccaccio's conception of love, which he thought similar to his own (*SL* 121–2). Besides the figure of Demogorgon, perhaps derived from *De genealogia*, the influence of *Teseida* has been traced in *Epipsychidion* (E. Viviani della Robbia, 'Shelley e il Boccaccio', *Italica*, XXXVI, No 3, Sept 1959, 181–97). On Foscolo, Branca (1964) 63, and all the chapter on Boccaccio's style.

56　The *Furioso* was a favourite of Agostino Isola, Wordsworth's teacher of Italian at Cambridge, who edited it 1789; Wordsworth had a copy of Ariosto's poem with him on his tour of the Alps in 1790, and began to read it in the original in 1796; in 1802–3 he translated long passages from the *Furioso*. See Schneider, *Wordsworth's Cambridge Education*, pp. 103–5; Sturrock (1984–5) 798–811; on Wordsworth's Italian studies, *Cormorant* I 201 nn. 22, 23; and I 439. Ariosto in *The Prelude*: see bk. IX, lines 454–6; J. Sturrock, 'Wordsworth's Translations of Ariosto', *Notes & Queries*, XXVI (Jun 1979), 227–8. He regarded Spenser's genius as superior to Ariosto (*W Prose* III 67 (1815)). The influence of Ariosto on Wordsworth's view of epic and romance, as *Peter Bell* and *The Prelude* show, should not be overlooked (see B. Wilkie, *Romantic Poets and Epic Tradition*, Univ. of Wisconsin Press: Madison and Milwaukee, 1965, the ch. on Wordsworth).

57　The influence of *Orlando furioso* can be traced in Southey's long poems, especially *Thalaba the Destroyer* (1801). On Southey's early reading, *Cormorant* I 49; 20 n. 2; 62; and Praz, *Machiavelli in Inghilterra*, p. 327. On Ariosto and

Thalaba see Gibaldi, 'The Fortunes of Ariosto in England and America', in *Ariosto 1974 in America*, ed. A. Scaglione, Longo: Ravenna, pp. 147–8; and Brand (1957) 74–5. In 1793 Southey acknowledged his ignorance of the minor epic poets of Italy (Wilkie, *Romantic Poets and Epic Tradition*, pp. 33–4). Although he complained that 'even Tasso is often an imitator', Wilkie points out traces of Tasso in Southey's works (ibid., pp. 47–8; 237 n. 58). Southey claimed his poems bore no resemblance to Milton, whereas 'with Tasso, with Virgil, with Homer, there may be fair grounds of comparison' (*The Life and Correspondence of Robert Southey*, ed. C. C. Southey, 6 vols., London 1849–50, vol. IV, p. 105, 16 Feb 1815). On Southey's view of epic, see Wilkie, ibid., pp. 36–9, 110–1. On the role of Southey's romances in the context of romantic literature, M. Butler, 'Repossessing the Past', in *Rethinking Historicism: Critical Readings in Romantic History*, ed. M. Levinson, Blackwell: Oxford 1989, pp. 82–3.

58   *CN* II 2670 (15 Sept 1805). In *Biographia* Ariosto was charged with 'degrading and deforming passion into appetite', unlike Shakespeare ((*CC*) II 22; *CN* III 4115 (1811)), a remark he repeated in Lecture III of the 1818 course.

59   *On the Name 'Chestnut Grove'* (*PW* (*CC*) No 375 (1805)). He was probably using Wordsworth's vol. IV of Ariosto, *Opere in versi* (Venice 1741), which he had brought with him from England (*CN* II 2770 (1815); and 2670 n.). Other editions he consulted include *Opere* (6 vols., Venice 1783) and Harington's translation (*CN* III 4115 n.). See also Coffman 8.

60   L. Caretti, intr. to Ariosto, *Opere minori*, ed. C. Segre, Ricciardi: Milano–Napoli 1954, pp. IX–X.

61   L. Blasucci, *Studi su Dante e Ariosto*, Ricciardi: Milano–Napoli 1969, p. 82; see also pp. 78–9. On Ariosto's style, see W. Binni, *Metodo e poesia di Ludovico Ariosto*, D'Anna: Messina 1947, pp. 128–9, 136; and G. Contini, 'Come lavorava l'Ariosto', in *Esercizi di lettura*, Einaudi: Torino 1974.

62   Wordsworth had difficulties with *ottava rima* when he translated Ariosto. Like Coleridge, he preferred Spenser's stanza, though he thought it inferior to the open, flowing movement of Homer, Virgil or Milton. He found Tasso's stanza rigid and unsuited to the subject of his poem (Brand (1965) 270), although he admired him as one of the great epic poets (Wilkie, *Romantic Poets and Epic Tradition*, p. 60).

63   Coleridge's lectures on Ariosto are something of a mystery. Ariosto often appeared as a subject in his plans, as in 1812, when he promised to lecture on 'Dante, Ariosto, Don Quixote, Calderon, Shakspeare, Milton, and Klopstock', but remarks on Ariosto are occasional in the early lectures (*CL* III 364; *L Lects* (*CC*) I 415). In 1816 he asked Murray for any edition of Ariosto, probably with an eye to some critical project (*CL* IV 637, 647). Coleridge's attitude is strange, since he said he discussed the Italian poets as precursors of the English; otherwise 'Ariosto alone would have required a separate lecture' (*L Lects* (*CC*) II 92). Elsewhere, he called the whole romance tradition an 'Ariosto–traditions' (*CN* IV 5075 (Dec 1823)). The syllabus of the 1819 course on Shakespeare etc. promised a lecture on Spenser, Chaucer and Ariosto, but the newspapers announced a lecture on 'Spenser, the *Italian School of Poetry*, and the nature of Allegory' (*L Lects* (*CC*) II 406). No reports have been found, and his notes concern only Spenser, so that it is not known whether he discussed Ariosto. Yet

some written remarks on Ariosto must have existed, since Ariosto appears in his later plans to collect and edit some volumes of the best criticism from his notes, (*CL* V 26 (30 Mar 1820)). Thereafter, comments on Ariosto became occasional (*CN* IV 4968 (1823); *CL* VI 726 (1828)).

64   Several critics and poets defended Tasso against French strictures – Boileau's in particular – already in the first half of the century. Muratori, Rolli and Pope in England were admirers of Tasso. See Brand (1965) 259–66; and Marshall 52–61. Brand ((1957) 89) points out that in the early nineteenth century 'it was quite customary for the student of Italian, after learning the grammatical essentials, to begin working through Tasso's poem'.

65   Brand (1965) 205.

66   Brand (1965) 205 ff.; and Marshall 318–21. Childe Harold (Canto IV, st. 36) had already visited Tasso's cell in Ferrara, which became a traditional place for English tourists in Italy.

67   See *L Lects* (*CC*) I 431 (1812); he referred twice to *Gerusalemme liberata* XIII sts. 38 ff. (*BL* (*CC*) II 217; *CL* VI 605 (17 Aug 1826)). For the remark on Addison, see *C on Bruno* 433. On Fairfax, see Brand (1965) 242–9. Coleridge probably knew also Hoole's translation (Coffman 211).

68   Hunt pointed out that Tasso, and especially *Le sette giornate del mondo creato*, had been one of Milton's sources in this respect. Italian was haunted by the monotony of vowel sound, which Tasso's frequent assonances, as in his use of proper names, rendered even worse (Hunt (1956) 234).

69   Coleridge owned Sannazaro, *Opera omnia* (Frankfurt 1709) (*Cormorant* II 462–3), which he was reading in the August of 1805 (*CN* II 2633). Like Samuel Johnson, he found Sannazaro's piscatory eclogues too improbable to be acceptable (*CM* (*CC*) I 60–1).

70   Hazlitt replied to this kind of objection in his review of Sismondi's *Literature of the South of Europe*, where Boccaccio's style was praised and his licence blamed. Hazlitt was one of Boccaccio's champions, but his interest was limited to a few tales of the *Decameron*, like most of his contemporaries. Hazlitt did not read Boccaccio in the original; his knowledge was founded on the 1620 English translation. Wright argues that his view was as one-sided as Coleridge's in spite of his enthusiasm (Wright 347–49).

71   Wright 339.

72   Despite the fact that Coleridge considered the chivalric reverence for women as a German element, he did not oppose Italian eroticism to German idealizing love. He borrowed from the Schlegels the idea of northern gallantry (*CN* III 4388 n.; *L Lects* (*CC*) II 91) and the definition of Petrarch as 'the final blossom & perfection of the Troubadours' (*L Lects* (*CC*) II 95; cf. F. Schlegel, *Geschichte* 183). Both observations, on which he did not insist, show his limited knowledge of the medieval tradition. Eroticism is often overt in medieval love poetry, as Sismondi and Hallam pointed out (*South* I 78–9, 215–6, 220–1; Hallam II 459, 463–4).

73   Partial translations from Italian romances appeared in several anthologies between 1795 and 1815 (Marshall 309–11).

74   Brand (1957) 76–7; Gibaldi, 'The Fortunes of Ariosto in England and America', p. 148. Scott read Ariosto and Tasso in Hoole's translation before he was fifteen;

Ariosto and Boiardo were his favourites. Foscolo's famous remarks appeared in 'Narrative and Romantic Poems of the Italians' in the *Quarterly Review* (Apr 1819). The occasion for Foscolo's long essay was the review of Rose's and Frere's mock-heroic poems.

75 Coleridge's comments on Boccaccio show that he admired his art of narrative and psychological insight and disliked his mythological machinery. But if so, he should have turned to *Decameron*. Most of Boccaccio's early romances contain an unaccomplished combination of Classical mythology and romance subject matter which makes them often clumsy, whereas the *Decameron* is a more medieval work, in which the Classical literatures are secondary sources. However, Coleridge disliked the crude realism of Boccaccio's tales as much as the mythological syncretism of the romances, so that he portrayed him as a scholar rather than a poet in *The Garden of Boccaccio*. See Branca (1964) 9–10, and 30, and A. E. Quaglio, Introduction to *Filocolo*, in Boccaccio, *Tutte le opere*, vol. I, tr. R. Monges, in V. Branca, *Boccaccio. The Man and His Works*, New York UP: New York 1976.

Coleridge knew few Italian *novellieri* besides Boccaccio. He mentioned Antonio Francesco Grazzini called il Lasca (CN IV 4535 (Apr–Jun 1819)); and he owned an anthology of sixteenth-century burlesque writers which included works by Agnolo Firenzuola (Coffman 155).

76 *CM* (*CC*) I 543–4; *PW* (EHC) I 480 n. Coleridge's knowledge of Boccaccio's Latin works must be considered; see ch. IV below. S. Johnson and F. Schlegel shared his view (see *Life of Milton*; and *Geschichte* 210), even though both had a genuine interest in mythology (see J. Boswell, *The Life of Dr Johnson*, Dent: London 1933, II, pp. 327, 585). Hunt found *Teseida* prolix (*The World of Books and Other Essays*, p. 46); Sismondi blamed the incongruous mixture of Classical and Christian mythology, which already existed in the Middle Ages, but that Boccaccio and other Humanists had carried to extremes (*South* I 299); Warton, who dealt with Boccaccio as a source of Chaucer, argued that the latter 'has often abridged the Italian poet's ostentatious and pedantic parade of ancient history and mythology' (Warton 235 n. 1). Like Coleridge, Warton preferred the frame of Chaucer's tales to Boccaccio's (Warton 262). Warton justified Chaucer's unpolished taste as a consequence of his age, and Boccaccio's licence as an effect of the black death, which led to a general debauchery (Warton 280). Boccaccio's merit was that he 'gave a stability' to the *novella*, 'which had existed in a rude state before the revival of letters in Italy' (Warton 930).

77 See Brand (1957) 78–83; King, 'Italian Influence on English Scholarship and Literature', pp. 302–4; Churchill 40–3. Byron translated Canto I of *Il Morgante maggiore* in 1819–20; *Don Juan* was begun in 1818. He was influenced by other Italian mock-heroic poets, especially Ariosto, Berni and Casti, as well as by William Stewart Rose's *The Court of Beasts* (1816), an abridged version of Casti's *Animali parlanti*, which helped to create the vogue for satiric poetry. Coleridge was a good friend of Rose, to whom he referred for example in *The Friend* (*CC* I 12). The best study of Byron and Italian poetry is P. Vassallo, *Byron. The Italian Literary Influence*, Macmillan: London 1984.

78 In the same period he referred to Casti's 'gay spirit', though he regretted that 'the prurient heroes and grotesque monsters of Italian Romance' were preferred to Milton (*Friend* (*CC*) I 12–13; Coffman 45).

79   He defined Pulci's poem as 'the first proper Romance'; his story was based on 'the fabulous History of Turpin', although Boccaccio's *Teseida* may have been its model in the way of rereading its source. Pulci's attitude to the subject matter of his poem was ironic and sometimes reminded the reader of Rabelais. Irony rendered improbable Ficino's and Poliziano's contributions to the composition of the work, as Ugolino Verino reported, though Coleridge had some doubts about Poliziano because of his licence (*L Lects (CC)* II 96). F. Schlegel found evidence in Pulci's ironic attitude to his subject that the true Romantic spirit was alien to the Italians (*Geschichte* 218). Schlegel is not a source for Coleridge's lecture, which is based on Ugolino Verino's introduction to *Il Morgante maggiore* (3 vols., Firenze 1732) (*CN* III 4389 n.).

80   Like everybody before Panizzi's 1830 edition of the *Orlando innamorato*, Coleridge knew Berni *rifacimento* of Boiardo, but did not mention it in the lecture (*CN* III 4133 (1811–12); *CL* III 363 (1812); IV 801 (1818)). For Coleridge's copy of *Orlando innamorato, Cormorant* II 187; Southey owned two copies of the poem. When Coleridge resumed the study of Italian in 1808, he noted that in learning a language it is advisable to read from the beginning complex texts, like Ariosto's satires, Berni and Dante (*CN* III 3283).

81   Pulci's treatment of sacred subjects reminded Carwardine of Voltaire's (*L Lects (CC)* II 104). Sismondi was uncertain whether to charge Pulci with 'gross bigotry or profane derision' (*South* I 324 n.). By way of concluding his lecture, Coleridge quoted some passages from the first Canto of *Il Morgante maggiore* to illustrate his observations (*L Lects (CC)* II 97–8).

82   Coleridge was presumably referring to Tasso's *Allegoria della Liberata* (1576). Tasso, who had formerly expressed dislike for allegory, was compelled to defend the supernatural and unclassical elements of his poem against the attack of contemporary criticism. The allegoric interpretation applied not only to the characters (for example, Goffredo was said to represent intelligence, Tancredi and Rinaldo irrational passion, Armida temptation, etc.), but also to some events and objects in the poem.

83   See Shaffer (1975). I cannot understand what Shaffer means by 'His [Coleridge's] criticism of *Paradise Lost*, and of the other major epics, especially Tasso's . . . and Dante's . . . makes it clear why *The Fall of Jerusalem* was the only fit subject left' (p. 34). I have not found any confirmation of this in his observations on Dante and Tasso.

84   L. Caretti, intr. to Ariosto, *Opere minori*, p. XIX.

85   Baretti set Ariosto above every other Italian poet, and even David Hume enjoyed the variety of his invention, his style and his picture of the passions, though he deplored his digressions and improbable fictions (Gibaldi, 'The Fortunes of Ariosto in England and America', pp. 144–5). Another eighteenth–century fanatic admirer of Ariosto was William Huggins, whose translation of Ariosto (1755), completed with the help of Henry Crocker and Baretti, attracted little public attention (ibid.). Coleridge's view was like that of S. Johnson, who in his *Life of Milton* criticized both allegory and Ariosto's and Tasso's morals.

86   On Hurd and Hayley, see Brand (1965) 260–3. Arthur Johnston points out that Thomas Warton's knowledge of medieval romances depended on the use Boiardo, Ariosto, Spenser and Milton had made of them; their interest justified

the recovery of those forgotten works (*Enchanted Ground. The Study of Medieval Romance in the Eighteenth Century*, Athlone Press: London 1964, pp. 106, 62). On Tasso, see Praz, *Machiavelli in Inghilterra*, pp. 326–9.

87 His translation of *Orlando furioso* (1783) in heroic couplets enjoyed at least eight editions until it was superseded by William Stewart Rose's version (8 vols., 1823–31), which became the English Ariosto for over a century. Hoole's *Jerusalem Delivered* (1763) was reprinted nine times before 1815 (Brand (1965) 146; Marshall 156–61). On Rose, Gibaldi, 'The Fortunes of Ariosto in England and America', p. 151. On Tasso, Marshall 58–60. It is worth pointing out that Hoole modified or omitted all passages containing erotic elements (Marshall 161–2).

88 Brand (1965) 266. See also pp. 220–5; and Brand (1957) 90–1.

89 Few were as enthusiastic as Sismondi, whose favourite was Ariosto, but who placed Tasso above all modern poets for his subject, the most engaging for an epic poem (*South* I 335–42, and 356 ff.). Landor's admiration, for example, was not unconditional (*Landor as Critic*, pp. 52–5, 76); nor did the Schlegels introduce a new perspective, as they did on other poets. August Wilhelm, who thought Ariosto overvalued in Germany (for example by Goethe), and defined Tasso as a 'Romantischer Dichter malgré lui', seemed to prefer Guarini to both (*Geschichte der romantischen Literatur*, p. 221). Friedrich believed that 'Tasso must undoubtedly be preferred to Ariosto', although Camoens was superior to both (*Fragmente zur Poesie und Litteratur, Kritische Ausgabe* XVI, (XII) (4)). See also *Geschichte* 267–70, and *Wissenschaft der Europäischen Literatur, Kritische Ausgabe* XI 151. Interestingly, the Schlegels criticized the structure of Ariosto's poem as formless and praised Tasso's, as Classicists had always done. Hazlitt resumed the prevailing opinion when he wrote that Tasso was the greater technician, Ariosto the greater genius (Brand (1965) 272–5).

90 *CL* V 25–7 (30 Mar 1820). Though he mentioned the plan again, in 1826 he was still asking a year or two to bring 'the substance of my Lectures on Shakespear, Milton, Dante, and Cervantes into publishable shape' (*CL* V 36 (8 Apr 1820); V 166 (19 Sept 1820); VI 541 (Jan 1826)).

91 It is noteworthy that Coleridge ignored Sismondi, who provided an historical model based on eighteenth-century principles. However, he made use of him through Henry Hallam, whose study of the Middle Ages is based on Sismondi.

Philology and Philosophy

1 See for example Kristeller, 'Humanist Learning in the Italian Renaissance' ((1965) 1). On painting and the Platonic revival, see *CL* IV 759; *P Lects* (1949) 167, 193, 393; and my ch. III. It is not surprizing to see Dante as part of the Platonic Renaissance; the idea was common in the fifteenth and sixteenth centuries (E. Garin, *Medioevo e Rinascimento*, Laterza: Bari 1954, p. 103). It was only in the nineteenth century that the age of Dante began to be distinguished from the age of Petrarch and his followers (for instance by Foscolo); see H. Weisinger, 'The Study of the Revival of Learning in England from Bacon to Hallam', *Philological Quarterly*, XXV, No 3 (Jul 1946), p. 237.

2 *CRB* I 200; *P Lects* (1949) 317; *CN* IV 5081 (Dec 1823); *Friend* (*CC*) I 467–8 n. Pantheist tendencies prevailed in those who for Coleridge became 'pagans'; on the other hand, conversions to Roman Catholicism were due to its appealing pietism, 'that VIE INTÉRIEURE – THAT SAN-THERESIANISM that attracted our CRASHAW' (*P Lects* (1949) 317).

3 *CN* III 4352 (29 Apr 1817). Coleridge once argued that the Schoolmen were 'the true dawn of the restoration of literature' (*CM* (*CC*) II 12), but elsewhere he noted that Scholasticism was defended by monks, who 'were the enemies of all Genius & liberal Knowledge'. They were 'laughed out of the Field as soon as they lost the power of aiding their Logic by the Postpredicaments of Dungeon, Fire & Faggot' (*CN* III 4352). In any case, they had not solved the problem of philosophical language: he hoped that Greek, 'that flexible Tongue', would sooner or later replace Latin and French (*CN* III 3365 (Sept 1808)). On the subject, see P. O. Kristeller, 'The Scholar and His Public in the Late Middle Ages and in the Renaissance', in his *Medieval Aspects of Learning*, tr. E. P. Mahoney, Duke UP: Durham (N. C.), 1974.

4 Though it does not modify the substance of the present discussion, it is worth pointing out that Coleridge considered Lecture X of the philosophic course, in which he dealt with the Italian Renaissance, as the worst he had ever given (*P Lects* (1949) 59).

5 In the early 1790s, he conceived of a selected edition of modern Latin poetry to raise money for the Pantisocratic project. He abandoned the plan but not the interest in 1795. See *CN* I 161 and n.; and Southey's letter to Joseph Cottle (5 Mar 1836, *New Letters of Robert Southey*, ed. K. Curry, Columbia UP: New York and London 1965, vol. II, p. 447).

6 As George Whalley noted, the marginalia suggest an exploration rather than a systematic reading (*CM* (*CC*) II 7–10); and this is confirmed by other notes Coleridge made on the subject. Most annotations concern sixteenth-century poets, even though his selection ranged from the fifteenth to the seventeenth century (*CN* II 2626). The poets annotated are: Marco Girolamo Vida (*c.* 1485–1566) (*CN* I 161 n.; II 2590; III 4178), Marcantonio Flaminio (1498–1550), Girolamo Fracastoro (1483–1553), Berardino Rota (1509–1575), Faustino Avogadro (fl. sixteenth century), Ignazio Albani di Merate (fl. early seventeenth century) (*CM* (*CC*) II 7–10). Stay's satire was part of his *Philosophiae recentioris* (1755–60), a didactic poem on Newton's philosophy Coleridge read at Cambridge (*Lects 1795* (*CC*) 215–17; *Friend* (*CC*) II 11–12; I 7–9). The subjects involved were equally various: religion (Vida and Vergerio), love – in relation to the 'Soother of Absence' (Avogadro, *CN* III 4110 (?1811–6); Rota, *CN* III 3319 (1808)), metrics (Albani di Merate), science and politics (Stay).

Vida, praised by Milton and Pope, was well known in eighteenth-century England. Translations and editions of his works, especially *De arte poetica*, were numerous (see M. Di Cesare, *Bibliotheca Vidiana*, Sansoni: Firenze 1974). A copy of his works was inscribed by Wordsworth and Coleridge (*Cormorant* II 548; Coffman 223). In Flögel's *Geschichte der komischen Litteratur* Coleridge read of Lelio Capilupi (1497–1563) and the satirical prose of Pietro Paolo Vergerio (1498–1565) (*CM* (*CC*) II 763–5). Besides, Coleridge owned a copy of Ubertino Carrara's *Columbus, carmen epicum* (1715) (*Cormorant* II 213). It is worth remembering that many of these poets also wrote in Italian (for example, Rota was a pastoral and Petrarchist poet).

7 Its Latin was rude and its versification harsh and feeble, despite the 'endless centos and ends of lines from Virgil, Ovid, and Statius'. But such flaws were tolerable in comparison to the poverty of its imagery and the absence of any beautiful passage, which were all the more surprising in a poet whose Italian works, even 'the most indifferent of them', always possess 'a fascinating delicacy in the choice and position of the words and the flow of metre'. Coleridge considered it as an example of the interference of scholarly prejudices on poetic genius (*L Lects* (*CC*) II 92). On Warton's view of *Africa*, see n. 15. Landor regarded *Africa* as a failure and Petrarch's Latin poetry in general as unoriginal, even though he thought that Latin versification had never been so correct since Boethius (Corrigan 159, 170). Hunt mentioned Petrarch's failed epic together with Ariosto's and Fracastoro's Latin poetry in 'On the Latin Poems of Milton' (Hunt (1956) 177).

8 *CN* III 4178; *BL* (*CC*) I 14 and 222; combined with some lines from Milton's *Epitaphium Damonis* in *Friend* (*CC*) I 144.

9 L. Spitzer, 'The Problem of Latin Renaissance Poetry', *Studies in the Renaissance*, II (1955), pp. 125, 137. Most neo–Latin poets contented themselves with evoking 'sentiments already exploited by the ancient poets'; only the best poets, like Pontano or Giovanni Cotta, were able to give new life to traditional poetic conventions (p. 138). For another view, see F. Arnaldi, intr. to *Poeti latini del Quattrocento*, Ricciardi: Milano–Napoli 1964.

10 John Barclay's *Argenis* was a masterpiece in terms of poetry and style of which 'it is awful to say, that it would have been well if it had been written in English or Italian verse', even if 'the Event seems to justify the Notion' (*CM* (*CC*) I 221).

11 *L Lects* (*CC*) II 91. The opinion was widespread in his time. Wordsworth, for instance, said that 'Miserable would have been the lot of Dante, Ariosto, and Petrarch if they had preferred the Latin to their mother tongue' (Toynbee (1909) II 2). In consequence of the Romantic vogue for the Middle Ages, the revival and imitation of the Classics were considered as having had a noxious effect on Italian literature (see e.g. Sismondi, referred to by Ferguson 168; and Hale (1954) 132).

12 1808–9: *CN* III 3360, 3364, 3366 (quoted *EOT* (*CC*) II 400 (1814); *Friend* (*CC*) I 77 (1818 only); and *Friend* (*CC*) I 7 and 9), 3467, 3633 (also *Friend* (*CC*) I 75–6), 3727; see also *Friend* (*CC*) I 51, *EOT* (*CC*) II 270 (1811): *CN* III 4178 (quoted *BL* (*CC*) I 14; and, combined with some lines of Milton, *Friend* (*CC*) I 144); *BL* (*CC*) I 222 and II 16. Coleridge was familiar with all the letters (*Familiares, Seniles, Metricae*, and *Variae*).

13 *De otio religioso* contains the same principles as *De vita solitaria*, of which it is a kind of continuation. *De vita solitaria* is constructed on the contrast between commercial life and the life of knowledge. Some passages transcribed by Coleridge concern this point: they are ironical descriptions of people's inconstancy, greed, superficiality, and above all their unawareness of them (*CN* III 3364, 3467, 3727). A consequence was the contrast between the city and the country – an attractive theme for Romantic sensibility. In a passage transcribed by Coleridge, Petrarch argues that nature inspires poets and philosophers. If

they want to speak a superhuman language, they must be carried beyond the limits of the human mind, which happens more easily 'locis apertissimis'. In such places Cicero wrote his *De legibus*, Plato his *Republic* and Virgil his eclogues (*Prose* 366–8; *CN* III 3467).

14 G. Martellotti, introduction to *Prose*, p. XV. Interestingly, Coleridge ignored book II of *De vita solitaria*, in which Petrarch related examples of saints and Classical figures who lived in solitude.

15 See *P Lects* (1949) 293–4. Giovanni da Ravenna lived with Petrarch between 1364 and 1368 (*Prose* 1014–15 n.). Coleridge's information on Giovanni Malpaghini derived from Meiners and probably Tennemann. In the lecture on Dante, Giovanni Malpaghini was said to have read the *Comedy* as a philosophical work (see my ch. III).

16 E. H. Wilkins, *Studies in the Life and Works of Petrarch*, Mediaeval Academy of America: Cambridge (Mass.) 1955, pp. 280–1. In Italy, the wave from the Latin works 'reached its peak in the late fourteenth and early fifteenth century, diminished thereafter, and virtually disappeared in the sixteenth century'. In the Northern European countries the chronology is similar though belated. Coleridge noted that Petrarch spent most of his time on the works neglected by his posterity (see *Cormorant* I 444).

17 However, Petrarch's antiquarian interests did not grow out of nothing, as he induced posterity to believe; they developed what other grammarians and scholars had begun (G. Billanovich, *Petrarca letterato: I. Lo scrittoio del Petrarca*, Edizioni di Storia e Letteratura: Roma 1947, pp. 405–6). As an instance of the Humanistic image of Petrarch, Garin mentions Johannes Herold's presentation of the 1554 Basle edition of Petrarch's works, which Coleridge used. Herold portrays Petrarch as the father of the revival of Classical learning outside the schools. Petrarch's works are an encyclopedia of the liberal arts. Those who possess this kind of culture are philosophers, and as such they are regarded as guides and models for well–ruled cities ('Il filosofo e il mago', in *L'uomo del Rinascimento*, ed. Garin, Laterza: Bari 1988, pp. 174–5).

18 'Le poetiche del Trecento in Italia', in *Momenti e problemi di storia dell'estetica*, Marzorati: Milano 1968, vol. I, p. 293. Petrarch's defence of poetry in the *Invective contra medicum quemdam* is unorganized and based on medieval concepts. Boccaccio developed them in the *Genealogia deorum*.

19 *Prose* 1018 (*Familiares* XXIII, 19).

20 It was translated and frequently reprinted in several European languages, and constituted 'one of the most famous reference works down to the nineteenth century' (Branca, *Boccaccio. The Man and His Works*, p. 109). The other Latin works of Boccaccio were popular until about 1700 (ibid., p. 110). Chapter VI of Branca (1964), 'Motivi preumanistici' (pp. 185–205), is an excellent introduction to Boccaccio as a scholar and his role in Humanism. Boccaccio's Latin works were almost forgotten in Coleridge's time. Sismondi argued they were superseded, though they had contributed to the advancement of letters. Their style was less polished than Petrarch's. Boccaccio's greatest merit was the reintroduction of Greek to Western Europe (*South* I 302–4).

21 See D. C. Allen, *Mysteriously Meant*, The Johns Hopkins UP: Baltimore and London, 1970, p. 216. Demogorgon and his progeny are described in book I of

the *Genealogia*. Boccaccio derived his notion of Demogorgon from Lactantius Placidus' annotations on Statius' *Thebaid*. Demogorgon, a name that does not appear in Classical mythology, is used in Boccaccio's corrupt manuscript of Lactantius for '*de⁻miourgón*'. The case is not isolated in early Italian literature (*Genealogie deorum gentilium libri*, ed. V. Romano, Laterza: Bari 1951, p. 793). For Coleridge's copy of the work, *CN* II 2737 n. Coleridge mentioned Demogorgon in *Limbo* (l. 4) as an evil spirit, a demonic character. Demogorgon appears in Jonson's *The Alchemist*, in *The Faerie Queene* and *Paradise Lost*. The source of Shelley's Demogorgon in *Prometheus Unbound* is uncertain (Wright 38–41; an extensive account in *Prometheus Unbound*, ed. L. J. Zillman, Univ. of Washington Press: Seattle 1959, pp. 313–20). The figure was mentioned by Giordano Bruno in *De la causa* (*Dialoghi* 220).

22 See *Trattatello* (which in the *CC* edition is referred to as 'Origine, vita, studi e costumi del chiarissimo Dante Alighieri', one of his various titles – Boccaccio never fixed a definitive one), in Boccaccio, *Opere in versi, etc.*, ed. P. G. Ricci, Ricciardi: Milano–Napoli 1955, pp. 614–21. See also Barberi Squarotti, 'Le poetiche del Trecento in Italia', in *Momenti e problemi di storia dell'estetica*, I, p. 308; R. Stefanelli, *Boccaccio e la poesia*, Loffredo: Napoli 1978; Allen, *Mysteriously Meant*, pp. 212–17.

23 Poliziano appears in Meiners' *Lebensbeschreibungen* as part of the intellectual circle of Lorenzo de' Medici's Florence (*CN* I 374 (1798–9)). Coleridge does not seem to have known Poliziano's Italian poetry, whereas he quoted his Latin verse (*CN* I 1673 (Nov 1803); *BL* (*CC*) I 21). Coleridge learned, probably from a secondary source, that Poliziano collected his letters during his lifetime in 1494 (*CM* (*CC*) II 476 (*c.* 1816–9 and 1827–8)). Poliziano was mentioned in the 1818 lectures as proxy for fifteenth-century Humanists intoxicated with Classical learning (*L Lects* (*CC*) II 94). On Coleridge and the Humanists, see the confused account of the revival of learning in *P Lects* ((1949) 294–5).

24 *CL* IV 648 (4 Jul 1816). Coleridge transcribed some maxims of Scaliger in 1801 (*CN* I 880; I 908; I 1000C; I 1125 (1800–2)). He quoted them in *Friend* (*CC*) I 177; in *Omniana* 125–6; and *BL* (*CC*) II 31, *BL* (1907) II 228, *CM* (*CC*) I 533. Coleridge made a note on Scaliger's interpretation of the *Apocalypse* (see *Cormorant* II 464; *PW* (*CC*), commentary to poem No. 101). He quoted Scaliger's opinion that hieroglyphs were partly a pictorial language (*P Lects* (1949) 111). Scaliger's *Poetices libri septem* (1561) exercized an immense influence on French Classicism (an outline in B. Weinberg, *A History of Literary Criticism in the Italian Renaissance*, Univ. of Chicago Press: Chicago and London, 1961, pp. 743–50).

25 *BL* (*CC*) I 56. He thought Milton's project of a Christian epic was stimulated by Strada rather than by Andreini's *Adamo*. The borrowings of Milton from Andreini pointed out by Hayley in his *Life of Milton* were inessential (*CM* (*CC*) II 973–5 (Jun–Sept 1807)). On Strada, see *CN* III 3276 and n. (Feb 1808).

26 Coleridge may have read of them in Meiners or Roscoe (for example, *Life of Lorenzo*, II, ch. vii). He transcribed a passage of Valla's *Dialecticae disputationes* on the theory of translation from the King James Bible (N 39.3 f.6 (1829)). On Poggio Bracciolini, Valla's opponent on the attitude to Classical Latin, see Field. In 1802 Coleridge met Shepherd, the author of the *Life of Poggio Bracciolini*

(1802) (*CN* II 1849 n.); see also Hale (1954) 93. Coleridge transcribed a passage of Pico della Mirandola's letter to Ermolao Barbaro in which Pico defended medieval philosophy, despite its unpolished style, against philology (*CN* I 1068 (Dec 1801); quoted *Omniana* 129). On Ermolao Barbaro, see *Logic* (*CC*) 231–2.

27 The impact of Valla's philology on northern Humanism and Reformation was immense. Erasmus praised him as the founder of the new Biblical philology (E. Garin, *Italian Humanism. Philosophy and Civic Life in the Renaissance*, tr. P. Munz, Blackwell: Oxford 1965, p. 199); Erasmus paraphrased Valla's *Elegantiae* in his *Paraphrasis, seu potius Epitome*; Luther thought his own doctrine of will identical to Valla's (C. Trinkaus, Introduction to Valla's 'On Free Will', in *The Renaissance Philosophy of Man*, Univ. of Chicago Press: Chicago 1956, p. 153). Garin points out that Valla's rejection of Scholastic Latin was motivated, like Descartes', by the desire to revive a philosophic language closer to common language (Garin (1989) 85–7).

28 M. Baxandall argues that whereas for Petrarch 'Ciceronianism was an intellectually adventurous and muscular undertaking in itself, by the time of Erasmus it could no longer be that, since the important grammatical routes through classical consciousness had been explored and mapped' (*Giotto and the Orators*, p. 6). On fifteenth-century Latin and its relationship to Italian, see R. Spongano, *Due saggi sull'Umanesimo*, Sansoni: Firenze 1964. Spongano points out that fifteenth-century Latin was a living language and, 'in idioma diverso dal volgare, una lingua – ossia un atteggiamento del pensiero – non diversa dal volgare.' In the following centuries, Latinists intentionally detached from modern mentality to lock themselves up in the ivory tower of classicism (ibid., pp. 52, 57). The religious overtones of the attacks to Erasmus as a precursor of the Reformation must not be overlooked (see M. P. Gilmore, 'Italian Reactions to Erasmian Humanism', in *Itinerarium italicum*, eds. H. A. Oberman and T. A. Brady Jr, Brill: Leiden 1975, 61–115).

29 L. Baldacci, introduction to *Lirici del Cinquecento*, Longanesi: Milano 1975 (rpt. 1984), p. XXII. Baldacci reminds us that 'the most direct impulse to the theory of imitation originated in the context of Classical eloquence' (ibid.).

30 He owned a Greek manuscript containing 'over sixteen works' of Plato, which he could not read (see *De sui ipsius et multorum ignorantia, Prose* 756).

31 C. Vasoli, *La dialettica e la retorica dell'Umanesimo. 'Invenzione' e 'Metodo' nella cultura del XV e XVI secolo*, Feltrinelli: Milano 1968, p. 14. Although 'the experienced eye of the historian can discover certain subtle analogies between the extremes of Nominalism and the new philological and rhetorical interests' (Garin, *Italian Humanism*, p. 24), basic differences remain (see E. Auerbach, *Literary Language & Its Public in Late Antiquity and in the Middle Ages*, tr. R. Manheim, Routledge and K. Paul: London 1965, pp. 273–5).

32 Klibansky 68. As he wrote in *De sui ipsius et multorum ignorantia*, man cannot know God fully, but he can love him. The love of God is always happy, whereas knowledge is sometimes painful (*Prose* 748).

33 *The Poet as Philosopher*, p. 14.

34 Klibansky 69. In a letter, Petrarch pointed out that Augustine found 'in libris Platonicorum magnam fidei nostre partem' (*Familiares* II, 9) (*Prose* 820).

35 Klibansky argues that

'If the origin of the impulse which produced the humanist translations be sought, it appears that this is to be found, not in a foreign Greek influence, but in Petrarch's veneration of Plato, which inspired Boccaccio, and afterwards Coluccio Salutati … who was the first to order, from a Florentine in Byzantium, a complete text of Plato. … The admiration for Plato, which was handed down by Coluccio to the next generation of noble Florentines, accounts for Cosimo de' Medici's reception of Pletho in 1439. The fresh inspiration given by the Byzantine Platonist would hardly have borne fruit had it not fallen on ground already well prepared by a century old enthusiasm. (Klibansky 32)

36 *Eight Philosophers of the Italian Renaissance*, Chatto & Windus: London 1964 (rpt. 1965), p. 12.

37 Trinkaus, *The Poet as Philosopher*, pp. 24, 111 and 84. The doctrine of the primacy of the will was developed by the Franciscan School, with which Petrarch was in touch. It eventually led to Ockhamism (ibid., p. 111). Some of Petrarch's works were put on the *Index* (see P. P. Gerosa, *Umanesimo cristiano del Petrarca. Influenza agostiniana, attinenze medievali*, Bottega d'Erasmo: Torino 1966, p. 360 n. 1).

38 *LS (CC)* 173; *CL* IV 759 (25 Jul 1817). He quoted from the *Trionfi*, which was not his favourite work, the lines on Plato, who 'came closest to the goal/Whereto by Heaven's grace men may attain' (*CM (CC)* II 868; *AR (CC)* 42 n.).

39 Sismondi thought that Petrarch's philosophical works are bombastic and display 'neither truth nor depth of thought. They are merely a show of words, on some given subject.' The letters were too official and devoid of sentiment; the metrical epistles were insignificant and bombastic (*South* I 291). He also blamed Petrarch's vanity and submission to princes, but acknowledged his merits as a scholar (*South* I 292). For Warton, see Warton 106 n. 2.

40 *Friend (CC)* I 75 n. The discussion of Petrarch in lecture 3 of the 1818 course was brief, but a lecture on Dante and Petrarch was announced for the 1819 course on Shakespeare &c (*L Lects (CC)* II 343–4). On 27 February, he asked J. H. Bohte for Meiners' *Lebensbeschreibungen berühmter Männer aus der Zeiten der Widerherstellung der Wissenschaften* (3 vols., 1795–7), probably with an eye to the lecture on Petrarch. He in fact described the book 'by saying that it contains the Life of … Johannes Somewhat, the Eleve and Scholar of Petrarch', that is Giovanni Malpaghini da Ravenna (*CL* IV 922). He did not receive the volumes, and only lectured on Dante, since he had never revised his notes on Petrarch and the time available was little. In 1816 he had included Petrarch in his planned reviews of old books that had caused important changes in taste or ideas (*CL* IV 648). In the last year of his life, Coleridge still advised the new series of the *Gentlemen's Magazine* to include the learned criticism and 'the Biography of the middle age & the Restoration of Literature – Hugo de St Victore, Ambrosius, Petrarch &c &c &c.' (*CL* VI 976 (4 Jan 1834))

41 Garin (1989) 117.

42 Klibansky 73.

43 *Plato's Parmenides in the Middle Ages* (Klibansky 48). On Coleridge, Proclus and Taylor, see my section on Bruno. Coleridge found references to the Greek Neoplatonists and Ficino in Dupuis' *Origine de tous les Cultes* (1795) (Lowes 232–3).

44   Coleridge read several editions of Ficino's Plato: Lyons 1557, Lyons 1567, Lyons 1590, Zweibrücken (Biponti) 1781–7 (Coffman 163–4). In 1796 he asked Thelwall for a volume of Neoplatonists and 'Plotini Opera, a Ficino' (*CL* I 262). For Plotinus' works, ed. and commented by Ficino (Basel 1580), see Coffman 164. Lowes indicates that Iamblichus and Julian are still owned by the Coleridge family (Lowes 231). The volume includes Iamblichus, *De mysteriis*; Proclus, *In platonicum Alcibiadem*; Porphyry, *De divinis atque daemonibus*; Psellus, *De daemonibus*; Hermes Trismegistus, *Pimander* and *Asclepius* (*Cormorant* II 268; *CN* I 180 n.). The doubts expressed by Fruman and Haven about the extent of Coleridge's early acquaintance with Neoplatonism are unfounded (*Coleridge, the Damaged Archangel*, p. 118; see my section on Bruno below). Ficino's version of Iamblichus was quoted *CL* II 682 (18 Feb 1801); he used it while taking notes from Tennemann's chapter on Porphyry (*CN* IV 5081 n. (Dic 1823)). For quotations from Ficino's Plotinus, see *Friend* (*CC*) I 418; *CN* IV 4909. Coleridge thought Plotinus deserved a new edition, since the only one available was Ficino's. Creuzer's new edition was published in 1835 (*BL* (*CC*) I 114–15; I 240 n.; *CN* IV 4839 (1821–2)). On Proclus, see *CN* III 3276 n. Coleridge quoted a passage from Simon Grynaeus' introduction to the 1557 Leyden edition of Ficino's Plato (*CN* III 3951 (Jul 1810); *BL* (*CC*) I 165; *Friend* (*CC*) I 23); another quotation, *CN* III 3824 (May 1810). Whalley suggests that the book may have been in Southey's library (*Cormorant* II 269).

45   *BL* (*CC*) I 144. As far as I know, Coleridge did not have a first-hand knowledge of Plethon. He may have read Plethon's commentary on Zoroaster's *Oracles* as it appears in Stanley's translation of Francesco Patrizi's 1593 edition, which also included Psellus' commentary (*CN* III 4424 n. (1818)). Coleridge noted that the oracles contained the fundamentals of Schelling's system (*CL* IV 874 (30 Sept 1818); McFarland (1969) 159). He used an oracle as a motto for *The Friend* (*CN* III 4446, 4447 (Oct 1818); *Friend* (*CC*) I 2; *CL* IV 884; *CM* (*CC*) I 660–1). He thought the metrical structure of the oracles showed they were not ancient, and believed their author was a Christian (*CN* III 4424; *Friend* (*CC*) I 433 n. 1). On Plethon, see P. O. Kristeller, *Renaissance Concept of Man, and Other Essays*, Harper: New York, Evanston and London, 1972, pp. 96–107.

46   *CN* IV 4617 (Oct 1819). Charles Lamb relates that when visitors saw young Coleridge walking in Christ's Hospital's cloisters while unfolding 'the mysteries of Jamblichus, or Plotinus', they weighed 'the disproportion between the speech and the garb of the young Mirandula' ('Christ's Hospital Five and Thirty Years Ago', *The Works of Charles and Mary Lamb*, ed. E. V. Lucas, Methuen: London 1903–5, vol. II, p. 21). Coleridge first read of Pico in Meiners' *Lebensbeschreibungen*, from which he transcribed some of Pico's 900 theses. The notes include the Averroist idea that 'una est anima intellectiva in omnibus hominibus' (which is a pantheist problem); and examples of Scholastic philosophy (*CN* I 374 (1798–9); quoted *CM* (*CC*) I 573–4, 633–4). Pico's *Conclusiones LV secundum Proclum* was included in the edition of Proclus owned by Coleridge (*CN* IV 4744 n.). Coleridge disagreed with Pico's neoplatonic definition of happiness, related by Donne, as the return of all things to their principle. It should have been: 'the completion of any Soul in that, in which it feels itself insufficient . . . Hence – nec amet quemquam – nec ametur ab ullo –

is the most comprehensive Curse ever uttered against a human Soul' (*CN* III 4050 (Mar 1811)). The frequency of Coleridge's objections to most diverse thinkers on grounds of ethics and the philosophy of love makes his agreement with Petrarch in this respect all the more relevant.

47 *CN* I 943 (Apr–Nov 1801); on Shakespeare, *Friend* (*CC*) I 457; *BL* (*CC*) II 185. The source of Coleridge's quotation is unknown; Coffman indication is probably hypothetical (Coffman 165). Pomponazzi is cited from *On the Immortality of the Soul*, tr. W. H. Hay II, revised by J. H. Randall Jr, in *The Renaissance Philosophy of Man*, p. 319. The first part of the work discusses Aristotelian psychology and the conception of imagination in particular. Pomponazzi opposed the dualism of soul and body; on his psychology, see E. Cassirer, *The Individual and the Cosmos in Renaissance Philosophy*, tr. M. Domandi, Blackwell: Oxford 1963, pp. 136–41; 'Ficino and Pomponazzi on the Place of Man in the Universe' (Kristeller (1965) 106–7). Pomponazzi's book, which caused a long controversy because it denied the immortality of the soul, was burnt publicly in Venice.

48 *CN* IV 5007 and n. (Oct 1823). Kathleen Coburn points out that Tennemann mentions a 'divine' but not an 'active' imagination. In any case, Pomponazzi rejected Averroes, especially in psychology (Cassirer, ibid., p. 136).

49 *AR* (*CC*) 241. See Cassirer, ibid., p. 105. Coleridge thought *De fato* contained nothing dangerous to the Church or offensive to a believer, but elsewhere he spoke of the 'Italian Aristotelian Infidels' (*CN* IV 5006 (Oct 1823)). Ernst Cassirer points out that *De fato, libero arbitrio et praedestinatione* (such is the complete title) enumerates all the motifs on the subjects in Scholastic fashion without adding anything substantial to it (ibid., p. 75).

50 Yates (1964) 163. She quotes as examples Petrarch's and Erasmus' hostility to magic. However, 'the atmosphere very rarely was unadulterated and elements from the one tradition infiltrated into the other' (ibid.).

51 On the Roman Church and magic, Thorndike vol. V, ch. xiii. On Ficino and magic, Yates (1964) ch. IV; on Pico, ch. V, and Thorndike IV, ch. lix. Pico went so far as to state: 'Nulla est scientia, que nos magis certificet de diuinitate Christi, quam Magia & Cabala' (Yates (1964) 105). On Ficino, Pico and magic, E. Garin, *Ermetismo del Rinascimento*, Ed. Riuniti: Roma 1988, pp. 18, 49–50, 63–7.

52 *CN* III 3737 (Mar 1810). Coleridge owned Girolamo Fracastoro, *Opera omnia* (Venezia 1574) (*Cormorant* II 275–6). In 1824 he asked his wife for the book (*CL* V 328). On Fracastoro, Thorndike V, ch. xxii.

53 Coleridge claimed he had studied mesmerism for nine years (*IS* 57; *TT* (*CC*) 31 Mar 1830; and II 78 n.). See Whalley, 'Coleridge and Vico', p. 231; T. H. Levere, *Poetry Realized in Nature*, CUP 1981; J. Beer, *Coleridge's Poetic Intelligence*, Macmillan: London 1977.

54 *CN* IV 4908 (Jul 1822). See n. 42. As Frances Yates points out, Pico rejected the idea that Christ's miracles depended on magic, but other magicians took it up again later (Yates (1964) 106).

55 On Cabbalistic magic, see Yates (1964) ch. V; and Yates (1966) 188–9. Coleridge rejected all attempts to associate the Cabbala with Christianity (*P Lects* (1949) 317; McFarland (1969) 228).

56 *SM* (*CC*) 84–5. Meiners was his probable source of information on Pico.

Erasmus was not a friend of Pico and is not known to have disapproved of Pico's dismissal of astrology, even though he was sceptical of it (*LS* (*CC*) 84–5 nn.). In his *Disputationes adversus astrologiam divinatricem* (1493–4), Pico attacked vulgar astrology, the astrology of the horoscope, but defended Ficino's astral magic. The book is an apology of natural magic (Yates (1964) 114–15). See also Garin, *Ermetismo del Rinascimento*, pp. 50–1; Thorndike IV, chs. lxi and lxiii.

57 *Omniana* 123. Coleridge included Cardano, Paracelsus and old Fuller as 'positively amusing matter' among the reviews of old authors he proposed to Murray (*CL* IV 648 (4 Jul 1816)). Southey owned a copy of Cardano's *De rerum veritate* (*Cormorant* II 33). Lowes argues that Cardano's *De subtilitate* may be a source of the *Ancient Mariner* (Lowes 485). Cardano was included in a reading list of philosophers Coleridge recommended to Basil Montagu (*CL* V 332 n. (1824)). On Cardano, Thorndike V, ch. xxvii. Another alchemist known to Coleridge was Jacopo Berengario da Carpi, who 'indeed made gold out of Mercury', since his use of mercury as a remedy for syphilis made him rich (*CN* III 4414). He mentioned Giovanni Battista della Porta *Friend* (*CC*) I 486; *P Lects* (1949) 336; *CN* III 4392 (Mar 1818); *L Lects* (*CC*) II 201.

58 *Friend* (*CC*) I 57–8; *P Lects* (1949) 182; *CN* IV 5020 (Oct 1823); *AR* (*CC*) 245. For the works of Galileo he may have read, see Coffman 85. Garin points out that Bruno, Vanini and Galileo were a kind of lay trinity of martyrs in positivist time (Garin (1989) 260–1; cf. e.g. Algernon Swinburne's poem *For the Feast of Giordano Bruno, Philosopher and Martyr*). A passage on the value of scientific debate from Galileo's *Dialogus de systemata mundi*, which Coleridge transcribed in 1801 (*CN* I 937D), is quoted *Friend* (*CC*) I 42. In Darwin's *Zoönomia* he may have read that Galileo supported the principle of the incompenetrability of physical bodies (*CN* III 3370 (1808)). A vision of Galileo was part of the 'best attested stories of Ghosts and visions' (*L Lects* (*CC*) II 138; *CN* III 4065 and n. (Apr 1811)); he even planned a poem on it (*CN* III 3585 (Jul–Sept 1809)). Wordsworth's library contained *Mathematical Collections and Translations* (5 vols., 1661–5), a book marked as belonging to Coleridge which includes works of Galileo and Benedetto Castelli (*TT* (*CC*) 8 Oct 1830 n. 1).

59 On Cesalpino, *Friend* (*CC*) I 468. On Vesalio and Morgagni, *CL* IV 614 (Dec 1815); VI 740 (5 May 1828). Coleridge preferred their 'organicist' approach to contemporary studies 'in *defunct* Anatomy'. Coleridge knew Francesco Redi's observations on insects (*CN* IV 4880 (Apr 1822)). Southey knew something of Lazzaro Spallanzani (*Cormorant* I 108); the Bristol library contained a French translation of Spallanzani's *De' fenomeni della circolazione*, which Coleridge mentioned twice in 1800 (*CL* I 649, 651). Besides, he referred to Spallanzani's *Tracts on the Nature of Animals and Vegetables* (Edinburgh 1799) (*CN* IV 4620 (Oct 1819)). Other references: Luigi Cornaro, *Discorsi della vita sobria* (Padua 1591) (*CN* III 4461 (1818)); Antonio Minasi (fl. 1773) on the *fata morgana* (*CN* I 431 (May 1799)); Antonio Maria Jaci, whom he met in Sicily (*Friend* (*CC*) I 252; Sultana (1969) 373); Giovanni Rasori (*CN* I 389 (Feb–May 1799)); Giovanni Battista Amici's improvement of the microscope (*CL* V 523 (Dec 1825)).

60 Coleridge borrowed Boscovich's *De solis ac lunae defectibus* (1760) at college in 1793 (J. Mays, 'Coleridge's Borrowings from Jesus Library College, 1791–94',

Transactions of the Cambridge Bibliographical Society, VIII, 1985, p. 572). He read Priestley's *Disquisitions Relating to Matter and Spirit*, which are founded on Boscovich's conception of matter, in the autumn of 1794 (*Lects 1795 (CC)* I 216–17). Coleridge knew Boscovich's commentary to Benedetto Stay's *Philosophiae recentioris*, which contained the *Fable of Madning Rain*, a satire he admired (see the section on humanistic writing above). References to Boscovich: *CN* III 3370 (Sept 1808); III 3953 (Jul 1810); III 3962 (Jul 1810); also III 4455 n.; *CM (CC)* I 177 n.; I 568–9.

61 McFarland (1969) 187, 245.

62 W. Saenger, *Goethe und Giordano Bruno*, Ebering: Berlin 1930, pp. 252–3. See also H. Heimsoeth, 'Giordano Bruno und die deutsche Philosophie', *Studien zur Philosophiegeschichte*, Kölner Universität Verlag: Köln 1961, pp. 120–51.

63 Lessing intended to publish an anthology of Bruno's, Cardano's and Campanella's works with commentary (Saenger, ibid., pp. 254–5). Hamann was above all interested in the principle of *coincidentia oppositorum* (Saenger, p. 260; Heimsoeth, ibid., pp. 133–4). On Herder, see Saenger, ibid., pp. 41 and 261–2. Goethe first read of Bruno in 1770, but the peaks of his interest were between 1812 and 1816, and in 1829 (ibid., pp. 32, 37–8, 43, 57). His early interest focused on the personality of philosophers rather than on their thought (ibid., p. 33). Fülleborn wrote in 1796 that Bruno's works were 'in den Händen aller Freunde der Philosophie' (Heimsoeth, ibid., p. 138).

64 Saenger, ibid., p. 264; Heimsoeth, ibid., pp. 136, 144–5. See also McFarland (1969) 246–7. German Romantic interest led to Adolf Wagner's edition of Bruno's works (1830), which sold out in a few years (*Dialoghi* xxxix–xl).

65 *CN* II 2264 (Nov 1804). Whalley, however, thinks the entry should date from before November 1804 (*Cormorant* I 442).

66 Coffman (p. 34) includes also *De imaginum, signorum et idearum compositione* (1591), another work on the art of memory, among the works Coleridge read. If so, it is strange that he never mentioned it. *De immenso* is Bruno's most extensive cosmological work; its cosmology is the same as in the Italian dialogues (*De la causa* and *De l'infinito, universo e mondi* in particular), but shaped into a Lucretian poem (*Opere* I 41–2).

67 *BL (CC)* I 161–3; *CL* IV 775 (1817); *AR (CC)* 400 n.; McFarland (1969) xxxiii.

68 *CN* III 4189 (1813–15); *BL (CC)* I 246, *CM (CC)* I 602–3 (1818).

69 *CN* I 928. Bruno's conception of how blood circulated in the human body is a consequence of his panpsychism and has little to do with Servet's early observation of the phenomenon, as Coleridge believed. Leonardo had intuited blood circulation (Garin, 'Il filosofo e il mago', in *L'uomo del Rinascimento*, p. 193). Coleridge referred to Bruno in an article on blood circulation in *Omniana* (131–2 (1812)).

70 Yates (1964) 236–44. She points out that elements of solar mysticism appear also in Copernicus, but that the mathematical parts of his theory are immune from them. Bruno 'pushes Copernicus' scientific work back into a prescientific stage, back into Hermetism, interpreting the Copernican diagram as a hieroglyph of divine mysteries' (Yates (1964) 155). Bruno rejected some aspects of Copernicus' solar system: for instance, he believed that the orbits of Venus and Mercury around the sun were not smaller than that of the Earth (*CN* I 928;

Olc I i 395; *Opere* l 682 n.). M. Ciliberto (*Giordano Bruno*, Laterza: Bari 1990, p. 60) argues that Bruno's interpretation of Copernicus is based on Cusa's infinite universe and Bruno's own view of life as an eternal production of innumerable finite forms and as perpetual animation. On Copernicus and Cusa, see *De immenso* (*Olc* I i 381–2). A combination of Copernicus and the infinity of the world appers also in Thomas Digges (1576) (see Yates (1964) 244; McFarland (1969) 288).

71 Yates (1964) 251–2. It is worth pointing out that Bruno attacked Aristotle's metaphysics and natural philosophy, but admired his works on logic and rhetoric (*Dialoghi* 260 n. 2).

72 Cassirer, *The Individual and the Cosmos in Renaissance Philosophy*, pp. 188–9. The 'unique *value* of man' was jeopardized by the infinity of worlds, a concept which was for Petrarch the peak of insanity. 'For Bruno, instead, the intellectual and moral dignity of the Ego . . . requires a new concept of the world' (p. 189). On Petrarch's opposition to pantheism, see *De sui ipsius et multorum ignorantia* (*Prose* 730, 736–40).

73 P. Rossi, *La scienza e la filosofia dei moderni*, Bollati Boringhieri: Torino 1989, pp. 163–5; 168. Rossi pinpoints that the discussion on the inhabitability and the infinity of worlds was lively in the fifteenth and sixteenth centuries (p. 177). It is noteworthy that such ideas destroyed the view of the earth as a unique place and of humans as privileged beings, which were Christian but also Hermetic principles – that is, they destroyed one of their own sources. The theme appears in Spinoza, seventeenth- and eighteenth-century materialism (pp. 182–3).

74 *Olc* I i 218, 318–19; I ii 199, 257, 280. Carlo Monti points out that 'what the Atomists (Leucippus, Democritus, Epicurus) called absolute vacuum does not exist for Bruno'; vacuum was for him not nothingness, but '"all that which is not body and resists sensibly"' (*Opere* l 54).

75 Christian dualism is clearly in the background of Bruno's attacks on the chimeras of incorporeal light, on the world of archetypes separated from the world of matter, and on the distinction between essence and existence – which was merely logical (*Olc* I ii 312–14). Kristeller doubts 'very much that (Bruno) wanted to be an extreme pantheist or naturalist', although he acknowledges that 'in comparison with his favourite sources, Plotinus and Cusanus, Bruno goes much further in the direction of a pantheistic or immanentistic conception' (*Eight Philosophers of the Italian Renaissance*, p. 135).

76 *P Lects* (1949) 323. Coleridge claimed that many parts of Bruno's chemistry 'seem wonderful in his age as anticipations of modern discoveries': Bruno described oxygen 'with the greatest accuracy', and gave 'many of the most striking attributes of our modern electricity' (*P Lects* (1949) 326–7). I am inclined to believe that Coleridge's assertions are unfounded, since I have not been able to find such ideas in Bruno. On Bruno's cosmology and modern science, see *Opere* l 415 n.

77 O. Barfield, *What Coleridge Thought*, OUP: London 1972, pp. 263, 186; McFarland (1969) 381–2; K. M. Wheeler, *Sources, Processes and Methods in Coleridge's Biographia Literaria*, CUP 1980, pp. 49–51.

78 Barfield, ibid., p. 186; Wheeler, ibid., pp. 48–51.

79 Barfield, ibid., pp. 186–7. See for instance: 'quoniam constat contraria

totum/Perficere, ut calidam naturam frigida sempei/Oppugnet, nec non succedaiil ista vicissim/Perpetue, iustasque vices certo ordine servent:/ Multum unde etiam genitant refoventque potenter' (*De immenso, Olc* I ii 240). 'Everything consists of contraries', and 'where contraries coincide they become one and indifferent' (*De gli eroici furori, Dialoghi* 974, 977). But 'a contrary is the principle of the other' (*De la causa, Dialoghi* 338); 'Quidquod, et unum quodlibet, absolutione, respectu, tensione, contractione, prasentia [*sic*], absentia, conversione, adversioneque fit duo, fit diversa, fit contraria, fit contradictoria' (*De monade, Olc* I ii 537).

80 *CM (CC)* I 568. Bruno applies to his cosmos the principle that God is a circle in which centre and circumference coincide. Gentile points out that the same metaphor appears in Hermetism, St. Bonaventura, Cusa, Montaigne, Pascal, Leibniz and Heinrich Steffens (*Dialoghi* 321; see also *Opere I* 500).

81 Raymond Klibansky highlights that the medieval Latin translation of Proclus' commentary on Plato's *Parmenides* in particular was 'of marked influence on the conception of Platonism and and gave rise to some fundamental concepts of modern philosophy, such as Cusanus' and Bruno's doctrine of the "coincidentia oppositorum"' (Klibansky 26). Cusanus included marginalia he had made to Proclus' commentary on *Parmenides* in some of his philosophical sermons. Bruno borrowed Cusa's ideas without acknowledging their source.

82 Barfield, *What Coleridge Thought*, p. 182.

83 *CN* I 928. It must be pointed out, however, that the same relation between Beginning, Middle and End as expressed in *De monade* appears in other works (see e.g. *De lampade combinatoria lulliana, Olc* II ii 270; *De umbris idearum, Olc* II 26; *De progressu et lampade venatoria logicorum, Olc* II iii 39–43). Coleridge wrote that the most perfect example of a philosophy like Boehme's, Fox's and Bruno's 'is to be found in the Platonic Theology by Proclus'. It 'endeavours to explain all things by an analysis of Consciousness, and builds up a world in the mind out of materials furnished by the mind itself.' Taylor, however, 'translated that difficult Greek into incomprehensible English' (*CL* III 279 (21 Jan 1810)).

84 In 1810 he wished exceedingly that he could 'procure from Malta the Logica Venatrix of Giord. Bruno' for a project on logic which should have led to what Bacon called *ars inveniendi* (*CN* III 3825). He found Tennemann's analysis of Bruno 'a mere skim from one or two only of Bruno's writings – while his interesting attempts of (on?) Logic and Mnemonic are passed over altogether – tho' they would have thrown a light on his whole philosophy' (*C on Bruno* 436).

85 *CL* V 331–2 n. (Feb 1824?). Coleridge advised Tulk to consult the Greek 'Oneirocritici', medieval mystics like the Victorines, 'the Lullian Logical and Mnemonical Treatises of Giordano Bruno', and Campanella before reading Hartley (*CL* V 326 (26 Jan 1824)).

86 Yates (1966) 251. Lullism derives from Augustinian Platonism and the Neoplatonic tradition. It was admired in the Renaissance, since it had several points in common with the Florentine Neoplatonism (pp. 175, 187).

87 See Yates (1966) 259, 379–89; and P. Rossi, *Clavis universalis. Arti della memoria e logica da Lullo a Leibniz*, Il Mulino: Bologna 1983, pp. 131–45.

88 Barfield, *What Coleridge Thought*, p. 193.

89 Frances Yates considered *De progressu et lampade combinatoria logicorum* and the

other mnemonic works Bruno wrote in Germany as important but 'dull indeed' in comparison to the Italian dialogues (Yates (1964) 307). On *De umbris idearum*, which she defines as a book of solar magic, see Yates (1964) 194–9.

90 Yates (1966) 379–88. On Leibniz, see also Rossi, *Clavis universalis*, pp. 259–81. The originality of Coleridge's ideas on Bruno's mnemonic works is clear if they are compared with James Joyce's, whose interest in Bruno is well known. Joyce believed they 'have an interest only because they are so fantastical and middle-aged' ('The Bruno Philosophy', 1903, *The Critical Writings of James Joyce*, eds. E. Mason and R. Ellmann, Faber and Faber: London 1959, p. 133).

91 McFarland (1969) 381. McFarland reminds us that the primary source of Romantic dynamism were Kant's *Metaphysische Anfangsgründe der Naturwissenschaften* (1786). Bruno is quoted by Priestley in *Matter and Spirit*, which rejected Newton's conception of matter (P. Deschamps, *La formation de la pensée de Coleridge*, Didier: Paris 1964, p. 412). Wellek's remark that Coleridge 'never properly understood the inner principle of every dialectic' is too drastic (*Immanuel Kant in England, 1793–1838*, Princeton UP: Princeton, N. J., 1931, p. 86).

92 On Sidney and Greville, *Friend (CC)* II 81; I 117; on Bruno's style, *CN* I 928; *SM (CC)* 19.

93 In November 1803 he planned a series of philosophical essays, the first of which should have been on Bruno, Boehme and Spinoza (*CN* I 1646; and 1369 n.). In 1809 he intended to give an account of Bruno's life in *The Friend* ((*CC*) II 81–2). The problem he had to face was the rareness of Bruno's works, although it was not so great as some bibliographers claim (*CM* (*CC*) II 976) – he had in fact discovered that censorship was inefficient in Italy. The project later became a comparison between the characters of Boehme, George Fox and Bruno (*CL* III 279 (21 Jan 1810)). The fifth treatise of his planned *Logosophia* would be on 'the Lives and Systems of Giordano Bruno, Jacob Behmen, George Fox, and Benedict Spinoza' (*CL* IV 590 (27 Sept 1815); and IV 592). The same project reappears with the exclusion of Fox in 1816 (*CL* IV 687). Coleridge complained that a Mr Hare refused to lend him a unique collection of Bruno's works, though he intended to discuss Bruno's life and system in *The Friend* (*CL* IV 656 (16 Jul 1816)). In 1817 he asked for details of Bruno's death and German period, since *La cena de le ceneri* contained 'a highly curious & interesting account of his adventures in London' (*CL* IV 742; *Friend* (*CC*) II 82). Tennemann's history of philosophy was 'a mere compilation from common books, and the article of (on?) Giordano Bruno heartless & superficial . . . O for a real Life of Bruno, and analysis of his writings!' (*C on Bruno* 436). In 1819 he was still hoping to avail himself of Hare's books (*CL* IV 926). He recommended Gioacchino de' Prati, an Italian exile who lent him a copy of Vico's works, to write a series of critical and biographical sketches of revolutionary minds 'in the manner of Meiners's Work'. Bruno and Cornelius Agrippa were advisable subjects to begin with (*CL* VI 579 (9 May 1826)). In 1827 he intended to write a 'Vindication of Great Men unjustly branded': Bruno, Boehme, Spinoza and Swedenborg (*CL* V 136 n.).

94 The passage, 'Ad ist haec quaeso vos, qualicunque primo videantur aspectu, adtendite, ut qui vobis forsan insanire videar, saltem quibus insaniam rationibus cognoscatis' (*De immenso, Olc* I i 208), is quoted variatim *CL* III 127, 133

(1808); *Friend (CC)* I 125; *SM (CC)* 3, 112; *Cl.* V 228 (1822). For other defenses of philosophical obscurity, *CN* I 1647 (1803); *CM (CC)* I 621–2; *CM (CC)* II 13 n.; *Omniana* 136, in which Bruno is said to have shared with Plato, Aristotle, Kant and 'with every great discoverer of the human race' the charge of obscurity.

95   'Let others lust to bind to naked shoulders/Daedalus' wings . . .' (tr. G. Whalley, *P Lects* (1949) 324–5). Bruno affirms in the poem that he is a genius enlightened by God; he tends to the highest truths and despises the vulgar mass and the empty versification of grammarians. According to Coleridge, the poem portrays 'the human mind under the action of its most elevated affections', and it has 'a fair claim to the praise of sublimity' (*Omniana* 135). He transcribed it *CN* I 929 (Apr 1801); he quoted it in full *Omniana* 135–6, and in his lecture on Bruno (*P Lects* (1949) 324–5). A partial quotation appears in *Friend (CC)* II 282; and *CM (CC)* I 183. Coleridge also quoted the 'rhapsody' from the conclusion of *De immenso* (*CL* II 809 (1802)).

96   Yates ((1964) 246) points out that Bruno modified the original passage 'on the miraculous and godlike power of man to know the world, extending it into a power to know an infinite god and an infinite universe'. The excerpt from Bruno is quoted *Friend (CC)* I 115–16.

97   *Omniana* 135; *Friend (CC)* II 81–2; I 117–18; *AR (CC)* 400 n.

98   See *The Expulsion of the Triumphant Beast*, tr. and ed. A. D. Imerti, Rutgers UP: New Brunswick (N. J.) 1964, pp. 251, 255: the Jews are 'the excrement of Egypt'; Christ taught that 'white is black, that the human intellect . . . is blindness, . . . that Nature is a whorish prostitute, that Natural law is ribaldry, that Nature and Divinity cannot concur in one and the same good end . . . that they . . . are contraries'. Bruno attacked Christ using Orion as a symbol for him. The symbolism is transparent, even though he denied it at the Venetian trial (ibid., p. 308 n. 4). On Bruno's attitude to the Reformation, see Ciliberto, *Giordano Bruno*, pp. 127–32. Bruno reversed Luther's *De servo arbitrio* point by point. Humans are responsible and free: destiny, merit and guilt are inter-dependent. The best religion is that which creates a link between man, nature and God, and which gives value to human responsibility. Such a religion was Roman religion. Significantly, when Bruno extolled Luther in his *Oratio valedictoria* before leaving Wittenberg, he did not mention theological issues (Ciliberto, ibid., p. 214).

99   See for example, *De la causa, Dialoghi* 270–2, 316, and especially 324 ('every production . . . is alteration, since the substance is always the same: because the substance is one, a divine and immortal entity. Pythagoras understood it. He did not fear death, but expected mutation'). Bruno quoted Solomon's 'Nihil sub sole novum' in support of his theory (*Dialoghi* 324). Matter changes because 'she likes the absent form as much as she hates the present one' (*De gli eroici furori, Dialoghi* 979).

100 On the relationship between Humanism and Renaissance philosophy, see Yates (1964) ch. IX; E. Garin, *Ritratti di umanisti*, Sansoni: Firenze 1967, the ch. on Poliziano. On Bruno's theory of love, J. C. Nelson, *Renaissance Theory of Love. The Context of Giordano Bruno's 'Eroici Furori'*, Columbia UP: New York and London, 1955 (rpt. 1963). Bruno identified 'Petrarch's love with the lower, "bestial" kind of love in Ficino's classification' (that is, bestial – human – divine

love) (ibid., p. 173). Bruno's language and imagery are nonetheless Petrarchan, though he transfigured them into a metaphysical Baroque (ibid., p. 220 ff.; see also F. A. Yates, 'Il contenuto simbolico negli "Eroici furori" di Giordano Bruno e nei canzonieri elisabettiani', in *Giordano Bruno e la cultura europea del Rinascimento*, Laterza: Bari 1988, pp. 59–90).

101   'La poesia non nasce da le regole, se non per leggerissimo accidente; ma le regole derivano da le poesie: e però tanti son geni e specie de vere regole, quanti son geni e specie de veri poeti' (*Dialoghi* 958–9). Bruno thought that art shaped its matter from without, whereas nature shaped it from within (*De la causa, Dialoghi* 264–5; *De immenso, Olc* I ii 312–3).

102   He occasionally referred to conventional Machiavellism as a way of attributing a devilish character to the politics of Napoleon or the Roman Church (e.g. *EOT (CC)* I 421 (Jan 1803); *CN* III 4494 (Mar 1819)), but he otherwise took Machiavelli seriously. After reading the *History of Florence* and *The Prince* during his Italian sojourn, he became aware of Machiavelli's historic importance. On his reading of Machiavelli, *CN* II 2385 (Dec 1804); II 3015 (May 1807); a quotation from *The Art of War, CN* III 3535 (Jul–Sept 1809). For the editions of Machiavelli's works he used, Coffman 134–5. Machiavelli was for Wordsworth 'one of the greatest of men' (*TT (CC)* I 546); on Machiavelli and the Romantics, Brand (1957) 128. Coleridge also knew Guicciardini and Paolo Sarpi, the similarity of whose styles he found 'very interesting' (*TT (CC)* 10 Mar 1827). On Sarpi, *CM (CC)* I 843, 846; *EOT (CC)* II 406; *BL (CC)* I 198.

103   Machiavelli's epigrammatic power struck Coleridge, who quoted some of his maxims. He noted there were both advantages and disadvantages in Boccaccio's and Machiavelli's Italian in comparison to Latin, though he did not specify what they were; both Latin and Italian were superior to the uniformity of French (*CN* II 2512 (Mar–Apr 1805)). Quotes from Machiavelli: *Friend (CC)* I 274; *CN* II 2385; on the mediocrity of the mass, *CN* II 3015, quoted *SM (CC)* 13, *Friend (CC)* I 122–3, *CL* VI 742 (8 May 1828), *C&S (CC)* 74 and n. Other references: against tyrannicide, *Friend (CC)* I 324; Greville, *CN* III 3713 and n. (Mar 1810); *CN* IV 5115 (1824), *Omniana* 354.

104   *Friend (CC)* I 123. For example, England would not have acted as it did against revolutionary America and France had its rulers borne in mind Machiavelli's remarks on the conduct to be pursued in such situations (*CN* III 4117 (Dec 1811), where he probably refers to a passage transcribed *CN* II 3015). He made the same point in the *Statesman's Manual*, in which he added that every important political truth pre-existed in the Bible in a clearer form (*(CC)* 17). He complained that 'Bacon, Harrington, Machiavelli and Spinoza are not read, because Hume, Condillac, and Voltaire *are*' (*BL (CC)* I 54). With reference to the Reform Bill, Coleridge argued it was vain to discuss how to make laws, considering what 'to make' and 'law' meant in the eighteenth-century philosophical tradition (*CL* VI 903 (7 May 1832)).

105   On Coleridge's philosophy of history, C. De Paolo, 'The Lessons of Wisdom and Caution: Coleridge's Periodization of Western History', *The Wordsworth Circle*, XVII, No 3 (Summer 1986), 119–30; and S. V. Pradhan, 'The Historiographer of Reason: Coleridge's Philosophy of History', *Studies in Romanticism*, XXV, No 1 (1986), 39–62.

106 Cf. Pradhan, ibid., pp. 60–1. Coleridge's philosophy of history, he summarizes, 'is idealistic and elitist and belongs to the Christian tradition of historiography' (p. 61).

107 *CL* V 424 n. The edition (3 vols., Milan 1816) included Vico's *Autobiography*. Prati, who studied law and medicine, had a deep knowledge of Boehme, Bruno, Schelling and Spinoza; he was personally acquainted with Jacobi, Schelling, Friedrich Schlegel, Ritter and Oken; and he had a direct experience of mesmerism. See M. H. Fisch, 'The Coleridges, Dr Prati, and Vico', *Modern Philology*, XLI, No 2 (Nov 1943), 111–22; and G. Whalley, 'Coleridge and Vico', in *Giambattista Vico. An International Symposium*, The Johns Hopkins UP: Baltimore 1969, 229–31. See also *CL* V 452–3 (14 May 1825); VI 964–6 (29 Oct 1833).

108 Fisch and Bergin, introduction to *Autobiography of Giambattista Vico*, Cornell UP: Ithaca 1944, p. 84.

109 *TL* 35–6. See also *Friend (CC)* I 476. Fisch and Bergin traced the story of Jacobi's quotation. Gaetano Filangieri gave Goethe a copy of the *New Science* when he was in Naples in 1787. In 1792 Goethe lent the book to Jacobi, who later got hold of other works by Vico. Coleridge's quotation was the first appearance of Vico in England (ibid., pp. 68–9; see also I. Berlin, *Vico and Herder. Two Studies in the History of Ideas*, Hogarth Press: London 1976, pp. 90–2).

110 *Scienza nuova* § 331. The origin of Vico's doctrine of *verum-factum* has been discussed widely. It can be traced back to Augustine and Aquinas, and was a theological commonplace in Vico's time (Berlin, *Vico and Herder*, pp. 116–17; K. Löwith, '"Verum et factum convertuntur": le premesse teologiche del principio di Vico e le loro conseguenze secolari', in *Omaggio a Vico*, Morano: Napoli 1968, pp. 73–112). Paolo Rossi points out that the doctrine is central in seventeenth-century mechanicism (*Immagini della scienza*, Editori Riuniti: Roma 1977, p. 153). Jacobi cited the doctrine as an anticipation of Kant (Vico, *Autobiography*, p. 68).

111 The only *Degnità* he remembered was that mutes 'send forth indistinct sounds in a sing-song: and Stammerers by chaunting gradually unloose and accustom or facilitate the tongue to pronounce freely' (*Scienza nuova* § 228). He noted children stuttered when prevented from singing their words (*CL* V 465 (23 May 1825)). For other observations on phonetics, see *CN* IV 5232; *CM (CC)* II 1091–2, and my Appendix below.

112 *CRD* II 5 (1825). See *CM (CC)* II 892, and *TT (CC)* I 559–60. Henry Nelson Coleridge was the source of Samuel Taylor's knowledge of Wolf, whom he never read. It was Vico who induced him to adopt the Homeric theory we are discussing (*TT (CC)* 9 May 1830). Wolf, whose *Prolegomena ad Homerum* was published in 1795, was irritated when in 1802 he discovered that Vico had anticipated him (Vico, *Autobiography*, p. 69; Berlin, *Vico and Herder*, p. 92). For other reports of Coleridge's discussion of Vico's Homeric theory in his conversations, see Fisch, 'The Coleridges, Dr Prati, and Vico', pp. 114–7.

113 It is worth pointing out that Vico did not decide whether the rhapsodes composed the poems which formed the *Iliad* or merely put together available material (*Scienza nuova* § 852 and n. 4 p. 1700). Nor did he decide whether Homer was a real poet who became a symbol for the poetry of his age, or

whether he had never existed and was a symbol for anonymous, collective poetry (*Scienza nuova* § 873 and n. 4 p. 1703).

114 Fisch and Bergin note the presence of Vichian principles in Coleridge's biblical exegesis in the *Confessions of an Inquiring Spirit*, which was written at the time when he was reading the New Science (Vico, *Autobiography*, pp. 84–5). Graham Davidson points out the great 'emphasis in the late notebooks on historical patterns of development – from the individual to the nation – that echo the Vichian scheme'. Such emphasis is particularly evident in his reading of Hebrew history (*Coleridge's Career*, pp. 242–3). Davidson argues that what distinguishes Coleridge's scheme from Vico's is Coleridge's intepretation of 'each stage as representative of the life of man ideally conceived'.

115 See P. Rossi, 'Vico e il mito dell'Egitto', in *Omaggio a Vico*, pp. 25–36. Rossi points out that despite Vico's rejection of the antiquity of the *Hermetica*, his way of criticizing the reactionary hermeticism of authors like Kircher and Fludd is different from that of Conrig, Bianchini, Moreri, Montfauçon, Voorbroeck and Warburton. Rossi thinks that Vico's preoccupations with Hebrew cultural primacy are a sign of his belatedness. See Andrea Battistini's summary of Vico's old-fashioned learning in Vico, *Opere*, pp. 1473–4. Vico's greatness does not depend on his obsolete materials, but on the way in which he organized them. George Whalley noted similarities between the opening of Coleridge's *Prometheus* essay and the 'Tests of Tradition' in *CN* IV 5232 ('Coleridge and Vico', pp. 236–7).

116 N Q.6 f6 p. 44 (after 1829). Coleridge regarded Vico's idea that 'Sacra i.e. secreta' as a 'capital stroke of Jesuitry', all the more surprising considering that Vico admired Bacon and Grotius (*CN* IV 5204, 5207). To estimate Vico's greatness, one should remember that he lived as a Roman Catholic in Naples in the 18th century (*TT (CC)* 23 Apr 1832).

117 Other non-Christian doctrines are the natural origins of language and the rejection of timeless values implied by his historicism (Berlin, *Vico and Herder*, pp. 77–8, 84). For a deeper discussion, F. Nicolini, *La religiosità di Giambattista Vico*, Laterza: Bari 1949. Nicolini shows that the idea of an animal phase of humanity, derived from Lucretius, Grotius, Hobbes and Pufendorf, is irreconcilable wih the Genesis. The doctrine was condemned by the Neapolitan Inquisition when Vico was young; the same idea appears in La Mettrie, D'Holbach, Dupuis and Rousseau (ibid., pp. 67–8, 79–80).

118 *CRD* II 5 (1825). The comparison later appeared in *C&S* ((*CC*) 25). For similar statements, see *CN* IV 5208, 5211 (May 1825), which focus on the systems of marriage in Rome and the colonies. Coleridge thought Niebuhr's Roman history was based on Vico (*CL* V 470 (16 Jun 1825)). In effect, Niebuhr's case was the same as Wolf: he developed his theories unaware of Vico, and was annoyed when Orelli and Leopardi pointed out that Vico had anticipated them (Berlin, *Vico and Herder*, p. 92).

119 *TT (CC)* 8 Apr 1833. The passage seems to recall in particular *Scienza nuova* § 1026 (cf. also §§ 1089–94). Vico emphasized that he had refuted both the Epicureans (Hobbes, Machiavelli) and the Stoics (Zeno, Spinoza). He presented his political theory as Platonic (*Scienza nuova* § 496, 1097, 1109; see however p. 1258, and n. 3 p. 1668). He spoke disparagingly of Spinoza's 'republic of

merchants' (*Scienza nuova* § 335). On Vico's Platonism, see N. Badaloni, *Introduzione a Vico*, Laterza: Bari 1984, pp. 5, 26.

120 *PW* (EHC) I 478 ll. 26–34. On the composition of the poem and its editorial history, *PW* (*CC*), editorial commentary; Wright 335, 341–2; *CL* VI 749, 756–7, 778–9, 783 (1828–9); *Samuel Taylor Coleridge. An Annotated Bibliography of Criticism and Scholarship. Volume II: 1900–1939*, eds. W. S. Crawford, E. S. Lauterbach, A. M. Crawford and G. K. Hall: Boston (Mass.), 1983, p. 25. The poem was meant to illustrate the engraving of F. Englehart after Stothard's drawing which appeared in *The Keepsake* in 1829. The poem includes fragments composed at different times (*CN* IV 4623 (Oct 1819); *EOT* (*CC*) III 308). On the poem, Brooks, 'Coleridge's Poetic Technique', p. 606; Whalley, '"Late Autumn's Amaranth": Coleridge's Late Poems', pp. 173–5; Wilson Knight, *The Starlit Dome*, pp. 117–18, points out parallels with *Kubla Khan*; Ridenour, 'Source and Allusion in Some Poems of Coleridge', pp. 82–3; Suther, *Visions of Xanadu*, pp. 182–5, 268; McFarland (1969) 112–13; Beer, 'Coleridge and Poetry: Poems of the Supernatural', in *S. T. Coleridge. Writers and Their Background*, pp. 86–7; Dorenkamp, 'Hope at Highgate', pp. 60–1. John Hamilton Reynolds, Keats' friend, published *The Garden of Florence* (1821), based on a tale of Boccaccio (Brand (1957) 113–4).

121 The quotation is from *The Confessions of St Augustine*, tr. F. J. Sheed, Sheed & Ward: London and New York, 1944 (rpt. 1960), p. 30. The original is: 'Nondum amabam et amare amabam . . . Querebam quid amarem, amans amare' (*Confessionum Libri XIII*, ed. Lucas Verheijen, Brepols: Turnhout 1981, III. I. 1). Shelley used Augustine's sentence as a motto to *Alastor*.

122 *PW* (EHC) I 480 n. The passage runs as follows: 'And having taught them to read, he made them read the holy book of Ovid, in which the great poet shows how the sacred fires of Venus can speedily be kindled in the coldest hearts' (tr. *CM* (*CC*) I 544). Cf. *Alice du Clos*, lines 35–9: 'O! Alice could read passing well,/And she was conning then/Dan Ovid's mazy tales of loves,/And gods, and beasts, and men.' Mays points out that the word 'mazy' possessed erotic, amoral feelings for Coleridge (*PW* (*CC*), commentary to poem No 643). Coleridge specified that Classical literatures and mythology were '*worked* in & *scripturalized*' in the minds of Renaissance poets and scholars. The Bible and the Classics were taught with equal zeal; what was 'publickly *taught* of Aristotle, was individually & perhaps more generally, *felt* of Homer' (*CN* II 2670 (Sept 1805)).

123 He was 'much in the dark' about the problem, and although he noted that Scholastic philosophers were quoted both by Protestant and Catholic divines (*P Lects* (1949) 318), he argued that the Reformation was attributable to Scholasticism 'far more than to the revival of classical literature, except as far, indeed, as it produced a general impulse and awakening over society – nay, even more to the scholastic philosophy that to the MORE genial school of Platonism in Italy' (*P Lects* (1949) 316–17). On the subject, see A. McGrath, *The Intellectual Origins of the European Reformation*, Blackwell: Oxford 1987, p. 195; and H. Weisinger, 'English Attitudes toward the Relation between the Renaissance and the Reformation', *Church History*, (1945), 167–87. The relations between the Scholastic tradition and the Platonic revival have been much debated by twentieth-century scholarship. The neat contrast affirmed by

Coleridge is unfounded: even for Ficino, Plato integrated rather than replaced Aristotle (Garin (1989) 206 n. 3). Plato was the leading authority in metaphysics, Aristotle in logic, physics and ethics ('The Moral Thought of the Renaissance', Kristeller (1965) 34–5). In general, it has became indisputable that all Renaissance thinkers and scholars had at least some knowledge, and many a considerable knowledge, of Scholastic philosophy. Moreover, Coleridge overlooked the philological contribution of Humanism (see McGrath, ibid., pp. 59–60, 67–8).

124 Kristeller points out that, though Classical myths were popular in the Renaissance, 'there were few, if any, thinkers who seriously thought of reviving ancient pagan cults'. Atheists and pantheists were rare; some can at most be considered as precursors of eighteenth-century free-thinkers. On the whole, he believes that the attitude is not 'distinctive of the Renaissance period', in which nonreligious interests were not opposed to religious interests, but competed with them in attracting public attention. Kristeller argues that the Renaissance was 'a fundamentally Christian age'; the Humanists themselves supported the notion. Humanism was 'in its core neither religious nor irreligious, but a literary and scholarly orientation that could be and, in many cases, was pursued without any explicit discourse on religious topics by individuals' who were fervent or nominal Christians ('Paganism and Christianity', *Renaissance Thought. The Classic, Scholastic, and Humanistic Strains*, Harper: New York 1955, rpt. 1961, pp. 72-5).

125 See E. Panofsky, *Renaissance and Renascences in Western Art*, Harper & Row: New York 1972, pp. 82–100. On the allegorical interpretation of the Classics in the Renaissance, Allen, *Mysteriously Meant*, ch. VII.

Afterword

1 On Sismondi, see Marshall 391–2; Ferguson 165–8; Hale (1954) 128–30. Recent historiography confirmed that the flourishing of the arts in the high Renaissance was not the result of a healthy political life: politics was characterized by an extreme decadence (C. Vasoli, 'Il concetto di Rinascimento nel pensiero contemporaneo', in *Il Rinascimento. Aspetti e problemi attuali*, p. 37). On Hallam, H. Weisinger, 'The English Origins of the Sociological Interpretation of the Renaissance', *Journal of the History of Ideas*, XI (1950), pp. 335. Ginguené's history of Italian literature is based on eighteenth-century, Voltairian principles: dislike for the Middle Ages, neoclassical taste, and a view of literature as part of political history.

2 Ferguson 90–3.

3 Weisinger, 'The English Origins of the Sociological Interpretation of the Renaissance', p. 328. It was only in 1820 that George Miller noted that the commercial spirit which was supposed to have stimulated the Florentine literary enterprizes failed to produce anything comparable in Venice (ibid., p. 337). A detailed account is provided by Hale (1954) 42–57, who points out that Shaftesbury was a precursor of the eighteenth-century interpretation (Hale (1954) 80–1). These ideas were taken up by Burckhardt through Voltaire

(P. Burke, *Culture and Society in Renaissance Italy 1420-1510*, Batsford: London 1972, p. 8).

4 See Marshall 208–9; Ferguson 104–6; Butler (1981) 24–5; Churchill 8–9; Hale (1954) 84–5. However, Gibbon still admired the Medicis (Ferguson 106; Hale (1954) 85).

5 On Roscoe, Hale (1954) 85–103; Marshall 275–7, 285; Weisinger, 'The Study of the Revival of Learning in England from Bacon to Hallam', pp. 234–5. Foscolo complained that contemporary taste and travel literature neglected the fifteenth century (Hale (1954) 136).

6 Roscoe indeed had contributed to *The Watchman* soon after his *Life of Lorenzo* was published, and had subsequently noted the discontinuance of Coleridge's periodical with regret (*Watchman* (*CC*) 351 and n.). As Ferguson (165) points out, Roscoe overrated the influence of single individuals and was lacking in general principles. His view of history seems almost the opposite of Coleridge's, which was all principles and few (sometimes too few) facts.

7 *LS* (*CC*) 172. Among the ideas discussed in Renaissance Florence, Coleridge mentioned the '*Ideas* of Will, God, and Immortality' (*SM* (*CC*) 101; *LS* (*CC*) 172; *Logic* (*CC*) 236 n.). In *C&S* ((*CC*) 64–5), 'Immortality' is replaced by 'Freedom'. See also *CN* I 374 (1798–9)); and Field 8–9, 14–15. Roscoe pointed out that Platonism was not a mere matter of discussion, but was applied to practical use (*Life of Lorenzo* I 160). It is not relevant in this context that Coleridge disagreed with Pico's conception of will (*CM* (*CC*) II 678).

8 *P Lects* (1949) 394. Coleridge does not seem to have known Lorenzo il Magnifico as a poet. On the change of Lorenzo's image in early nineteenth-century England, see Hale (1954) 130, 136–9.

9 Ficino's prefaces to Lorenzo were affecting in comparison to the present time (*CN* II 2746 (Nov–Dec 1805)). The darkest continental despotisms had done more for the arts than contemporary England, where only sensational artists, like Paganini, became popular, whereas a Mozart would pass unnoticed (*TT* (*CC*) 7 Jul 1831). Coleridge seemed to overlook the extent of English patronage in the eighteenth century, which was very influential even in Italy. He thought commercial patronage tended to turn mediocre artists into geniuses for reasons of profit (*CM* (*CC*) II 235). Elsewhere he noted that the flourishing of Italian painting was due to wealth and not the Church, since 'to have Raphaels there must be a sale even for such things even as Raphaels in their *beginnings* must do' (*CN* II 2844 (May 1806)). He was aware the older patronage had its negative sides, of which the mediocre devotional painting he found distasteful in Italy was an example (*CN* II 2420 (1805)). Great patrons like the Renaissance popes imposed censorship, as Pico's case showed. It is historically not clear if, and to what extent, Renaissance patronage favoured the development of the arts (see Burke, *Culture and Society in Renaissance Italy*, pp. 109–11, 281–2). Burke points out that Lorenzo's patronage was in the tradition of the wealthiest Florentine families (p. 111). The appendixes of Roscoe's *Life of Lorenzo* include some Humanist prefaces dedicated to Lorenzo.

10 Hale (1954) 99. As Ferguson points out, Roscoe's historical model was Voltaire, for whom an enlightened despotism was acceptable; Sismondi was instead a disciple of Rousseau (Ferguson 165).

11   For Hunt, see Weisinger, 'The English Origins of the Sociological Interpretation
      of the Renaissance', p. 336. Byron's attitude was not clear. He wrote in *Hints
      from Horace* (lines 509–12): 'Unhappy Greece! thy Sons of ancient days/The
      Muse may celebrate with perfect praise, / Whose generous children narrowed not
      their hearts/With Commerce, given alone to Arms, and Arts'. Shelley wondered
      in *Marenghi* (line 23): 'Was Florence the liberticide?' He was probably referring
      to the Florence of the Medicis, whom he defined in *A Philosophical View of
      Reform* as 'flattered traitors [and] polished tyrants' (*SCW* VII 5).

12   Marilyn Butler's argument appears in *Peacock Displayed*, pp. 63–5; and Butler
      (1981), the ch. 'The Cult of the South'.

13   The view of Florence as a modern Athens, for instance, first appeared in
      Leonardo Bruni's *Laudatio florentinae urbis*, which was written when Florence
      was threatened by the Milanese monarchy in the early fifteenth century. Bruni's
      work was inspired by Aelius Aristides' *Panathenaicus*. On Bruni, see H. Baron,
      The Crisis of the Early Italian Renaissance, Princeton UP: Princeton (N. J.) 1955
      (rpt. with rev. 1966).

14   The classical study on early Humanism and politics is Hans Baron, ibid., which
      ought to be integrated by Field; see also Garin (1989) 118–21.

15   Butler (1981) 136–7. Butler argues that the Greek taste of the younger
      Romantics was intended to oppose the German and medievalist taste of
      Coleridge's *Biographia* (Butler (1981) 123, 128). But Coleridge's *Biographia* is
      German in some premises of vol. I and medievalist nowhere. Its *taste* is much
      more Renaissance and in part even eighteenth century, as is evident in vol. II,
      than German and medievalist. On Coleridge's supposed medievalism, cf. *Lines
      . . .* (1826), line 21: 'That age how dark! congenial minds how rare!' (*PW* (EHC)
      I 461) Besides, one cannot help observing that in their youth the older
      Romantics had developed their own primitivism – Pantisocracy and the like –
      without drawing inspiration from 'southern' sources, with the sole exception of
      Rousseau.

16   Webb, *The Violet in the Crucible*, pp. 57–8.

17   Landor, *Poems*, p. 199 (1853). See Shelley's description of his visit to Pompeii
      (*SL* 71 (23–4 Jan 1819)). I have extended Timothy Webb's observation that
      Shelley's image of Greece was formed on his knowledge of Greek culture and
      Italian setting (*Shelley: A Voice not Understood*, p. 191).

18   On Shelley's Platonism, see J. A. Notopoulos, *The Platonism of Shelley. A Study of
      Platonism and the Poetic Mind*, Duke UP 1949 (rpt. Octagon Books: New York
      1969); and Webb, *Shelley: A Voice not Understood*, and *The Violet in the Crucible*.
      Notopoulos (ibid., pp. 52, 54, 89) points out that the Platonism of the younger
      Romantics was based on that of Thomas Taylor, who did not reject the pseudo-
      Platonism of Ficino and More, as Webb believes (*English Romantic Hellenism
      1700–1824*, Manchester UP: Manchester; Barnes & Noble: New York, 1982,
      p. 181). Taylor's view of Plato as the inheritor of a *prisca theologia*, as Webb
      describes it immediately below, is Ficinian. Shelley made use of Ficino's version
      of Plato for his translation of the *Symposium*. He translated from the original
      when he could; otherwise he turned to Ficino (Notopoulos, ibid., p. 398). On
      Byron's view of Shelley's Platonism, see *BL&J* IX 119 (4 Mar 1822): with
      Shelley's 'speculative opinions I have nothing in common, nor desire to have'.

19 An example can be found in the recent *Cambridge Companion to British Romanticism*, ed. S. Curran, CUP 1993, who includes Webb's chapter 'Romantic Hellenism' and hardly anything on the Romantics and Italy, even though Webb himself acknowledges that 'Shelley never reached Greece, and his experience of Italy . . . strongly influenced his views of classical Greece' (p. 155), not to mention the rest of his view of the 'south'. This is not meant to undermine Webb's admirable studies, to which we are all indebted.

20 See J. J. McGann, 'Rome and Its Romantic Significance', in his *The Beauty of Inflections. Literary Investigations in Historical Method and Theory*, Clarendon Press: Oxford 1985, p. 325. McGann recalls that Stendhal's attitude in this respect was similar to Byron's.

21 See Foscolo, *Epistolario*, vol. VII, ed. M. Scotti, Le Monnier: Firenze 1970, p. 289 (20 Feb 1818). Foscolo emphasized that everything was understood in terms of fashion in England. He found English ladies elegant and proud, and could not stand those over forty for their hypocrisy (p. 422, 29 Oct 1818); young ladies were instead 'vereconde e schiette – e un po' civette, benché schiette' (*Epistolario*, vol. VIII, Le Monnier: Firenze 1974, p. 212, 7 Oct 1820). Foscolo noticed a widespread interest in Classical poetry which surprised him (vol. VII, p. 386, 30 Sept 1818).

22 *C&S* (*CC*) 25–6. The link had been noticed by C. Woodring, *Politics in the Poetry of Coleridge*, Univ. of Wisconsin Press: Madison 1961, p. 41 and n. 12 p. 245. Coleridge shared the idea that Italy was 'rich in the proudest records of liberty'. Its history was 'all alive with the virtues and crimes of hostile parties, when the glories of ancient Greece were acted over again in the proud republics of Venice, Genoa, and Florence'. But 'not a pulse' of the liberty of Dante's or Machiavelli's Florence survived under the Austrian and Spanish domination (*C&S* (*CC*) 26). The contrast between the past liberty of Italy and its present slavery was a commonplace repeated by all Romantics, English and Italian.

23 This was the prevailing Renaissance attitude. The common denominator of the numerous political treatises written at the time was 'not a set of opinions, but a cultural and educational ideal' ('The Moral Thought of Humanism', Kristeller (1965) 49). See also my section on Petrarch's prose works above.

24 With reference to Plato's *Republic*, Shelley wrote: 'His speculations on civil society are surely the foundations of true politics, & if ever the world is to be arranged upon another system . . . it must start from such principles' (*SL* 360 (22 Oct 1821)). Godwin's *Political Justice* prepared Shelley to accept the doctrines of the *Republic*, which he considered the summa of Plato's philosophy (Notopoulos, *The Platonism of Shelley*, p. 146). The ambivalence which characterizes Romantic attitudes to classical Athens also appears in Romantic interpretations of the Italian Renaissance, which in political terms is an example of enlightened despotism, though it was republican in its early phase.

Appendix

Coleridge's Knowledge
of the Italian Language

(i)

Modern languages were not part of the normal curriculum of study in Coleridge's time. A special arrangement introduced in 1724 existed for the universities, where the Professor of History could appoint two teachers of modern languages, which were usually French and Italian.[1]

Whereas some students like Hayley, Mathias and Wordsworth profited from the opportunity, Coleridge's academic interests at Cambridge did not extend beyond Greek and Latin. When he later developed an interest in modern languages, he learnt them in the same way as other Romantics, that is, by teaching himself.[2] Italian was a reasonable task for a student who had already mastered the Classical tongues, the rich Latinate vocabulary of English and some French, as it was common at the time. Coleridge began the study of Italian in late 1802 (*CN* I 1269); Lowes' suggestion that his understanding of an Italian pun in 1798 could testify to an earlier acquaintance with the language is unconvincing.[3] Although Coleridge was critical of learning 'Italian through the medium of French' (*CL* II 802, 3 Jun 1802), he began his study with the aid of a tetraglot edition of Pascal's *Provincial Letters* he found in Southey's library (*CL* II 994, 22 Sept 1803). He was also helped by the Wordsworths, who had developed their good knowledge of Italian in the 1790s. However, their influence alone cannot be considered as decisive.

It was Coleridge's desire to read authors like Bruno, Dante, Petrarch and Boccaccio that stimulated him to learn Italian. Before leaving for Malta he asked Wordsworth for 'Dante & a Dictionary' (*CL* II 1059, 8 Feb 1804), and received an Italian grammar and a dictionary from Lady Beaumont (*CL* II 1107 n.). On board he decided to 'fag Italian after dinner' and before breakfast time; he later wrote to Daniel Stuart he had done little else than read the Italian grammar on his way to Malta (*CL* II 1129, 1133; *CN* II 1993, Apr 1804, 2070, May 1804). He was using Trigny's *A New Method of Learning the Italian Tongue* ... (1750), the grammar Wordsworth had sent him.[4]

Two long notebook entries show that he devoted his first months in Malta to studying and improving his Italian. The annotations are a list of phrases he copied out from the tetraglot edition of Pascal on account of their difficulty or utility.[5] In July he wrote confidently that he would 'soon be able both to speak & write both F(rench?) and Italian' (*CL* II 1146), but his optimism was frustrated by the difficulties he met in the following weeks.

The main problem was pronunciation: for instance, he could not understand his guides on his first ascent of Mount Etna in August 1804, even though he learnt much from them in a short time (*CN* II 2174). In other words, the contact with native speakers made him aware of the distance between the literary and spoken language: 'Difficulty of learning Italian in Sicily – I. from the utter want of distinct Ideas & of Judgment which makes a muddy *stream* of sound, 2. bad It.' (*CN* II 2179, Aug 1804). The 'bad Italian' was probably the Sicilian dialect or Italian spoken with a strong Sicilian accent.

Coleridge could never reconcile himself to spoken Italian, which he found from the beginning 'shrill but melodious' (*CN* II 2174). He thought the Roman accent sweet, but was disgusted at the Florentine. The characteristic aspiration of the Florentines made him think they 'appear to have lost the roof of the mouth', so that they gargle rather than speak (*CN* II 2862, Jun 1806). He concluded that Italian was 'a most harmonious at least melodious Language' if pronounced by the English, while in the mouths of the Italians 'it is beyond all comparisons the most ear-insulting chaos of shrill and guttural, up and down, sounds I have ever heard'. The widespread ignorance, due to 'Despotism & Priestcraft' and to sensuousness, was responsible for the lack of harmony in speaking (*CN* II 2812, Mar–Apr 1806). If Coleridge found Italian as pronounced by Italians unpleasant, he paradoxically argued that the pronunciation of Greek and Latin ought to be as close as possible to Italian, as Milton had suggested. English people spoke Greek with 'a most sound-murdering confusion of vowels' (*CM* (*CC*) II 1092 and n.).

One is left with the impression that Coleridge never became fluent in spoken Italian while he was in Italy. I do not know how much credit ought to be given to his assertion that in Malta he read a chapter of St Paul to the Romans to the Chief Judge 'translating it literally into Italian' (*CL* V 1, 4 Jan 1820). As far as is known, he did not have many contacts with Italians: he spent most of the time in the circles of English travellers, artists, politicians and sometimes with Italian people associated with them. He referred to his own experience in Germany and Italy when he later advised Thomas de Quincey not to travel with too many English companions in Spain if he intended to learn the language (*CL* III 248, 16 Oct 1809). His proficiency in speaking cannot have improved after his return to England, since he never practised the language with native speakers again. When he met Italians in England, he always conversed in English or German, as with Gioacchino de' Prati in 1824.[6] Although he was more familiar with German than Italian, his German was also not perfect. When he met August Wilhelm Schlegel in 1828, they spoke English, since Schlegel's English was better than Coleridge's fluent but mispronounced German (*TT* (*CC*) II 418, 421).

His writing skill was equally uncertain. The basic mistakes which appear in his rare notes in Italian make it probable that the public documents in Italian he is supposed to have written in Malta were merely drafted or signed by him.[7]

If Coleridge never attained a real proficiency in speaking and writing, he improved his reading knowledge of Italian after 1804. Italian was and remained for Coleridge a book language. I am inclined to believe that Metastasio must have been one of the first poets he read on the basis of the recently recovered edition of Metastasio's works, his transcriptions of operatic arias for metrical purposes and his interest in the opera in the latter half of 1804. Metastasio was commonly used by beginners, since he is easy and pleasant to read. The numerous accents Coleridge misplaced in the arias he analysed show the limits of his knowledge at the time.

Thereafter, his progress was rapid: by the March or April of 1805 he was reading as complex a writer as Boccaccio, whose style he compared with Machiavelli's (*CN* II 2512). His linguistic confidence was much greater when he transcribed and analysed some sonnets of Giambattista Marino in the summer of 1805 (*CN* II 2625). His reading of Petrarch's Italian poems, to which he wrote some marginal notes, probably dates from the same period, since the main plans he was developing were an essay on metrics and the 'Soother of Absence', a collection of love poems.

Coleridge made use of various dictionaries and grammars for his study of Italian. He consulted the Della Crusca dictionary in Malta (*CN* II 2134,

Jul 1804); in 1805 he purchased Giuseppe Luca Pasini's *Vocabolario italiano-latino* ... (Venezia 1794), of which he noted the humorous prudery (*CN* II 2074 n.; II 2658 and App. A); another dictionary he consulted was Lorenzo Franciosini's *Vocabolario italiano, e spagnolo* (Geneve 1636), a copy of which was in Wordsworth's library. Franciosini's was 'the most entertaining dictionary' he 'had ever looked into';[8] he returned to it when he tried to learn Spanish and Portuguese in 1808.[9] He owned Adriano Politi's *Dittionario toscano* (Venezia 1728), and may have used Baretti's *English and Italian Dictionary* (1778), a copy of which was in Gillman's library.[10]

Coleridge owned Franciosini's *De particulis Italicae Orationis* and *Grammatica spagnuola, ed italiana* (Venezia 1734), which was probably acquired when he was learning Spanish in 1808.[11] Gillman's library contained other grammars he may have consulted: D. F. Lates's *Italian Tongue* (1762), Evangelista Palermo's *Italian Language* (1779), and *Veneroni's Grammaire Italienne, par Zotti* (1811).[12] Veneroni's was the most popular Italian grammar in eighteenth-century England.[13] The grammars Coleridge certainly used were Trigny's and Mussolini's. Trigny's was so full of oddities that it induced him to plan an essay 'on the morals and manners of the makers of Dictionaries and Grammars' (this notebook entry also contains the first hint at the project for *The Friend*) (*CN* II 2074). He returned to the idea after reading Cesare Mussolini's *Italian Exercises* in 1813, when he taught his daughter Italian (*CN* II 2074 n.). He found the book's 'folly & immorality ... laughably gross'.[14]

(ii)

Coleridge took up his Italian again in the *Friend* period, although his reading of Italian poetry was not interrupted by his return to England: for example, he read Dante's lyric poetry from late 1806 to 1808 (*CN* II 3017-19, 3201). If his command of Italian was sufficient for Marino, Giambattista Strozzi and Petrarch, Dante still resisted him. He was reading him in 1805, since he wrote that Dante, Ariosto and Bruno would be his Italy (*CN* II 2598, Mar 1805). However, it is significant that there are no marginalia on his Italian copy of the *Comedy*, which may suggest he found it too difficult at the time. When he took up Italian again in 1808, he noted that in learning a language it is advisable to read difficult writers as soon as possible; otherwise one becomes content with the easiest and never goes beyond them. He included Metastasio, Tasso and part of Ariosto in the former; Berni and Dante in the latter (*CN* III 3283).

His confidence and interest in Italian were remarkable if, in George Whalley's words, when *The Friend* 'came to an end in the spring of 1810 Coleridge was incapable of anything but to teach Italian to his wife and his daughter'.[15] The Italian grammar for his daughter Sara, which will appear in the *Shorter Works and Fragments* of the *Collected Coleridge*, was probably sketched at the time. Diverse reasons may underlie his decision to teach Sara Italian. Italian was included in the normal curriculum of girls' schools from the latter half of the eighteenth century, and by the 1810s it was considered an indispensable part of ladies' culture.[16] Under the influence of the opera, Italian was regarded as an effeminate language, and therefore as suitable for women. Coleridge seems to have shared the view. In the *Logic* he argued that the harsher sounds of a language drop along with the development of civilization, as in modern Greek and Italian; however, 'a nation may rebarbarise into the opposite extreme of effeminacy', which is what happened to Italian though not to Greek (*Logic* (*CC*) 26). Italian was the 'language of Love itself' if spoken by 'an accomplished, *self-respecting*, and therefore of necessity *reflectionate*, English Lady' (*CN* II 2812).

Gianfranco Folena, who has traced the idea of the effeminacy of Italian back to the seventeenth century, remarked that the evaluation of a language on the basis of its sound qualities is a variation of popular commonplaces.[17] Wordsworth noted that Dante and Michelangelo showed that Italian was not necessarily effeminate;[18] Macaulay and Hunt were also critical of this prejudice.[19] As it stands, the idea of effeminacy did not dominate Coleridge's view of Italian.

In 1805 he made a long note on the character of the European tongues, among which Italian was 'the sweetest' but not effeminate – an opinion he also expressed in the fragment of Italian grammar he sketched for Sara. Italian was second only to Spanish and Greek 'in the narrative Epic and all the simpler modifications of Thought, and passion, and general Imagery'. Italian can represent common things naturally and yet with dignity because of its sweetness and pomp of sound, and because it is not spoken by the lower classes (*CN* II 2431, Feb 1805). Ariosto was an instance of this peculiarity (*L Lects* (*CC*) I 291). Wordsworth agreed with Coleridge about the musicality of Italian, but thought it a disadvantage, since a more dissonant tongue like English prevents the writer from neglecting thought for music.[20] The greater defect of Italian for Coleridge was the scarce variety of its terminations. Greek was the most perfect language in this respect (*TT* (*CC*) 7 Jul 1832).

To sum up, Coleridge's attitude to the quality of Italian was ambivalent. He thought, like many English people, that it was a melodious tongue, but he was also struck by the harshness of the native pronunciation. The contrast was due to a literary approach to the language. His attitude to modern languages was always that of a classicist: modern languages were for him not indispensable in early education, and he did not favour the introduction of any of them in schools (*TT* (*CC*) 1 Jul 1833).

(iii)

Coleridge's interest in Italian continued after the *Friend* period, but his command of the language does not seem to have improved further. In 1811 he said to John Payne Collier that he admired Dante, but was not 'sufficiently master of the language to form a proper estimate' (*C Talker* 174). It is significant that his interest in Dante revived when he read Henry Francis Cary's translation of the *Comedy* in 1817. However, he retained the considerable reading knowledge of Italian he had developed in the 1800s, since he was able to read Vico's *New Science* without difficulty as late as 1824 (*CN* IV 5204). It may be observed that the style of Vico's main work is very difficult – so difficult that it finds few readers even in modern translation.

Coleridge made some remarks on the Italian language in the context of European linguistics, a subject he did not know in depth but with which he dealt in his lectures. He discussed the mixed character of the Romance languages when he compared classical and modern drama in the 1812 lectures. The modern tongues were less homogeneous than Latin, but richer and more various (*L Lects* (*CC*) I 466). The Romance languages consisted of a mixture of Latin, Celtic and Gothic elements. Italian was 'the Ruin of the Latin the Blocks remaining but with the greater part of the Cement dropt out' (*CN* IV 4934, 1822–3). The definition of the Romance tongues had not only a linguistic value, but also a bearing on his view of Shakespeare as a Romantic poet (*L Lects* (*CC*) I 481, 490–1, 519, 1812–13). His remarks derived in part from August Wilhelm Schlegel. He recommended the Schlegels' dialogue on the character of the European languages in *Athenaeum* (*TT* (*CC*) 2 Sept 1833). It is noteworthy that Coleridge was unaware of the discoveries of modern German linguistics (Rasmus Rask, the Grimm brothers, Humboldt), despite his interest in contemporary German culture and his personal acquaintance with Humboldt.[21] His linguistics was impressionistic, the linguistics of a poet.

Italian stimulated Coleridge to reflect on the concept of the language of poetry. He observed that a poetical language exists whenever the majority of the population is ignorant, as in Italy from Dante to Metastasio (*CN* III 3611, 1809). It was not important that English did not possess a poetic dialect, like ancient Greece or modern Italy: even in Greek and Italian the language of poetry differs from spoken language in the forms of declension and conjugation rather than in the words themselves. The language of poetry is not essentially different from the language of prose, if essence is understood in its philosophic sense. The material is the same for both (*BL* (*CC*) II 62).

There was a primitivist strain in Coleridge's idea of linguistic purity. He thought the golden age of Greek ended with Theocritus; of Latin, after the Augustan age; of Italian, before Tasso; and of English, before the Restoration (*TT* (*CC*) 8 Jul 1827).

If Coleridge's knowledge of the Italian language might seem modest or insufficient to make him a reliable critic of its literature, it should not be forgotten that the average expertise of his contemporaries was not greater. Some, like Hazlitt and Clare, did not know Italian at all. Among those who did, Thomas J. Mathias and Byron were exceptional: the others – for example Wordsworth, Southey or Hunt – read extensively but had a modest or negligible command of the written and spoken language.[22] Nor did interest outside literary circles lead to greater results. Panizzi and Rossetti, who held the two chairs of Italian Language and Literature instituted in London in 1828 and 1831, found very few students. Brand points out that 'in no university was Italian treated as a serious or principal subject of study'. Foscolo was justified when he complained that many studied Italian, all thought they knew it, few learnt it and could understand his own writing.[23] However, Foscolo himself always had his essays translated, since he never learnt to write English decently.

Notes to the Appendix

1   E. H. Thorne, 'Italian Teachers and Teaching in Eighteenth Century England', *English Miscellany* (Rome), IX (1958), p. 148; Brand (1957) 39.
2   Brand (1957) 41, 44.
3   Lowes 527 n.
4   *CN* II 2074 n.; *Cormorant* I 436.
5   *CN* II 2133-6, 2142; Sultana (1969) p. 154 and n. 8, pp. 157–8.
6   Fisch, 'The Coleridges, Dr Prati, and Vico', p. 120.
7   See for example *CM* (*CC*) II 976, *CN* IV 5047 (Oct–Nov 1823).
8   *Cormorant* I 199–200 n. 14; *CN* II 2625.
9   *CL* III 58; *Cormorant* I 199–200 n. 14. He last asked for it in 1823 (*CL* V 302).
10 *Cormorant* I 437.

11   Ibid. II 276.
12   Ibid. I 199 n. 14.
13   Thorne, 'Italian Teachers and Teaching in Eighteenth Century England', p. 149; Marshall 304.
14   *CM* *(CC)* III 930; see Thorne, ibid., p. 153.
15   *Cormorant* I 462.
16   Brand (1957) 37, 40; see *CN* IV 5328 n.
17   *L'italiano in Europa*, Einaudi: Torino 1983, p. 222.
18   Rossiter Smith, 'Wordsworth and His Italian Studies', pp. 249–50.
19   Brand (1957) 43.
20   Sturrock, 'Wordsworth's Italian Teacher', p. 807.
21   Neumann, 'Coleridge on the English Language', pp. 642–3; *TT* *(CC)* 28 Aug 1833.
22   Mathias alone was fully bilingual; Byron's letters show that his writing in Italian was always imperfect. On Hazlitt, see H. Baker, *William Hazlitt*, Harvard UP: Cambridge (Mass.); OUP: London 1962, p. 123.
23   Foscolo, *Epistolario*, vol. VII, p. 289 (20 Feb 1818).

Select Bibliography

Manuscripts

N F°: San Marino (California), H. E. Huntington Library, HM 17299.
N 37: London, British Library, Add. MS 47532.
N 39: London, British Library, Add. MS 47534.
N 40: London, British Library, Add. MS 47535.
N 41: London, British Library, Add. MS 47536.
N 45: London, British Library, Add. MS 47540.
N 49: London, British Library, Add. MS 47544.
N 50: London, British Library, Add. MS 47544.
N 52: London, British Library, Add. MS 47547.
N 54: London, British Library, Add. MS 47549.
N Q: New York, Public Library, Berg Collection.

(From: *Index of English Literary Manuscripts. Volume IV 1800–1900*, Pt. I Arnold-Gissing, compiled by Barbara Rosenbaum and Pamela White, Mansell: London and New York, 1982. Coleridge entry by B. Rosenbaum.)

J. C. C. Mays made available to me Kathleen Coburn's transcripts of the original for *CN*, vol. V; references to notebooks in possession of the British Library have been checked against the originals.

Other unpublished material

Coleridge's marginalia on Pietro Metastasio, *Opere*, London (Leghorn) 1782–3, 12 vols., now in the Coleridge Collection, Victoria College, University of Toronto.

Primary Sources

Italian

ALIGHIERI, Dante. *Tutte le opere*, ed. Luigi Blasucci, Sansoni: Firenze 1965 (rpt. 1989).

_____. *Dante's Lyric Poetry*, eds. Kenelm Foster and Patrick Boyde, 2 vols., Clarendon Press: Oxford 1967.

_____. *Rime*, ed. Gianfranco Contini, Einaudi: Torino 1946 (rpt. 1987).

ARIOSTO, Ludovico. *Opere minori*, ed. Cesare Segre, Ricciardi: Milano–Napoli 1954.

BOCCACCIO, Giovanni. *Genealogie deorum gentilium libri*, ed. Vincenzo Romano, Laterza: Bari 1951.

_____. *Opere in versi. Corbaccio. Trattatello in laude di Dante. Prose latine. Epistole*, ed. Pier Giorgio Ricci, Ricciardi: Milano–Napoli 1965.

_____. *Tutte le opere di Giovanni Boccaccio*, ed. Vittore Branca, 12 vols., Mondadori: Milano 1967–.

BRUNO, Giordano. *The Expulsion of the Triumphant Beast*, tr. and ed. Arthur D. Imerti, Rutgers UP: New Brunswick (N. J.) 1964.

FICINO, Marsilio. *Commentary on Plato's 'Symposium' on Love*, tr. Sears Jayne, Spring Publications: Dallas (Texas), 1985 (rpt. 1988).

_____. *Teologia platonica*, ed. Michele Schiavone, 2 vols., Zanichelli: Bologna 1965.

FOSCOLO, Ugo. *Epistolario*, vols. VII and VIII, ed. Mario Scotti, Le Monnier: Firenze 1970 and 1974.

_____. *Lirici del Cinquecento*, ed. Luigi Baldacci, Longanesi: Milano 1975 (rpt. 1984).

METASTASIO, Pietro. *Opere*, 12 vols., London (Leghorn) 1782–3.

_____. *Tutte le opere*, ed. Bruno Brunelli, 5 vols., Mondadori: Milano 1943–54.

PETRARCA, Francesco. *Canzoniere*, ed. and intr. Gianfranco Contini, notes by Daniele Ponchiroli, Einaudi: Torino 1964.

_____. *Le rime*, eds. Giosué Carducci and Severino Ferrari, Sansoni: Firenze 1899 (rpt. 1965).

_____. *Petrarch's Lyric Poems. The 'Rime Sparse', and Other Lyrics*, tr. Robert M. Durling, Harvard UP: Cambridge (Mass.) and London, 1976.

Poeti latini del Quattrocento, eds. Francesco Arnaldi, Lucia Gualdo Rosa and Liliana Monti Sabia, Ricciardi: Milano–Napoli 1964.

The Renaissance Philosophy of Man (texts by Petrarca, Valla, Ficino, Pico, Pomponazzi, Vives), selections in translation eds. Ernst Cassirer, Paul Oskar Kristeller, and John Herman Randall, Jr, Univ. of Chicago Press: Chicago 1948 (4th edn 1956).

STROZZI, Giovan Battista il Vecchio. *Madrigali inediti*, ed. Marco Ariani, Argalia: Urbino 1975.

TASSO, Torquato. *Discourses on the Heroic Poem*, tr. Mariella Cavalchini and Irene Samuel, Clarendon Press: Oxford 1973.

VASARI, Giorgio. *The Lives of the Painters, Sculptors and Architects*, tr. A. B. Hinds, ed. W. Gaunt, 4 vols., Dent: London 1927 (rpt. 1980).

VIDA, Marco Girolamo. *De arte poetica*, tr. with commentary by Ralph G. Williams, Columbia UP: New York 1976.

English and Others

ADDISON, Joseph. *Remarks on Several Parts of Italy, &c., In the Years 1701, 1702, 1703*, in *Works*, London 1741, vol. II.

AUGUSTINE, St. *Confessionum libri XIII*, ed. Lucas Verheijen, Brepols: Turnhout 1981 (Engl. tr. F. J. Sheed, *The Confessions of St Augustine*, Sheed & Ward: London and New York, 1944, rpt. 1960).

BLAKE, William. *Blake Records*, ed. G. E. Bentley, Jr, Clarendon Press: Oxford 1969.

BOSWELL, James. *The Life of Dr Johnson*, 2 vols., Dent: London 1933.

BOWLES, William Lisle. *Fourteen Sonnets. Sonnets Written on Picturesque Spots. Verses to John Howard. The Grave of Howard. Verses on the Philanthropic Society. Elegy Written at the Hot Wells. Monody Written at Matlock. A Poetical Address to Edmund Burke. Elegiac Stanzas. Coombe Ellen.*, intr. Donald H. Reiman, Garland Press: New York & London, 1978.

CARY, Henry Francis (tr.). Dante, *The Divine Comedy*, London 1805–14 (rpt. OUP: London [1910] 1950).

GOETHE, Wolfgang. *Italienische Reise*, Berliner Ausgabe, vol. XIV, Berlin 1961 (rpt. 1978).

GRAY, Thomas. *The Correspondence of Thomas Gray*, eds. Paget Toynbee and Leonard Whibley, 3 vols., Clarendon Press: Oxford 1935 (rev. edn by H. W. Starr, 1971).

HAZLITT, William. *The Complete Works of William Hazlitt*, ed. P. P. Howe, 21 vols., Dent: London and Toronto, 1930–4.

HUNT, Leigh. *The Autobiography of Leigh Hunt*, ed. J. E. Morpurgo, Cresset Press: London 1949 (orig. edn London 1850).

_____. *Dante's Divine Comedy. The Book and Its Story*, George Newnes: London, n.d.

_____. *A Jar of Honey from Mount Hybla*, Smith, Elder & Co.: London 1897 (orig. edn London 1848).

_____. *The World of Books and Other Essays*, Gay & Bird: London 1819.

JOHNSON, Samuel. *Lives of the English Poets*, ed. G. Birkbeck Hill, 3 vols., Clarendon Press: Oxford 1905.

JOYCE, James. *The Critical Writings of James Joyce*, eds. Ellsworth Mason and Richard Ellmann, Faber and Faber: London 1959.

KANT, Immanuel. *Sämmtliche Werke*, ed. G. Hartenstein, 8 vols., Voss: Leipzig 1867–8.

LAMB, Charles. *The Works of Charles and Mary Lamb*, ed. E. V. Lucas, 7 vols., Methuen: London 1903–5.

_____. *The Letters of Charles and Mary Lamb* (1796–1817), ed. Edwin W. Marrs, Jr, 3 vols., Cornell UP: Ithaca and London, 1975–8.

LANDOR, Walter Savage. *Landor as Critic*, ed. Charles L. Proudfit, Routledge & K. Paul: London and Henley, 1979.

____. *The Pentameron and Other Imaginary Conversations*, ed. Havelock Ellis, Walter Scott: London (1889).

____. *Poems*, selected and intr. Geoffrey Grigson, Centaur Press: London 1964.

____. *Selections from the Writings of Walter Savage Landor*, ed. Sidney Colvin, Macmillan: London 1882.

MOORE, John. *A View of Society and Manners in Italy*, 2 vols., London 1781. *The Norton Anthology of English Literature*, vol. II, ed. M. H. Abrams, Norton: New York and London, 1962 (5th edn, rpt. 1986).

PRESTON, William. *The Poetical Works of William Preston*, 2 vols., Dublin 1793.

de QUINCEY, Thomas. *The Collected Writings of Thomas de Quincey*, ed. David Masson, 14 vols., Black: Edinburgh 1889–90.

REYNOLDS, Joshua. *Discourses on Art*, Collier: New York 1961.

ROSCOE, William. *The Life of Lorenzo de' Medici*, 2 vols., London 1795 (rpt. 1797).

____. *The Life and Pontificate of Leo the Tenth*, 6 vols., London 1805 (rpt. 1806).

RUSKIN, John. *The Works of John Ruskin*, eds. E. T. Cook and Alexander Wedderburn, Allen: London; Longman, Green and Co.: New York, 1903–12.

____. *Ruskin in Italy. Letters to His Parents 1845*, ed. Harold I. Shapiro, Clarendon Press: Oxford 1972.

SCHELLING, F. W. J. 'Ueber Dante in philosophischer Beziehung', *Sämmtliche Werke*, vol. VI (1802–3), Cotta: Stuttgart und Augsburg, 1859, pp. 152–63.

SCHLEGEL, August Wilhelm. *Geschichte der romantischen Literatur* (lectures given 1802–3), ed. Edgar Lohner, Kohlhammer: Stuttgart 1965.

____. *Vorlesungen über dramatische Kunst und Literatur*, ed. Edgar Lohner, 2 vols., Kohlhammer: Stuttgart, Berlin, Köln, Mainz, 1966 (orig. edn 1809–11).

SHARP, Samuel. *Letters from Italy*, London 1766 (rpt. 1767).

SHELLEY, Mary. *The Mary Shelley Reader*, eds. Betty T. Bennett and Charles E. Robinson, OUP: New York and London, 1990.

SHELLEY, Percy Bysshe. *Poetical Works*, ed. Thomas Hutchinson, rev. by G. M. Matthews, OUP: Oxford 1905 (rpt. 1988).

____. *Prometheus Unbound*, ed. L. J. Zillman, Univ. of Washington Press: Seattle 1959.

SMOLLETT, Tobias. *Travels through France and Italy*, ed. Frank Felsenstein, OUP: Oxford 1979 (orig. edn London 1766).

SOUTHEY, Robert. *The Life and Correspondence of Robert Southey*, ed. Charles Cuthbert Southey, 6 vols., London 1849–50.

____. *New Letters of Robert Southey*, ed. K. Curry, 2 vols., Columbia UP: New York and London, 1965.

WALPOLE, Horace. *The Letters of Horace Walpole, Fourth Earl of Oxford*, ed. Mrs Paget Toynbee, 19 vols., Clarendon Press: Oxford 1903–25.

WORDSWORTH, William. *Descriptive Sketches*, ed. Eric Birdsall, Cornell UP: Ithaca and London, 1984.

____. *Poems, in Two Volumes, and Other Poems 1800–1807*, ed. Jared Curtis, Cornell UP: Ithaca (N. Y.) 1983.

Secondary Sources

Coleridge

i. Bibliography

Samuel Taylor Coleridge. An Annotated Bibliography of Criticism and Scholarship. Volume I: 1793–1899, eds. Richard and Josephine Haven, and Maurianne Adams, G. K. Hall: Boston (Mass.) 1976.

Samuel Taylor Coleridge. An Annotated Bibliography of Criticism and Scholarship. Volume II: 1900–1939 (with additional entries for 1795–1899), eds. Walter B. Crawford, Edward S. Lauterbach and Ann M. Crawford, G. K. Hall: Boston (Mass.) 1983.

ii. Criticism

BARFIELD, Owen. *What Coleridge Thought*, OUP: London 1972.

BARTH, Robert J. *Coleridge and Christian Doctrine*, Harvard UP: Cambridge (Mass.) 1969.

BEER, John. 'Coleridge and Poetry: I. Poems of the Supernatural', in *Writers and Their Background: S.T. Coleridge*, ed. R. L. Brett, G. Bell & Sons: London 1971, 45–90.

_____. *Coleridge's Poetic Intelligence*, Macmillan: London 1977.

BODKIN, Maud. *Archetypal Patterns in Poetry. Psychological Studies of Imagination*, OUP: London 1934.

CHAYES, Irene H. 'A Coleridgean Reading of "The Ancient Mariner"', *Studies in Romanticism*, IV (1965), 81–103.

COOKSEY, Thomas L. 'Dante's England, 1818: The Contribution of Cary, Coleridge, and Foscolo to the British Reception of Dante', *Papers on Language & Literature*, XX, No 4 (fall 1984), 355–81.

DARCY, C. P. 'Coleridge and the Italian Artist, Migliarini', *Notes & Queries*, XXIII, No 3 (Mar 1976), 104–5.

DAVIDSON, Graham. *Coleridge's Career*, Macmillan: London 1990.

DESCHAMPS, Paul. *La formation de la pensée de Coleridge (1772–1804)*, Didier: Paris 1964.

DE PAOLO, Charles. 'The Lessons of Wisdom and Caution: Coleridge's Periodization of Western History', *The Wordsworth Circle*, XVII, No 3 (summer 1986), 119–30.

DORENKAMP, Angela G. 'Hope at Highgate: The Late Poetry of S. T. Coleridge', *Barat Review*, VI (1971), 59–67.

DUNSTAN, A. C. 'The German Influence on Coleridge', *Modern Language Review*, XVII, No 3 (July 1922), 272–81.

FISCH, Max Harold. 'The Coleridges, Dr Prati, and Vico', *Modern Philology*, XLI, No 2 (Nov 1943), 111–22.

_____. and BERGIN, Thomas Goddard (eds.). Introduction to *The Autobiography of Giambattista Vico*, Great Seal Books, Cornell UP: Ithaca 1944.

FOGLE, Richard Harter. *The Idea of Coleridge's Criticism*, Univ. of California Press: Berkeley and Los Angeles, 1962.

FRUMAN, Norman. *Coleridge, the Damaged Archangel*, G. Braziller: New York 1971.

GATTA, John Jr. 'Coleridge and Allegory', *Modern Language Quarterly*, XXXVIII (1977), 62–77.

HAASE, Donald P. 'Coleridge and Henry Boyd's Translation of Dante's *Inferno:* Toward a Demonic Interpretation of "Kubla Khan"', *English Language Notes*, XVII, No 4 (Jun 1980), 259–65.

HAYTER, Alethea. *A Voyage in Vain. Coleridge's Journey to Malta in 1804*, Faber and Faber: London 1973.

JASPER, D. *Coleridge as a Poet and Religious Thinker*, Macmillan: London and Basingstoke, 1985.

KESSLER, Edward. *Coleridge's Metaphors of Being*, Princeton UP: Princeton (N. J.) 1979.

KNOWLTON, Edgar C., Jr. 'A Coleridge Allusion to Angelica Catalani (1780–1849)', *Notes & Queries*, XXV, No 3 (Jun 1978), 221.

LEVERE, Trevor H. *Poetry Realized in Nature. Samuel Taylor Coleridge and Early Nineteenth-Century Science*, CUP 1981.

LOCKRIDGE, Laurence S. *Coleridge the Moralist*, Cornell UP: Ithaca and London 1977.

MAYS, James C. C. 'Coleridge's Borrowings from Jesus College Library, 1791–94', *Transactions of the Cambridge Bibliographical Society*, VIII (1985), 557–81.

_____. 'Coleridge's "Love": "All he can manage, more than he could"', in *Coleridge's Visionary Languages*, Boydell Press: Woodbridge 1993, 49–66.

McLAUGHLIN, Elizabeth T. 'Coleridge and Milton', *Studies in Philology*, LXI (1964), 545–72.

MENDILOW, A. A. 'Symbolism in Coleridge and the Dantesque Element in "The Ancient Mariner"', *Scripta Hierosolymitana* (1955), 25–81.

NEUMANN, Joshua H. 'Coleridge on the English Language', *PMLA*, LXIII (1948), 642–61.

OLIVERO, Federico. 'Dante e Coleridge', *Giornale Dantesco*, XV, No 5 (1908) (rpt. in his *Saggi di letteratura inglese*, Laterza: Bari 1913, 61–74).

PRADHAN, S. V. 'The Historiographer of Reason: Coleridge's Philosophy of History', *Studies in Romanticism*, XXV, No 1 (1986), 39–62.

RAYSOR, Thomas M. 'Coleridge and "Asra"', *Studies in Philology*, XXVI (Jul 1929), 305–24.

REED, Arden. *Romantic Weather. The Climates of Coleridge and Baudelaire*, University Press of New England: Hanover and London, 1983.

RIDENOUR, George M. 'Source and Allusion in Some Poems of Coleridge', *Studies in Philology*, LX (1963), 73–95.

SCHULZ, Max F. 'The Wry Vision of Coleridge's Love Poetry', *The Personalist*, XLV (1964), 214–26.

_____. 'The Soother of Absence: An Unwritten Work by S. T. Coleridge', *Southern Review*, II (1967), 289–98.

SERONSY, Cecil C. 'More Coleridge Marginalia', *Studies in Philology*, LII, No 3 (Jul 1955), 497–501.

SHAFFER, Elinor S. '"Infernal Dream" and Romantic Art Criticism: Coleridge on the Campo Santo, Pisa', *The Wordsworth Circle*, XX (1989), 9–19.

_____. 'Coleridge and the Object of Art', *The Wordsworth Circle*, XXIV (1993), 117–28.

STILLINGER, Jack. '"Kubla Khan" and Michelangelo's Glorious Boast', *English Language Notes*, XXIII, No 1 (1985), 38–42.

SULTANA, Donald (ed.). *New Approaches to Coleridge: Biographical and Critical Essays*, Vision: London; Barnes & Nobles: Totowa (N. J.), 1981.

SUTHER, Marshall. *Visions of Xanadu*, Columbia UP: New York and London, 1965.

WHALLEY, George. 'The Bristol Library Borrowings of Southey and Coleridge 1793–8', *Library*, IV (Sept 1949), 114–31.

_____. *Coleridge and Sara Hutchinson and the Asra Poems*, Routledge & K. Paul: London 1955.

_____. '"Late Autumn's Amaranth": Coleridge's Late Poems', *Transactions of the Royal Society of Canada*, II, No 4, Section II (Jun 1964), 159–79.

_____. 'Coleridge and Vico', in *Giambattista Vico. An International Symposium*, eds. Giorgio Tagliacozzo and Hayden V. White, Johns Hopkins UP: Baltimore 1969, 225–44.

WHEELER, Kathleen M. *Sources, Processes and Methods in Coleridge's Biographia Literaria*, CUP 1980.

WOODRING, Carl R. *Politics in the Poetry of Coleridge*, University of Wisconsin Press: Madison 1961.

_____. 'What Coleridge Thought of Pictures', in *Images of Romanticism. Verbal and Visual Affinities*, eds. Karl Kroeber and William Walling, Yale UP: New Haven and London, 1978, 91–106.

ZALL, P. M. 'Coleridge and *Sonnets from Various Authors*', *Cornell Library Journal*, II (1967), 49–62.

Italian Art, Literature and Philosophy

ALLEN, Don Cameron. *Mysteriously Meant: the Rediscovery of Pagan Symbolism and Allegorical Interpretation in the Renaissance*, Johns Hopkins UP: Baltimore and London, 1970.

AMATURO, Raffaele. *Petrarca* (Letteratura Italiana Laterza vol. VI), Laterza: Bari 1971 (rpt. 1974).

ANTAL, Frederick. *Florentine Painting and Its Social Background. The Bourgeois Republic before Cosimo de' Medici's Advent to Power: XIV and Early XV Centuries*, K. Paul: London 1947.

ARGAN, Giulio Carlo, and CONTARDI, Bruno. *Storia dell'arte classica e italiana*, diretta da G. C. Argan, vols. III and IV, Sansoni: Firenze 1981 and 1983.

ASOR ROSA, Alberto. *La lirica del Seicento*, Laterza: Bari 1975.

AUERBACH, Erich. *Literary Language & Its Public in Late Latin Antiquity and the Middle Ages*, tr. Ralph Manheim, Routledge & K. Paul: London 1965 (orig. edn Franke: Bern 1958).

BADALONI, Nicola. *Introduzione a Vico*, Laterza: Bari 1984.

BALDACCI, Luigi. *Il Petrarchismo italiano nel Cinquecento*, Liviana: Padova 1974.

BARON, Hans. *The Crisis of the Early Italian Renaissance*, Princeton UP: Princeton (N. J.), 1955 (rev. edn 1966).

BAXANDALL, Michael. *Giotto and the Orators. Humanist Observers of Painting in Italy and the Discovery of Pictorial Composition 1350–1450*, Clarendon Press: Oxford 1971.

BELLOSI, Luciano. *Buffalmacco e il Trionfo della Morte*, Einaudi: Torino 1974.

BERLIN, Isaiah. *Vico and Herder. Two Studies in the History of Ideas*, Hogarth Press: London 1976.

BIALOSTOCKI, Jan. 'The Renaissance Concept of Nature and Antiquity', *Studies in Western Art. Acts of the Twentieth International Congress of the History of Art*, Princeton UP, 1963, II (*The Renaissance and Mannerism*), 163–73.

BIGI, Emilio. 'La lirica latina del Poliziano', *La Rassegna della letteratura italiana*, VII, No 2 (Apr–Jun 1956), 265–83.

BILLANOVICH, Giuseppe. *Petrarca letterato: I. Lo scrittoio del Petrarca*, Edizioni di Storia e Letteratura: Roma 1947.

BINNI, Walter. *Metodo e poesia di Ludovico Ariosto*, D'Anna: Messina 1947.

BLASUCCI, Luigi. *Studi su Dante e Ariosto*, Ricciardi: Milano–Napoli 1969.

BONORA, Ettore. 'Il Classicismo dal Bembo al Guarini', in *Storia della Letteratura Italiana*, diretta da Emilio Cecchi e Natalino Sapegno, vol. IV: *Il Cinquecento*, Garzanti: Milano 1966 (rpt. 1970).

BOSCO, Umberto. *Francesco Petrarca*, Laterza: Bari 1946 (rpt. 1961).

BOYDE, Patrick. *Dante's Style in His Lyric Poetry*, CUP 1971.

BRANCA, Vittore. *Boccaccio. The Man and His Works*, tr. Richard Monges, cotr. and ed. Dennis J. McAuliff, New York UP: New York 1976.

BURKE, Peter. *Culture and Society in Renaissance Italy 1420–1540*, Batsford: London 1972.

CASSIRER, Ernst. *The Individual and the Cosmos in Renaissance Philosophy*, tr. Mario Domandi, Blackwell: Oxford 1963.

CILIBERTO, Michele. *Giordano Bruno*, Laterza: Bari 1990.

CONTINI, Gianfranco. *Esercizi di lettura* (Nuova edizione aumentata), Einaudi: Torino 1974.

DI CESARE, Mario A. *Bibliotheca Vidiana. A Bibliography of Marco Girolamo Vida*, Sansoni: Firenze 1974.

FAGIOLO, Marcello, and MADONNA, Maria Luisa (eds.). *Roma 1300–1875: La città degli anni santi*, Mondadori: Milano 1985.

FERRERO, Giuseppe Guido. Intr. to *Marino e i marinisti*, Ricciardi: Milano–Napoli 1954.

FLORA, Francesco. 'Poetica del madrigale cinquecentesco', in his *Saggi di poetica moderna (dal Tasso al Surrealismo)*, D'Anna: Messina–Firenze 1949, 3–10.

FOLENA, Gianfranco. *L'italiano in Europa. Esperienze linguistiche del Settecento*, Einaudi: Torino 1983.

FORSTER, Leonard. *The Icy Fire. Five Studies in European Petrarchism*, CUP 1969.

GARIN, Eugenio. *Medioevo e Rinascimento*, Laterza: Bari 1954.

_____. *Italian Humanism. Philosophy and Civic Life in the Renaissance*, tr. Peter Munz, Blackwell: Oxford 1965 (first publ. Franke: Bern 1947).

_____. *Ritratti di Umanisti*, Sansoni: Firenze 1967.

_____. *Ermetismo del Rinascimento*, Ed. Riuniti: Roma 1988.

_____ (ed.). *L'uomo del Rinascimento*, Laterza: Bari 1988.

GEROSA, Pietro Paolo. *Umanesimo cristiano del Petrarca. Influenza agostiniana, attinenze medievali*, Bottega d'Erasmo: Torino 1966.

GETTO, Giovanni. *Barocco in prosa e in poesia*, Rizzoli: Milano 1969.

GILMORE, Myron P. 'Italian Reactions to Erasmian Humanism', in *Itinerarium italicum. The Profile of the Italian Renaissance in the Mirror of its European Transformations*, eds. Heiko A. Oberman and Thomas A. Brady Jr, Brill: Leiden 1975, 61–115.

GILSON, Etienne. *Dante the Philosopher*, tr. David Moore, Sheed & Ward: London 1948.

GOMBRICH, Ernst H. 'Introduction: The Historiographic Background', intr. to section 'Recent Concepts of Mannerism', *The Renaissance and Mannerism*, vol. II of *Studies in Western Art. Acts of the Twentieth International Congress of the History of Art*, Princeton UP: Princeton (N. J.), 1963, 163–73.

_____. 'The Renaissance Theory of Art and the Rise of Landscape Painting', in his *Norm and Form, Studies in the Art of the Renaissance*, Phaidon: Oxford 1966 (rpt. 1985), 107–21.

GUSS, Donald L. 'Petrarchism and the End of the Renaissance', in *Francis Petrarch, Six Centuries Later. A Symposium*, ed. Aldo Scaglione, Dep. of Romance Languages, Univ. of North Carolina: Chapel Hill; The Newberry Library: Chicago, 1975, 384–401.

HEIMSOETH, Heinz. 'Giordano Bruno und die deutsche Philosophie', in his *Studien zur Philosophiegeschichte*, Kölner Universität Verlag: Köln 1961, 120–51.

JONARD, N. 'Giuseppe Baretti e la critica johnsoniana', in *Problemi di lingua e letteratura italiana del Settecento*. Atti del quarto Congresso dell'Associazione Internazionale per gli Studi di Lingua e Letteratura Italiana (Magonza e Colonia, 28 apr.–1 maggio 1962), Steiner: Wiesbaden 1965, pp. 276–92.

KRAUTHEIMER, Richard. *Rome. Profile of a City, 312–1308*, Princeton UP: Princeton (N. J.) 1980.

KRISTELLER, Paul Oscar. *Il pensiero filosofico di Marsilio Ficino*, Sansoni: Firenze 1953.

_____. *Renaissance Thought. The Classic, Scholastic, and Humanistic Strains*, Harper: New York 1961 (first publ. 1955).

_____. *Eight Philosophers of the Italian Renaissance*, Chatto & Windus: London 1964 (rpt. 1965).

_____. *Renaissance Concept of Man, and Other Essays*, Harper: New York, Evanston and London, 1972.

_____. *Medieval Aspects of Renaissance Learning*, ed. and tr. Edward P. Mahoney, Duke UP: Durham (N. C.), 1974.

LEE, Rensselaer W. *Ut Pictura Poesis: The Humanistic Theory of Painting*, Norton: New York 1967.

LONGHI, Roberto. *Lavori in Valpadana* (*Opere complete*, vol. VI), Sansoni: Firenze 1973.

LÖWITH, Karl. '"Verum et factum convertuntur": le premesse teologiche del principio di Vico e le loro conseguenze secolari', in *Omaggio a Vico*, Morano: Napoli 1968, 73–112.

McGRATH, Alister. *The Intellectual Origins of the European Reformation*, Blackwell: Oxford 1987.

MEISS, Millard. *Painting in Florence and Siena after the Black Death. The Arts, Religion and Society in the Mid-Fourteenth Century*, Harper: New York, Evanston and London, 1964 (first publ. Princeton UP 1951).

MIROLLO, James V. *The Poet of the Marvelous: Giambattista Marino*, Columbia UP: New York and London, 1963.

_____. 'Mannerist and Baroque Lyric Style in Marino and the Marinisti', *Forum Italicum*, VII (1973), 318–37.

Momenti e problemi di storia dell'estetica, Marzorati: Milano 1959 (rpt. 1968), vol. I.

MONTANARI, Fausto. *Studi sul Canzoniere del Petrarca* (2nd edn), Editrice Studium: Roma 1972.

MORGAN, Lady S. *The Life and Times of Salvator Rosa*, London 1824 (rpt. 1855).

NELSON, John Charles. *Renaissance Theory of Love. The Context of Giordano Bruno's 'Eroici Furori'*, Columbia UP: New York and London 1955 (rpt. 1963).

NICOLINI, Fausto. *La religiosità di Giambattista Vico. Quattro saggi*, Laterza: Bari 1949.

PANOFSKY, Erwin. *Idea. A Concept in Art Theory*, tr. J. J. S. Peake, University of South Carolina Press: Columbia 1968 (orig. edn, Teubner: Leipzig 1924).

_____. *Renaissance and Renascences in Western Art*, Harper & Row: New York 1972 (first publ. Stockholm 1960).

PESTELLI, Giorgio. *L'età di Mozart e di Beethoven*, vol. VI of *Storia della musica*, EDT: Torino 1979 (rpt. 1980).

PEVSNER, Nicolaus. 'The Genesis of the Picturesque', *Architectural Review*, XCVI (1944), 139–46.

PRAZ, Mario. *Mnemosyne: The Parallel between Literature and the Visual Arts*, The National Gallery of Art: Washington D.C.; OUP: London, 1970.

PREVITALI, Giovanni. *La fortuna dei primitivi dal Vasari ai neoclassici*, Einaudi: Torino 1964.

_____. *Giotto e la sua bottega*, Fabbri: Milano 1967.

Raffaello a Roma. Il Convegno del 1983, Elefante: Roma 1986.

ROSSI, Paolo. *Clavis universalis. Arti della memoria e logica combinatoria da Lullo a Leibniz*, Ricciardi: Milano–Napoli 1960 (rpt. Il Mulino: Bologna 1983).

_____. 'Vico e il mito dell'Egitto', in *Omaggio a Vico*, Morano: Napoli 1968.

_____. *Immagini della scienza*, Editori Riuniti: Roma 1977.

_____. *La scienza e la filosofia dei moderni. Aspetti della Rivoluzione scientifica*, Bollati Boringhieri: Torino 1989.

SAENGER, Werner. *Goethe und Giordano Bruno. Ein Beitrag zur Geschichte der Goethischen Weltanschauung*, Ebering: Berlin 1930.

SALERNO, L. *Salvator Rosa*, Edizioni per il Club del Libro: Milano 1963.

SAPEGNO, Natalino. *Antologia storica della poesia lirica italiana nei secoli XVI e XVII*, ERI: Torino 1964.

SCAGLIONE, Aldo. *Nature and Love in the Late Middle Ages*, Univ. of California Press: Berkeley and Los Angeles, 1963.

_____. 'Cinquecento Mannerism and the Uses of Petrarch', in *Medieval and Renaissance Studies* (Proceedings of the Southeastern Institute of Medieval and Renaissance Studies, Summer 1969), ed. O. B. Hardison Jr, Univ. of North Carolina Press: Chapel Hill 1971, 122–55.

_____. *The Sistine Chapel: Michelangelo Rediscovered*, Muller, Blond & White: London 1986.

SMART, Alastair. *The Dawn of Italian Painting 1250–1400*, Phaidon: Oxford 1978.

SMITH, Albert James. *The Metaphysics of Love. Studies in Renaissance Love Poetry from Dante to Milton*, CUP 1985.

SPITZER, Leo. 'The Problem of Latin Renaissance Poetry', *Studies in the Renaissance*, II (1955), 118–38.

SPONGANO, Raffaele. *Due saggi sull'Umanesimo*, Sansoni: Firenze 1964.

STEFANELLI, Ruggiero. *Boccaccio e la poesia*, Loffredo: Napoli 1978.

SUMMERS, D. *Michelangelo and the Language of Art*, Princeton UP: Princeton (N. J.), 1981.

TADDEO, Edoardo. *Studi sul Marino*, Sandron: Firenze 1971.

_____. *Il manierismo letterario e i lirici veneziani del tardo Cinquecento*, Bulzoni: Roma 1974.

TOESCA, Pietro. *Il Trecento*, UTET: Torino 1951.

TOYNBEE, Paget. *Dante Studies*, Clarendon Press: Oxford 1921.

TRINKAUS, Charles. *The Poet as Philosopher. Petrarch and the Formation of Renaissance Consciousness*, Yale UP: New Haven and London, 1979.

VASOLI, Cesare. *La dialettica e la retorica dell'Umanesimo. 'Invenzione' e 'Metodo' nella cultura del XV e XVI secolo*, Feltrinelli: Milano 1968.

_____. 'Il concetto di Rinascimento nel pensiero contemporaneo', in *Il Rinascimento. Aspetti e problemi attuali*. (Atti del X congresso dell'Associazione Internazionale per gli Studi di Lingua e Letteratura Italiana, Belgrado 17–21 aprile 1979), Olschki: Firenze 1982, 19–43.

WEINBERG, Bernard. *A History of Literary Criticism in the Italian Renaissance*, 2 vols., Univ. of Chicago Press: Chicago and London, 1961.

WHITE, John. *Art and Architecture in Italy 1250 to 1400*, Penguin: Harmondsworth 1966.

WILKINS, Ernest Hatch. 'A General Survey of Renaissance Petrarchism', *Comparative Literature*, II (1950), 327–42 (rpt. in *Studies in the Life and Works of Petrarch*, Mediaeval Academy of America: Cambridge, Mass., 1955, 80–99).

_____. *The Making of the 'Canzoniere' and Other Petrarchan Studies*, Edizioni di Storia e Letteratura: Roma 1951.

YATES, Frances A. *Giordano Bruno e la cultura europea del Rinascimento*, tr. Mariella De Martini Griffin and Ales Rojec, Laterza: Bari 1988.

English and Others

BAKER, Herschel. *William Hazlitt*, Harvard UP: Cambridge (Mass.); OUP: London, 1962.

BLANSHARD, Frances. *Portraits of Wordsworth*, Allen & Unwin: London 1959.

BLOOM, Harold. 'First and Last Romantics', *Studies in Romanticism*, IX (1970) (rpt. in his *The Ringers in the Tower. Studies in the Romantic Tradition*, Chicago UP: Chicago & London, 1971).

BURD, Van Akin. 'Background to Modern Painters: The Tradition and the Turner Controversy', *PMLA*, LXXIV (1959), 254–67.

BUSH, Douglas. *Mythology and the Renaissance Tradition in English Poetry*, Univ. of Minnesota Press, 1932 (rpt. Norton: New York 1963).

BUTLER, Marilyn. *Peacock Displayed. A Satirist in His Context*, Routledge & K. Paul: London 1979.

_____. 'Myth and Mythmaking in the Shelley Circle', in *Shelley Revalued. Essays from the Gregynog Conference*, ed. Kelvin Everest, Leicester UP, 1983, 1–19.

_____. 'Repossessing the Past: the Case for an Open Literary History', in *Rethinking Historicism. Critical Readings in Romantic History*, Blackwell: Oxford 1989, 64–84.

CROLL, Morris W. *Style, Rhetoric, and Rhythm*, eds. J. Max Patrick and Robert O. Evans, with John M. Wallace and R. J. Schoeck, Princeton UP: Princeton (N. J.) 1966.

CURRAN, Stuart. *Poetic Form and British Romanticism*, OUP: New York 1986.

ELWIN, M. *Landor. A Replevin*, Macdonald: London 1958.

FORD, Brinsley. 'James Byres: Principal Antiquarian for the English Visitors to Rome', *Apollo*, NS XCIX, No 148 (Jun 1974), 446–61.

_____. 'The Earl-Bishop. An Eccentric and Capricious Patron of the Arts', *Apollo*, NS XCIX, No 148 (Jun 1974), 426–34.

_____. 'The Grand Tour', *Apollo*, NS CXIV, No 238 (Dec 1981), 390–410.

FRIEDLÄNDER, Max J. *Landscape, Portrait, Still–Life. Their Origin and Development*, tr. R. F. C. Hull, Cassirer: Oxford 1949.

GERDTS, William H. 'Washington Allston and the German Romantic Classicists in Rome', *Art Quarterly*, XXXII, No 2 (1969), 167–96.

GITTINGS, Robert. *John Keats*, Heinemann: London 1968.

HAYTER, Alethea. *Opium and the Romantic Imagination*, Faber and Faber: London 1968 (rpt. 1969).

JOHNSTON, Arthur. *Enchanted Ground. The Study of Medieval Romance in the Eighteenth Century*, Athlone Press: London 1964.

LIGHTBOWN, R. L. 'Italy Illustrated', *Apollo*, NS XCIV, No 115 (Sept 1971), 216–25.

LIPKING, Lawrence. *The Ordering of the Arts in Eighteenth-Century England*, Princeton UP: Princeton (N. J.) 1970.

MARTIN, Philip A. *Byron. A Poet before His Public*, CUP 1982.

NOTOPOULOS, James A. *The Platonism of Shelley. A Study of Platonism and the Poetic Mind*, Octagon Books: New York 1969 (first publ. Duke UP 1949).

POPPER, Karl. *Logica della scoperta scientifica*, Einaudi: Torino 1970 (orig. edn Vienna 1934).

PRICE, Hereward T. 'Functions of Imagery in Venus and Adonis', *Papers of the Michigan Academy of Science, Arts and Letters*, XXXI (1945), 275–97.

SUTTON, Denys. 'Magick Land', *Apollo*, NS XCIX, No 148 (Jun 1974), 392–407.

_____. 'Aspects of British Collecting, Part I', *Apollo*, NS CXIV, No 237 (Nov 1981), 282–339; Part II, NS CXVI, No 250 (Dec 1982), 358–420; Part III, NS CXIX, No 267 (May 1984), 312–72; Part IV, NS CXXIII, No 282 (Aug 1985), 84–159.

WEBB, Timothy. *Shelley: A Voice not Understood*, Manchester UP: Manchester 1977.

_____. *English Romantic Hellenism 1700–1824*, Manchester UP: Manchester; Barnes & Noble, New York, 1982.

_____. 'Romantic Hellenism', in *The Cambridge Companion to British Romanticism*, ed. by Stuart Curran, CUP 1993, 148–76.

WELLEK, René. *Immanuel Kant in England, 1793–1838*, Princeton UP: Princeton (N. J.) 1931.

WILKIE, Brian. *Romantic Poets and Epic Tradition*, University of Wisconsin Press: Madison and Milwaukee, 1965.

WILSON KNIGHT, G. *The Starlit Dome. Studies in the Poetry of Vision*, OUP 1941 (rpt. Methuen: London 1959).

ZECCHI, Stefano. *La fondazione utopica dell'arte. Kant Schiller Schelling*, Unicopli: Milano 1984.

Anglo-Italian Relationships

ASH, John, and TURNER, Louis. *The Golden Hordes. International Tourism and the Pleasure Periphery*, Constable: London 1975.

BARROWS, Herbert. 'Convention and Novelty in the Romantic Generation's Experience of Italy', *Bulletin of the New York Public Library*, LXVII, No 6 (Jun 1963), 360–75.

BOSTETTER, Edward E. 'The Original Della Cruscans and the Florence Miscellany', *Huntington Library Quarterly*, XIX, No 3 (1956), 277–300.

BRAND, C. P. 'Dante and the English Poets', in *The Mind of Dante*, ed. U. Limentani, CUP 1965, 163–200.

CHANDLER, S. B. 'La fortuna del Tasso epico in Inghilterra 1650–1800', *Studi tassiani*, in *Bergomum*, V, No 5 (Sept 1955), 69–105.

CUNNINGHAM, G. F. *The Divine Comedy in English. A Critical Bibliography 1782–1900*, Oliver and Bush: Edinburgh and London, 1965.

CURRY, Kenneth. 'Uncollected Translations of Michelangelo by Wordsworth and Southey', *Review of English Studies*, XIV (1938), 193–9.

de PALACIO, Jean, 'Byron traducteur, et les influences italiennes', *Rivista di letterature moderne e comparate*, XI, Nos 3–4 (Dec 1958), 209–30.

DOUGHTY, Oswald. 'Dante and the English Romantic Poets', *English Miscellany* (Rome), II (1951), 125–69.

FENNER, Theodore. *Leigh Hunt and Opera Criticism. The 'Examiner' Years, 1808–1821*, Univ. of Kansas Press: Lawrence, Manhattan, Wichita, 1972.

FISCHER, Erika. *Leigh Hunt und die italienische Literatur*, Trute: Quakenbrück 1936.

FISKE, Roger. *English Theatre Music in the Eighteenth Century*, OUP: London 1973.

FRIEDRICH, Werner P. *Dante's Fame Abroad 1350–1850. The Influence of Dante Alighieri on the Poets and Scholars of Spain, France, England, Germany, Switzerland, and the United States*, Univ. of North Carolina Press: Chapel Hill 1950.

FUCILLA, Joseph G. 'European Translations and Imitations of Ariosto', *The Romanic Review*, XXV, No 1 (Jan–Mar 1934), 45–51.

GALIGANI, Giuseppe (ed.). *Il Boccaccio nella cultura inglese e anglo-americana* (Atti del Convegno internazionale di studi, Certaldo 14–19 Sept. 1970), Olschki: Firenze 1974.

GIBALDI, Joseph. 'The Fortunes of Ariosto in England and America', in *Ariosto 1974 in America. Atti del Congresso Ariostesco – Dicembre 1974, Casa italiana della Columbia University*, ed. Aldo Scaglione, Longo: Ravenna, 135–77.

HALE, John Rigby. 'Cosimo and Lorenzo dei Medici: Their Reputation in England from the 16th to the 19th Century', *English Miscellany* (Rome), VIII (1957), 179–94.

HARGREAVES–MAWDSLEY, W. N. *The English Della Cruscans and Their Time, (1783–1828)*, Nijhoff: The Hague 1967.

KING, R. W. 'Italian Influence on English Scholarship and Literature during the "Romantic Revival"', *Modern Language Review*, XX (1925), 48–63 and 296–304; XXI (1926), 24–33.

KIRBY, Paul Franklin. *The Grand Tour in Italy (1700–1800)*, Vanni: New York 1952.

von KLENZE, Camillo. *The Interpretation of Italy during the Last Two Centuries. A Contribution to the Study of Goethe's 'Italienische Reise'*, Chicago UP: Chicago 1907.

KUHNS, Oscar. *Dante and the English Poets from Chaucer to Tennyson*, Henry Holt: New York 1904.

MANWARING, Elizabeth Wheeler. *Italian Landscape in Eighteenth Century England. A Study Chiefly of the Influence of Claude Lorraine and Salvator Rosa on English Taste 1700–1800*, OUP: New York 1925 (rpt. Frank Cass: London 1965).

McGANN, Jerome J. 'Rome and Its Romantic Significance', in his *The Beauty of Inflections. Literary Investigations in Historical Method and Theory*, Clarendon Press: Oxford 1985, 313–33.

MELCHORI, Giorgio. *Mighelangelo nel Settecento inglese. Un capitolo di storia del gusto in Inghilterra*, Edizioni di Storia e Letteratura: Roma 1950.

MOURET, François J.–L. *Les traducteurs anglais de Pétrarque 1754–1798*, Didier: Paris 1976.

248 *Coleridge in Italy*

MOZZILLO, Atanasio (ed.). *Viaggiatori stranieri nel Sud*, Edizioni di Comunità: Milano 1964.

Noble and Patriotic. The Beaumont Gift, 1828, The National Gallery of London (3 Feb–3 May 1988), National Gallery Publications, 1988.

PARKS, George B. 'The Turn to the Romantic in the Travel Literature of the Eighteenth Century', *Modern Language Quarterly*, XXV (1964), 22–33.

PERELLA, Nicolas J. *The Critical Fortune of Battista Guarini's 'Il Pastor Fido'*, Olschki: Firenze 1973.

PERINI, Giovanna. 'Sir Joshua Reynolds and Italian Art and Art Literature', *Journal of the Warburg and Courtauld Institutes*, LI (1988), 141–68.

PETTY, Frederick C. *Italian Opera in London: 1760–1800*, UMI Research Press: Ann Arbor (Mich.) 1980.

PINE–COFFIN, R. S. *Bibliography of British and American Travel in Italy to 1860*, Olschki: Firenze 1974.

PITE, Ralph, *The Circle of Our Vision. Dante's Presence in English Romantic Poetry*, Clarendon Press: Oxford 1994.

PLUMB, J. H. 'The Grand Tour', in *Men and Places*, Cresset: London 1963, 54–66.

PRAZ, Mario. 'Dante in Inghilterra (e in America)', in *Maestro Dante*, ed. Vittorio Vettori, Milano 1962, 63–94.

_____. *Machiavelli in Inghilterra ed altri saggi sui rapporti letterari anglo-italiani*, Sansoni: Firenze 1962.

_____. *The Flaming Heart: Essays on Crashaw, Machiavelli, and Other Studies in the Relations between Italian and English Literature from Chaucer to T.S. Eliot*, Doubleday Anchor Books: New York 1958 (rpt. Smith: Gloucester [Mass.] 1966).

_____. *Il giardino dei sensi. Studi sul Manierismo e il Barocco*, Mondadori: Milano 1975.

QUENNELL, Peter. *Byron in Italy*, Collins: London 1941 (rpt. 1951).

RAAB, Felix. *The English Face of Machiavelli. A Changing Interpretation 1500–1700*, Routledge & K. Paul: London; University of Toronto Press: Toronto, 1965.

ROSSI, Sergio. 'Wordsworth e l'Italia', *Letterature moderne*, IV, No 5 (Sept–Oct 1953), 532–547.

ROSSITER SMITH, H. 'Wordsworth and His Italian Studies', *Notes & Queries*, CXCVIII, No 6 (Jun 1953), 249–50.

SAMUEL, Irene. *Dante and Milton. The 'Commedia' and 'Paradise Lost'*, Cornell UP: Ithaca (N. Y.), 1966.

SCHNEIDER, Ben Ross. *Wordsworth's Cambridge Education*, CUP 1957.

SHACKFORD, M. H. 'Wordsworth's Italy', *PMLA*, XXXVIII (1923), 236–252.

STURROCK, June. 'Wordsworth's Translations of Ariosto', *Notes & Queries*, CCXXIV (Jun 1979), 227–8.

_____. 'Sigismunda and Ghismonda: Wordsworth and Scott on Dryden and Boccaccio', *English Studies*, LXIII (1982), 134–8.

THORNE, E. H. 'Italian Teachers and Teaching in Eighteenth Century England', *English Miscellany* (Rome), IX (1958), 143–62.

TILLYARD, E. M. W. *The English Epic and Its Background*, Chatto and Windus: London 1968 (first publ. 1954).

TOYNBEE, Paget. *Britain's Tribute to Dante in Literature and Art. A Chronological Record of 540 Years* (c. *1380–1920*), British Academy: London 1921.

VALLONE, Aldo. *La critica dantesca nel Settecento ed altri saggi danteschi*, Olschki: Firenze 1961.

VANCE, William L. *America's Rome*, 2 vols., Yale UP: New Haven and London, 1989.

VASSALLO, Peter. *Byron. The Italian Literary Influence*, Macmillan: London 1984.

VINCENT, E. R. *Ugo Foscolo. An Italian in Regency England*, CUP 1953.

_____. 'Fortuna di Dante in Inghilterra', in *Enciclopedia Dantesca*, 6 vols., Istituto della Enciclopedia Italiana: Roma 1970–8, vol. III, 445–8.

VIVIANI della ROBBIA, Enrica. 'Shelley e il Boccaccio', *Italica*, XXXVI No 3 (Sept 1959), 181–97.

WEBB, Timothy. *The Violet in the Crucible. Shelley and Translation*, Clarendon Press: Oxford 1976.

WEINBERG, Alan M. *Shelley's Italian Experience*, Macmillan: London and Basingstoke, 1991.

WEISINGER, Herbert. 'English Attitudes Toward the Relationship between the Renaissance and the Reformation', *Church History*, (1945), 167–87.

_____. 'The Study of the Revival of Learning in England from Bacon to Hallam', *Philological Quarterly*, XXV, No 3 (Jul 1946), 221–47.

_____. 'The English Origins of the Sociological Interpretation of the Renaissance', *Journal of the History of Ideas*, XI (1950), 321–38.

Index